DOSTOEVSKY

TO
ANDY VON ZSOLNAY

DOSTOEVSKY

THE MAN AND HIS WORK

JULIUS MEIER-GRAEFE

Author of
Vincent Van Gogh, The Spanish Journey,
etc.

Translated by
HERBERT H. MARKS

HASKELL HOUSE PUBLISHERS Ltd.
Publishers of Scarce Scholarly Books
NEW YORK, N. Y. 10012
1972

HASKELL HOUSE PUBLISHERS Ltd.

Publishers of Scarce Scholarly Books

280 LAFAYETTE STREET

NEW YORK. N. Y. 10012

Library of Congress Cataloging in Publication Data

Meier-Graefe, Julius, 1867-1935.
 Dostoevsky, the man and his work.

 Reprint of the 1928 ed.
 Translation of Dostojewski, der Dichter.
 Bibliography: p.
 1. Dostoevskii, Fedor Mikhailovich, 1821-1881.
I. Title.
PG3328.M413 1972   891.7'3'3   77-38843
ISBN 0-8383-1390-6

Printed in the United States of America

LIST OF ILLUSTRATIONS

PREFACE

So much interest has been shown in the life and works of Dostoevsky that no apology is offered for presenting Mr. Meier-Graefe's work to the English reader. Mr. Meier-Graefe needs no introduction as Mr. Holroyd-Reece's translations are already well known.

Mr. Meier-Graefe's prose is a strange medley of spirited and racy narrative, metaphor which is picturesque, though at times mixed and somewhat overbold, and the latest precipitate of modern German idiom. Mr. Holroyd-Reece, in his Preface to his translation of the *Vincent Van Gogh*, has drawn attention to the difficulties of a literal rendering. In the translation of *Dostoevsky The Man and his Work* an attempt has been made to follow the original even in its elliptic flights. This experiment may have led to harsh results, but the Translator thought it his duty, not only to interpret faithfully Mr. Meier-Graefe's remarks on Dostoevsky, but also to give as exact a rendering as possible of Mr. Meier-Graefe's vivid narrative. Such has been the method, though often a free rendering was inevitable, and the charm of the original has thereby had to be sacrificed.

Some of Mr. Meier-Graefe's theories may startle English critics of Dostoevsky. On the other hand it seems to the Translator that no such careful analysis of Dostoevsky's work has so far been made in the English language.

In conclusion it should be observed that much of any success which may have been attained by this translation is due to the generous help of Mr. Frederick Norman, of University College.

H. H. M.

LONDON,
February 1928.

vii

DOSTOEVSKY

THE MAN & HIS WORK

CHAPTER I

DOSTOEVSKY opens up new worlds: the regions he explores were previously unknown to literature. And he creates Upheaval.

Our activities have become highly specialized, a fact which has made life extremely complicated. In Dante's time the hall in which the Muses feasted was spacious—there was room to breathe; now it is nothing but a nest of compartments, each partitioned off: there is the perpetual click of the typewriter. Nothing is left of the original architecture except a few disconcerting fragments and shafts of antique marble columns piercing the *bourgeois* stucco ceiling. Here and there the columns have been painted over as part of the general colour-scheme and look rather like fat water-pipes; some of them have been hidden behind woodwork which has given the room an even more angular appearance. The vast hall has completely vanished behind these built-in partitions. Not only has there been building-in but also building-up. When there was no more space on the ground-floor a few storeys were tacked on; the result to-day is a complicated sky-scraper. Life is like that. An accurate impression of all these countless compartments is rarely possible; a so-called artistic impression even more rarely possible, only possible in fact if we climb to the twentieth floor or indeed to the artificial garden on the roof of the sky-scraper. Up there will be found what used to take place in the festive hall with the high windows and marble pillars. Up there in the vicinity of heaven is a world of thought and feeling which, because it is perched on the top of the building, imagines itself to be the crown of the whole. But even so its cry, however loud and tragic, cannot pierce the nearest concrete layer; it certainly cannot reach the lower storeys, where people are occupied with serious affairs. A complete artists' colony has settled on the roof and is leading a lively existence. They discourse to the people and to God and dangle their limbs. They can be seen from the street in fine weather. Soon another storey will be tacked on, and then the Lord knows where the colony will move to !

Dostoevsky opens up new worlds. Doubtless his principal appeal is still to the roof-garden of Europe, but his influence is not confined to the artists' colony. His art has long been trickling from the roof down to the lowest storeys of the building. That is without precedent since the days of our classical writers and, let us not forget, in those days the hall was in the middle of the house and there were no limitations. In those days, so it seems to us now, there was little else to do than listen to poets, and when someone wrote of the sorrows of Werther all the young folk sorrowed with him. It is no exaggeration to assume that in the near future Dostoevsky will exert as much influence as Goethe or Schiller, if indeed he has not already done so—perhaps even as much as Shakespeare, and we shall have to consider how far this is true. What remains of the others ? The richness and texture of French literature in themselves deny such power to any one person; on the other hand the necessary effect cannot be attained by collective creation. In their world-history task the encyclopædists of the eighteenth century carried too much scientific and political baggage. Even Voltaire's influence appears limited compared to that of the Russian, and completely lacking in popular appeal. In our time it is impossible even to imagine a writer exerting such influence on his fellow-countrymen, least of all on Europe. Again, the language he employed was not European. None of us can read him in the original. Only a Russian could acquire this influence, this all-European influence, and only our age

IMPRESSION

in which spiritual values are not allowed to exercise any kind of popular appeal has fashioned the conditions for his popularity. Whence the influence? Perhaps the most cogent factor is the more or less conscious superstition that Dostoevsky's creations are not literature and that he must not be counted amongst the poets.[1] This fallacy is by no means based on the supposed plausibility of his plots, on the so-called naturalistic truth ; on the contrary the plausibility is often a matter of doubt to the naïve reader. Moreover, Dostoevsky's outlook in no way justifies classifying him as a naturalist. Detailed description of externals is entirely eliminated. There is no painting of a *milieu* in its modern sense. The *milieu* grows with the action, or rather out of the action. Where Dostoevsky goes into details every external factor is merely auxiliary to an easily recognizable object, and this object, frank tension or tendency, is rejected by the naturalistic school. This partly constitutes the distinction between his writing and the current notion of modern literature. Such exciting stories are considered by the cultured reader as inartistic, particularly when coarse material is introduced. Dostoevsky seems to prefer this coarseness. It is nearly always a matter of crime or the possibility of crime. The plot of *Crime and Punishment* (which can be reduced to quite a simple theme) is the very thing for admirers of Sherlock Holmes. The same applies to the central *motif* of *The Brothers Karamazov*. In *A Raw Youth* the tension depends on a hardly tolerable film-trick, the famous letter which is never delivered and finally stolen. In *The Idiot*, *The Eternal Husband*, *The Possessed*, there is murder or attempted murder. The disguising of the gruesome *motif* does not render these stories different from the most vulgar concoctions of their kind. Blood flows, not behind the scenes, but in the full blaze of the footlights. In spite of that we read, we devour eagerly every line. Mature, cultured people who possess their Goethe, their Hölderlin,

[1] In the original this word means " creative writer " for which there is no exact English equivalent; the word " poet " is therefore used here (and in other places) in this wider sense.—TRANSLATOR'S NOTE.

DOSTOEVSKY

their Molière, their Baudelaire, and Verlaine, abandon themselves to the excitement as youngsters to their stories of
Red Indians, and murder does not repel. We despise those
who are repelled as weaklings, who miss the fundamental
meaning. Blood suddenly looses its reek, not indeed because
we consider it unnecessary, as in *Hamlet*, where it becomes
mere historical claptrap. In the *Hamlet* of our imagination
the killing-off in the last Act plays no part—in fact the effect
is tedious, and, in our thoughts, we have already gone home.
In Dostoevsky's novels blood is of the very essence of the
mystery, always an indispensable factor. The action gains
impetus from it, it produces a fascinating play of light and
shade and, at times (consider the end of *The Idiot*), consecration. If we can tolerate this gory atmosphere, if murder
not alone does not blunt but actually refines our spiritual
senses—so refines them that they become sensitive to the
most secret, the most delicate things of a complexity hitherto
unpresentable—then it must be because the gruesome *motif*
is introduced in some other way than is usual in stories of
murder ; it must be because the significance of what is
revealed, not in spite of but by means of this *motif*, sweeps
us beyond the point of blood-shyness.

These methods by which the murder-stories are brought
to a higher level can be generally termed psychology ; it is
the psychological element which distinguishes these stories
from commonplace productions, though they are not necessarily on that account brought within the realm of literature.
Nietzsche asserts that he learnt psychology only from
Dostoevsky. Let us ignore the pretentiousness of this
phrase. If it is a matter of psychology one could say that
one single book of Dostoevsky stands higher than the whole
of European novel-literature since Diderot. Why a book?—
a chapter, a few lines suffice : the page with the dialogue
between Ivan Karamazov and Smerdyakov, before the latter
goes off and hangs himself ; one of Versilov's conversations
with his son, or when, in *The Idiot*, the prince opens his
heart; when, in *The Double*, the unfortunate petty official
enters society; when, in *An Unpleasant Predicament*, the

councillor fights against his drunkenness. These are trifles, not the famous incidents.

It is true, there would be only this one man if literature were exhausted in psychology, but fortunately both for mankind and for Dostoevsky that is not so ; for, because we all know or at least instinctively feel that it is not so Dostoevsky is able to conceal his personality under the garb of a psychologist whose only concern is to reveal associations, the dark threads between thought and action, between heart and countenance, between two men who love one another whilst their hearts are overflowing with hatred, between enemies who smile while they rend one another, between two adjacent chambers of the same human heart. If this were regarded as literature, his arbitrary methods could not be overlooked; he could not be forgiven his reckless transitions, his apparent lack of economy, his irrelevancy and offences against the good manners of European prose. And still one thing more, the most important ; it is because we look, not at the literary, but at the psychological side, that our interest is held. Of course, we are susceptible to " real literature "—we can be quite enthusiastic about it since we regard ourselves as cultured people; but, in spite of our spiritual elevation, we never lose touch with market-prices; contact with the roof-garden and its artists is an indulgence outside the normal range of our work-a-day lives. But listening to Dostoevsky is an entirely different proposition. He almost becomes an opponent at a committee-meeting whose intentions we have to divine before coming to any conclusion; or else the dreaded banker on whose whim depends the credit of the whole business. We do not say too much, do not show too much enthusiasm, but keep our wits about us. It might be worth while. Who knows?

That is just the point : we foresee certain advantages. Naturally we shall not imitate Stavrogin's vile deed and from pure boredom torture a child of twelve to death. Who would think of attacking an old woman with a hatchet and then killing another one? And surely no one would be so

5

mad as to stab in her bridal dress the woman he adored. That sort of thing happens at most in Russia, outside Europe, a fact which yields us a certain satisfaction. But we are too eager about establishing our innocence, there is too audible a sigh of relief. Though we may be innocent theoretically, our deeds do not always quite bear this out. Let us confess that in certain circumstances, in circumstances which, thank God, have not yet arisen and are hardly likely ever to arise, we could perhaps behave similarly —in fact in a sense we have already done so. We do not tell every Tom, Dick, and Harry; but in the privacy of our own thoughts we admit it. Our whispered confession is of more moment than the tirades of the roof-garden. Up there another masterpiece has just been recited and the shriek of enthusiasm split the clouds. But a cynical wag laughed inwardly at this enthusiasm and declared that the masterpiece did not concern him in the slightest.

If we allowed the wag in us, who to-day behaves more cynically than ever, to do as he pleased, a strange state of affairs would arise. Our appreciation of the masterpiece seems to be merely skin-deep. Our innermost being remains unmoved. We are not indifferent, it is true ; this masterpiece certainly reminds us of other masterpieces ; but this whole net of relationships is loose. Dostoevsky, on the other hand, cuts deep into us. Possibly other writers want, or are compelled, to remain on the surface because that is their only means of revealing their nature. On that surface which is affected by the nobility of an *Iphigenia* there must lie wonderful organs, organs more delicate, more carefully tended than the outstretched fingers with which we snatch the Karamazovs to us ; organs which enable us to remain calm, to bring a smile to our furrowed countenance and to give dignity to our burdened gait. Let us not bother for the time being whether or not these organs are independent of our lacerated hearts, whether or not their functions, their capacity for enjoying works which have no tangible connexion with the driving forces of our existence, are a gift of little value. We cannot dispute the existence of the organs, though the existence requires consideration. It might be said that the *Iphigenia* appeals to other senses—for example to the musical sense—whilst Dostoevsky's appeal is to sight or touch. But that does not explain the different reaction of our spirit. Doubtless there are in the *Iphigenia* rhythmic notes which cannot be heard by Dostoevsky's reader. Is there adequate compensation in Dostoevsky? This question is discussed with fervour in the roof-garden. Those who miss the world of tone assume that Dostoevsky entirely lacks form. They assert that the spirit which finds refreshment in beautiful forms receives no nourishment from him. That is true to a certain point, up to the point, namely, when form becomes an end in itself. If we grant that form is a means to an end—and we shall have to find out how far this is possible—then form as commonly understood requires modifications which we shall have to accept even if the whole roof-garden stands on its head. Musical form is ignored by Dostoevsky, apparently if not actually. That is partly how he succeeds—in fact an indispensable factor of his success. He ignores the obvious as if he had more important things to attend to than to bother about the sound of his words. All the same, sound is not eliminated, for that is not possible —it is only subordinated to other conditions. If a relationship with the reader exists at all, it becomes so intimate that the traditional conception of narrator, event and listener acquires quite a new significance. In Dostoevsky's novels not alone is the hero's existence at stake, but also our own. The narrator, this being from a distant land, informs us of the secrets of our own lives, knows our most intimate thoughts, seems to have lived with us, at times even with our parents : hence a peculiar intimacy whereby language is not always necessary to expression ; what we learn is in part not new at all, but was only lying dormant in our subconsciousness. What is new is the light which suddenly guides these things out of chaos ; a light whose brilliance at first hurts our eyes, a light which perhaps we ourselves could have kindled, had we not fled in our weakness. Ultimately it illuminates the most disconcerting factors in our existence. We may consider this light as a substitute for the waves of sound. It has far greater rhythmical force.

There are, then, three consecutive effects ; first the crude tension of a detective story, which is carried to its climax with the utmost subtlety; secondly, the enigmatic and intimate relationship of the stories to latent parts of our own existence which suddenly become roused and torment us ; thirdly, the gladdening relaxation bringing spiritual harmony. It is understood, of course, that to the poet the most essential of these is the third. With the first two he wounds us, like a surgeon who is compelled to cut open the body in order to see what is inside it. The wound would soon heal again were it not that now follows the real interference, the laying bare of diseased and stunted organs. At last comes the promise of a healthier existence.

The painful operation is performed almost without anæsthetic. Our suffering is at times so agonizing that we feel like falling upon and murdering the man who is rummaging inside us. Hatred is our only redress. Sometimes he seems to torment us unnecessarily, prolonging the torture only because it gratifies his virtuosity. He is guided not by consideration for our well-being but by a hellish science, and we are the victims of his experiments. But every time we are on the point of condemning this as revolting literature, there is the dawn of a new salvation, and again we surrender. We become more and more convinced that his treatment is good for us and that we must endure it at any cost. In the end we bless the surgeon.

This benefaction renders his delving into souls something quite different from the usual psychology, and it thus brings his work a step nearer to the accepted standard of literature, though it is not in itself confined to art ; a conscious moral aim might indeed depreciate literary value.

This tendency is as little concealed by Dostoevsky as murder and film-tricks. None of his books would have needed defending by the advocate of *Madame Bovary* who, in the famous lawsuit, strained every nerve to prove that Flaubert was moral. He saved the author and betrayed

DOSTOEVSKY'S FATHER

his work. Flaubert, even in his wildeſt dreams did not, as M. Senard asserted, think of the " excitation à la vertue par l'horreur du vice." Didaċticism was quite foreign to him. His principle was to portray things as they were without adding to or detraċting from them, without drawing conclusions; to evolve a highly finished ſtyle for the purpose of objeċtive representation. Were this the only juſtifiable aim, Doſtoevsky could not be considered an artiſt.

The German subtitle of the firſt big novel is *Guilt and Penance*. The French principal title, *Crime et Châtiment*, is a more faithful rendering. We ought also to have called it *Crime and Punishment*, though Raskolnikov sounds better and is less banal.[1] To judge by the titles of other books the author seems to have attached importance to labels reminiscent of popular melodrama.

All Doſtoevsky's ideas ascend from moral motives into the realm of art, and not, it would seem, from art into the realm of morals. All his principal works are tendentious. He wants to teach and to reform. But to him a doctrine is not an immutable law, it is a living organism in perpetual motion; it avoids a rigid formula because that would weaken its effeċt. A thoroughly Russian inſtinċt. In The Beginning there is not the Word coined by invisible powers, but communion with others, with the whole people ; and since this people is numerous and provided by nature with peculiarly associative organs, with the whole world. Anxiety for this communion makes him speak out without forcing him into the limelight. He does not rise to becoming the spokesman of the community but remains so essentially a part of it that he has only to talk to himself in order to speak to them. When Doſtoevsky says " we," it is not the poetic licence of the Weſterner who means only himself ; Doſtoevsky indicates a tangible living mass. The sinner does not stand isolated but is part of the mass. We all sin. Even the perpetrator of the moſt heinous crime is always surrounded by a crowd which is in some way his accomplice,

---

[1] The principal German title is *Raskolnikoff*.—Tʀ.

which sins with him and encourages him. The greatest sinner is Dostoevsky himself; at all events he accepts that responsibility. He understands everything and, in the rôle of an older man who has once done the same himself, would not dream of reproaching the younger sinner. We must cling together, he says, we must take mutual counsel how to escape from this muddle. I cannot say to you, don't do it, for you would merely scoff. I understand, in fact, that you must do it, for I too had to do it. If you do it, at least you shall know that I'll stick to you. Afterwards we shall see. This lack of prejudice makes the moral purpose more palatable; it does not override it, on the contrary it broadens it, takes the edge off a narrow-minded sermon. The moral tendency becomes an integral part of our experience.

So much for the present about the so-called content. Incidents, full of excitement, which give us a vivid picture of the Russian and are, at the same time, of immediate concern to us Europeans become a foundation on which we can build afresh.

CHAPTER II

Now for the so-called form. That there is unity of content and form is obvious from the fact that it is necessary only to substitute form for morality in the previous chapter in order to be clear about the most essential factor in Dostoevsky's artistic construction. The form and the moral tendency are correlative. His form is not a rigid formula, but arises spontaneously out of the needs of the moment, which are numerous on account of the uncommonly complicated situations, and, above all, on account of the peculiarities of the Russian temperament which necessitates a thoroughly popular, colloquial style. One has to become accustomed to that (1). Lessing and Goethe would be horrified at the looseness of the phrasing. Most Frenchmen are horrified even now. When at the end of the eighties in a book on the Russian novel, de Vogüé mentioned Dostoevsky for the first time publicly in France, he apologized for his presumption in introducing so vague and nebulous an author whose doubtful progress seemed to have come to an end with *Crime and Punishment.* Of *The Brothers Karamazov* he stated that even few Russians had entirely read this endless story. There is scarcely anything more opposed to the Gallic instinct than Dostoevsky except perhaps the second part of *Faust.* In the fine fragment *Nyetochka Nyezvanov,* the story of an orphan girl, there is a discussion of educational methods. The French governess employs the standard classical method ; gradual instruction, neither too little nor too much at a time. Alexandra Michailovna, the adopted mother, wants to teach the little girl everything at once and overwhelms her with knowledge as with gifts. The child does not know where to begin and is completely at a loss. The French governess wears a smile of victory but they do not give in. The mother, so recently become a teacher,

11

DOSTOEVSKY

is still opposed to a system which crams the head with "dead principles" and suggests that after a few trials a method will automatically be found for developing the pupil's natural capacities : and after a few false starts that is what actually happens. The child and the grown-up woman learn together like two friends. The woman often behaves as if she were being taught by the child. They have other teachers. Each of them brings his new curriculum, but the real study only begins when these learned gentlemen are out of the way again and they can set about their tasks alone. The geography teacher would have made them ruin their eyesight by continual scrutiny of the map for towns and rivers. After he has gone they travel through fabulous countries and go right round the world. They have new books sent them. Very soon the little girl is teaching geography to the teacher. To do him justice, in so far as he can give the geographical bearings and number of inhabitants of every township, he retains his superiority.

In relation to Western requirements, this method is unpedagogic in the extreme, but for Russia and the Russians, the only reasonable system. There the loss of time becomes a gain and disorder orderly. Of what use is knowledge of towns and townships if I have not the world as well? Of what use the lucid exposition of European literature if obscure, many-sided human nature remains ignored? Of what use the fine meshes of the net which the comfortable fisherman dips into the water if he cannot catch fish worth while? Dostoevsky saw living things in the dark waters which unquestionably had to be brought to the surface, not only because they were his objectives, but also because a knowledge of this wild life was bound to be to the utmost advantage of every living being. Dostoevsky's departure from the literature which preceded him was no less considerable than Shakespeare's departure from Greek tragedy. Was Shakespeare more orderly? Let us remember all the criticisms of the eighteenth century, for which there was more justification than for the reproaches of our contemporaries against Dostoevsky; actually both sprang from the same source of error. Even to-day in spite of universal recognition, Shakespeare is still a target for fresh objections. Dostoevsky himself, the most unassuming and appreciative of all poets, dared in one of his essays to reproach him with carelessness and lack of taste. He felt that the creator of *Hamlet* could have done more justice to his genius. This criticism is enlightening. Dostoevsky must have had something else in mind than, for example, Voltaire, who levelled the same criticisms without, as is well known, refraining from admiring Shakespeare and making use of him for his own tragedies. But Dostoevsky was none the less appreciative and that is the decisive factor. To-day a whole world treats Dostoevsky in much the same way, for all of us copy him, not only the enthusiasts on the roof-garden. Every creator remains under the shadow of his creation; that and that only is his immortality. The work goes on. New thought is always running counter to the world; there is richness in disorder; disorder is only an expression of a new order, new, not yet collated material. The Russian who brought the form of a new humanity challenged the whole old world.

In any criticism it is important to remember that Dostoevsky was often driven to haste by the direst need. He was a prolific and rapid writer. " Often the beginning of a chapter," he himself confesses, " was already in the compositor's hands whilst the end was still in my head and had, without fail, to be written by the following day " (2). From the speed of his writing it would seem that the conception was also too rapid. His epileptic attacks are well known.

But though his whole literature soon became epileptic and though he wrote at this stupendous speed, there must have been some sort of coherence behind these disorderly ideas and indiscriminate details, otherwise it would mean nothing to us at all ; whereas we succeed in following every detail and in making sense of apparent incoherence. Consequently there must be some system. We are forced to assume that Dostoevsky's work could only come to fruition

on the path which he saw himself compelled to tread.
Perpetual ill-health, want, which dogged him till within a
few years of his death, and many other obstacles, were the
mainsprings of his creativeness and the determinants of his
form ; an eminently contemporary form, the only one suitable to convey his stories to us. That must be discussed
in detail, as well as the question how far his writing either
was or appears to have been handicapped by want and
illness. We have to picture a being to whom existence in a
world of chaos was not painful. He may constantly have
needed chaos to control the order which he sought to
create. Naturally he feared epilepsy for it interrupted his
work. Attacks, which recurred generally every four to six
weeks, sometimes more frequently, and each time deprived
him for several days of his memory, perpetually threatened
to destroy the harvest. He became inured to it, may even
have welcomed the attacks, for the momentary exaltation
which preceded them cleared his field of vision and brought
him into fresh relationships with chaos, out of which his
energy wrenched his conception into the light of day.
Dostoevsky neither considered literature in any way the
reflex of an inner harmony, nor sought to bestow harmony
by means of it. He struggled and endeavoured to make
men fellow-strugglers. The aim of his creation was unrest
from which others fled. And he knew what he was doing.
To none of the great visionaries has the task been clearer.
Though some detail often escaped his notice or even here
and there some task, he was never unmindful of the significance of his calling. To no one has it come more naturally
to turn the spirit of unrest to account in creative literature,
unambiguously and without any element of vagueness. In
spite of that, unrest drove him to the most ambitious aims.
Most critics miss in Dostoevsky's works some limit to his
demands on a reader's power of comprehension. The
reproach is justified, but there is no justification for con-
cluding that he was therefore totally lacking in moderation.
It is true that in many respects Dostoevsky was immoderate,
but not in his claims on others, and he should not in any

FORM

sense be considered egocentric. His supposed failing was not the result of egotism but of a boundless respect for the realm of phenomena which prevented him from being satisfied with mere cleverness. What Dostoevsky saw was more interesting to him than himself, and he was restrained by nothing but his idea, which he regarded as common property. The limits which one misses would often considerably narrow the scope of his idea, a fact which has repeatedly been substantiated (3). Right to the end there are instances of immoderacy. Dostoevsky constantly strove after more intensive composition, but this by no means led either to the simplification which an ideologue would desire for an adequate insight into his idea, or to a lessening of the unrest. *The Brothers Karamazov*, Dostoevsky's zenith, is the most complex as well as the most restless work of all.

There is a fundamental and easily recognizable idea in each of Dostoevsky's novels, as well as a few well-worked-out principal characters. Other ideas are ranged round the fundamental idea and secondary figures encircle the principal characters. The connexions between these secondary ideas and characters are often arbitrary or abstruse but never commonplace. We are never wearied by irritating, secondary figures usurping the functions of the principal actors. The object of padding is, as in Shakespeare, to complicate, retard or spread out the action and to contribute to the creation of the *spiritus loci*. If direct relationships to previous occurrences are at times scanty, indirect connexions with the author are so much the more convincing, for the latter depend on the dynamic force of Dostoevsky who never allows himself to be completely dominated by the idea underlying the work. At this juncture we will not stop to consider either the interpretation of his ideas or his dynamic force. Suffice it to observe that he was always reaching out beyond the things portrayed, and carried away by a momentary inspiration, yielded to the temptation. This method is as far removed from customary literary forms as is Rembrandt's drawing from the calligraphy of the Primitives or the Classicists, and it is at bottom the same argument

which justifies the canvas technique of Rembrandt and his
followers and the amorphous prose of the Russian. Dostoevsky aimed at illuminating a darkness of gigantic volume
without thereby detracting from its inherent value. It was
not his vocation as a poet which drove him to that, but his
mission, as a Russian, Christian, servant and brother of
mankind. In the darkness lay boundless possibilities of
salvation and Dostoevsky's perceptive faculty rendered him
a visionary in the twilight. It was not till he had dragged
the particular incident into the light of day that he became
the creative artist, and then he would mould it, toy with it,
and forget the darkness for a time. That would never last
very long. The passion of the artist would yield before his
yearning for that mysterious treasure-chamber and once
again he would plunge into the darkness. That was his
fanaticism for toil. He was not a maniac, not a glutton for
work, not a Balzac, but a seer who knew what the treasures
of the darkness would one day mean to his people and to
mankind. Of course, if it is true to say that nothing can
be added to or taken away from a work of art, Dostoevsky
wrote nothing perfect, at least not till *The Brothers Karamazov*,
and perhaps even in that book something could have been
cut out here and there. But even an ideal Dostoevsky could
not have attained our ideal standard; the very nature of so
comprehensive a work precluded that possibility. There is
admitted vastness in the atmosphere of Rembrandt which
early Italian art did not need ; it is even agreed that what
is suppressed by a painting in the Rembrandt manner is
more important than what earlier artists express. On the
other hand Dostoevsky's form still invites criticism. In
theory that cannot be silenced. It was not by the efforts of
art-experts that the revolutionary, Rembrandt, won recognition, but by the pioneer labour of modern artists who
followed in his footsteps and proved in practice the possibility of his forms. The same thing cannot fail to happen
with Dostoevsky; it has, in fact, long since begun. His
influence on creative minds grows hourly. Soon he will be
indispensable. Theoretical objections to Dostoevsky's form

are unconvincing, often contain contradictions and recoil on
the reader. Most of them are levelled against a quality
on which we have already touched. Even admirers of
Dostoevsky frequently criticize his lengthiness, though not
always in the manner of the opportunist Strachov[1] who
censured his lavishness (3). Some people share the view of
de Vogüé who considered the scope of a literary work just
as definitely determined as the height of a hat and who was
eventually simply too lazy to read *The Brothers Karamazov*.
Others take exception to the relative length, though that
does not prevent them from giving Dostoevsky every
possible due, psychological insight, discretion, a sense of
variety in dialogue; in fact where possible they declare these
qualities to be unique. Lack of proportion must of necessity
lessen the artistic worth of a work, can, indeed, ruin it, and
all the excellent qualities attributed to Dostoevsky could not
make up for this shortcoming. It is questionable whether
the much lauded merits are even conceivable in conjunction
with the equally censured failings.

Lack of proportion can only indicate an uneven relationship between content and extent, insufficient concentration.
Instead of acting the author reflects, laments, regrets or
rejoices, or recounts in ten sentences what ought to be given
in one. Dostoevsky was at times long-winded, a fact which
will be stressed in considering his works. There are many
long-winded passages but they certainly do not belong to
the species just mentioned. Dostoevsky's content, or at
least parts of it, could not be set out more briefly. It may
be thought that these parts are the most essential and that
on that account Dostoevsky ought to have renounced the
padding. That is quite possible.

But however much his lengthiness may irritate us,
however obscure its object may seem at times, it was never

---

[1] Nikolay Nikolaevitch Strachov, critic and philosopher, 1828-1896, a
close friend of Dostoevsky and collaborator with him on the *Vreyma*; joint
author of a biography of Dostoevsky. He was also closely associated with
Tolstoy, and his scathing letter to Tolstoy of November 1883 on the subject
of Dostoevsky is notorious.—TR.

merely the outcome of loquacity, least of all when it most appears so. Something very different behind it is soon enough noticeable. Dostoevsky's idea was guilt. His nervous tension could not resist the flow of his phantasy, and he seems at times to have been veritably obsessed by an aversion to all method, as though it were a cloak for lies and hypocrisy and everything which he found ridiculous and pernicious in the institutions of Europe. His digressions never resemble the long-winded passages of Western novelists, for example Balzac's prolix introductions which Marcel Proust has ridiculed in his *Pastiches*. That sort of thing, tolerated on the roof-garden, is not to be found in any of his work; never the convenient prop which every *virtuoso* has at hand. His lengthiness did not lighten his task, nor was it an ornament, although one can, or at least thinks one can, imagine the novel without it ; it was a medium, one of the thousand mediums of unrest. This leads to a curious result. The more one reads Balzac, the more tedious he becomes. If he relates the history of the paper industry in order to create a background for a pair of lovers, one feels tempted to apply the scissors. The roof-garden is appalled, but of what use is that ! The second time the scissors are inevitable. Each time a little bit comes away. Amazing how the parings accumulate and the rest of it vanishes.

At first sight many of Dostoevsky's situations seem to invite similar treatment ; the scissors are always applied on the first reading. Every one has done it. Every one begins by devouring and wants to reach the murder story as rapidly as possible. There are gluttons who never attain the poet because the path to the detective is too wearisome. This sensual craving has first to be satisfied ; then in certain circumstances, circumstances which do not always exist, the other can come. There are two classes of people, those who read Dostoevsky once and those who read him again. If his long-drawn passages were inapposite they would be intolerable at the second reading ; but they have the opposite effect ; long as they are, long as Jupiter's nose

LENGTHINESS

and El Greco's saints, they shrink, and we scarcely notice their length. The more often we take up *The Brothers Karamazov* the more compact it appears. Dostoevsky needed length to ensure room for the action, to give himself, as well as us, a start, because there are never any of the normal links in the form of descriptions of nature or other transitional matter. If we look back, the country which at first sight seemed barren, is verdant, and we see it inhabited by the very people who later fascinate us. Thus the action started long ago whilst we thought we were still involved in an unnecessary introduction, started surreptitiously with the first page, indeed with the first word.

The reproach that Dostoevsky is prolix is frequently the result of mental sloth. One can just as well censure him for the often exaggerated terseness of his descriptions, particularly in specially important parts where the psychologist is carried along by the impetus of the action and the story-teller supplants the novelist. The classical unity of space and time—unique in this unclassical novelist, a fact which must give food for reflection to over-zealous critics—forced him to concentrated action. This terseness endangers particularly those situations which cannot, in any circumstances, attain complete realization. Somewhere in every work is the point at which the thread must become disconnected, when the finiteness of the work must be separated from the infinity of the idea. The story-teller can more easily determine the beginning of his book than the end, and this is truer of Dostoevsky than of any. We shall see why. The parts which seem defective are to be found particularly where the action, intensified by many subordinate incidents, has at last reached its final issue. Dostoevsky was fully alive to these omissions. Think of the chapters which precede the conclusion of *The Idiot* and *A Raw Youth.* Moreover, in the course of the novels there are passages in which it seems the author wants to shake off his technique and burlesque it with an old-fashioned gesture, as if driven by delicacy to add a commonplace to the inevitable seriousness of his words, to enable his reader to recover.

19

DOSTOEVSKY

One would be more easily reconciled to Doſtoevsky's lengthiness—after all, whole works, which to the *bourgeoisie* have only one meaning, are borne with the patience of an angel—if only it were not bound up with one annoying charaċteriſtic which has invited universal reproach ; his obscurity. There are long and obscure passages which are heartily welcome to the European intent on education and sound sleep. The convention of Weſtern literature satisfies this double requirement in that it evolves all kinds of pleasant theories and introduces symbolism of universal import without bothering the reader. The method sweetens the pill. It is possible to recognize already in the second part of *Faust* a firſt tremor of that Europe from whose collapse Doſtoevsky's obscurity emanates; recognition, however, is not obligatory, beautiful piċtures might suffice, whilſt the mind is soothed by the rhythm of the words. The whole of Weſtern literature might be interpreted in that way. Unintelligibility is often highly prized to-day. There is a warm reception for every geſture from the dark realm of metaphysics whose myſterious powers can ward off reality. Superſtition flourishes between telephone and adding-machine. The more the narrow field of the specialiſt is illuminated, the obscurer becomes the whole, and altars spring up to every *Deus ex machina*.

But in Doſtoevsky there is none of this pseudo-obscurity which is a mere illusion. With his obscurity he rouses somnolent emotions; the tired eyelid may will itself to recognize only obscurity; aċtually his is a sonorous colour scheme; it illuminates the darkness out of which it has arisen. But to perceive its brilliance the spirit muſt be willing.

DOSTOEVSKY'S MOTHER

CHAPTER III

DOSTOEVSKY the poet was new in so far as any literary form can be considered new; new, because he employed existing methods more profoundly than had hitherto been done, in order to attain a more forceful characterization of the developing new human type. As the father in *A Raw Youth* said of the Russians, he possessed the faculty of "having a presentiment of the future man," possessed it to a degree bordering on the mystical, a factor which somewhat overshadowed other characteristics.

Even to-day, nearly half a century after his death, after Europe has felt his influence and the generation with which he was dealing has grown up, his words ring depressingly true in the light of history. Consider what has resulted from the activities of other revolutionaries. At first the distinction between him and other writers was attributed to the distance between Europe and Asia and he was to be treated as an ethnographic phenomenon. Even now he seems to be lacking in literary manner to a degree impossible in an author amongst any other cultured people; not only amongst the Latins but even amongst us formless Germans; indeed, the difference between French form and German formlessness almost disappears before the groping efforts of this " autodidact." It is true that that applies not to him alone, but also to the Russians, his people.

Dostoevsky was everything, even Russian, to an unusual extent. He was more Russian than the whole of Russia herself ; there are a hundred proofs of that. He represented Russia quite otherwise than Dante Italy and Homer Greece. That fact is, of course, no criterion for an appreciation of the artist, particularly in view of the tragi-comic fact that to-day he ranks amongst the best-hated of the intellectuals of his country ; but it is certainly very remarkable when it is remembered that his voice could penetrate to few of his fellow-countrymen and that he lived in our age of unbridled individualism; even more remarkable when we consider that in his popularity is reflected the psychology of the modern European ; and almost beyond comprehension when it is realized that the aim of this psychology was a world of ideas which the modern European considers antiquated.

But it is just these factors which are enlightening. He was not a *littérateur* employing current methods. If his tracks are found far and wide, if Russian snow becomes his snow and the Siberian steppes his steppes, if every peasant and every Lenin speaks his language, that is not thanks to his keen sight or sensitive hearing. He never troubled about Russian steppes or Russian snow, and in none of his novels does a peasant appear. Certainly his gift of observation was considerable, that is palpable, and he must have been abundantly equipped for creative literature. Nevertheless to describe his writing as a step in the development of literature would unwarrantably depreciate him or the others, particularly the others. What he had in common with his contemporaries is quickly told. Apart from Russia it is necessary first to look to France, the land of the novel, where at a cursory glance there are analogies in plenty, for example, Balzac. What contemporary prose is not in some way connected with his gigantic creation ! Balzac collected, with insatiable energy, the characteristics of definite social strata of a particular country in a certain defined epoch. He was not lacking in imagination for he invented many of his incidents ; but he only drew on his imagination for what might have been found outside it. He evinced particular interest in human beings, their deeds and motives, as well as in customs and manners. His collection contains vast material arranged with care and industry ; though the sense of the arrangement escapes us, as in a museum of unknown objects. An artist would find something to be done here. He constructed an admirable universe in which things go on more or less as in the real world, a marvel of technical accomplishment ; but in consequence of a far-reaching co-ordination the small universe contains all the countless repetitions of the great. The contents, it is true, had to be reduced to so many volumes, but that involved merely cutting out a little. People were labelled and inscribed on a gigantic card-index, a marvel of modern organization. Balzac has rendered chaos more tractable without seeking to build anything out of it. He has gathered material for the historian. The weaving of the fabric was not his affair. And finally he cheated chaos of its vastness. He was too sane, too little obsessed to carry the interplay of his characters to the point where reality becomes merely a sloughed-off snake skin. Dostoevsky was one of the many who visited and admired this collection. He was enraptured with *Eugénie Grandet* and appears to have translated it into Russian. There is poetry in this story of the miserly father and abandoned heiress. There is poetry between the lines of all Balzac's stories. Dostoevsky only needed to write what Balzac omitted and to put between the lines what Balzac wrote. The father, who does his utmost to give proof of his avarice and finally, despite immense details, becomes an impossible study, because, naturally, humanity is not defined by a collector's card-index, would have become a living character and Eugénie would not have remained a mere name.

Admiration of Georges Sand sprang from a similar source. According to Dostoevsky's scanty utterances his association with Flaubert was purely negative ; it could not indeed be otherwise, for Flaubert is the Western symbol of all that is mathematically opposed to the aims and ideas of the Russian. Like Balzac, Flaubert stood, at least in his essential aim, beyond creative literature. But he knew where he stood. Whereas Balzac was never clear about the hybrid nature of his creation, the author of *Madame Bovary* quite consciously tried, in weaving his fabric, to suppress the many opportunities of becoming subjective. He wanted to be anything rather than creative. Creative literature was a travesty of the truth. " Probité " involved a complete renunciation of every unauthenticated assertion. Better to be a scholar if objective truth could not be recognized in any other way ! The collector's mania of Balzac developed into a demand for " impersonal art."—" Il ne faut pas conclure ! " There followed as a matter of course the " spleen " to which the proudest hope of France eventually succumbed. Had we reproached him with his self-destruction he would not have deigned to answer us barbarians, and the pride with which he pursued his painful career justified him. The contrast between Dostoevsky and Flaubert is not without dignity ; the extremes meet ; Flaubert's ingrained generosity savours of the Russian. His psychology, a marvellous instrument, turns on itself and kills the action which it ought to animate. He preferred to say nothing rather than to be compelled to say what was not relevant to the chance situation. Chance is not a mere subterfuge to a constructive realist, but the very purpose of the action, its god, its law. Dostoevsky's most significant argument began where Flaubert saw himself condemned to silence. With some justification the whole of Western fiction could be put in Flaubert's place, particularly that class of fiction which, unlike Flaubert, not alone does not voluntarily fetter itself but does not even know where to look for the psychological factor which Dostoevsky discovered. At times the novels of even the greatest writers are intolerable if we do not force ourselves to forget Dostoevsky. Whoever is brought up on Dostoevsky can object to *Elective Affinities :* it ended where it ought to have begun. That is not applying present-day judgment unreasonably. He must be an enthusiastic admirer of *Werther* who is not put out by any objections to *Elective Affinities.* At all events whoever disavows *Elective Affinities* must defend himself against the reproach of appraising too little the world of Goethe which permeates the novel. It is just this limitation which is not applicable to Flaubert, because his error was wonderfully organized. He suppressed precisely what we should have to hear to be rescued from the mechanism of clockwork. His style is as clear as crystal.

FLAUBERT

Nevertheless there is a point in which their spheres have met, and that is of importance for a knowledge of both. Once Flaubert does attain the level of the Russian, once they do come into contact, not indeed in the similarity of apparently psychological situations behind which each has concealed his glowing heart but, it almost seems, with their very hearts. The intensity of the contact is like the infinite fervour with which at the end St. Julian embraces the leprous wanderer. Flaubert's masterpiece, a masterpiece of Europe of that time, grew out of a conception quite contrary to the spirit of the Russian. For chance there was substituted an æsthetic experience which was equally unsuitable to the Russian, the stained-glass window, from which Flaubert thought he could read the legend ; naturally fiction, at bottom as little appropriate as the divinity of the incident, only having the advantage of loosening Flaubert's wings without forcing him to disavow the impersonal. As a matter of fact he made fun of the glass window which he wanted to put at the head of his short-story as a " document historique." All the same the legend had the effect of allaying spleen. For once the crystal clockwork was set a worthy task. There is the true spirit of Dostoevsky in this story, not his psychology but his legendlike mysticism, a church window illumined by his fervour. The affinity is considerable in this one single moment. The French mediævalism of the one and the modern Russianism of the other are irrelevant draperies. If there is anything in French literature which bears comparison with an Alyosha, an Idiot, or a Raw Youth, figures whose vital impulses only enhance the purity of their lives, it is St. Julian. The digression enchants us as, in Ivan Karamazov's conversation with the Gentleman, the scintillating parallel to Faust and Mephistopheles, or as the hidden relationship of a Foma Fomitch with characters from the world of Tartuffe, as the deep connexion between Dostoevsky and Shakespeare ; or as we are delighted, despite all probability, to find a Werther in the murderer Raskolnikov. Moreover Dostoevsky knew the legend of the hospitable St. Julian. In the fifth book

DOSTOEVSKY

of *The Brothers Karamazov* Ivan Karamazov quotes the story of " Ivan, the Charitable " who went to bed with the plague-infected beggar. It is part of the paradox of the relationship that Ivan Karamazov perceives in the act of the saint " a self-violating lie."

Dostoevsky read as only young people in his country can read, possessed all important European authors and devoured every line of every Russian. Only those of his fellow-countrymen whose eyes were not set exclusively on the West could have given him anything, and what Russian in Dostoevsky's time was not tainted with the West? This tendency was rife amongst Russian *littérateurs*, just as German painters in the first half of the century looked towards Rome and in the second half towards Paris. They wrote about the life of the Russian of means. Existence which was worth while began on the far side of the frontier and Russia was just a place for a summer holiday on an estate. Turgenev and the young Tolstoy portrayed the homeland in the spirit of eminent tourists and utilized the Russian element as a preparation for a pleasant atmosphere. The smell of Russian leather created a furore everywhere. Dostoevsky, without the least intention of being malicious, invented for it the pertinent name of " literature of the squirearchy." By way of retaliation Turgenev called him the Russian Marquis de Sade and thought, presumably, that he was being just as objective (4). Flaubert's friend had lost his sense of fundamentals. But Tolstoy remained, even after discovering the Russian peasant, a renegade German, whose ideas were ruined by Protestant ethics ; besides being a renegade aristocrat. Thomas Mann, who admires him and includes him in his homage to Goethe, without meaning ill calls Tolstoy's dream a noble passion and puts it in the eighteenth century (5). That seems to me to be ingenious and pertinent and at the same time demonstrates the fundamental difference between Tolstoy and Dostoevsky. It is inexplicable how Merejkovsky could possibly find complementary beings in these two Russians as though they were flesh and blood of one body (6). When

RUSSIAN PREDECESSORS

Tolstoy learned of Dostoevsky's death he wrote to Strachov that the dead man had been the dearest and the most necessary to him, deplored that he had never seen him, and read with emotion the only one of his novels which was a complete failure (7).

At the end of 1883 he wrote again to Strachov saying that Dostoevsky suffered from eccentricity and that therefore Turgenev would outlive him (8). Later he unburdened his heart to Gorky and expressed the opinion that things were really much simpler in Russia than Dostoevsky made them out. That savours of smug complacency.

Of the contemporaries amongst his compatriots probably only Goncharov struck a similar note, although in a very minor key. Oblomov might have lived on the first floor over the den of the man of memoirs " in the darkness of the great city " (9).[1] But of the new man he had no conception.

Gogol and Pushkin are deemed forerunners and probably with good cause. Gogol is supposed to have inspired that tender first work, *Poor Folk*. Dostoevsky himself said that, and he was not unbiassed, for in his eyes the whole of literature had a hand in his works. Once he even called Tolstoy his teacher.

We also feel that there is a connexion between Gogol and Dostoevsky though we can trace nothing in individual works; at most they are sprung from the same soil. It is surprising to learn that Dostoevsky had already written a great deal when the darkness in which Gogol's mind was shrouded came to an end. Great as the distinction may be between Gogol and Dostoevsky, it is of a nature altogether different from that between the contemporaries Tolstoy and Dostoevsky. Gogol exercised considerable influence on the early Dostoevsky. The latter once said : " We are all derived from *The Cloak*." That is difficult to contradict, for Gogol's *Cloak* is of universal significance and Dostoevsky's

---

[1] Oblomov, the title-rôle of Goncharov's novel. " In the Darkness of the Great City " is the German title for a translation of the last five chapters of part two of the *Letters from the Underworld*. For further reference see Chapter Nine.—Tr.

humour may well have been indebted to it. And all the others? It seems to me that Turgenev and Tolstoy were not derived from *The Cloak*, were not sprung from the same soil. Gogol did not write literature of the squirearchy. Rudolf Kassner calls him the conqueror of the eighteenth-century man. He is of opinion that Gogol's story had the same significance for the great Russian story-tellers as Masaccio's frescoes for the Renaissance (10). In this comparison the disparity between Dostoevsky and the other Russian masters is overlooked. Dostoevsky is not *primus inter pares* but must be placed beside Michelangelo.

Even further off non-Russian eyes can catch a glimpse of the Russian idol, founder of their new literature. Pushkin's untranslatable lyrics, considered by Russians the culmination of their poetry, elude us and we hardly get beyond their historical importance. The fundamental connexion seen by Merejkovsky and others between *Crime and Punishment* and Pushkin's masterpiece, *Queen of Spades*, is a matter of internal history. Dostoevsky, because he read himself into Hermann, the hero of the story, could see in him " a tremendous figure." We cannot do that. His pæans on Pushkin, Gogol, Tolstoy and even Turgenev were the outpourings of his unique family sense which ranged even to the remotest of his own relatives and at times reached absurdity. Only Van Gogh was his equal in enthusiasm. Dostoevsky did not criticize unless he considered that an author's influence was detrimental to Russia. Only then did he fill his quiver. His invectives, which were at times violent against Belinsky,[1] Turgenev, Gradovsky and others whom he considered disloyal, were always directed against their attitude, not against the individual. The acidity of the cuts at their native land of the Russians who at that time were living abroad, the immeasurable contempt with which Turgenev, for example, in the novel

---

[1] A Russian critic of extreme views who was interested in Dostoevsky's work and with whom Dostoevsky was in close contact as a young man. The reading aloud of a letter which Belinsky had written to Gogol was the main pretext for Dostoevsky's arrest.—Tr.

PREDECESSORS IN PAINTING

Smoke attacked his country, explain the political element in Doštoevsky's literary criticism (11). He was able to express literary opinion with impunity. What also contributed to embitter him was the often coarsely underlined atheism of cosmopolitan Russians. His vicious attacks on Germans and Frenchmen can be explained in no other way. They were his reply to the vulgarization of things which were sacred to him, by his fellow-countrymen, dazzled by life abroad (12). Never once have his embittered words touched the spiritual treasures of other nations. He kneeled before them and required his people to do likewise. Versilov's dream of the Golden Age is in the realm of Weštern immortal values.

Pushkin and Gogol are compatriots. They have Russian beards, Russian gait, speak with the accents of their country, and literary hištorians in Russia suffer from an imperfeᶜt sense of differentiation such as charaᶜterizes Weštern art-hištorians in their attitude towards El Greco and Velasquez.

One is often tempted to seek equivalents in other realms of art. El Greco's Spain is a cognate case. The faᶜt that El Greco was not born a Spaniard but, as a Greek, immigrated through Italy and discovered the country of his choice, does not neutralize the comparison but rather facilitates our insight into the poet's Russian heritage. Doštoevsky's daughter has enlightened us about his Norman-Lithuanian origin which she has made the principal theme of her biography (13). Even if her *motif*, which leaves out of account the influence of his purely Russian mother, is an exaggeration, we mušt make use of it. It would be quite fitting to imagine that Doštoevsky was born not in Moscow but in some Crete; and that he migrated thence, possibly by way of Weimar. One should think of a Crete sufficiently far away, a Crete in Mongolia or some even more dištant and hieratic Asia, where are conserved not only the remotešt reflexes of a Chrištian Byzantium but the earliešt germs of religious feeling which, by contaᶜt with virgin soil, can buršt forth exuberantly into flower. One mušt imagine Dostoevsky with that gift which rendered the Greek more successful than a native in finding Spanish spirit, Spanish faces, Spanish landscapes, Spanish mysticism, because it was his chosen land, the soil most fitted to his emotions. And just as only loose thinking could lead us to call El Greco's discoveries Spanish, that is, belonging to a class which existed there before him, so what we call Russian in Dostoevsky's creation, is, at bottom, nothing more or less than his breath, his humanity, his creativeness. The Crete of the Greek is small and more easily determinable than the origin of Dostoevsky, and El Greco's Spain, luxuriant as his colours may be, a tiny province beside the Russia of the poet. Even El Greco's revelation of the essentials of modern conventions, three hundred years before Renoir and Cézanne, is scarcely more amazing than the prophetic vision of Dostoevsky in his handling of current problems.

I believe it was André Gide who, in one of his studies, compared Dostoevsky's novel to a painting, the novel of earlier writers to a panorama. That contains a great deal of truth but sounds a little hard on the others. I think the difference is more accurately illustrated by the great gulf between art of the fifteenth to the sixteenth century and that of the seventeenth, by the final emancipation of painting from the bonds of architecture when El Greco, Rubens, Rembrandt, freed themselves from their stern task and exalted the decorative handmaiden of the church and of great lords to the medium of personal confessions. This gulf, which reveals its breadth when we leave in Florence a fresco of the *Quattrocento* and step before a portrait by Rembrandt, is hardly greater than the step from Balzac or Pushkin to Dostoevsky, and the relatively insignificant difference in time renders the case even more astonishing. New aims demanded a new picture, stimulated the invention of new mediums. There arose a new art of painting. Contemplation became action. Not a line remained in its previous position. Action was crowded into every corner. Reverent ideas were exploded. The object portrayed became disintegrated. A man's countenance was no longer circular and puppetlike with eyes, nose and mouth ſtuck in, covered with a smooth skin, almoſt plaſtic in form, but a whirl of intraćtable lines, chaos. It was not a face but grew to a face, remained always in motion, pressed forward out of the frame. This reſtlessness needed careful handling if the artiſt was to recognize and selećt the essential, and success was its own reward.

The novel writer before Doſtoevsky employed conceptual figures. The differences between the conceptions produced the differences between the representative types and from that sprang the aćtion. The differences were not always black and white but such that every reader could see them with his eyes shut. If someone was avaricious, he was fundamentally so. Balzac crammed into his Grandet everything appertaining to the type money-lover, creating him exclusively from that aspećt. As he was punćtilious, as every detail could be verified, every chapter was convincing in its truth to life. What was not true to life arose only from the complete work.

Doſtoevsky renounced the usual ſtrićt separation of these types. The evil man was also good, the dirty one clean, the fool wise, and avarice revealed aspećts which were not suspećted in an avaricious man. This insight was not the result of vapid idealization, even less of transvaluation beyond good and evil. Nothing was more foreign to Doſtoevsky. Black remained black, white white, but black and white are never found true in nature, they are the produćt of mixtures and the possibilities of mixture are unlimited to the sensitive eye. That accounts for the faćt that one single figure now embodies all the charaćteriſtics which formerly were allotted to a variety of charaćters and qualities introduced which no one had thought of before. The charaćters were no longer set in a groove. Ivan or Dmitri might murder juſt as well as Smerdyakov.

Possibly Smerdyakov was leaſt of all a murderer, merely the inſtrument of another will. Nevertheless the aćtion goes breathlessly on, an aćtion of flitting shadows and quivering lights and, despite the swarming crowd, the characters stand before us, each one separately, like a bronze cast, no, like the visions of Rembrandt.

Everything which was said yesterday against Dostoevsky's gloom and obscurity and which to-morrow one will no longer venture to say, was said with equal bitterness a few centuries ago about Rembrandt, and less than a hundred years ago was still repeated with fervour. And the peculiar splendour surrounding Rembrandt, whatever the brilliance of other artists, sets him in high relief from the rest.

There are pictures by Rembrandt whose relationship to Dostoevsky shoots like a flame out of the darkness. There are phrases of the Russian, occasional, arbitrary, contorted, acute-angled phrases like drawings by Rembrandt. It is not alone the similarity of the *motifs*, not those self-portraits which both repeat in more and more powerful variants, not those more profoundly conceived legends, but the uniformity of the stage on which the play is set, this thoroughly theatrical drama carried right into the midst of life with the unmistakable central illumination ; all that we, with our satellite understanding, call form and technique. They are mutually helpful. The one states the moral of the other's works. This operates even more marvellously than the relationship to Shakespeare. Rembrandt contains more of Dostoevsky than of any painter, and the Russia of Dostoevsky is at the same time the Jewish quarter of Amsterdam where are enacted the stories of poor people. A close relationship can be discerned at the point where Dostoevsky becomes unliterary and Rembrandt supersensual. Painting begins to speak and frees itself from the burden of events concentrated on a narrow canvas. Literature overcomes the sequence of words and becomes an undulating surface. The Russian emerges from the dusk surrounding the prodigal son and blesses the blessing hands on the shoulder of him who has returned home. He also sits at the weird round table at the feast of Claudius. Is not the Polish officer on horseback a Karamazov? Is not that a lively Katya masquerading in the garb of Hendrickje Stoffels?

REMBRANDT

Potiphar's wife could have laughed like Grushenka, and behind those heavy curtains lurks murder. People pray in Rembrandt's pictures as only Dostoevsky's Russians can pray. The outcome is what the incomprehensible Orient stands for in biblical pictures, incense, glittering fairy-tale of the orthodox church, which annoy the bolsheviks.

But Rembrandt, if anyone, belonged to the insulted and injured. It was only in their company that he would have felt at home, and he would not have fitted badly into the *katorga*,[1] where men laughed and jested whilst their limbs were in chains, and many a one contorted his branded face into the grin of an old toper. He loved dirt and disorder like a true Muscovite. In his youth he lied and cheated, indulged in orgies and squandered money. As his years increased he made himself even older and uglier than he was, and delighted in it. He debased himself so much that he attained Christ and lived with him. He had humility and pride and was a great tormentor. Out of his misery grew his art which dissipation and depravity only served to develop. He saw and laughed and his laughter was born of sorrow. He had the wit of the drunkard who in the end could fiddle better than the best violinist from Petersburg and urged his young daughter to purloin her mother's last farthing for a glass of gin.

To-day we recognize Rembrandt's creativeness. It has already been mentioned that we owe this knowledge to the painters of the nineteenth century. Art without God, without patron, without guild, art of the middle class and finally of the pariahs, in a word the whole succession from Corot, Delacroix to Marées, Cézanne and Van Gogh, has, brick by brick, erected the monument. With every significant work of a master of our age a veil was drawn from the work of Rembrandt. This precedent points to what may happen to Dostoevsky. He was at once the Rembrandt and the whole gamut of the nineteenth-century painters. However independently each one struggled, all of them had a hand in the

---

[1] Russian: hard labour, punishment inflicted in extreme cases involving at that time imprisonment in the remotest part of Siberia.—Tr.

DOSTOEVSKY

work. Each one handed a piece to the other and, unequal as the pieces may have been, they were mutually helpful. Dostoevsky, as a poet, was alone in his generation and, apparently, without forerunners. The whole of European prose was virtually useless to him. Shakespeare was his only guiding star. To carry the analogy into the world of painting we should have to imagine a Michelangelo as the only predecessor of a Van Gogh.

CHAPTER IV

COMPARED to the artist the writer suffers the disadvantage of being more visibly in the public eye. No one is interested in tracing the origin of a painting, which is a pity because of the modern tendency to select the purely sensual interest. Unquestionably the written confessions of Van Gogh, the grandchild of Rembrandt and nephew of Dostoevsky, have helped to a clearer understanding of his relationship to art. To the violent sweeps of his brush has been added the nervous tension of his letters. The unpretentious *motif* of his pictures gained force from his own tragic experience. His painting is to-day not up to the standard of many other masters, but the figure of a struggler has been revealed, and that is worth more. Perhaps we should be helped by a greater knowledge of the dramatic incidents in Rembrandt's life of which there cannot but have been many, though, of course, that would not change the colour of the Brunswick family portrait, and it is impossible to say whether any light would be thrown on the legend of the Stockholm fragments.

One examines a writer minutely and, through superfluity of personal detail, arrives at the opposite extreme. One of Dostoevsky's biographers asserts that, beside his work, his life is insignificant. It would be difficult to say anything more perverse. Perhaps it is intended to make the utmost of his work, but therein lurks the danger of playing into the hands of the roof-garden. It is, of course, implied that Dostoevsky's life had virtually no meaning for his work, well-known facts are given the lie, and one might just as well ponder on the New Testament without thinking of the life of Christ. Had Dostoevsky led the life of a peaceful citizen in some country house near Petersburg his novels would never have been written. He had amazing experiences, experiences which only a man of his emotion and

intellect could have lived through; and he was not satisfied
to rest on the laurels of these experiences and to ignore
them in his novels in fa,our of fiction ; he wrestled with
those enormities and embodied them in his own works.
Everything written by him can be directly or indirectly
ascribed to actual incidents in which he was involved.

The intensity of Dostoevsky's representations leads
frequently to the inference of a closer connexion between
the man and his creation than actually exists, and to the
very antithesis of the roof-garden's enthusiasm. This error
is far more dangerous. It has been sought to impute to
him his heroes' crimes. One of these legends has recently
been revived in Paris (14). These attempts are to be condemned even if they are the result of scientific research.
But as a matter of fact there is, up to the present, not the
minutest spark of probability, least of all any definite proof.
The coarseness of this materialistic conception of his work
is rather more symptomatic of our times than of Dostoevsky.

The distinguishing events of his life wear an exclusively
gloomy hue. The spring which fed him, rendered him
great and powerful and never quite dried up, was suffering.
It is hardly exaggerating to call Dostoevsky's burden the
heaviest which any man has had set upon his shoulders.
Every kind of suffering tormented him ; bodily misery,
social misery, spiritual misery, everything in excess. He
was born an invalid. His dipsomaniac father laid epilepsy
in his cradle, the most terrible of scourges to the mental
worker. It afforded him lightning-visions and bestowed on
him *The Idiot.* He was born (1821) in unpretentious but
tolerable circumstances, lived in Moscow, where his father
had an appointment at a workhouse-hospital, through a
severe but happy childhood, and was prepared for a military
career at the engineering school in Petersburg, where,
thanks to the morbid stinginess of his father, he already
had to struggle with poverty. He was not free of want for
fifty long years. His was not the calm misery of the poet
in a garret ; it had immense, almost mystical features, was
also a form of epilepsy peculiar to him, from which he

could not and, so it seems at times, did not even wish to escape. Naturally he was spendthrift and knew how to enjoy himself. The starveling for fifty years was a *bon-vivant* for minutes. He scattered gifts like a prince, won and gambled away large sums, was perpetually fleeing from his creditors and, in addition, unnecessarily shouldered his relatives' huge burden of debt. He knew how to make himself a meal out of anything, even out of want. He fed on his poverty, fattened on it, made it tasty, moulded it, borrowed from it the theme of many a novel, laughed and wept about it. His life was determined by financial operations. Money assumed the importance of a guiding spirit which drove him to constructive work.

The Dostoevskys were an old and noble family. There was no trace of it in him. He was the first modern proletarian of the pen. Merejkowsky makes an amusing comparison with Tolstoy. " Dostoevsky loved money, or imagined he loved it, but money did not love him. Tolstoy hated money, or believed he hated it, but money loved him and came of its own accord into his hands." (15).

He grew to know capital crime from living next door to it. After the death of his mother his father abandoned himself wholeheartedly to his avarice and dipsomania and became the prototype of old Karamazov, except that he was not tainted with erotic sensuality. When the youth was scarcely grown up, his father was murdered by maltreated serfs. The principal work can be traced back to that. He came personally to learn the ways of justice. The young writer, who had joined in an apparently nihilistic plot, was sentenced to death by court-martial. Opinions differ about the Petrachevsky conspiracy and the part which Dostoevsky played in it (16). The documents create the impression that they were only a band of youthful and thoroughly harmless babblers, of great immaturity. It is clear that in the meetings of the revolutionaries described in *The Possessed*, Dostoevsky turned to account his experiences as a conspirator. Dostoevsky's revolutionary demand was the abolition of serfdom, which in any case was decreed soon afterwards. The first Court of Justice apparently found no evidence for prosecution. It was only the special court set up by the Tsar which promulgated this draconic sentence. In the last minute before the execution the condemned were reprieved and the sentence commuted to hard labour in Siberia. Dostoevsky received four years, and after that had to serve the same time in Siberia as a private soldier. The hard punishment did not break him; on the contrary, it elevated him. The convict prison prepared the way for the works of his maturity.

Two eventful love affairs succeeded his release from the House of the Dead. The first began in Siberia and led to an unfortunate marriage. What details we know are from the biography of the daughter of his second marriage who herself had to rely on reports and whose impartiality was certainly put to a severe test. Baron Vrangel, the sole surviving witness who was able to observe this relationship from its inception, has expressed himself in his Memoirs with remarkable reserve as to Maria Dmitrievna. Nevertheless there is no trace of any contradiction of the daughter's portrayal. Dostoevsky himself refrained from any accusation and attributed the misfortune of their marriage to incompatibility and the " fantastic " temperament of his wife. At the same time it seems that they loved one another passionately and that their love grew with increasing adversity. A truly Dostoevskian theme ! He was clearly concerned about ensuring a happy memory of the dead woman. That reverence outweighed love follows from Dostoevsky's behaviour during the last part of their married life.

Only the outlines of their relationship are at all clear. He was already in love with Maria Dmitrievna when she was still married to a consumptive captain in Semipalatinsk, the penal garrison where Dostoevsky was stationed after his release from Omsk. To Dostoevsky's despair the captain was transferred to Kusnezk, another Siberian garrison, died there, and his widow became engaged to someone else very soon afterwards. Dostoevsky must have suffered a great deal at this, but did not oppose the alliance, sought in fact to help his fortunate rival and made considerable sacrifices to enable the couple to marry. But the engagement was broken off and the widow approached the writer again, made him come to Kusnezk and married him. She had a son, a good-for-nothing, who caused Dostoevsky much anxiety and to whom he remained a devoted father till the last. According to his daughter, Maria Dmitrievna, during the whole of her married life with Dostoevsky, kept up a *liaison*, begun before her marriage, with a, so it is said, handsome but insignificant teacher named Vergunov. According to Dostoevsky himself he esteemed him " as his own brother." Vergunov followed the couple on their journey to Petersburg. The crude details of this affair were perhaps exaggerated. The fact itself is almost beyond dispute. The faithless woman contracted tuberculosis and the couple separated, ostensibly because the wife could not endure the Petersburg climate. She went to Tver. There her condition grew worse and Vergunov deserted her. Dostoevsky hastened to the invalid who was beyond all hope. In a paroxysm, which can be interpreted in various ways and which Dostoevsky certainly did not interpret as did his biographer, Maria Dmitrievna confessed her deception to the unsuspecting man and spared him nothing. Dostoevsky tended her with self-sacrifice till the end.

The second love affair, of which we know even less but about which we shall shortly have detailed information, took place partly during the unhappy marriage but ended more harmlessly, though it was not more merciful to Dostoevsky's longing heart. According to his daughter, Pauline Suslov, a pretty student, was attracted to the famous author by a superficial ambition (?). She induced him to follow her to Paris and there had an affair with someone else. Dostoevsky became reconciled, but as soon as Pauline had finished her interlude, one of many, he was again caught, this time with threats of suicide and so forth. All these details must be taken with a grain of salt. Since Polina in *The Gambler* (the forerunner of Nastasya in *The Idiot*) bears essential traces of his *inamorata*, a fact admitted by his daughter, she cannot have been a commonplace creature (17). The couple travelled to Wiesbaden, where Dostoevsky gave himself up to roulette. Evidently this love affair was also taken very seriously. His daughter's assertion that only eroticism drove her father to Suslov is more than improbable. Russians who are acquainted with the circumstances assert the contrary. According to them their intercourse was platonic, whether with or without Dostoevsky's concurrence. Anyway, his beloved's incalculable moods led to bitter strife. Pauline Suslov is supposed to have remained constant to the poet till her death.[1] Thereafter Dostoevsky once more came to grief as a suitor till finally (in the spring of 1867), not far short of fifty years of age, he found in Anna Grigorevna, his nineteen-year-old stenographer, a worthy wife and companion.

The zigzag path to the happy haven was not fruitless. The *Eternal Husband*, incidents in *The Insulted and Injured* and *The Gambler*, the dual love of the prince in *The Idiot*, and some of the female characters in *The Brothers Karamazov* are unmistakable fruits. Moreover in a certain degree the reverse is true. Many an experience seems to be the outcome of his writing. Before fate brought him his first wife he made the hero of his early story, *White Nights*, behave as he himself behaved half a dozen years later.

His life seems to have been a cup overflowing with bitterness. No wonder that many people imagine him to have been a ruined man whose glance was unsteady, whose thought was sombre and whose words were poison. His personal utterances to the contrary, for example his repeated protestations of gratitude to the Tsar, who inflicted on him the severest punishment thinkable, they regard merely as humbug, a further sign of his misfortune. As a result they approach his works with bias and ignore the gleams which pierce the darkness, see only infernal devils with whom he battled and not the God who led him to victory.

[1] In 1881 she married V. V. Rozanov, but the union was unhappy and they parted in 1886.—Tr.

INFLUENCE OF MARRIAGE

This man was not unhappy; a few of his heroes, perhaps, but not he. He would have been incapable of writing about their sufferings had he not been above them. Can a man of such vehement creativeness possibly be unhappy? It was not only as a creator, not only in the peculiarly ecstatic moments, which he paid for with epileptic breakdowns, that he enjoyed the raptures of heaven; even in his normal daily life he found more than ample protection against pain and want. His brow was wrinkled early, he grew old quickly, his neck was bent, but that was all. The more robust Rembrandt behaved no differently and laughed beneath his surface heavy with sweat and sighs. Dostoevsky's power of resistance was greater, he was more serene. To think him melancholy is to judge on the surface. He was excitable and moody and at times found difficulty in chasing off in the morning, which for the others was midday, the worries of his nocturnal work. But anyone might have been like that, and on the slightest pretext he changed and laughed. Laughter and tears were very close neighbours in him. His wife calls him an eternal child in good and evil. She sometimes suffered under his incalculable ideas and his violence, under the outpourings of which his excitement stood in need, particularly when she was still very young and had not yet grasped that excitability was inevitable in a man of his susceptible mentality. She came to him at a critical time when his economic circumstances bordered on catastrophe and his creative faculties were strained to their limits. In spite of that no intelligent reader of his wife's *Reminiscences* and *Diary* (18), written in the worst period with palpable sincerity by a quite simple person, will gain the impression that he was an unhappy being, condemned to nourish both himself and others on gloom. The twenty-year-old Anna Grigorevna was obviously unfitted to comprehend many of Dostoevsky's shadows which fell across them just in the first year of marriage; and, likewise, at the beginning, the profound simplicity of his comrade may have passed unrecognized by the poet. In spite of that Anna Grigorevna never seriously doubted, nor had reason to doubt, her good fortune. Her womanly instinct recognized in the childlike mind of her Fedya an elementary safeguard against all danger, and a sure guarantee of a successful wedded life. She was not mistaken. If ever there was an ideal marriage it was this (18).

Apart from his illness which grew with it, his central experience was the Siberian *katorga*. Without the House of the Dead there would be no Dostoevsky. Even the execution scene, the most gruesome moment in his life-story, can be disregarded. It never became a salient factor in his work and, what may seem more remarkable, did not oppress him to any appreciable extent (19). On the other hand the years of the convict's hard labour at Omsk, those four full years on every day of which something was shattered and something was created, that spiritual and physical chafing to the marrow, fortified the man and magnified tenfold the poet.

It is in such circumstances that the study of *milieus* becomes imprinted. He did not fail to turn them to account. His iron chains did not prevent him noting certain characteristics of his comrades' language, and he used his notes in *The House of the Dead*. These memoirs have a biographical and sociological value, but do not count as a decisive factor in his work. Little or nothing of this environment has been introduced into the novels.

On the other hand the whole experience, hammered into him, took possession of the man, not as a strange background for the setting of his works, but as a complete stage for a life entirely changed after the *katorga* ; there was nothing or nearly nothing left of the former man, nothing of the ideas of the Petersburg literary circle, nothing of the one-time social level or of the former politician. Even his body gained, though it had previously succumbed to much slighter exertions. His nerves were strengthened, the intervals between the epileptic attacks became longer. Forced contact with new people, the gloomy stations of Ostrogg renewed his whole being. He was conscious of this rehabilitation and was finally moved by it to bless the constraint of his situation. The Siberian experience, alike in its effect on the man and the poet, was of immense importance: the transformation of a position universally regarded as the lowest stage of human existence into one, not only tolerable, but actually beneficial, and eventually welcome. He acquired a new outlook, the idea of community so indispensable to this poet. The decisive factor in this instance was that such a man, an artist, in short, an individualist of our time, accepted the idea of community, that he attained community as a result of compulsory and perpetual association with a mass of complete strangers. The composition of the *katorga* of convicts who had been deported, not, as Dostoevsky and very few others, for political crimes, but for common felonies, mainly for murder, rendered the situation more difficult.

As he bid his brother farewell in Petersburg he said that, after all, he was not going amongst wild animals. That was naturally said for his brother's consolation because there were tears in his brother's eyes and because one always says something of that kind. As a matter of fact he entered a den. In Ostrogg dwelled all kinds of wild beasts in human form. Amongst them were slavering wolves which constantly circled round and were amused if you shrank at not altogether accidental contact. The dark silent ones in the corner, who did not stir and did not take their eyes off you, were the worst brutes, to whom murder was a pastime. The *milieu*-studies began with the question how to behave in order not, on occasion, to be struck dead. The enemy was not watchful authority, not the dissolute major's sadism; all that was of no account beside the real enemy, the inscrutable mass, into which you were hurled, to which, as a noble, educated, one-time gentleman you did not belong, a mass which was in no mind to accept the new-comer without further ado. The peasant whom patricide had brought there was on good terms with the whole company from the first hour, had immediately acquired their tone, felt as if he had lived there years. The criminal with six murders to his credit was received with applause.

43

DOSTOEVSKY

This political offender, however, who could boast of no crime, was at most ridiculous and contemptible, and his half-shaved head, his chains, his bi-coloured trousers, did not suit him, were a foolish masquerade about which the true inmate of Ostrogg was under no delusion. It seemed not far short of mockery to them.

The problem of how to behave was far more arduous than any hardship. These roughs had an amazingly delicate instinct for certain things—for example, for timid attempts at cultivating friendship. He soon perceived that they had altogether astonishing instincts; therefore restraint was imperative, quite apart from the fact that, for the time being, physical incapacity prevented him from undertaking his share in the compulsory labour and the rest of the *katorga* routine. But if he had wanted to renounce every bond of union with the others, it would have meant, for a man such as he, nothing less than gradual death in a fog of hatred. Such a position throws a man back on his own resources; his companions also allowed themselves to be guided by their nature, a coarse and free nature; hence training in self-discipline and observation and particularly in discretion, a quality so essential in intercourse with the outside world. Dostoevsky preferred the small circle of condemned Polish nobles who never mixed with the crowd and were to him only one of the many curiosities of the den. It was only from the others that he could learn.

One thing he noticed very soon. Men there were actuated only by impulses which it was considered bad form not to curb in the world whence he came. They were thoroughly debased impulses, but surrender to them there was on a totally different plane. The variety was astonishing. No two convicts looked alike in spite of the fact that they constituted a homogeneous mass. On closer inspection the mass was more harmless than the individual. Their instincts did not differ specially from well-known mass-instincts, they stood in fact relatively higher. When the *katorga* appeared *en masse* it seemed as inquisitive as a crowd of school-girls, intent on every stupidity, chattering, romantic, open-hearted, a bit cowardly, and, naturally, stupid as schoolboys. When a new horse was bought or the general paid a visit, when Kulikov and his comrades escaped, they were like a crowd of school-children at play. The mass was calculable like every mass and, what is incredible, easier to influence and to lead than any other. They would all have let themselves be quartered for the colonel, who was only half human. A slight gesture sufficed to animate them and make them forget the insane torture of flogging. There was something childlike in these brutes so soon as they became a mass.

Slowly his eyes became accustomed to the gloom and began to discern gradation in the blackness. Brutes were not the only inhabitants of this den any more than black is the only colour in nature; nature does not paint in monochromes whether it be in the *katorga* or in the shaded forest. These criminals were still in some way human since their humanity could survive such crimes. Anyway the human element in this darkness must have been of peculiar power. Their life must have been a peculiar life.

Dostoevsky gained experience here for his later work. If it was possible to converse humanly with the *katorga*-beings, it was not in his customary language. It would have been useless to approach them with Fourier or Herzen, Schiller or Balzac. You have to delve much more deeply than that, to get down to rock bottom. He came into contact with men from every quarter of the gigantic realm, even with foreigners who could not speak Russian. It was not civilization, not even a semblance of civilization, which held them together, but Ostrogg, their chains and, not least, the pride of their chains. This pride was not the outcome of cynicism, it sprang from a natural and necessary class-consciousness. Most of them were not criminals till they came there, committed deliberately for the first time in Ostrogg the deed for which quite fortuitously the opportunity presented itself outside; and would have repeated it now with their eyes open. No one dreamt of remorse, that is expressed quite definitely in the Memoirs.[1]

[1] The Russian title is *Memoirs of the Dead House.*—Tr.

Even at the place of execution in Petersburg none of the conspirators thought of remorse. That had nothing to do with the deed, but only with the instinct of self-preservation. Dostoevsky thought just as little of attempting to make converts, even amongst his intimates. They would not have welcomed such Protestantism and he would have considered it unjustified encroachment on another's domain. Deprive them of their crime and you impoverish their existence. It is not men who can be changed, but Ostrogg. It is not human instincts alone which are guilty, but the chains on their limbs. Another Ostrogg with less clanking chains drove them to manslaughter when previously they were living in apparent freedom.

That was the great experience which laid the foundation. It did not lead to the easy doctrine that the perpetrator is exonerated; he is guilty, but the others are guilty too; all are guilty for each. There is no difference between one man and another, and Dostoevsky stood by the insulted and injured.

Glances were their first medium of approach. In the eyes of these convicts there was something different from the filth which their mouths muttered as we say Good-day and Good-evening. This language of looks could be cultivated. The language could be acquired only by over-coming dumbness. If that succeeded this language became superior to the usual language, at least for the poet's purposes.

Dostoevsky discovered the necessary idiom for his purposes. It was the immediate outcome of his experience, of his perception, without generalizations and metaphor. The language broadened with the extension of his relation-ships. Possibly the childlike manner was in the individual as well as in the mass. It appeared here and there, generally when least expected. Often a man would forget the crimin-ality of which he boasted, and it seemed as though his pride were only a makeshift for the consciousness of tremendous diabolic force. There in Ostrogg with its unconventional notions it was possible to catch a glimpse of the human element because of the absence of labels, good and evil. It could happen there that suddenly such a purity of feeling should be revealed in the monster as to justify the conclusion that his criminality was only a cloak for his chastity.

This proximity of apparently conflicting feelings was only to be found in such rich and numerous examples in Ostrogg. The thinker trained himself by means of them and acquired an objectivity biassed by no conventional consideration. The Russian and the Russian Christian practised himself on them. In Ostrogg one was a Christian. They rejoiced at every outrage against humanity, but no one would have entertained the thought of an act against God. An atheist, denying Christ with the habitual candour of the outside world, would have been slain without further ado; but no one thought of such a thing. Monstrous brutalization was the order of the day, but they prayed to the Saviour with childlike devotion. And had it been the last tie with the outer world, a tinsel, a mere habit which they had neglected to discard, they would have let themselves be crucified for it.

Could the poet have had such a training in the outside world? Would the four years have passed more easily in communion with a more *bourgeois* type of criminal? Certainly not. In the rough side of the *katorga*-being there were advantages not to be found elsewhere. But you had to be Dostoevsky to benefit by them. A lesser being would have brought away only a superficial tinge of the *milieu*, some picturesque incident, a " subject." Dostoevsky laid in Siberia the foundation of his moral and spiritual existence. A Crusoe discovered his island in Ostrogg. It was the realization which was new, not the problem. Tolstoy, in an early work of his youth, *The Cossacks*, portrayed a Petersburg aristocrat, enfeebled by civilization, who escapes into the Caucasian wilderness and tries to convert himself to a pure humanity, amongst the primitive mountain-folk. Love for Marianka, the bride of the Cossack Lukaschka, becomes the pillar of the action. The story does not rise beyond the nature worship of a man who has read Rousseau. It is only the body of Olenin, the Crusoe of this wilderness, which travels; his head stays behind in accursed civilization. Perhaps that is what Tolstoy wanted to show. What escaped him was the doubtful reality of his island. Like foot-notes whose purpose is to give weight to the text, this Caucasus, which he decks out with ethnographic details, does not exist. His Cossack girls flirt just like young ladies of Petersburg, and Lukaschka is a Guards officer in disguise.

Tolstoy has written better novels with more effective Lukaschkas and Mariankas. So long as he remained a poet he never overcame the use of disguise, and when he abandoned it we would have entreated him quickly to adopt it again, for every one's benefit. He never found and underwent an Ostrogg.

Many have played the part of Crusoe. The whole of European culture is doing that to-day. The flight from Europe drove a Gauguin to remote regions. He thought that far away he could abjure the past and preclude all possibility of return by adopting sinister idols, but all the same he clung to the boulevards till his dying day.

Repudiation is not possible. The structure of the atoms is not transformed by violence. You can only develop what you bring. Van Gogh could complete as a painter only what he had begun as instructor and teacher; he could not change his vocation. Dostoevsky was carrying the germ of his Ostrogg experience when, as an unsuspected *littérateur*, he wrote the story of *The Double*. Only such a fanatic of second sight could discover the unity underlying the demonic man. Everything followed from this discovery. What happened in the den, happens everywhere. Fine and base instincts are everywhere fingers of the self-same hand; but in the outer world we are wont to wear gloves and society insists on them; they can only be dispensed with in a world which does not need a mask to conceal the ruin to which it is tottering. And whoever survives the *katorga* without losing his faith in humanity can judge the world from a very different angle.

From Siberia Dostoevsky discovered Russia. The *katorga* was the Venice where this El Greco went to school before he embarked for his Spain. The discovery of this unity was bound eventually to lead to the conception of the Russian universal man, Dostoevsky's legacy in his swan-song, his speech on Pushkin.

There can be no doubt about the good-fortune which Dostoevsky met with in Siberia. His gratitude for Siberia is therefore thoroughly legitimate, and no one can be astonished that he gave expression to it. The Tsar who sent him there became his benefactor. Devotion to the Tsardom was part of the Russian Christian religion. From now onwards Dostoevsky began a struggle for the Russian creed. His appreciation of its manifest blessing added not inconsiderably to his own articles of faith. Another considerable influence, long after Siberia, was his personal contact with foreign countries; first the short journeys to Paris, London, Germany and Italy in the first half of the sixties, and then his sojourn abroad from the spring of 1867 till the summer of 1871. Those four years of travel constituted a kind of educational tour during which he was able to put his new attitude to a practical test and, in that sense, though comparatively unspectacular, they were an essential complement of the four *katorga* years which had resulted in his conversion and the introduction of a powerful literary stimulus. His distance from the *milieu* for which he had to create broadened his imagination and finally rendered distinct the last and highest step in his development. Connected with this tour were severe shocks which would have been spared him in his homeland and it bequeathed him his most brilliant work. *The Idiot* was written in Italy.

Karl Nötzel, in his biography, finds, as a result of the four years in the West, " spiritual concentration such as he had never yet experienced and such as he could attain only in foreign countries which, because they were inwardly

strange to him, diverted him far less from his true self."
That is the main reason, he adds, why many Russians
travelled abroad at that time; to give themselves a rest from
Russia and to enable them to meditate on matters with
which they were in too close contact at home. That is
peculiarly true of Dostoevsky. In the first years after
Siberia Dostoevsky seems indeed to have been too near
to Russia to discharge the tension which was the fruit of
the *katorga*. His first works after Siberia, in part unsteady,
in part thoroughly sceptical, bear testimony to disillusionment, even if it be only at not finding the freedom he had
hoped for on his return. In his first travels there was something of the ferment of accumulated desires. But the first
great novel followed immediately on these confused and
extravagant works. *Crime and Punishment* was published
shortly before his big journey. Its success was unprecedented. This first exhaustive work of the *katorga*-poet
became the foundation for everything which succeeded it.
That fact must be firmly grasped in order to appraise at
their true worth subsequent events in his life, his second
marriage and the big journey.

The journey was very welcome to his young wife,
because she hoped thereby to extricate her husband from
the intrigues of his relatives. The couple went first to
Dresden, then to Switzerland. They passed the first
winter in Geneva where Sonia was born and, to her parents'
despair, died after a few months; the second in Florence,
the last in Dresden, where the second daughter was born.

Their sojourn abroad was not entirely of their own
free-will. It was not only the disagreeable friction with
the family which made it desirable; there were much more
cogent economic considerations. The financial success of
Crime and Punishment was negligible, so great had become
his debts since the death of his brother Michael and the
failure of the periodical *Epoca* which Dostoevsky had considered it his duty to carry on. He was prevented from
returning to Russia by fear of his creditors who constantly
threatened imprisonment. This state of affairs gradually

became intolerable. Dostoevsky has himself stated that in the last years his exile became scarcely less easy to endure than the *katorga*.

He was not unsusceptible to the enjoyments of the tourist, he liked music and was fond of art. The curious drawings of Gothic arches here and there between the lines of his manuscripts suggest that he had a taste for architecture. But that was not so; in fact buildings of earlier periods repelled him. Everything he could consider an antiquity left him cold. His interest in literature was unbounded. He seems to have appreciated painting. Wherever he went he visited the museums, if only hurriedly, and, during their first stay in Dresden, often accompanied his young wife to the gallery of which she was an *habituée*. He adored the Sistine Madonna, symbol of the ardently hated Roman Catholicism. He always came across pictures which seem opposed to his temperament. Rembrandt was not mentioned. On the other hand the cool idylls of Claude Lorraine impressed him. His favourite picture was the coast-scene in the Dresden Gallery, with its glistening sea and pair of lovers under the tent. It plays an important part in Versilov's dream of the Golden Age.

Nevertheless these stimulants were no compensation for absent friends. His distress was more pressing than at home. His epilepsy grew worse and rendered his work more difficult and, above all, at the beginning of this period he was in the clutches of a gambling mania. But still his harvest came. Those four years gave birth to *The Idiot*, *The Eternal Husband* and the major part of *The Possessed*, besides a number of smaller things. Work accumulated, particularly in the second half of the journey.

More than from illness, privation, sorrow for little Sonia, or working against time, he suffered from nostalgia; at times he must have been a martyr to it. The glistening lake did not smile on him and the mountains oppressed his soul. In all seriousness he went as far as to consider the climate of Geneva detrimental to him. He would have given Rome and the Two Sicilies for a corner in some remote Russian province. He devoured every Russian newspaper. His letters to people in Petersburg invariably turned on only two things, money and news. His health depended on whether a periodical containing a Slavophil article had been forwarded to him. He did not beat about the bush. The urgency of this need can be felt in every line. He would have worked frantically, even if time had been no object, merely to create for himself a Russian atmosphere. His novels were rags around his own nakedness. Distance from home had accentuated this typical attitude. To him art and culture were not educational requirements but the last escape from isolation. Science counted only in so far as it served that purpose. His creative advance can be recognized. He was always frightened of losing touch with Russia, a fear born not of a *littérateur's* concern about his own position but of anxiety about spiritual nourishment which only Russian soil and the Russian people could give him. In so far as he had the people with him in the *katorga*, the *katorga* was more desirable. He seems to have missed his country less in Italy. German orderliness jarred on his nerves. The stolid tone of the Swiss was intolerable to him. He found men poor and wretched and a prey to mass-instincts of no importance. Finally he lived in Dresden like a prisoner.

Longing consumed the man but strengthened his creative power, and whilst reality was denied him he fortified himself in dreams. The distance from Russia may have assisted in the tenderness with which he surrounded *The Idiot*. It palpably injured *The Possessed*.

Abroad his love for everything Slav was his main support, fortified by comparisons with the world around. On his first travels he had already intuitively drawn a marked distinction between East and West, a factor which was in no way in conflict with his own universality. The West possessed, from earlier times, all manner of values not found in Russia, but was not in a position to build on them. Russian civilization was an historic relic, like cathedrals and temples no longer used for prayer, and enthusiasm for an exuberant though obsolete form led to humbug and to the divorce of man from humanity. But the famous civilization of the West accomplished much the same. Its vivacity, however, did not escape Dostoevsky. Although the æsthetic element was dead, yet there was a living urge to improve conditions of physical existence. In comparison the East could show nothing but inertia. But what resulted? Did not the West with its industry widen the gulf between one man and another? Was not the unclean East on the whole far more uniform? What was understood by life in East and West was not the same thing. Before the Russian eye the complex clockwork of Europe lost its glamour. Western culture became an antique and its civilization commercialism. What they called education was furniture in a best room, and they sat down on the cushion of religion. The chains with which machinery threatened mankind were heavier than had ever been threatened by the forces of Russia, opposed, as were the latter, to culture.

The politician Dostoevsky, in realizing that, was lured into many doubtful inferences, and he mistook trifles for essentials, especially in the beginning. His essays after his first journey abroad, *Winter Notes on Summer-impressions*, waged a truly naïve polemic against France, and, later, Germany too received several hits. Later on the poet overcame his narrow-mindedness.

CHAPTER V

WE have already seen that the literary element was not the only factor in Doſtoevsky, a fact which he himself deliberately ſtressed. In the course of time he attached less and less importance to his literary mission, if such an expression can be applied to him at all. In this sense he bears a certain resemblance to Goethe who also did not believe that exclusive devotion to literature fulfilled one's human obligations, though Doſtoevsky was guided by a conception totally alien to Goethe. The urge of the encyclopædiſt Goethe to excel in many spheres in order to perfect himself and thus to become an example to others, to be educator, if possible scientific teacher of himself and of his people, was in direct conflict with the notions of Doſtoevsky who, though he too did not confine his intereſt to literature, did not feel attracted to any other activity, and scientific method was altogether foreign to him. The energy which was withheld from his writing was directed towards the inveſtigation and cultivation of relationships with his neighbour, thus contributed to spiritual exercise, and, in that way, remained in conſtantly accessible and serviceable proximity to his main calling. The by-way always led back into the main road and afforded fresh nourishment to his creative literature.

This procedure had advantages. It was only in his imagination that his activity was directed along devious routes, a self-delusion to which his renunciation of all formal æſthetics lent support. In reality no poet has ever concentrated so exclusively on his main purpose. His apparent extravagance is economy.

Goethe's manifold activities, his contributions to the sciences, his actions as ſtatesman and courtier, were of no direct service to him as a poet; rather they became a bar to the development of his genius. What he created on the by-paths would have been done without his efforts and, though a matter for admiration, merely illustrated a breadth of mind which needed no proof; it can only count as a faint reflex of his incomparable literary powers which explored the finite on the by-paths instead of creating the unique. The universality generally admired in Goethe is far below the ideal standard he set himself, and was the educational ideal of precisely that class which to-day is the enemy of all ideals.

Dostoevsky went to the people with no thought of making them *bourgeois*. The pitiable condition of *bourgeois* Europe did not tempt him. The simple people who lived by the toil of their hands should remain what they were. You went not to reform them, but to reform yourself and to receive as much as possible from them. In spite of that it was possible to remain an intellectual, there was no need to revert to a primitive state, and sophistication followed all the more readily. It was decidedly no advantage that the people could neither write nor read, but those short-comings did not prevent them from feeling, thinking, loving, suffering and coping with life. The simple people were more successful than the civilized man who obstructed the view with a thousand trifles, and lost touch with the soil. The people were in touch with the soil. They were not a prey to unnatural brooding, but thought seriously and about serious matters. Their feeling bound them together. Community of instinct, feeling, experience was paramount, and no one ever stood alone. Dostoevsky admired those qualities above all. Doubtless he considered it a good thing to lessen the number of the illiterate, himself did his utmost to that end, in Ostrogg taught reading and writing and recommended such instruction wherever he had the opportunity. "Go and teach reading and writing if only to one Russian youth!" he told many a visitor who came to him with problems, but he was thinking not only of what the instructor imparted but also of what he would thereby acquire. Teaching was a different proposition in vast Russia from what it was in Dresden or in Geneva. It meant going out into the steppe with its tiny villages, miles apart, and reading and writing became neither a weapon for the struggle for existence nor a medium of contact with the outer world but a means of shortening the distance from village to village and from town to steppe in order to be nearer together.

Together ! That was his entire aim. People were to be good, as good as possible, and eschew evil, as far as possible, but, above all, to be together. The whole of morality and of beauty turned on that. Communion was worth more than the whole of thought and knowledge put together; any idea which did not emanate from the closest union with the people was moonshine. A thought which I alone comprehend is not a real thought. Literature was the people's literature or nothing at all. Doubtless as much as possible was to enter the circle, and Russians are capable of embracing the whole world. But the circle had to be Russian. Communion was conceivable by Russians only in the Russian manner. What the Russian manner is and what it signifies cannot be explained in two words. It is soon known on reading Dostoevsky. But this nationalism was able to inspire a universal outlook which was not merely a cultural notion. It led Dostoevsky to an activity which we would call political and distinguish as a separate vocation and which, to a Russian, is a matter of course, be he poet or dentist. Since Dostoevsky could write, he did not confine the expression of his nationalism to the spoken word. The extraordinary thing was the intensity of his political writing. He was occupied with journalism at a quite early stage and wanted, in his very first years, to take a hand in the foundation of a satirical journal. After his return from Siberia he became a journalist. In 1861 he and his brother Michael founded the periodical *Vremya*, and he devoted himself to it with energy. After two successful years the periodical was suppressed as a result of an error of the censor. In 1864 it was followed by the *Epoca*. Dostoevsky overloaded himself with editorial work and, after the death of his brother, vainly sacrificed a fortune to carry on the paper. After his return from abroad he began again and in 1873 joined the editorial ſtaff of the *Grajdanin*. In 1876 he published the firſt *Journal of an Author*, written entirely by himself, which appeared at irregular intervals. The proofs of the laſt number were correĉted on the day before his death and appeared on 31ſt January 1881, the day of his burial. It dealt with the relationship of the intelleĉtuals to the people, a theme which had already been broached in the preliminary announcement of the *Vremya*.

Journalism was the foundation of his literature. Once he frankly ſtated that he considered the journaliſt more important than the poet. An example taken from everyday life could be more valuable to him than an abſtraĉtion. Coming from any other mouth one might objeĉt to this diĉtum. The Petersburg æſthetes who turned to the Weſt vented their indignation. In reply he cited the example of the murderous earthquake in Lisbon which did not prevent a lyric poet composing to the dawn a well-rhymed hymn " without verbs " and putting it in the newspaper the day after the disaſter. Thereon the poet was lynched in the open market-place. " Not because he wrote a poem without verbs, but because yeſterday, inſtead of the trill of the nightingale, there were heard quite different trills under the earth, and the dreamy rolling of the waves at that moment when the whole city shook was felt to be an insult on the part of the poetaſter." It was possible, of course, calmly to accept the consummate beauty of the poem. It is possible that later it was even of great advantage to the inhabitants of Lisbon since it enhanced their sense of beauty. In faĉt the next generation ereĉted in the same market-place a memorial to him who was lynched. And one generation was juſt as much juſtified as the other. " It was not art which was guilty but the poet who applied it at a moment when it was bound to become an abuse." This classical inſtance in which Doſtoevsky came to grips with the roof-garden indicates the nature of his journalism, an experi-

mental pedagogy which his quick mind extemporized.
There was not a grain of narrow-minded prejudice in his
reference, and his underlying nationalism had not only the
Russian but all people in view, and not only Russian
æsthetes but æsthetes in general. Even to-day anyone
might profit by this example. It is truer now than ever.

Doſtoevsky's periodicals, full of such indications of
sound common-sense, also contain banalities. The journaliſt
was not concerned with niceties. Unambiguous expression
of opinion was more important than *esprit*. He laughed at
the all too scrupulous who, in every *feuilleton*, had their
collected works in mind. If one adminiſtered a ſtrong pill
to the reader, it had to be made palatable with two or three
milder ones. Doſtoevsky confessed to such guiding principles with the utmoſt candour. For those who were not
cognizant of the ultimate editorial objeɛ̌t—and how could
contemporaries have known !—the conduɛ̌t of the *Vremya*
at times came perilously near to the usual newspaper
method which regards the acquisition of subscribers as the
goal of all its desires.

He shrugged impatiently when he was reproached
and went on. What he published was an infinitesimal part
of his journalism; he could have furnished ten publications
with ideas. His notebooks swarmed with topical themes.
He assumed a definite attitude towards every utterance of
the daily press which affeɛ̌ted his circles. He had few free
minutes in Petersburg.

In his novels this journaliſt was concerned only with
the task he set himself; they were not intended to serve
any personal end, though there is a certain familiarity of
tone which, judged by accepted ſtandards, is scarcely
worthy of the poet. This tone was Doſtoevsky's invention,
his secret, his technique, the natural garb of the people's
writer, and, in spite of its banality, it succeeded in revealing
the sublime. It is by this means that he attains intimate
contaɛ̌t with his reader in such a way that the latter entirely
fails to notice the gradual development of profound thought
and expansion of the theme. It is a bungling process, like

a child trying to draw, but he groped his way gradually to the complete manifeftation. " To force a way to truth through lies ! " That profound di&um of the philosopher Doftoevsky explains his writing and conftantly proves that there were no barriers between the man and the poet, between his ethics and æfthetics. There was no pedantry in it; he was a humble man who admitted his kinship with eternally groping and bungling humanity; there was wisdom in his words. His journalism did not show to advantage compared to that of writers before him but, as we have seen, he was equal to the great bunglers in other realms of art whose journalism had become a source of inspiration and a path to ultimate success. Certainly his inftin& might have appealed to the greateft man in the world, to the person he revered before all else. With a like journalism Chrift built His church.

But there is a cry from the roof-garden. There is only one law, the law is supreme; and however deep the feeling, however great the humility, journalism cannot be transformed into creative literature. Doftoevsky may have been a profound thinker, a Chriftian, a benefa&or, but it does not therefore follow that he needed to produce creative literature. You can point to the development of painting, it is true, but painting is in decay, and the very fa&ors which aided its growth in the nineteenth century have later on accompanied its decline. Therefore, philosophizes the roof-garden, if Doftoevsky's procedure is a criterion, precisely the same thing may happen to literature.

That may be, indeed it is quite probable; possibly with Doftoevsky began the collapse of European literature, but that indicates nothing more or less than the spirit of the age and does not show who is responsible. The disintegration of the arts is a social phenomenon which no individual by himself can bring about, and the roof-garden cannot judge it adequately. Already before Doftoevsky enlightened minds were forced, by unmiftakable signs, to reckon with this decay. This movement is beyond the control of any individual. The loss has to be made good and, if made good, may be borne with the same equanimity with which we dispense with costumes of bygone ages. If we cannot find a substitute for artistic and literary values we shall be standing naked, face to face with chaos.

Dostoevsky was devoted to literature, whatever its period or nationality, but did not consider that the sleeping souls of men could be awakened by use of traditional form. He was more conscious of the danger than others, and had a deeper sense of responsibility, not towards literature, but towards humanity, and therefore, rather than be cramped by obsolete forms, he sought to discover his own method of delivering his message. To discover, not to invent, for personal intervention lessened the prospect of success. Colloquial expression was the best means to this end. First content and coherence, then æstheticism. Did this lead to some form of art or to a substitute for art? Or must Dostoevsky's creation be defined in some other way? What's in a name? Creative literature is the highest human achievement because it requires the least equipment. Even its possibilities of development surpass those of the other arts and its æsthetics are the least tied to fixed norms. But however loose the norms may be, Dostoevsky's creation must always be subject to æsthetic consideration if it is to be brought into any, even if only a substitutional relationship to art. Dostoevsky's indifference to this point of view does not alter facts.

In any attempt at considering this point we shall have to revert to the separation of idea and form. Effectively as Dostoevsky's methods may have served their inspirational purpose it cannot be said that they necessarily have the permanent value of literature. There may be limitations to the idea of Dostoevsky as benefactor or perverter of present-day humanity, and then what remains of the creator?

The idea cannot be separated from the work and the question is: what has Dostoevsky done for the formation of the idea? That leads us to the history of his development. An insight into the development of Dostoevsky may make it possible to perceive a literary canon which we regard as essential in order to render his art acceptable to us. But anyone regarding as futile, formless matter the world of thought comprised in his novels would be taken aback, could organic growth be proved, were it possible to demonstrate how, connected with it, composition, expression and everything we call literary method are developed in the course of time, were he to discover a widening of vision and elevation in the numerous works. In that case he could not fail to remember that such elevation and generalization have been constituted criteria by great masters of Europe. Then he would, in certain circumstances, have to recognize in the Russian manner of representation an admissible, perhaps even necessary form, legitimate in its own sphere, and fear of journalism would be overcome. Yet the fact of the collapse of literature might have to stand all the same. That would then be a matter in itself which we should have to endure.

It is far easier to trace the development of Dostoevsky than that of any other writer. There were two distinct and unequal stages. In the first he accumulated material, sifted and prepared it. The *katorga* fell in this period and helped to bring the preparation to fruition without, however, setting any limit on it. In the spring of 1854 Dostoevsky was released from the convict prison and in the spring of 1859 from compulsory service in Siberia. But the first stage did not come to a natural conclusion till 1864 with the *Letters from the Underworld*. The second period began with *Crime and Punishment*, written in 1865 and 1866, and ended with *The Brothers Karamazov*, which appeared in 1880 shortly before his death. The significance of the four-year sojourn abroad is reflected in the higher level of work in this period. There is a distinct parallel here: just as Siberia may have been of importance to his analytical tendency, so voluntary exile may have hastened the development of his synthetic process.

The young Dostoevsky was an enthusiast. Many of his utterances recall writers of the German romantic period, and every lover of French literature of the same period hears familiar echoes.

DOSTOEVSKY

He would have been glad to have been like these writers. He was fond of them all. Many of the early letters sound like the youthful outpourings of Delacroix. In conversation, on the other hand, he proved himself reserved, of that perverse obduracy of which all Vincent van Gogh's friends had to complain. If he were misunderstood he found a certain pleasure in magnifying the motive of the error. He was oppressed by his inability to express or restrain his feelings. Van Gogh must have been like him in many respects, and this similarity, whose limits are easily recognizable, can assist us in our portrayal of Dostoevsky's beginnings (20). One cannot help feeling that just as Van Gogh fruitlessly sought resonance, just as unrest drove him from one vocation to another and finally to death, so Dostoevsky was threatened, and withstood the threat. But in the Russian cadet the yearning was still more confused and lacked the directing motive of Van Gogh's aims which, though they were evanescent, were fruitful for at least a short time.

Dostoevsky's ambition, which was unknown to Van Gogh, yielded a greater power of resistance and enabled him to lay his soul bare. Writing was not the last resort for Dostoevsky as was painting for Van Gogh, but it was his one and only means of expression. Van Gogh's vagaries from art-dealer to teacher, from teacher to theologian, to lay-preacher, to painter, were accomplished by Dostoevsky in his writing. Van Gogh's vagaries were not the caprice of a *dilettante*, he was forced to them by the desire to escape from the fraud of his calling, flights which really every conscientious person ought to venture; in the same way Dostoevsky was driven to his prolific productivity. That was the only way of enduring Dostoevsky's world of problems.

He began with a great deal of sentiment but with no definite aim. It is true that there are elements of his genius in the two early works, *Poor Folk* and *The Double*, and they can be considered two distinct preludes to the whole of his later works; but in their relationship to the first period they may appear merely as lighthouses in the midst of an ocean. Dry land is not sighted till much later. Moreover although they were the first printed, they were not the first written works; they were preceded by a short and entirely different phase in which Dostoevsky tried his hand as a dramatist. This phase, of which unfortunately nothing is preserved, is palpable throughout his development.

In the early days he was indiscriminately enthusiastic about literature, particularly Western literature and, a true romanticist, sought emotion everywhere. His youthful admiration for Schiller must be borne in mind. He raved about everything he read and passed judgment with boyish swiftness. The love for Schiller, particularly for the Schiller of *Don Carlos* and *Maria Stuart*, was more deeply embedded and for a time attained fanaticism. He himself spoke of " possession." Schiller must have been the earliest and most potent experience of his youth, and exerted on him a highly paradoxical influence which can be traced throughout his life.

The Russian element in Dostoevsky set up varying degrees of resistance against this sentimentality; in course of time it grew more effectual and eventually overcame the Western heritage. The powers of resistance owed their origin to the clear-sighted realism of a young race which was not muzzled by any *bourgeois* convention; there was, however, no recourse to the materialistic scepticism of the West which ultimately flings every feeling overboard as useless ballast, but strong feeling supplanted a feeble sentiment. Even when from time to time Dostoevsky overflowed with bitterness he did not fall to the temptation of neutralizing his creative instinct, although his specific tendency to psychology could have tempted him particularly. With his psychology grew his all-embracing power of feeling, for, in the Russian, psychological insight is fed by emotion. The feeling utilized the analytical results, "Atoms tracked out in the depths " (21), as building material for the synthesis. Eventually we perceive the purest expression of human greatness.

CHAPTER VI

LET us examine his development. He made his public *début* in the winter of 1845 to 1846 with the novel *Poor Folk*. The work immediately assured Dostoevsky a place in literature; not only amongst his contemporaries, who overwhelmed him with unprecedented applause, but also amongst all those who to-day take up the book. Were it possible to regard this first work as a criterion there would be no discussion about the character of Dostoevsky's creation. Whether good or bad, it owes its existence exclusively to poetic impulse and is nothing but literature, is entirely free of disturbing or even surprising psychological effects and almost without action. It is only the portrayal, the tone of the letters between the poor man and the poor girl, to which the unusual charm is due. I know of no other author's *début* of such inward as well as outward success. The book created a furore amongst public and critic alike. There were a few genuinely Russian scenes; the one when Nekrasov and Grigorovitch, having read the manuscript during the night, and scarcely knowing the author, rushed to him at four o'clock the next morning, awakened him and told him what they thought of the book; the second scene when Belinsky, the dreaded master of criticism, lost all control and excitedly declared that Dostoevsky himself had not the least conception of the importance of the work.

It is strange that Dostoevsky so often calls artists to our minds and so seldom writers. The success of *Poor Folk* with the public recalls the triumph of Delacroix's first picture, Dante's Bark, which twenty years earlier stirred another public in the same way. Another standard was promptly set. People suddenly knew what art was; everything else was nonsense. All at once the Russians, even Russians who had never troubled about literature, possessed

a poet. They set no store by its artistic merit, had no
notion of its meticulous structure with which Dostoevsky
had been experimenting for a year; the only work which
was worked out with care. They did not think of that at
all. What excited them was the charm, the crystal purity
of its sentiment, the poet's devotion. He had surrendered
himself, and since his surrender had not been in vain it
became intoxicating in its effect. Every one wanted to
surrender himself in the same way. As once Dante's Bark,
he aroused ideas which had long since existed unconsciously
and established unusual associations between giver and
receiver. The Dante's Bark set loose a flood of romanticism
in whoever looked at it. Every one, more especially every
Frenchman, perceived sublimity in the action, and every one
had pictured this remote incident in exactly the same way.
The barrier which had previously been associated with
pictorial art was removed. In the same way familiarity
with these poor people thrilled the reader who had never
considered them worthy of representation. Every one was
familiar with the submissiveness of this broken-down clerk
and insignificant girl. Every one became a writer for every
one believed he too could write such letters. Every one
felt the tenderness of this trampled official who dared not
even confess his love. Every one saw through the dutiful
impulse of the girl who behaves as best she can in the
circumstances and finally acts as any other woman would.
That was reality. But apart from the realism there arose in
the reader's mind a spontaneous sympathy, quite detached
from the book, which illumined their sorrows and yearnings,
and yet remained restrained because the poet was restrained.
Later, in *The Insulted and Injured*, Dostoevsky alluded to the
psychological effect of this novel; first astonishment at the
commonplace features, then sympathy, and finally common
joy with the silent poet who knew how to describe pity.
Indeed the Russian felt this exaltation, which had an appeal
similar to the Dante's Bark. Both poet and reader were
inspired. People drew together and smiled although the lot
of the poor folk was really sad.

DOSTOEVSKY

The enthusiasm of contemporary criticism was not so naïve. Belinsky, the father, and Nekrasov, the poet of nihilism, were attracted only by the poverty of the poor folk and were delighted with the propaganda they read into it. Belinsky's attitude towards Dostoevsky was the same as that of the socialist Proudhon towards Gustave Courbet whose ambition led him to profit by the misunderstanding, though this was of no ultimate benefit to his painting. Belinsky acquired a short-lived and limited influence on Dostoevsky's political thought and may have prepared him for Petrachevsky. He was more sensitive than Proudhon to artistic worth which was a pleasing adjunct in a novel in which he perceived a new form of protest. Dostoevsky, on the other hand, was not concerned with this protest; all he sought to portray in the novel was the intimacy of two persons steeped in sentimentality within narrow intellectual boundaries; their joint relationship to the outer world was a given background.

The literary world spoke of a new Gogol. It would have been just as fitting to call Delacroix a new Gros. The entirely new source of light was overlooked. Gogol never illuminated. He may have furnished the nucleus of the action. That does not mean much in this actionless story. The inspiration was more probably of Western origin, though it is difficult to indicate precisely whence it emanated.

The second novel sounded like a recantation of *Poor Folk*. Instead of the calm illumination there was an unsteady flicker like street-lamps in the breeze. This work shared the fate of Delacroix's second *salon*-picture, the Massacre of Chios, and for much the same reasons; it was as great a failure as his first book had been a success. In Paris they talked of the massacre of painting. In Petersburg *The Double* was banished from the realm of literature.

With *Poor Folk* Dostoevsky struck out on a new path of tenderness and sentimentality of universal appeal. One's thoughts turn to Western literature as well as to Gogol and Pushkin, but these pleasant thoughts are soon dispelled; a new person appeared, the psychologist, an uncanny fellow,

who interrupted the course of the sentimentality just as
Delacroix, in the Massacre, interrupted his surfaces.
Delacroix did that in order to enhance the brilliance,
because he was a painter and loved colour. Actually the
colours glowed quite otherwise than in Dante's Bark, but
the composition lacked concentration and became problematic. There were people who foresaw the need for this
development and retained their confidence in the painter.
In Petersburg even the enlightened assumed an attitude of
opposition towards the new work. Very few read it to the
end and finally Dostoevsky himself fell to regarding it as
a failure. The political critics who had read into *Poor Folk*
socialistic propaganda were sorely disappointed; this story
puzzled them, the author seemed to be as mad as his hero.
A variant of *Poor Folk* would have been welcomed, possibly
in a more lively key, and Dostoevsky would have been able
to settle down as a popular writer. No one noticed what
this unexpected turn augured for the future, even though
the first work was more perfect in form. With *Poor Folk*
the author might have exhausted himself; its very merits,
the restrained tone and chiselled details, might have led
sceptics to believe that the artist was satisfied with this note.
With *The Double* his genius went off at a tangent. This
bold experiment had its counterpart in the prancing steed
in the human throng seen in a divine second which positively
had to be painted even if it were senseless. Youthful
enthusiasm is and must be unbridled. That is what we
must bear in mind, Delacroix's prancing steed and not the
psychology of *The Double*.

But the psychology must not be ignored. The steed
leaps on solid ground, could otherwise not be realized. It
is only the space surrounding it which sways, only the
dimensions which are not harmonious. Those are trifles.

In so far as *Poor Folk* is a true picture of the people it
portrays and not a fortuitously successful piece of writing,
The Double is its organic sequel. Golyadkin, like Dyevushkin
in *Poor Folk*, is a sentimental and unassuming official who
regards oppression as inevitable, but all the same reflects on

it and thereby does something to his detriment, a thing which would never have occurred to Dyevushkin; thus he is a fuller type, more resourceful and resisting and, as a consequence, less harmonious, not yet resigned in the positive way which pleased the reader of *Poor Folk*, although his good nature is prepared at any moment for any renunciation. He would agree to any sacrifice on one small condition, and it is this small condition which brings him to the madhouse.

The struggle with this small matter leads to a most fantastic tragedy. Golyadkin harbours in his breast the two souls which Cervantes fashioned in the costume of his period. Dostoevsky attempted the same thing in a modern Russian setting. Life has become extremely complicated since those days, and the windmills against which the knight tilted his lance have been replaced by other obstacles. Dualism can no longer be denoted by an arid Don and an obese Sancho. One of Golyadkin's souls endures Dyevushkin's disciplined obedience, is constantly in fear of giving offence, is cowardly and cringes. The other wants, not exactly the world, but a glimmer of it, a little recognition, without striving and cringing, recognition not only of the little bit of ability but of its hidden nobility of soul, of its goodness of heart. Golyadkin wants to play a part, even if only quite a small one. He wants that urgently, but does not think very seriously about it, by no means, would never make a move for it, remains quietly at his desk in the office of the Ministry, department so-and-so, till the double appears. A second Golyadkin, the image of the first, also becomes an official in the same department and sits opposite the first Golyadkin. The double realizes all the most secret desires of the hero and is a huge success with his colleagues and superiors, even with society. Golyadkin the first tries to come to an understanding with Golyadkin the second, wants to be his friend, his brother, wants to love him and kill him, but is unawares invariably displaced by the mean fellow.

The poet has not been forgiven for not having made Golyadkin the second a little more shadowy. The artistic blunder proves his independence of mind and does not detract from the artistic achievement. The casual manner in which the illusion torments the real Golyadkin and the simplicity with which he allows himself to be tormented, thereby becoming even more deeply involved, do not display the normal attributes of auto-suggestive fantasies; yet fantasies which lead to insanity must possess such reality. We are faced with Dostoevsky's uncanny familiarity with pathological conditions. His vision was far ahead of contemporary research and is still to-day considered a phenomenon by experts. He covered much of the ground of psycho-analysis and was most intimately familiar with the modern conception of the subconscious.

Purely psychological effect, as distinct from psychology as an artistic medium, doubtless pleased the public which eagerly concurred in any obliteration of the boundaries of art. Dostoevsky's artistic blunder, which he himself accepted as a matter of course, was his renunciation of the terminology of scientists and his attempt to generalize the pathological case. He stood by his hero, not as a physician, but as participator in his fate, himself believed in the corporeality of the double and only on the threshold of the asylum ridded himself of the illusion. It was just his art which was the artistic blunder, the break with analysis in favour of synthesis. Dostoevsky certainly had no desire to demonstrate a diseased case but, as he himself said thirty years later in the *Journal of an Author*, wanted to establish " a type of great social significance." That was a truly modest claim. There was more involved than that. After *Poor Folk* Dostoevsky wanted to create the tragedy of a humiliated type, and the portrayal of madness up to the point of the *alter-ego*-illusion, although conclusively worked out, was largely poetic licence. Nötzel's suggestion that Golyadkin's madness is an indictment of the State of Nicholas I in whose service officials were driven to madness as well as bribery, is open to question. It is improbable that such an accusation would have escaped the notice of contemporary revolutionaries and would not have tempered their criticism accord-

ingly. *The Double* reflects the drama of the lonely man of
our time as in an anaclastic glass. What is piquant is that
the costs of the fruitless emancipation are borne, not by a
hero, a great personage, but by an amusing little fellow,
one of the poor people. It was a prelude and the double
will often reappear equipped with a better brain.

The work was a prelude in two respects. First there
was the known " cruelty "[1] of Dostoevsky's psychology
which assumed every guise, sat down at every table and
crept into every corner to snatch at confessions. The poet
needed cruelty towards his people as much as love, and
unquestionably, at the beginning of his career, he was
moved not only by sympathy with the insulted and injured
but also, and particularly, by the interest of a diagnostician.
Nötzel has shown convincingly how both these tendencies,
the humanity of the poet and the objectivity of the psychologist, are combined in the novel. He asserts with reason
that he can prove in the portrayal of Golyadkin the idea of
" sentiment." Moreover the novel is characteristic of
Dostoevsky's habit of increasing the tension till the end and
then revealing to the reader, as he looks back, the essential
connexions.

The jump from *Poor Folk* to *The Double* was enormous.
Golyadkin already contained elements of the underground
brooder who, in the *Letters from the Underworld*, recklessly
challenges the world. This essential sequel did not follow
till nearly twenty years later. Till then he was unsteady
and produced a quantity of more or less stimulating but not
decisive works. *The Double* remained on a solitary height.

This gap testifies to his immaturity. *Poor Folk* was up
to his standard and was brought up to perfection by rare
diligence. With *The Double* his vision was extended beyond
his experience. Of this work Belinsky might more justifiably
have said that the young man had no idea what he had
written. In addition, success and failure had on this
ambitious man an equally oppressive effect. The fame

---

[1] A quality stressed by Mikhaylovsky, critic and writer 1842-1904.—
Tr.

which he won in a night ran to his head and ill-founded criticism did him no good. The letters to his brother in these years reveal an often astonishingly immature and ebullient being, dragged hither and thither by youthful desires whose sole aim appears to have been gratification of his immeasurable craving for glory. His confessions of vanity reached a low level but had grace. He sunned himself in social success, enjoyed being sought after by eminent people and voraciously consumed every form of flattery. His brother cannot imagine, he writes, how people chase after him. In Petersburg he is the only thing which counts, Dostoevsky here, Dostoevsky there, in the *salons* they are talking of nothing but of what he is saying, what he is thinking, what he will write next. During a recent conversation with Nekrasov he has conceived the idea of a novel in nine letters. The same night he has written it without a pause, taken it the following morning to the publisher and immediately received good payment. He is rolling in money and squandering it. "All the little Minnas, Claras and Marias are incredibly pretty but cost a heap of money." What does it matter? The publishers actually crave the honour of making payments in advance. Every one runs after him. Young Turgenev, the very first day of his return from Paris, has attached himself in intimate friendship. An excellent fellow ! His brother absolutely must read the story by this excellent fellow, this genius. There are other geniuses too, Goncharov and Herzen for example. Petersburg teems with geniuses, but Dostoevsky surpasses them all.

However his vanity and search for fame revolted him, he was fully aware that vain people went to rack and ruin. In a trice money and love and genius had vanished and he was bewailing his infinite ineptitude. Everything he had so far written repelled him. Nothing more commonplace could be imagined. But now he was going to write a story which should be really first rate. He had already begun. This story was to cast into the shade everything which had ever existed. People were to be *bouleversés*.

DOSTOEVSKY

One would never attribute *The Double* with all its perspectives to this boyish ecstasy. What had the dark-subconscious of a submissive official to do with an ardent pleasure-seeker? It must be assumed that he himself had at that time an *alter ego*, possibly even several. One of them masqueraded in the mask of Schiller and caused him the most trouble, spurred him to excesses and then chased him to the other extreme. Dostoevsky's state of mind at that time is sufficiently evidenced by the fact that, during his work on Golyadkin, he was seriously pressing forward with the project of publishing the works of Schiller, jointly with his brother (22).

Poor Folk was the beginning of a gifted career. It was a red-letter day for the roof-garden and the people. With *The Double* a visionary was venturing into an unknown land and the result was terrifying and almost miraculous. It is here, if anywhere in his work, that Dostoevsky's epileptic attacks can be said to have furthered the creative effect.

Poor Folk and *The Double* must be considered together. Nowadays people are inclined to regard the gloomy element as indicative of his subsequent development. That is wrong. The first work is full of episodes which foreshadow incidents in later works. In her life-story Dyevushkin's companion and correspondent speaks of an old drunkard named Pokrovsky, the father of the lover of her youth, who died of consumption. She collaborates with old Pokrovsky to give Pushkin's works as a birthday present to her beloved Peter who dotes on good books, and she subscribes thirty roubles, the whole of her savings. The old man does his best in raking together three roubles. A tender picture. The father, laden with books, running after his son's coffin is unforgettable. Nor did Dostoevsky forget him. This brief episode is one of many which embellish the work from beginning to end.

CHAPTER VII

In the years 1846 to 1849, between *début* and catastrophe, there appeared nine stories or short tales, all of which unquestionably bore testimony to his talent, but not one of them foretold Dostoevsky's unique significance. The main factor in these small works was a quality whose mysterious power of appeal was already noticeable in his early works; that was his happiest gift. Dostoevsky was not only a born psychologist; occupation in psychological problems must have come naturally to him, and he yielded to this inclination before he himself fully recognized its importance. Moreover he was a born humorist; even though he would peer into the depths of a tragic situation he could still see the humorous side. This fact neither strengthens nor weakens the argument of a positive element in Dostoevsky's underlying tendency; it is only that the gift was a rare possession which, amongst other things, he turned to account in the generalization of his problems. Humour served as a counterblast to sentimentality, curbed whilst at the same time supporting his irony, contributed to intensifying what to others seemed cruel and helped in no small degree to divert his self-torment. This gift alone sufficed to assure him a career; a Russian Dickens, if such were possible in Russian atmosphere; a Dickens inclined to the grotesque, more incisive, and free of the Englishman's *bourgeois* tolerance. But, as Stephan Zweig demonstrates in his book dedicated to the three great novelists (23), it was only in smug England that a Dickens, with his restraint, could become a national hero. Contemporary Russia was too vast for such humour, too full of tragedy; a writer pursuing such a course would have become nothing more than a jester, far inferior to the Englishman. This danger did in fact threaten the young Dostoevsky. It was due to his journalism, to his lack of bias and his proximity to the soil, that his sense of humour, which later was to become so vital a force in his greatest work, was once satisfied with light satire and modest comedy of situation. Again one's mind turns to the early days of Delacroix.

Two short stories foreshadowed the master. Mr Prohartchin, the avaricious maniac in the lodging-house, who also had his double, makes a most effective corpse on his straw-mattress stuffed with roubles which his sleeping companions encircle with mouths agape. A laugh from the underworld cheats death of its terrors and gives it new ones. In such scenes there is a touch of the comic relief of Shakespearean tragedy. The tragedy is too profound for tears. *The Honest Thief* illustrates another phase of his humour such as had already coloured *Poor Folk*. We should be overcome by emotion at the death of the honest breeches thief who succumbs to his sense of honour, and of the even more honest victim, were there not a rogue concealed behind the tenderness. Russian atmosphere alone would not overcome the Schilleresque, which is here so palpable.

The most remarkable of these stories, *The Landlady*, is completely outside the range not only of the others, but of his whole work. There is entire lack of construction. Dostoevsky renounces realism and substitutes the wildest romanticism for psychology; it is fantastic even in the dialogue and especially in the desultory, cinematographic action. People pass arbitrarily from one mood, one swoon into another. All Dostoevsky's usual qualities are swept aside. Ordynov, the madly enamoured youth, acts in a trance and remains formless. Katerina, his beloved, would prefer most to speak in verse which might have been culled from Scottish bards and translated by Schiller. There is a distinct feeling of foreign influence. The extravagant sensuality of this pair of lovers leads to pictures, but not to organic thought. Even the relationship of old Murin to Katerina, who is dominated by him, and Murin himself, remain shadowy, and Dostoevsky seems actually to have enjoyed this superficial mysticism. A painter could have written this story. It is only at the end, when Murin gives unwelcome notice to his subtenant, that, in this mixture of servility and mockery, the real Dostoevsky comes to the fore. It sounds like Smerdyakov. It is a mystery how Dostoevsky failed to see the shortcomings of this story and considered it superior to *Poor Folk* (24).

Dostoevsky sought with a greater work to escape from the storm and stress of this period. *Nyetochka Nyezvanov* was to become the first big novel. The fragment has left two charming portraits of children; Nyetochka, the drunkard's step-child, in a minor, and Katya, the radiant princess, in a major key. There is a melody of inimitable sweetness in the struggle of the two children for one another. The portrayal of their love touches on eroticism with the simplicity of Greek pastoral poetry. (That has not prevented adherents of psycho-analysis from arriving at vast inferences concerning Dostoevsky's sexuality.) Chopin has a similar melancholy sweetness. The novel promised much, even if not the greatness of the principal works; in fact a novel in Dostoevsky's sense could not possibly have sprung from it. The poet's imprisonment is supposed to have interrupted the work. During his long and oppressive detention in the Peter-Paul fortress pending the inquiry, he wrote the sunniest story of all, *A Little Hero*, the tale of a boy of eleven who, in the company of beautiful and elegant women, performs a daring feat of horsemanship and experiences the first revelation of his heart.

Nyetochka, Princess Katya, and the little hero were the beginning of a long row of child-characters which peopled his work till the end. If superficial thinkers believe that Dostoevsky distressed and tormented merely for the sake of distress and torment, they should pause to consider his children who constitute a small but by no means separate world in his creation, a world which in itself reflects enough of his will to live. Nötzel had the idea of excerpting and collating child-episodes from the later novels. They have resulted in a volume abounding in life (25), for which thanks are due to Nötzel's discretion; there are normally strong objections to the present-day passion for arbitrarily tearing specific passages out of the context and then flaunting them as evidence of the writer's perversions or peculiarities, a procedure which merely bewilders and contorts one's view.

Dostoevsky introduced the child into literature. Previously it had been granted only a supernumerary rôle with its stereotyped smile reminiscent of the *putti* of Donatello and Della Robbia, merely a pleasant ornament. Dostoevsky gave the little person his atmosphere, which was not limited to dolls and fairy-tales, and indicated his place in the world of adults. He dispelled the traditional notion and revealed countless living types, as well as versatility in the type. Dostoevsky's children live through their eyes; their sight is keener than that of adults, they visualize in the picturesque and simple relief of the Primitives. Their co-ordination is neither the result of psychological experience nor directed by any sense of personal interest. The child's restricted field of selection forces on it a more definite decision and disposes it to heroism. Dostoevsky's child is far less the young than the primitive being who does not need learning as a guide to thought and action. Dostoevsky loved children. That was the beginning of his philanthropic attitude; it commenced in his youth and was, in the period of storm and stress, the first quite unequivocal and positive discovery. There was none of the bygone " idealization " in his treatment of the child; he dismissed the social distinction between child and adult and other traditional limitations and approached it with an unbiassed mind. That objectivity was at bottom the most essential token of his love.

Dostoevsky comprehended the uncalculating and incalculable qualities of the child and its incorruptibility. He saw it wild and occasionally cruel, direct in speech, reserved and proud and always alert, distrustful and open-hearted. To him the child was like the simple people. If we cannot all be familiar with his conception of the people, at least we see his children with his eyes, whatever they may do. We are bound to love them since the driving force of their being is true in itself, a healthy organism which, even when it lays hold of rottenness, retains its unspoiled character. We love them as we love Renoir's flowers, overcome by the radiance of their nature, and love them in still another way. Renoir's children are less agile. Their radiant flesh makes a homely still-life of them. When they grow up they invariably become women destined to be loved by us. Those of Dostoevsky have something boyish about them even when they are girls. The boys, active youngsters, raise themselves stealthily on their toes in order to become bigger. The pensive schoolgirls turn somersaults. From both there bursts forth unexpectedly illuminating thinking and fabling, and thought does not trouble them.

Renoir painted them as blossoming plants, and that makes us happy. Dostoevsky's children have the quality which distinguishes the human being from plants and are children in spite of it, are in fact children for that very reason, and we are no less pleased. They have the human quality in pure form. The thought which is later suppressed, distorted, stuck into uniform and trained to drudgery, lives in them untamed, like a foal on luxuriant pasture, and again and again one supposes there must surely be some means of conserving in them this mobility of thinking. And become what they may, there is so much of mobility in this youth that something must be retained. That was Dostoevsky's confident belief. His last and most significant work does not for nothing conclude with a choral of youth to the future. He is lost who loses his childhood. The world without childhood succumbs.

In painting the child Dostoevsky selected the softest shades of his palette. They were always the colour-tones in which he painted adults, but in those delicate derivatives they reach us more easily and without perplexing contrasts. Doubtless there was already a cloud on the horizon of little Nyetochka, in whom were foreshadowed the tragic female parts of later works, but that only added to her childish

77

mysticism and increased the charm. In the princess is something of the kitten which shows its claws when we want to be kind to it. Her aristocratic quality, in striking contrast to her playmate, only accentuates the detachment of the future woman, which a man cannot understand, and when the senseless barrier between the children is finally broken down and they lie at last in each other's arms, laughing and weeping, we feel more out of place than ever. The clumsiness of those who scent out the sexual element in this child-love only confirms the normal incapacity of man to perceive in woman, be she only twelve years of age, anything but his docile complement. The same faculties which enabled Dostoevsky to comprehend the peculiar world of the child, revealed to him the mystery of woman, which is incomprehensible to the male. On that account modern doctors have declared him to have been impotent.

A Little Hero comprises the developing world of the male, but in this story there are truly banal elements, sometimes French, sometimes related to Schiller's Ballads; were these the only elements the work could confidently be reckoned amongst the " literature of the squirearchy." In the happy passages the boy's action is not described, not explained, but flows calmly forth and compels us to blink with the eyes of the little hero. How he restores to the lady of his heart the lost letter of her lover, the discovery of which would ruin her, the device to which he has recourse in order to conceal his rôle, the episode with the nosegay and the scene in the sun when he feigns sleep and she rewards her deliverer—what prose has ever created such lyricism? We are here a long way from the obscure East.

Such children are not to be found in the streets. They are more childlike than real children, just as Renoir's babies eclipse nature. Even the little hero is, as may be imagined, not an epitome of nature—for that Dostoevsky had not yet seen enough—but nature eclipsed. The vital factor here was not the poet's experience, but his own childlike temperament of which we have evidence. It is not by accident that it constitutes the pillar of the action in these early works.

BEFORE THE CATASTROPHE

It may well have been the essence of his talent, more essential than his psychology or his humour. A child had a hand even in the writing of *Poor Folk*.

This obvious source of inspiration must be borne in mind in order to guard against errors in Dostoevsky-literature of to-day. The great complexity lies less in the man's disposition, which nowadays people tend to regard as outrageous, than in his outrageous experiences; he had to face these and actually succeeded in coping with them.

The essentials of these early works are reflected throughout. Even a small work so relatively unimportant as *A Little Hero* was a preparatory step. The boy's devotion to the beloved of another and, particularly, the manner in which he endeavours to protect someone else's property, indicate almost imperceptibly a problem which Dostoevsky had already touched on in *White Nights*; he was personally faced with this problem which he repeatedly introduced in later works in many variants, from the tenderest lyricism to the most glaring grotesqueness. Such variations are perceptible in *Nyetochka Nyezvanov*, in *Mr Prohartchin*, and in other early works. The history of the development of these themes, a necessary research scarcely yet begun, would yield unique results and contribute in no small degree to clearer ideas about Dostoevsky's art.

Even if the wild confusion succeeding his *début* was to a certain extent justified and could be accepted as fruitful soil, that was thanks only to the later Dostoevsky, for the constructive tendency was entirely lacking in his period of storm and stress. He committed hurriedly and unselectively to paper whatever occurred to him, and seems only to have been set on letting his talent glitter in as many varied colours as possible. He was still a gifted writer, hot-blooded, sentimental, and full of roving desires. The central idea was still lacking. To no one was more necessary the great experience which enforced composure. In a letter, full of self-accusations, which he wrote in 1847 to his brother Michael, he says, " I can show myself a man of heart and spirit only when external circumstances tear me forcibly out

79

of the eternal commonplaces. If that does not happen I am always repellent. I explain this lack of proportion by my illness."

The poet was driven to Petrachevsky more by that romantic disposition than by his political impulses, which at that time were not yet awakened or at least quite indecisive and of which the letters of his youth give no inkling. He was led astray, not by the immature ideas of the circle of conspirators, to whom his intellect was far superior, but by the thrill of secrecy. The catastrophe came at the psychological moment. Even if it is true that Dostoevsky could not have attained his great synthesis without this brutal imprisonment, it is nevertheless certain that only the fortunate combination in him of lofty human qualities enabled him to benefit by this catastrophe which crippled him for many years. The harmony of *A Little Hero* is not disturbed by the merest shadow of that cell in which the poet's last work was created prior to a decade of silence. Was this trifle beginning or end? He never again wove such light garlands, but the story by no means brought his light-heartedness to an end. There is a radiance in it unexampled in any earlier work. The beginning of suffering seems already to have kindled a new light.

CHAPTER VIII

THERE was remarkable delay before his Siberian experiences had any positive effect on him; either Siberia alone did not suffice to elevate him or else he was too deeply stirred. He felt the worst restriction of the *katorga* to be the prohibition of any form of writing, and he spoke in a letter of the "inward seething work" on a significant story which was probably in his mind in the first period of imprisonment (26). The torture of such mental work must have served to train his memory, otherwise the manner in which later works began would be inconceivable. In the last prison-years this restriction certainly prevented the ferment of creation and must have had its effect long after it was removed. The experience obviously ate into him little by little, for he shrank at the touch of literature, even when later such action was no longer natural. Nearly everything produced in Siberia after leaving the *katorga* subsisted under the shadow of restraint. The works deemed literature do not betray the slightest sign of prison-influence, and are certainly not distinguishable to advantage from the most modest work of pre-prison days. At times they move on a very low plane. Had *Crime and Punishment* even been begun in Semipalatinsk, that would have been only toying with the main theme which could have been suggested to him by one of the many prison stories (27).

The House of the Dead, on which he worked in Semipalatinsk, stands strikingly higher than other writings of that period. It treats exhaustively of life and movement in the Omsk prison, has a high literary value, and is of great sociological and criminological interest, but was neither intended nor is to be appraised as literature. The writer of the work was possessed of a rare objective vision and was familiar with every nook and cranny of the cage, was

F   81

peculiarly fitted, both in mind and heart, to mix with the many types and to observe their every thought, word and action; the very limitations imposed by the nature of what he reports lend a certain significance to his words. In spite of the misleading introduction, the designation " Memoirs " must be taken literally although later Dostoevsky gave this title to a work of pure fiction.[1] Dostoevsky quite naturally refrained from a hybrid of truth and fiction.   But he attached little importance to the work. There is not much of the personal in these " Notes," he writes to a Petersburg friend while occupied on the work.

Semipalatinsk was not satisfactory soil, for it did not afford Dostoevsky the enjoyment of existing once again for himself alone. He was hindered not so much by military life as by the happiness which he found or believed he found: his love for Maria Dmitrievna. The intoxication of this kept him from work and he did not begin to write till separation ensued and the threatened loss tormented him. The result was exactly the opposite to what would be expected in such a situation: a humorous sketch and a humorous novel. The first work, *Uncle's Dream*, depicts the miscarried attempt of an ambitious mother to attach her daughter to a degenerate old prince. The prince is a mere puppet; nothing in him is genuine, not even his eye armed with a monocle; he is padded to the brain; he suffers from forgetfulness and is persuaded by the enemies of the provincial lioness that the betrothal forced on him is only a dream. One laughs. These exaggerations were intended for the circus-public of a Siberian provincial town. The daughter's seriousness is distasteful and the sentimental ending at the death-bed of her former lover is intolerable. Schiller survived the *katorga*.

We are approaching the lowest point of the curve and can gauge the immediate reaction of prison life. The poet wanted, before all else, to create again, sought contact with literary acquaintances of former days, sought any, even the

---

[1] See note on page 45. The other work alluded to is *Letters from the Underworld*, the Russian title of which is *Memoirs from Underground.*—Tr.

most banal pretext. Could not all that which previously
constituted his life be simply past? Was that not uncommonly natural to him after all those years in such a
cage? Write, write! echoed in him. And he must have
rejoiced like a child at once again having his pictures on
paper. He played with them like a child.

Uncle's Dream is in the same category as earlier stories
such as The Crocodile and Another Man's Wife and was
originally conceived and even begun as comedy. (In this
one instance, therefore, theatrical folk of our time may be
forgiven their unscrupulous violation of Dostoevsky's novels.)
Dostoevsky's mood is clearly shown in a letter to Maikov.[1]
" I began to write a comedy for fun. So many comic
persons and so much comic action occurred to me and my
hero amused me so much that, although I was well pleased
with comedy form, I gave it up merely to prolong the
pleasure of following my new hero's exploits and of laughing
over him." It is impossible to be on more childlike terms
with one's art. The comedy form goes back to the earliest
period. Shortly before Poor Folk Dostoevsky wrote a play
which has apparently been lost. He says further in the
letter: " This hero is related to me in many respects."

On reading this sentence for the first time it is difficult
to imagine that Dostoevsky could have meant himself in
the idiot of a prince. The tragic, mournful, inwardly
seething Dostoevsky and this puppet! But no other interpretation is possible and this association assigns a peculiar
significance to the unimportant début after Siberia: so far
could he carry his disguise. The work is a foolish sketch.
But in the disguise lies humour of unusual range. Dostoevsky's second wife has told us how it must be construed.
In her Reminiscences she mentions his partiality during their
betrothal to acting the part of an old man who wants to be
young. " For hours on end he would talk and think like
his hero, the old prince in Uncle's Dream, and at the same
time express all kinds of droll, unexpected, amusing and
profound thoughts." That was always unpleasant, she adds.

[1] 18th January 1856.

The remark, as well as her comment, speaks volumes for the intimacy between the artist and the man. Thus already at the time of his first marriage he was practising such self-mockery. At that time it was more necessary to him as armour against a lover's disillusionment.

The second Siberian work is more comprehensive and on a much higher level. *The Friend of the Family* can be considered the first real novel, at least with more justification than *Nyetochka Nyezvanov*, though no comparison with this tender story is intended. There was no delicacy in Siberia. For the first time he concentrated on a complicated pattern, rich in figures, and the novel was built round a carefully thought-out idea, whereas previously episodes were piled on episodes as the fancy seized him or, as he said of *Uncle's Dream*, were stitched to one another. The central figure is the amusing Foma Fomitch, an unfortunate *littérateur* of infinite conceit. His oily speech stands, according to time-worn precept, for the good, the beautiful and the true, and conceals a crass egoism in rapturous pictures. His surroundings are governed by his rhetoric. He is blindly obeyed by the entire establishment of the well-to-do uncle, a landowner, who has philanthropically adopted him. The women fly to him. What the uncle, the principal victim, reveres in this Tartuffe are lofty principles beyond the reach of his own uncultivated mind. Probably at times he sees through the more than suspected shortcomings of the apostle but, in his simplicity and good-nature, dares not breathe a word. Many a theme which Dostoevsky tackled in *Uncle's Dream* in the crudest form is considerably developed. The uncle is to make a good match and marry a man-mad old spinster who also lives in the house. Even this exotic figure is brilliantly drawn. But the uncle secretly loves the governess, so secretly that he dares not admit it even to himself, and therefore sends for his nephew whom he considers a worthier suitor. Again the well-known theme. The nephew is the narrator. This time Dostoevsky succeeds to some extent in overcoming the disconcerting weakness of many of his works, the false situation of the

THE FRIEND OF THE FAMILY

" I " which partly reports and partly participates in the
action, and this auxiliary figure is as far as possible suppressed. As the old spinster elopes with a dowry-hunter
the match is frustrated and the uncle gravitates towards the
governess. Foma Fomitch surprises the couple at a
nocturnal rendezvous, girds himself with the sword of
violated morality and casts grave aspersions on the girl, an
outrage which finally drives the uncle into a fury. Foma
is flung through the glass-door in a hail of abuse, and
resolves to wander homeless till the end of time. The old
mother prostrates herself at the feet of her irate son, begging
him to fetch Foma back. Everything which has legs kneels
too. In the face of this heavy storm the uncle yields on
condition that Foma apologizes to the injured innocent.
He does not need to look far. The rain has quenched
Foma's thirst for wandering and the uncle finds him a few
yards away. The joke of it is that Foma, by means of
masterly perversion of his ethical sense, changes his position
and climbs an unsuspected peak of magnanimity before the
enraptured eyes of the community. It is he who brings
together the uncle and the timid governess, and makes
everybody happy. Even his former adversaries bow before
his wisdom and sing his praises.

It has already been stated that this detached humour,
which surpasses the bounds of reality and raises this
Tartuffe to unshakable faith in his own extravagant projects,
attains the standard of Molière. *The Friend of the Family*
can be considered the only Russian production in the
tradition of the greatest of European comedy-writers; even
in humorous literature of the West there is not much of
the tradition of *L'Avare* and *Tartuffe*. This kinship with
Molière is no small safeguard for tradition in a chaotic
mind; moreover in his development the influence of
Shakespeare is perceptible, and he thus combined in his
work the two greatest dramatists of Europe. But his
relationship to the Englishman attained higher planes. It
is an open question whether he liked the Frenchman.
Molière's name is missing amongst the many writers whom,

85

as a young man, he absorbed and mentioned in his letters, whilst he extolled Corneille and Racine to the skies. That, of course, is an accident. He had certainly read Molière, but not as he had read Shakespeare. With Molière the Frenchman's finish permeated him; their literary polish detracted from his creativeness and robbed him of his ruggedness. Whilst the Frenchman was already widely familiar, he felt himself alone in his fruitful discovery of Shakespeare. As a successor to Molière Dostoevsky was tempted to write social comedies as well, on Molière's lines. *The Friend of the Family* is a transposed comedy like *Uncle's Dream*, only much better constructed, richer in thought and more reserved. The mature Dostoevsky has accustomed us to deem such criteria insufficient. Only the beginnings or subordinate factors in his strikingly novel vision are traceable. He was still essentially in an old world, and his new world was to arise from its collapse.

The struggle began around this world as soon as he set foot again on Petersburg soil. His journalism, which started with great energy as early as 1860, both aggravated and mitigated the struggles. Work on the *Vremya* began in the summer and was no light task. The monthly review comprised politics and every sphere of intellectual interest, as well as extensive *belles-lettres*. Every number contained four to five hundred printed pages. Dostoevsky saw to the essential part of the management and, in addition, had to contribute a great many articles. His brother superintended the business side. Of more interest to Dostoevsky than literature was the inner political situation at this moment, immediately before the abolition of serfdom, the most decisive moment in the history of the new Russia (28). Here he found fresh support for his entirely favourable attitude towards Tsardom which he had brought with him from Siberia. He again found in Petersburg the two old parties, the Westerners to whom he himself belonged or thought he belonged before Siberia, those who looked to Europe for salvation and regarded Russian civilization as degrading, and the Slavophils who swore by everything Russian even when it clashed with culture and reason. He consider the *blasé* attitude of the one party merely an artificial mask which could be laid aside were it known how to make use of the great moment, and then the others, whose obstinacy was only the outcome of their opposition, would have to come to reason. So it was a matter of forming a new party. It had to be unconditionally Russian, that is, to take its foundation from the Slavophils, but to renounce narrow-minded hostility to culture and lead Russia to universality. With that object the *Vremya* was started, the organ of the intellectuals, which was to assemble every available force at the service of the fatherland. It was not by accident that Dostoevsky came to found a periodical which, amongst other duties, imposed on him a political attitude, but because of his recognition of what was at stake in this turning-point in Russian history. His chief concern was his party. We possess adequate and enlightening evidence of that. Doubtless he foresaw the outlines of the party and was able intuitively to indicate its programme, and this he did in detail in the announcement of the *Vremya* which appeared in September 1860; on the other hand he was far from formulating definite claims, in fact even an expert, after mature consideration, could not easily have evolved them because they had to provide for an attitude to which both parties could be reconciled. These details could only be worked out after the situation had been cleared and Dostoevsky had become further absorbed in his political mission. His essays in the *Vremya*, at times thoroughly immature, illustrate how far he was from his goal.

He reaped a considerable benefit from this exacting work. It stimulated him, rendered him more earnest, broadened his task. All this indirectly served in good stead the poet who was bound to make the most of every gain to the man. But his political obscurity endangered him for a time. His many-sided activity threatened to dissipate his energy, compelled him to produce too hurriedly, and, for the time being, contributed nothing at all towards promoting the artist in him.

The political situation forced the poet's attention on the West and the issues involved. His outlook, borrowed from the essays, with which he sought to clarify both the reader and himself, was meant to be the background of a novel and of a serious novel at that. Humorous treatment would not have done justice to the task, would not have expressed his feelings unambiguously enough. His feelings drove him to look exclusively in the realm of ethics for the contrast between East and West, and thus he plunged more deeply than ever into sentimentality. It is on this that *The Insulted and Injured* is wrecked.

A penny-dreadful in the broadest meaning of the word ! The *naïveté* expected of us is astonishing. The cheapness is not a mask, not a jumping-off ground, but the quintessence of the writing. Any hack writer turns out his story like that, intent only on minimizing his own as well as his readers' mental task. The only difference between this story and a shocker is in a few unexpected subsidiary figures and the ingenuousness of the author who does not seek to justify the limitations of his scribbling.

The old theme, which no one has so effectually done away with as Dostoevsky, appears here in full dress. The prince, the scoundrel who represents the principle of evil and is only there to insult and injure, cannot be blacker. When he appears there is a smell of sulphur. He has to be as resourceful as the modern social brigand and by his accomplished manners to render the crime unnoticeable. The intriguer has the mind of a stock-jobber and goes about his business with the tricks of a petty thief, which would only catch people of the most incredible simplicity. His son Alexey says he is in love with Natalya, the daughter of a landowner whom the prince ruins by undisguised trickery, in order to thwart her association with his son. Natalya and her parents are only put there to be insulted and injured, although Natalya is supposed to be a capable person with her eyes open. Alexey is a graceful good-for-nothing, just as generally weak as his father is generally bad. He is supposed to be an innocent fool endowed with a charm outweighing all his weaknesses, but he is very nearly as infamous as his father, though none of the characters suspect it, or, for that matter, the author himself. Dostoevsky overlooked this parallelism in his haste; later in life he would have made it the main theme of the work. Alexey's sorest trial, having to endure all his father's outrages at the expense of his beloved, is not worked out and is endured almost as a physical necessity. Naturally Natalya hurries from her home to the weakling and is accordingly cursed by her father. The prince acquiesces in the marriage in order to trap Alexey and in fact visits his future daughter-in-law and makes a speech. At the same time he introduces his son to a rich and eminent heiress, as pretty as she is noble. Alexey is, of course, promptly infatuated with the new Katerina, and naturally the noble Katerina instantly reciprocates his love, puts up with all the young prince's mean actions towards his fiancée, and finally concludes a sisterly friendship with her unfortunate rival. Conversations ensue such as are only possible between people with stopped-up ears and blindfold eyes. Finally Natalya rouses herself, shows the pitch-black prince the door and quits the young prince with her blessings. That is the melodramatic climax. Thereupon the proud girl wants to return penitently to her parents. But the injured father sits hugging his curse and prefers to pine away rather than do the only reasonable thing. Nelly turns up. Nelly is the consumptive grandchild of a stubborn old man who had a poodle; he has already pined away and died, as well as the poodle, because he would not retract his curse of his daughter, Nelly's mother. One evening shortly before her death Nelly recounts this story of the grandfather's curse, and by means of her thoroughly vague narration induces the landowner to renounce his curse and sorrow and to embrace his contrite daughter.

This subsidiary story of Nelly, which has nothing whatever to do with the novel, is introduced by the narrator,

the I, called Ivan, who of all the unfortunate parts plays
the moſt unfortunate. At firſt he loved Natalya and ſtill
loves her, but retires magnanimously before the ſtupid and
faint-hearted young prince. Naturally he does his utmoſt
to promote the love between this rival and Natalya. He is
the only person capable of seeing through the prince's
father. In an infinitely improbable scene between Ivan
and the old prince in a *chambre séparée* of a reſtaurant the
scoundrel shows his true self and assents to whatever is
asked. The reek of sulphur so ensnares the intelligent Ivan
that he overlooks the obvious course and fails to have the
miscreant arrested. After all, it only needed this expedient
to occur to any one of the aċtors at any opportunity for the
novel to reach its end shortly after it had begun.

This weakness of the principal charaċter of the involved
ſtory seems to me even more serious than the Ivan whom
Russian criticism reproaches, not with his shadowy exiſtence
in the book, but with his altruism in love affairs, Doſtoevsky's
old theme, which is considered exaggerated.

We have arrived at the loweſt point of the curve. The
humorous ſtories are excused by his light touch; we cannot
take them seriously, and in any case a jeſter is always taken
at his face value. Here, on the other hand, Doſtoevsky
gives himself away or at leaſt pretends he does. He invents
a title which makes us prick up our ears, a very impressive
title, the sort of phrase which becomes a catch-word. The
title might be suitable for a great many of Doſtoevsky's
works from *Poor Folk* onwards, but it certainly does not
suit this shocker. The only person insulted in this inſtance
is Doſtoevsky himself, and the injured are we, his readers.

But doubtless this phase was inevitable; ſtrange as it
may seem, it was this morass of a ſtory with its sonorous
title which contained possibilities of *Crime and Punishment*,
The Idiot and *A Raw Youth*, and not the humorous sketches
or the far superior *Friend of the Family* which immediately
preceded it. If we ſtep closer to this turbid ſtruċture, we
shall soon see what the seeds are like and where they lie.

In the noċturnal conversation between Ivan and the old

prince who regales his satanism with caviare and champagne, the name of Schiller is constantly repeated. The scoundrel feels forced to explode because the " Schilleresque " of his environment has become intolerable. This attitude, judged by the standard of intrigue to which melodrama has accustomed us, shows itself in a most improbable way, but has a mysterious charm which takes our minds off the story. We suddenly give our attention, not very closely it is true, only with half an ear, but all the same not like the insipid Ivan who here reveals how entirely superfluous he is. The old prince is in the same position as we. After all the worthless nonsense of conscious and unconscious weaknesses and of unreality he wants to say something different. He does not say it well. How should he? Even the scoundrel has been infected by the atmosphere and is incapable of being half as wicked as he would like to be, as the insipid Ivan should require, as we should require in order to be deeply moved. There has been too much nonsense, we can scarcely keep our eyes open; but if anything of the story has been retained it is contempt for the Schilleresque.

It is not accidentally introduced into the discussion, it only falls accidentally from the lips of the old prince. Actually he is only an auxiliary figure, if not in the melodrama at least in the household of Dostoevsky for whom the entire novel was only a peg. Schiller is the true hero, the Schiller who obsessed the young Dostoevsky. The *milieu* of Natalya's parents is as stuffy as the *bourgeois* parlour in *Kabale und Liebe*.[1] The old prince does his best to look like the president. Louise and Lady Milford have disguised themselves a little, and the landowner curses like

[1] Schiller's *Cabal and Love.* Intrigue is the background of the action. Ferdinand, son of the president in a little state, is in love with the daughter of a musician. His father wants him to marry Lady Milford, cast-off mistress of the reigning duke. To separate the lovers the president has recourse to intrigue, and Louise, believing her father's life is at stake, is forced to write a letter from which she appears to be carrying on an intrigue with a court official. The letter is placed into Ferdinand's hands, and Louise's oath prevents an explanation till she has drunk the poison her lover has prepared for her and for himself.—TR.

the musician. Alexey alone in the age of Balzac dares not
assume the rôle of Ferdinand and must therefore be content
with his shadowy existence. The similarity of the material
is obvious and even more convincing, though less obvious,
is the consistency. We are flooded with the same sort of
sentimentality. But Schiller did it better. His sentimentality runs perfectly, and such a thing as the old prince's
idea in the *chambre séparée* never occurred to him. How
should it? He organized the unreal into a compact drama
in which not a screw was loose, and every loophole through
which common-sense could gain a disconcerting entry was
punctiliously stopped up.

Dostoevsky did this differently. He became more
intoxicated than Schiller, who was always conscious enough
to make his entries and exits at the proper place. A
drunkard staggers about, stumbles, smashes some glasses,
and then goes on drinking. After all that Dostoevsky had
already created, his choice of intoxicant at first sight bordered
on the absurd, indicated his artlessness, lay in the sphere of
his childhood which he tried very hard to remember at this
time, and corresponded with the emotional and rhetorical
needs of the political moment. Besides, Schiller was
regarded by the Russians of 1860 in quite another light
than in the France of Balzac and Flaubert, whose realism
had already had a very considerable effect on his reputation
even though they were still a long way off breaking him.
But Dostoevsky did not consider the scepticism of the
French realists any criterion, particularly at this moment.
It was the poison of the West and flung a challenge to his
spirit of contradiction. That was in Schiller's favour and
led to a second obsession. It had a salutary effect. Dostoevsky finished with Schiller's weaknesses because he did not,
like so many Germans, stick at half measures, but went the
whole hog, drank himself so thoroughly full that he was
absolutely driven to saying something quite different. He
exaggerated, if possible, the Schilleresque sentimentality and
so much the more easily reduced its prototype *ad absurdum*.
That was, of course, far from his intention, rather the

contrary; what he unconsciously discarded was only the negative part of the Schiller-chapter. A follower of no particular merit would have been satisfied with that or from now onwards the German poet would have been the object of his wrath. Now began the positive part of the Schilleresque.

Contemporaries excused this aberration, for they had in mind the *Vremya* in which in any case many a sin of Dostoevsky stood inscribed. Grigoriev, his collaborator on the paper, publicly proclaimed his brother Michael responsible, saying he had reduced the poet to the status of a beast of burden. In 1864 after Michael's death Dostoevsky strenuously contested this opinion in the periodical *Epoca*, defended with great warmth the brother whom he loved and assumed exclusive blame for the " serial-novel." He attributed the weaknesses of the work, which he readily admitted (" Puppets and walking dictionaries instead of human beings ") to his wonted hack-writing. He says that he was urged to the work by nothing but his own freewill. One gathers from his explanation that he was more concerned about the success of the *Vremya* than about the worth of the novel. But the *Vremya* can safely be left out of account. At most it had a beneficial influence in that it hastened a process which had to be undergone. Subconsciously the poet may have resolved on this hastening; the caricature-like allusion to the future, an allusion which has become distorted by overhaste and also, in a less degree, the still irresolute mockery of the Schilleresque through the mouth of the old prince who will soon play quite a different tune, all this affords us a glimpse of Dostoevsky's involuntary self-caricature. There are astonishingly banal characters and situations in *The Insulted and the Injured* which were sketches for much later works. Ivan's conversation with the prince is the crudest framework of the prolonged dialogues in the principal works where insults lacerate and injuries cut like knives. Prince Alexey is a faded arabesque of Prince Myshkin. Even a few fundamental features of the female characters foreshadow *The Idiot*. The prince, like Stavrogin, the hero of *The Possessed*, wants to command. His cynicism, forcibly developed, will be found again in the father of the Karamazov brothers. Nelly, a relative of the title-rôle in *Nyetochka Nyezvanov*, bears a faint resemblance to Sonia, Raskolnikov's beloved.

Seeds are rampant in this morass. Dostoevsky needed the morass and luckily was not called away too soon; just as Rembrandt needed the dangerous moment of his youth when in a frivolous posture and disguised as a fop he held Saskia on his lap and abandoned himself to wine, woman and song.

Such men always attain a ripe age, and thus fate affords them the widest scope. They are forced to steep their genius in the deepest humiliations because, at their zenith, their influence is universal. In order to comprehend everything they have to have been moved by the basest desires. Such banal moments safeguard them from drowning their greatness in a sea of shadowy abstraction.

From now onwards the curve rises. The dip caused by Siberia has at last been checked. We are at a new beginning. *The Insulted and Injured* is formless and as youthful as a first composition. If its immaturity were any criterion, it would have to be dated before *Poor Folk*. It appeared in 1861, the year in which *The House of the Dead* began in the same periodical, and towards 1862 the *Vremya* produced a short but perfect story entitled *An Unpleasant Predicament*, the humorist's masterpiece. A dignitary is on his way home after a drawing-room chat round a bottle of wine. A discussion of social obligations has left him unsatisfied and he resolves on a practical demonstration of his benevolence towards the people; he decides to honour with his presence a petty official's wedding festivities which are taking place that evening. His benevolence, which is only skin-deep, naturally achieves nothing, and his success consists in hopeless disturbance of the festivities—the wolf in the sheepfold. However fatherly little father may really be, he is none the less the wolf to them. The multifarious sheep are overcome by mixed feelings of terror and respect, and this unexpected turn takes the sting out of the well-wisher. In order to encourage both them and himself he gets as drunk as a lord, and the paralysis which gradually envelops him is like an inevitable death sentence. He slowly succumbs, to the horror of the young husband who foresees only too clearly the consequences of this undeserved misfortune. Even in this helpless condition the guest of honour is still the object of superstitious awe. Finally they pack him into the chaste bridal bed and the mother-in-law musters all her household remedies in order to bring the little father back to life.

This travesty of *The Insulted and Injured* is scrupulously realistic. Even when wolf and flock tumble over one another and we are carried away by laughter, not a muscle stirs in the author's face and the drunkenness is faithfully worked out to the end. None of the uproariously funny situations is overdone. The wonderful climax, little father in the bridal bed, is the most natural of results. The exaggeration is to be found behind the scenes, and it is not the poet, but the age of such wolf-and-sheep games, which is responsible. The grotesque shadow of such philanthropy stretches beyond the stifling *bourgeois* dwelling, beyond the realm of Petersburg officialdom, beyond that Russia with its laughter and tears. Such a thing can have happened, has happened hundreds of times, happens even to-day, and will go on happening all over the place, in China, in Rouen, in Timbuctoo, in fact everywhere where pretentious, Schilleresque, class-conscious people force their way into a lower social circle. This universal aspect of the local colouring lifts the humour above the level of the comic story. *Uncle's Dream* was a witty idea and there is a trace of Molière in the Tartuffe of Stepantchikovo. Finally what had Foma Fomitch and his flock to do with us? His sheep were too much like painted lambs, and there was something of the painted wolf about Foma. It is only now that the ornamentation is noticed. This foolish and uncommonly clever story brings us unexpectedly right into the middle of our problematic age. The people's well-wisher poking his nose into this flummery could be tragic. We laugh just as at many of Daumier's caricatures which suddenly render us speechless, as if in the echo of our laughter we were terrified at some shrill and irrelevant note. In Daumier has materialized as much of Dostoevsky as was possible in a Western contemporary. *An Unpleasant Predicament* is a great step in the conquest of Schiller's banal shallowness. After the infinite sentimentality of *The Insulted and Injured* Dostoevsky summoned himself to a conciseness and perfection as yet unattained. His progress was not hindered by the journalism which is said to have ruined the serial-novel. The story compelled laughter, but its moral could not be disregarded. The work of art was free from any clogging tendency, but nevertheless pointed its moral. He succeeded in reconciling the aims of the *Vremya* with the demands of good literature.

But it had only succeeded in satire; only in that can be found the perfection and precision which the novel lacked. Till the middle of the sixties there was an almost systematic interchange of sentimental and humorous writing, accompanied by a thick network of journalism. The primary factor was still sentimentality. It produced ideas and the ideas deposited new material. The poet forced the lock of the dark treasure-chamber and hurriedly dragged his finds into the light of day without bothering much about decking them out, and then the satire sifted them and moulded what it could make use of. Apart from the first work, *Poor Folk*, all the successful writings of any significance during that long interval owe their perfection to satire. It became the journalist's refuge. It was only when he freed himself of some of his impulses that he acquired balance between emotion and form. His satire is always bound to be a subject of admiration but, were it not for what followed, it might be thought that his genius had been nipped in the bud. What would be thought of Daumier if his work were confined to journalistic caricatures? But till 1864 there was still no material allusion to the *katorga*. With *The House of the Dead*, the poet seems definitely to have done with that experience. In the spring of 1862 he went abroad for the first time, to Paris, London, Germany and Switzerland. We know what drove him to Paris. The love-adventure with Pauline Suslov may have been a welcome diversion, and not only from his oppressive marriage. He played at the tables for the first time, and in 1863, during a second stay abroad, sketched the plan of *The Gambler*, another diversion. Both journeys, which were of great benefit to his health, were means of evading critical problems.

CHAPTER IX

In the spring of 1864 there began in the *Epoca*, the successor to the *Vremya*, the *Letters from the Underworld*. The seeds of *The Insulted and Injured* had taken root and the struggle with the " Schilleresque " began in bitter earnest. The form of the work is most unusual and falls into two distinct sections. The first consists of the extensive monologue of the " Author of these notes "; the second describes three loosely connected incidents in the life of the man of memoirs, likewise related by himself.

" I am a sick man, I am a vile man! " That is how the monologue begins, and it does not stop. After the first ten pages few persons will resist the temptation to fling it indignantly into the corner. We are not prepared for this tone in belletristic things. It is the reader who is addressed and who has to listen to this extravaganza. Flinging the object into the corner would be only pandering to the man of memoirs. The printed page goes on tittering in the corner, it still titters whilst we are at work or when we indulge in a well-earned respite. " All nonsense! only don't pretend! You're not better, you're not healthier, you're only a hundred times stupider, you haven't the faintest notion how ridiculous you are, you with your professional duties and your evening respite! "

A dozen times the book is hurled aside, a dozen times picked up again, and eventually the devil cannot be got rid of.

The sickness of the man of memoirs is a highly developed perception, and his vileness, the inability to overcome his perceptions; that is, the refusal to behave like the rest of humanity which eats its supper and plays cards. This sick and vile man draws conclusions. The result of his perception is hypersensitiveness, and of his hypersensitiveness inability to avoid feeling humiliated in intercourse both with himself and with others. The man of memoirs despises simple-mindedness, a shield against gnat-bites, called pride by one man and prudence by another. He has long since renounced mankind and is now sitting in his underworld den in Petersburg. Since in any case action can lead nowhere, he does nothing but think, thinks of the humiliations which he has suffered and could suffer and doubtless would have to suffer if he were to stick his nose out of doors, and enjoys it. This gloomy being is a real guzzler of thought. Since no one comes near him now he turns on himself and, as he has shorn himself of defence against his fellow-beings, he is extremely vulnerable to his own attack. The subtlety of his intercourse with himself far surpasses the *finesse* practised in dealings with people whom one likes or needs; a cat-and-mouse game of fool-hardy fantasy. Such things have never before been evolved by the human mind, at least not to this end, still less ever written. Wherever the unhappy soul discovers a hiding-place the gleam of the intellect mercilessly intrudes and chases the mouse out; this unhappy Schilleresque soul, which easily weeps and constantly thirsts after the sublime and the beautiful and wants, above all, to embrace the whole of mankind; this little soul from the flower garden, which cannot reconcile itself to the immutability of nature's laws, to Darwin and his monkey-business. Whilst the next-door intellect is on the most intimate terms with all these matters and has long since accepted them as infallible, this little soul still clings to the beautiful, even to Schiller, and struggles with might and main against the division of earth and heaven; this soul, hundredfold lacerated, which still survives in spite of everything, still hopes again at the last breath, still wants to convert humanity; truly an immortal soul. Everything is piled up on its sepulchre: the doctrine of world-preserving egoism and of the fiction of the will; all the logarithmic tables of mechanism. Trampled into the earth by machinery, submerged mile-deep, to-morrow it springs up again, the strumpet!

DOSTOEVSKY

The monologue of the sick and vile man is unfolded in a mass of closely printed pages. The *Faust* monologue is short in comparison and to the point; it has less to say, although there is a similar ring about it. The man of memoirs does not trouble about brevity. He is at laſt in a position to express himself and makes the moſt of the opportunity. He speaks without pathos as anyone might, but with more sagacity, is a universal spokesman to the point of genius. There is no time for the hocus-pocus of form. Even in this mass of pages he scarcely has room for the essential. It is the confession of a new Fauſt preparing a peculiar phial for his suicide, but there is no Mephiſtopheles or witches' cauldron to rejuvenate him before he goes to the devil. His capacity for speaking the truth borders on alchemy. He relates a few anecdotes of his life; firſt a minor quixotry in the ſtreet, the ſtory of the officer who, as he imagines, insults and injures him and againſt whom he muſters all his ſtrength to force him for once to make way on the pavement, an absurdity which cuts short our laughter. Then the carousal with former school-friends, who are now better off and on whom he forces himself in order to .show them—and ſtill more himself—his superiority; an Auerbach's cellar in modern setting. Naturally, all he succeeds in showing are his gnashing teeth. What would this disenchanted Fauſt not give to let flow Tokayer and fire inſtead of mordant rage; what would he not give to tie the idiots together by the nose! Thirdly the visit to an injured innocent in the brothel, which leads to a new novel in the darkeſt of darknesses. The aƈtors are men and masks, and the producer a Doſtoevsky of yeſterday, ſtruggling with Schiller, and a radiating Doſtoevsky of the day after to-morrow, a new Fauſt.

It is difficult to form any conclusion about this chain of episodes without beginning or end; it almoſt seems futile. The roof-garden, which on other occasions has been forced to recognition, takes bloody revenge on *The Insulted and Injured* and wants to attach to it responsibility for the form of this new work. Still morass, says the expert, Doſtoevsky never emerges from the morass. The expert refuses to be interested in morasses, that is not his subject. At a pinch he would rather accept *The Insulted and Injured* which, though a morass, is harmless. If this murk of the city[1] can be accepted, anything can be accepted. In the gloom lurks the danger of this new medium. Giving an inch means taking an ell and suddenly there is an end of literature.

There is a titter in the corner: literature!

We want to wall in the murk even at the risk of blundering, and to this end every argument is dragged from the realm of æsthetics. We are always suspicious of anything novel. Is there not a connecting link between this novel form and traditional form? Did not this novel form fail because of its inherent weakness? and since it is lawless it creates for itself new æsthetic values.

There is a titter in the corner: æsthetic values!

But that cannot be accepted without further ado. The monologue of the underworld man has more in it than merely unusual form. The monosyllabic introduction is continued in the episodes. The unprecedented tone of the discourse, against which the ear rebels, renders the whole work monological. The monologue in the den is spirited. Indeed one cannot but grant it spirit. What more? If, as has been said, the *Iphigenia* is a plea for the rights of society against the arrogance of the spirit, the den must be deemed the enemy of society.

And again there is a titter in the corner: society!

We cannot avoid the den. Once opened up it could not be closed by any power on earth. If we attempt to dispense with the art of the monologue the whole of our present age must be excluded. Society, literature, æsthetics must pass through the crucible of the den or are useless to us. It is only in this purgatory, in which superficial ideas instantly succumb, that any solid notion can stand the test and, beautiful or not, can carry the burden of the new creative literature. No rational being will consider murk a stereotyped model for any poet. Dostoevsky also did

[1] See note on page 27.

not stop at that. But doubtless there is scarcely any salvation for us which has not passed through this purgatory. This is not spiritual arrogance—even that notion is only a *cliché*—but a man crushed, beaten, crucified, steeped in insults and injuries which every one of us daily gives and receives; a man who lives in monologues because nothing else is left him, and whose poison unpoisons us.

A new idea is involved which, by its nature, demands a new medium of representation. What it represents and how it is represented has, for the moment, little to do with the matter. We are stimulated by it. If the memoirs, which Dostoevsky calls fragments, were even more fragmentary, if there were only one half, indeed only the first part, it would still suffice to enable us to recognize the possibility of a new poetical insight into the human soul.

It is just the monologue which is the novel and fruitful element in the work. It is unquestionably of a spiritual nature since it is able entirely to dispense with actuality. The author of *The Double* has fulfilled his promise. In dispensing with actuality the artist was not making any sacrifice, it was only the natural consequence of his experience. We have arrived at dramatization of thought. The thoughts are as physically real as the hero of the tragedy himself. The poet has mastered his facile inclination to the penny-dreadful. The vast prospect thus afforded is amazing.

The work remains fragmentary. A finished work would not have intensified the atmosphere. It is already perfect in itself. For that reason we have to accept the fragments in the spirit of toleration with which we admire the mutilated Gothic-like modellings of Michelangelo or the half-destroyed second Anatomy of Rembrandt. The rhythm is not alone not restrained by the limitation of incompleteness but is actually enhanced. Only in the first moments are the monologue and the loose linking-up of the episodes disturbing, just as in the first moment we are disconcerted by the missing limb of a *torso*. It is a mere superficiality. We ourselves can see to the rounding off

of the work without Doſtoevsky and we do it, as far as
necessary, inſtantaneously. Without our efforts to this end
no new synthesis can take place. But with these memoirs
Doſtoevsky has done more than set us on the new path.
He accompanies us almoſt to the end, running, it is true,
rather than walking. We muſt be careful not to jump to
premature conclusions on the ſtrength of passages which
have been skipped. All commentaries on the Russian which
are concerned with his idea and attempt to formulate it by
means of false inferences are exposed to this danger. Over-
haſte may lead to inferences such as those of Leo Sheſtov,
the reſtless Russian philosopher, who, from fragments only
half underſtood, deduced Doſtoevsky's kinship to Nietzsche
(29). The consequences of this typical blunder, largely
responsible for the antagonism againſt the poet both in
Russia and, recently, in Germany, may be so considerable
that further consideration of Sheſtov's work is imperative.

Sheſtov has educed from the *Letters from the Underworld*
a type of " underworldling " with whom he believes he can
identify Doſtoevsky. The memoirs are unqueſtionably a
more or less free autobiography of the period in which they
were written; it is quite unnecessary to refute the harmless
note at the beginning of the work in which Doſtoevsky
explains that the writer of the memoirs is a fiĉtitious person.
It is important to consider over what period of time the
work was spread, that is, whether it took one year, two years,
or only a few days. Sheſtov ignores this faĉtor. Of course
Doſtoevsky muſt have had the thoughts of the underworldling, otherwise he could not have expressed them.
Of course Shakespeare muſt have imagined himself into
every possible kind of rascal. His thoughts about humanity
muſt therefore be educed from his entire work.

Sheſtov fails to notice Doſtoevsky's development,
particularly this moſt important part, the inevitable ſtruggle
againſt sentimentality. He miſtakes the process of inure-
ment for the final renunciation of feeling. Because Doſtoevsky absolves himself from the Schilleresque—not from
Schiller, as we shall see—he is to disclaim all his ideals.

DOSTOEVSKY

Does that really happen even in these necessarily transient fragments which immediately succeed the most nauseous and disastrous work? They are neither written at the same time as nor do they precede *The Insulted and Injured*, as Shestov seems to suggest. The sequence is important. It must not be forgotten that Dostoevsky wanted to rid himself of the nauseous taste and to say something more important. It is perfectly clear from these fragments, brimful of mockery and scepticism, that he felt the need to purge himself of conventional notions. If the underworldling is feelingless, then so were Daumier, Rembrandt, and Grünewald.[1] Shestov compares Tolstoy's method of adjustment. We can dispense with that. It is just people like Tolstoy who prove how deep the acid must eat in before it reaches healthy flesh. That leads Michailovsky to the " cruel talent." Can a necessary operation be cruel? The underworldling was hard to himself and needed to be. Overwrought sentimentality leads him to despair. Who despairs? The " Schilleresque " underworldling, the Schilleresque Dostoevsky for that matter, thus a part of Dostoevsky! Even the people whom the underworldling addresses and who are very surely and speedily drawn, needed cruelty. Does Dostoevsky on that account murder hope? Shestov believes that the underworldling jeers at all construction because he sticks his tongue out at the indestructible palace of crystal. But in the tenth chapter of the first part there is a detailed discussion of the joys of sticking out the tongue, and it is not very far-fetched to assume that the crystal-castle stands for an indestructible notion of utter futility.

It is not necessary to have been in the *katorga* to share this aversion. But, for the rest, this sceptic is quite prepared to prefer a decent house to a hencoop in which, in case of need, it is possible to keep dry; indeed in certain circumstances to prefer a palace of crystal. " I would willingly," he says, " have my tongue cut right out in sheer

---

[1] Matthias Grünewald, German painter born in the latter half of the fifteenth century.—Tr.

gratitude if only I could be relieved of the desire to stick
it out. How can I help that it is impossible to make such
an arrangement and that one has to be satisfied with
lodgings? Why am I so constituted that I am compelled
to cherish such desires? Does then my whole spiritual
constitution only pursue the aim of bringing me to perceive
its own deception? Is that the whole intention? I cannot
believe it." He comes to the eulogy of seclusion. Since
he loathes normal beings, he finds isolation better, but, it is
doubtless understood, only because he does not find what
he seeks. "The best," he says, "is positively and certainly
not seclusion. To the devil with seclusion!"

All sorts of things can, of course, be deduced from such
spasms. To make the moods a basis of philosophy seems
to me a serious matter. In order to prove that the underworldling's egoism leads to Nietzschean master-morality,
Shestov quotes the cold repulse of Lisa, the poor harlot,
who comes for "moral support." "Do you know what I
really want?" he asks her. "That you all of you go to
the devil! That's all! I need peace. For a song I'd
instantly hand over the whole world. Is the world to go
to the dogs, or am I not to have tea? I say, let the
world go to the dogs, so long as I always have my tea!"
To which Shestov adds: "Who has ever thought of putting
words of such unexampled cynicism into his hero's mouth?
Just to the very Dostoevsky who not so long ago spoke
with such warmth and upright feeling concerning the destiny
of man."

And therewith Shestov seeks to prove an important
stage in the transformation of Dostoevsky's "humanity"
and couples with it far-reaching inferences.

It is difficult to grasp that Dostoevsky's tone in itself
did not perplex his interpreter. This lack of fine perception
is at the root of many errors. Moreover, if Shestov had
examined more closely an exactly parallel situation, Raskolnikov's first conversation with Sonia, the street-girl, in a
riper work, to which these memoirs served as an immediate
preface, he would have been convinced of the narrow-

mindedness and hastiness of his conclusions. He does, in fact, touch once on this parallel and imputes to the conversation with Sonia a special significance which Dostoevsky did not intend. Sonia is to give Raskolnikov what the knowledge of the " scholar " Razumihin cannot give him. (How does Shestov arrive at making Razumihin, the primitive man of feeling, the " blockhead " as he is called in the novel, the representative of knowledge?) He also quotes the climax of the conversation, Sonia's reading of the Bible, and refers to Raskolnikov's hope in the miracle of Lazarus, but merely in order to substantiate Dostoevsky's egoism in choosing, not a passage which was acceptable to recognized morality, but Lazarus, who fitted into Raskolnikov's situation, because, so at least Shestov believes, the immortality promised by the parable appears consistent with the belief in immortal egoism. He asserts that Dostoevsky was convinced " that a single passage torn from the context of the holy writing was perhaps not truth at all but became a lie." If only Shestov and his numerous followers could have been convinced that this procedure could not lead to creative literature, he would not have rejected, because it did not serve his purpose, such a masterpiece as *The Idiot*, would not have ignored *The Possessed*, a pamphlet, *A Raw Youth*, the impassioned protest against the superman, and would not have flung on to the rubbish-heap Alyosha, the purest of all affirmers. This philosophy destroys creative literature, and it is open to question whether the " idea " which Shestov evolves can offer sufficient compensation.

Let us keep to the underworld den and consider more carefully Shestov's important example, the above-mentioned words to Lisa " let the world go to the dogs——," because this passage is characteristic not only of the narrator's dialecticism but also of the author's method. The cynical words occur at a psychological moment which Dostoevsky has carefully prepared. The underworldling has awaited Lisa for days, has secretly indulged in hopes of saving and marrying Lisa and of thus saving himself. It must be remembered what has happened in the brothel. Lisa is

DOSTOEVSKY IN 1879

[*face p. 106*

perhaps his laſt refuge. She does not arrive. Therefore, after he has been scorned by his old school-fellows, in whose company his hopeless longing has brought him into an impossible situation, he is now rejected even by the whore. In the meantime he is, as usual, persiſtently wrangling with Apollo, his servant. This Apollo was expressly inſtalled by the devil to torment him. The scene with his " tormentor " degenerates almoſt into a brawl and drives the under-worldling into a violent rage. In the middle of this scene Lisa suddenly appears. Naturally he feels " crushed, ridiculous, in ignominious confusion." Then all his irritation is poured upon his visitor. Doſtoevsky says explicitly in the scene with Apollo, " If it were not for Lisa none of all that would have occurred," so that the tormentor owes his exiſtence to the yearning for Lisa. Moreover, this remark would certainly not have been necessary. The beginning of the scene with Lisa aggravates his exasperation. In order to entertain Lisa he is forced to make his peace with Apollo, to implore Apollo to buy tea and rusks as quickly as possible, and for three horrible minutes he does not know whether the brute will go or not. When the servant is at laſt out of the way and the underworldling returns to Lisa, he begins to wonder whether he should not simply go off, juſt as he is, in his tattered dressing-gown. In the presence of Lisa his fury with Apollo over-powers him.

" ' I shall kill him! ' I yelled, ſtriking the table. I was raving and at the same time had quite a clear notion of how ſtupid it was to rave like that.

' You don't know, Lisa, what this tormentor means to me. He is my torturer——'

And all at once I burſt into tears. That was a fit. I was horribly ashamed while I sobbed, but I could not control myself."

The cynical words to Lisa, to which Sheſtov objected, could long since have been introduced without incriminat-ing the unfortunate man, but Doſtoevsky is ſtill preparing. His psychology works faultlessly. After the " fit " Apollo brings the tea. This ordinary prosaic tea seems " wretched and unseemly " to the abnormally excited man after all that has happened. Who could not understand him? " Lisa, I suppose you despise me? " Only now comes the first attack on Lisa, not by any means a bolt from the blue. " I was angry with myself but, of course, she had to pay for it. A sudden wrath against her surged in my heart. She is responsible for everything, I thought."

But it still goes on. He struggles with himself, feels " the nauseous blackguardism of his spiteful stupidity," tries to conquer himself. If Lisa had not been so tactless at this moment, he would perhaps have been able to restrain himself. But it is just at this very moment that she informs him of her laudable resolve to quit the brothel. Nothing was more natural than to say it at this moment since she hoped thereby to free him of his suffering, and it is just as obvious that being informed at this moment was bound to be an intolerable profanity to him. And thereupon he razes the whole building and abandons himself to raving, in the course of which occur the words quoted by Shestov. These words are only few in a whole web which take the sting out of cynicism and yet sharpen it again and again. It suffices carefully to read such passages once, to follow the origin, the outburst and the dying down of the explosion, in order once and for all to be proof against the errors of Shestov and his colleagues. Dostoevsky's psychology always overwhelms us with a mass of detail, and only by means of his art does he succeed in retaining his spontaneity and in concealing the moral. It seems that he is too successful.

He is still saddled with the reproach of having portrayed, not the trill of the nightingale and blossoming roses and the beloved's amber-look, as it goes in the story of the Lisbon earthquake, but this underworld den. But since he had chosen the subject his task could not have been better fulfilled.

False interpretation, inadmissible isolation of the hero's phrases, which must not be removed either from their

atmosphere or, still less, from their psychological context if
they are to retain their original and quite definite significance,
misled Shestov into regarding the poet as a transvaluer of
all values. In effect, Dostoevsky, in his progress through
human nature, did come into contact with the region in
which supermen dwell. Unquestionably the topography of
this fever-region particularly attracted him all his life. He
recognized its immense significance for travellers weary of
Europe, and jealously inhaled its poisonous vapours.
Nietzsche may have believed that he leant on Dostoevsky
for support, and it can serve to enhance Nietzsche's psychology. It is of no importance to criticism of Dostoevsky.

This typical example proves how questionable is the
application of the epithet " cruel " to Dostoevsky's methods.
Actually his incentive was nothing more or less than the
unswerving devotion of a poet emancipated not from morals
but from the roof-garden. Instead of recognizing this path
to universality, a path across which thousands of candles
cast the light of day, Shestov considers Dostoevsky the
forerunner and relative of the philosopher " who was the
first to decorate his banner with the terrible words:
Apotheosis of cruelty." In so far as it is possible to
pervert facts it has here been done to perfection.

This procedure is a matter of course to-day and is
practised by every possible Shestov on every possible
occasion. This mental indolence proves how deeply we
are all sunk in an underworld den. We, on the other
hand, fail to benefit by the poison which stimulated the
underworldling. Old shibboleths are only flung aside to
make room for *clichés* which are more easily workable. A
poet whose very nature demanded bold leaps in the dark
and whose profile cannot be caught with a carpenter's
pencil, is not to be set on a Procrustes' bed. He needs to
become black just because he lights up the darkness.
Instead of letting him illuminate them, people paint him
over and perhaps even imagine that this adds to his greatness by rendering him more intelligible.

Attempts have been made to trace the experience which

provoked the fanatical exasperation of these memoirs. Shestov and others unjustifiably blame Siberia. It was not the *katorga* which gave birth to the underworld refuge. It dates back, as the reader already knows, to Dostoevsky's earliest emotions, first expressed in *The Double*. The rudiments of the underworld are found in Golyadkin's habitation, but Golyadkin is simple and stupid. His brain was not capable of generalizing his personal experience and lapsed into delusion. Not a little has been added to the hero's knowledge in twenty years. His power of resistance and his capacity for suffering have grown, but so has his tension. The anthropomorphic sentiment of the conservative Golyadkin is moderate beside the intellectual fantasy of the underworld man. The latter is certainly not disposed to soothe his twofold or manifold existence with the false product of a harmless madness, and to compound his claim on the world around with touching self-expropriation.

Naturally Siberia contributed to the preparation of this tension, and perhaps more than his experiences in the *katorga*, what followed the *katorga*. Still, it will not do to take isolated incidents in order to explain this turning-point in the poet's career. The tension is the natural consequence of every experience as well as of every quality of the man himself. Over the underworld den broods a sky of brimstone. The underworldling still squats in inactivity, meditates and chatters. How should I induce them not to laugh at my wretchedness? How should I show them that I am not a " little worm "? That is the sense of the monologue. The question swells and festers in the underworld den and presses towards an outlet. The monologue is not an outlet but merely a bridge to something else. Every line heralds the birth of tragedy.

CHAPTER X

ACCORDING to modern notions the *Letters from the Under-world* has no action. The incidents, brimful of movement, are strictly confined to this cage of reflection. It is just this characteristic which constitutes the literary setting. The man of memoirs preaches but never practises. His reflection disintegrates action before it begins to exist, even the activity absolutely essential to his moral existence. He feels he is a worm, less than a worm, and prostitutes himself in enjoying his knowledge of it. He is forty years old and was, or thought he was, or could have been, something else before; in the course of a slow process of decomposition he has become a worm. Somewhere in his hole lie possi-bilities of another existence, and at times, when the spirit moves him, he speculates on them and ponders on forms of action. At moments he is even on the verge of some such action, abnormal and unsocial to the point of childish-ness, such, for example, as this jostling with the arrogant officer who refuses to make way on the pavement: this escapade has only succeeded after many fruitless attempts. He shuts his eyes and assaults his adversary. That is just how he assaults others, invariably with closed eyes, merely for the pleasure of not feeling himself a worm for one short-lived moment. There is the germ of this under-world dweller in Raskolnikov, not forty but twenty years old, not an official but a student, sickly, though not yet ill, still possessing unimpaired vitality, not yet acclimatized to the underworld existence. The connexion is obvious. A man of memoirs of this kind is not bound to confine himself to monologues; in certain circumstances he is capable of other things. Jostling can result in murder; at such a point anything may happen. The monologue is transformed into lightning action. The scene becomes peopled by

III

DOSTOEVSKY

beings of flesh and blood whose activity is not confined to listening.

Twelve years after his release from the convict settlement he completed at last the *katorga*-book, the first of the five great principal works. In the eyes of many admirers of Dostoevsky it ranks even to-day as the most significant and the most astonishing of all five, contains the simplest action of all, and paved the way to the poet's universal success. It owes much to the fact that Dostoevsky discontinued a bad habit. He abandoned the *I*-form of narration, which for him was often only the leading-strings of the journalist, and compelled him to make the *I* an unimportant character. The author's own reflections are suppressed, and the facts reveal themselves, relentless as in ancient tragedy.

In many early stories the observant reader is bound to notice that, owing to the author's vision, owing to his mood, his humour and, above all, his psychology, several solutions were possible. Dostoevsky himself saw one of the several solutions, and might easily have chosen some other. The action moved in a narrow channel or swept along in a broad stream, was at times far-fetched and would suddenly stand still; a whimsical actor might behave much in the same way and begin to improvise with considerable skill. The author's high spirits were not beneath letting the puppets occasionally take control of the stage. All the same there was always, or nearly always, felt behind the multifarious action a force which could not be coerced. This force sometimes advanced, sometimes retarded the action. In favourable instances the force was a torrent on which events were swept along like floating craft. In the *Letters from the Underworld* the force showed up distinctly for the first time. The events were transparent, but we did not object to that so long as the force could be recognized through them. We saw a vast emotional force such as only Dostoevsky was capable of depicting, a force more important than action itself. We seemed to be experiencing that fascinating birth of rhythm which can be recognized in the few essential pencil strokes of a gifted artist.

COMPOSITION

This is changed with the new novel. Raskolnikov cannot be other than he is. Neither Dostoevsky nor anyone else could find another solution. It is not a story but an organic event. The dark torrent becomes action.

The central structure is built round a man who exists for himself only and whose essential source of action is his own inner being. Persky quite rightly denies any connexion between Raskolnikov and Turgenev's type of " nihilist," Bazarov[1] (30). There is no attempt at making society responsible for the crime. In the fifth chapter of the third part at the beginning of the tea-party at the house of the examining lawyer, Razumihin, Raskolnikov's friend, carries the excuse for murder *ad absurdum*. Raskolnikov follows his own impulse. On the other hand the influences of his intellectual *milieu* come into play; ideas current at that time play an important part in so far as Raskolnikov's impulse is formulated as a thought and, of course, in so far as he mentions his motives. The first idea is: is it permissible to murder a noxious, or, to say the least, useless and inferior creature who possesses considerable wealth, if the murderer believes he can thereby benefit humanity? The second: may extraordinary men break the law, by which ordinary mortals are governed, in order to create new values? Here, if anywhere, is the possibility of a link with Nietzsche.

The first idea, subjective opportunism, must always prove itself a deception, and it plays a subordinate part in the novel. When this theme is introduced at the drinking-table between the officer and the student the deed has already been decided on, and there is no real significance in the fact that Raskolnikov by chance overhears their conversation (31). Dostoevsky's statement, " this meaningless discussion in the tavern had an extraordinary influence on the further development of the matter," one of the few feeble passages of the novel, sounds like a rationalization of his previous intention. If the murderer had seriously attached any importance to this the incident would, in the

[1] In Turgenev's *Fathers and Children.*—Tr.

nature of things, have been worked out more fully. As a matter of fact opportunism is not for one moment a driving force, it is in direct opposition to Raskolnikov's temperament and to his behaviour, both before and after the deed. It is far more likely that the fortuitous conversation fostered his superstition.

The second doctrine, the idea of the superman, was for a long time accepted by European critics as the central theme of the novel. That opinion could be based on far more essential factors, for example on the ominous essay, the subject of discussion at the tea-party, which obliges Raskolnikov to explain his programme in detail. The doctrine stands and falls by the hero. He renounces it in the lap of his Sonia.

It is true that this doctrine gives much, very much of the idea of *Crime and Punishment*. Merejkovsky, in his amazing study of the modern Napoleon, has dealt with the subject exhaustively. But the doctrine does not exhaust this particular work. It could be compared to Napoleon's " Actes publics " of which only the prisoner of St. Helena stooped to speak when he dictated his memoirs to the faithful Las Cases, fearful lest going into personal details be interpreted as an attempt to defend his supposed crimes. Nevertheless there is the man behind them. But even were we to disregard the man, we could not overlook the fact that the most significant *Acte public* is that in which Raskolnikov declares his entire doctrine to be " idle chatter," " casuistry," and denounces, not the hyper-romantic folly of wanting to become a benefactor of mankind by means of a murder, but his demon. " Nonsense! I have simply killed. I have killed for myself, for myself only." Here the neurotic speaks the truth.

The decisive motive is the will to the deed, the deed at any price. It is true the ragged student is oppressed by poverty, particularly as he is generous and is always giving to other unfortunate beings, but he could escape poverty with a hundredfold less expenditure. A compromise would do it, a compromise for which there is an opportunity before the deed, one of those compromises to which every other middle-class family owes its continued existence. The proud aristocrat turns it down. Murder rather than this Luzhin as a brother-in-law! But even in that there is a touch of *Acte public*, from which you could tear yourself free with the same cynicism with which you call on the policeman calmly to leave to the mercies of the elegant gentleman the young girl you have just rescued from a street lover's appetite. But the urge within is unavoidable, as are also fear and loathing of the underworld hole, inability to cope with the complicated thoughts which fool you with ideas, with *Actes publics* which ring in your ears and are well on the way to obstruct your will with all kinds of subtleties. Unappeasable the desire which needs struggle more than daily bread; struggle for the good, if the good comes your way; for crime if no other course lies open. You want to leap beyond this wretchedness, beyond all so-called good, so-called evil. The whither does not worry you, only a way out of the underworld! Afterwards we shall see. Afterwards everything will be " repaid with immense interest." And the immensity rather than the interest is emphasized. Leap before everything, lay a vast distance between yourself and the rest of mankind and naturally spit on them. That is the superman all over.

Raskolnikov and the man of memoirs had different views of the rest of mankind. The man of memoirs really was in a bad way, had the plague in his very bones and already looked so uninviting that people ran away from him. Raskolnikov's fellow-beings are nice people. There is a charming mother and an adoring sister, both prepared for any sacrifice. There is Razumihin, the unswerving bungler of a friend, to whom he only has to nod. And there are others, there might be many others. This interesting young man has the mysterious faculty of attracting people and of dominating them. Indeed, there is something of a Napoleon about him, but his appeal is more subtle and not to the mass. He has a certain winning and ennobling way with him and an elevating influence on people with whom he comes in contact, whether friend or foe. He is handsome even in rags; well-built, of fine appearance, a splendid type, to whom even dirt gives a noble complexion, since nothing hinders his movement and his soaring spirit wards off every kind of ugliness; those who would hate him see only one side of him. He never gives himself away. Moreover his beauty is never a stumbling-block. He plunges headlong into the thick of danger, and at once a thousand arms are outstretched to rescue him. We tremble for him as for a brother, we are overcome by his beauty, the beauty of his spirit, his swift intellect which sees in a flash what others have to think about, his obdurate instinct which reason cannot sway, his intellectual altruism, culminating in a madness brought about by disgust at human weakness; above all by his incorruptibility and faithfulness to his own principles. It is almost possible to speak of this murderer's beauty of soul.

His beauty is his undoing; it is the rock on which is wrecked the ideology of the superman, the doctrinaire's vast experiment. He is straining every nerve when it is a question of rising above the level of " quivering creature," and proving whether he is of the " vermin " or of " human beings." There he struggles with the axe, this slender, delicate, fever-stricken youth whom conversation exhausts and who is too weak even to eat. He gets up, half in a trance, puts the sling under his coat in order to conceal the implement of murder, clasps it with an iron grip, and chases through the streets. Though his legs are unsure his eyes are wide open; his mad excitement does not prevent him from observing every minute detail. He manages to control his trembling voice in the presence of the money-lender, lifts the axe with both hands, and kills his victim. He steals because, if that was not the primary motive, at least he must make it appear so. Beauty is avenged, for it has degraded robbery to *dilettanteism.* Suddenly he raises the axe again on poor simple Lizaveta as she stands by the corpse, and murders his second victim;

an unpremeditated deed, and he accordingly thinks no more about it. Devilish mechanism of the mind! Then the mad minutes as the money-lender's two clients approach, find the door shut, finally notice from the door-hook that someone muſt be at home, and guess that there is something wrong. The æſthete's nerves are set on edge by the violent shaking of the insecure hook; on one side these pursuers eager on solving the myſtery, on the other the gruesome bodies of his prey. He saves himself by means of a film-trick rendered credible by its very improbability. He tears home and even manages to replace the porter's axe without being noticed. The whole thing is done mechanically. If the porter had happened to be there, he would simply have " handed him the axe." Then he is enveloped by the underworld from which he wanted to escape.

It is a hard beginning for a ' layman,' for this sensitive being whom ugliness confronts at every turn. He is physically repelled by the deed, and the prospeſt of madness or suicide hovers before him. It is in this ſtate of mind that he commits the well-known ſtupidities of the criminal, attraſts the attention of the insolent police-officer, and rouses the suspicions of Zametov, the diſtriſt-official, and Porphyry Petrovitch, the examining lawyer. Suspicion only serves to excite his anger, the anger of the artiſt. Fear is unknown to him except when he makes a mess of his part; he is frightened of nothing but hisses, nothing but the ridicule which the ſtupidity of his deed and his method of defence may invite; a snob, an artiſt and a Werther; the artiſt calls the tune. Pity that, inſtead of an axe, he did not set about with a pen or a brush; but his nerves would not have ſtood the ſtrain. It is obvious that he has long been a black coffee fiend, probably since he was a child, prattled over it, revelled in it, and smoked thousands of cigarettes; you could swear his fingers were ſtained with nicotine; and on top of this, so it is said, he bit his nails. The nerves! It is not remorse which drives him to self-accusation, but partly disguſt, at himself as well as at others, and mainly his nervous condition. If there had been a little

DOSTOEVSKY

less of the suspicious and "irritating" policeman about
Zametov, who catches him reading the newspaper reports of
the murder, Raskolnikov would have handed him the axe
in sheer absent-mindedness. Moreover, in the earlier scene
he actually makes a virtual confession in the course of
casual conversation. They are chattering about local
crime; Zametov is convinced that the murderer will be
found, just as a short while ago the gang of coiners was
found, quite simply, because the hands of one of the fellows
trembled in changing the money. Oho! thinks Raskolnikov, this coiner was a *dilettante*, and he straightway expounds, with the perspicuity of a retired criminal, how he
would have behaved in changing the money. The discussion
of the murder and Zametov's innuendo that the murderer
must have been a feeble novice spur his defiance. In
answer to the police-official's significant question how he
thought the murder was carried out, Raskolnikov, with
mad recklessness, goes into actual details. This boldness
completely allays the suspicion of Zametov, who is not
experienced enough for such bluffs. But Raskolnikov
rants on.

"What if I myself had murdered the old woman and
Lizaveta?" The question has a double effect. Zametov's
suspicion is again roused and Raskolnikov is brought to
his senses by the note of reality. He makes the most of his
vantage-point, behaves as though he were removing a
mask, convinces his adversary that he has been too hasty
and forces him to capitulate. Zametov's suspicion is again
dispelled and he tries to excuse himself. The examining
lawyer must have made a mistake, it must be a false track.
Raskolnikov has won the first battle. True, it is only an
outpost-skirmish, all the same it has proved his power; he
could give the police some hard nuts to crack if he wanted
to. It might be almost thrilling, and there would certainly
be a touch of Napoleon about it! If he wanted to! Possibly
it is not so much instinct for self-preservation as precisely
the opposite, desire for danger, which determines action;
an intoxicant, an eminently aesthetic excitement. He

THE DETECTIVE

abandons himself to it for a moment with real delight, with the artist's enthusiasm, and creates all kinds of wild fantasies. The excitement once over, he collapses. The effectiveness of even this stimulant depends on the type of person concerned. Is a Zametov worth it? Is it worth while at all? and what is left? His inner being scarcely figures, the inner being wherein rages the torment of disgust at himself and at the whole of mankind; and he is swayed by an entirely different impulse, the joy of self-destruction. Immediately after the discussion in the café he meets Razumihin, who does his utmost to save his sick friend. Raskolnikov can do nothing more pleasant than fling his kindness back in his face. " Leave me in peace! leave me alone! "

Away with the past! The past is dead, is lying by the red box of the money-lender, cannot help any longer. The past brings remorse in its train, remorse not perhaps so much at the murder as at the futility of all murder, always leads back to the underworld hole. Even his mother and his sister who have just arrived, whom he has not seen for years, even they are part of it; when they rush to him, overjoyed at seeing their idol once again, the broken link with the past is brought acutely home to him, so acutely that he cannot endure it, almost hates them, and falls insensible to the ground.

In this moment his torment reaches its climax, for it was exactly an hour earlier that he thought he saw the glimmer of a new life. He has come from the death-bed of Marmeladov, the drunkard who has been run over, has for the first time seen Sonia, the humiliated prostitute, his future companion. This glimmer of hope is scarcely intelligible to the reader, who cannot draw conclusions from later stages of the novel, and must be accepted as the poet meant it, and not as it is portrayed: an optimistic mood which intimates the main theme of the second volume, but which is, for the time being, only a fleeting thought (32). Raskolnikov's surprising, high-flown, almost declamatory announcement of his nascent hope seems to be a reflex of the " Schilleresque " (33) of which the gleam in this passage is symptomatic; a passage, incidentally, in which the psychologist's technique breaks down and the poet's rhythm tries to move on more quickly than the texture of the composition permits. Looking back later it is obvious that this lyrical element has been suppressed.

With Sonia Raskolnikov gains courage to try his strength with Porphyry Petrovitch, the examining lawyer.

A lesser writer would have attempted to indicate Sonia's moralizing influence. Dostoevsky disregards it. The only clear point is the fortifying influence of their first relationship. Porphyry Petrovitch is a dangerous antagonist, not because he is peculiarly fitted for his profession but because he deals with the ' layman ' as a ' layman,' in the only way valid in tackling a Raskolnikov, in a, so-to-speak, æsthetic way. Zametov could be played with. Zametov is a decent, clumsy fellow, of average intelligence, a Razumihin who cannot control himself, a blockhead. Porphyry Petrovitch is an artist. He knows it is not what is said that matters; all kinds of questions can be asked, all kinds of questions occur to the shrewd Porphyry, but he also asks questions because that is part of his job; omission to do so would be a technical error; he selects the choicest questions, but elicits only choicer answers. He comes quite spontaneously to the essay written by Raskolnikov a long while ago which he read as a matter of duty. The essay establishes the right to commit crime; extremely incriminating, of course. Raskolnikov modestly acknowledges himself the author. He corrects Porphyry's unreasonable inferences, simply and to the point, as though the last thing he were thinking of was the danger of this document. He recovers in the course of this skirmishing, and Porphyry Petrovitch makes no impression. Then he makes a masterly escape from the detective's second, truly professional trap, the question whether Raskolnikov happened to see the painters in the house of the murder. After that Raskolnikov is assured of getting away all right; a Zametov would have been put out of action, but not so Porphyry who really scorns all the minor tricks and is fully aware that if you want, not to prove, but to convince yourself, it is a matter of what is suppressed rather than what is said and done. Thereupon Porphyry fixes his gaze and nothing escapes him. If Raskolnikov talks too quickly or lacks restraint, because great people do sometimes lack restraint, Porphyry is wide-awake, but discreet, and not a movement betrays whether he has seen anything or how he construes what he has seen. In fact, when Raskolnikov lets himself go Porphyry intentionally looks away; he is too astute to take advantage of his adversary's lapse. One artist against another. What Raskolnikov cannot bear is his adversary's æstheticism. Porphyry relies for his effects on his physical appearance, on his positively feminine, ball-like, obese body, on his feminine restlessness; he is a caricature of the nervous, fidgety Raskolnikov himself. Gradually he drives Raskolnikov where he wants him; when Raskolnikov, the victor, makes his successful departure his adversary already knows everything: he is the murderer, he, and no one else. One little fact must still be established and everything else will follow mathematically.

Raskolnikov is not equal to such æsthetic torture and declines this *modus operandi* with blunt candour. That happens at the beginning of the second interview. He might just as well have asked his adversary in a duel to put away his pistol and let him do the firing. Naturally he achieves only the opposite effect. The rotund little man with the white eyelids rolls about the room, hugely tickled, becomes, indeed, a little too drastic; a cooler adversary would have seen through his game for, of course, his mirth is merely a cloak for his own feeble artifice, the apparatus behind the door which does not yet seem to function properly (the surprise with the little man).

But Raskolnikov, to his cost, is again much too clear-sighted, immediately divines the apparatus behind the door with the unknown witness who yesterday, as he passed by, whispered murderer; instead of being prepared for the surprise his imagination runs riot, and he is unnerved by the knowledge that he could not bear the sight of the terrible little man. Things which would leave a more or less professional scoundrel completely cold lead to his undoing. He constantly compromises himself and more often imagines he has done so, becomes wildly excited and begins to rave. Either a proper interrogation in legal form, facts, arrest, or drop it altogether! Porphyry is positively bursting with laughter. Legal forms! What an academician! Why arrest him? The butterfly cannot possibly escape, does not want to, is totally unable " psychologically to escape." He will flutter and flutter, gradually narrow his circle and " crash! fly straight into his mouth." " And I shall swallow him," laughs Porphyry, " and that is very pleasant, don't you think so? "

Raskolnikov is staggered. This ball-shaped person is reading his most intimate thoughts, his inmost agitation, is dissecting his brain and showing it to him as through a microscope, but transmitted, as on a kind of stage; really you might be in a theatre! He revels in keeping this game going although it has long been unnecessary. A young bull is in the ring, his head is down—plunge!

Then another respite. A *coup de théâtre*. Instead of the surprise with the little man, Porphyry's last trump, which he has kept back and almost forgotten, there suddenly rushes in the innocent prisoner, Nikolay, who confesses that he has killed the two women with the axe. It is Porphyry's turn to be surprised; but it only lasts a second. The experienced criminologist instantly recognizes that this is only a case of hysterical auto-suggestion, a thing of common occurrence, particularly in Russia, and is merely irritated at the interruption. Raskolnikov is dismissed. " *Au revoir!* hope to see you again soon! "

The scene is rather crowded and somewhat fierce. Dostoevsky sought ultimately to portray a monomaniac in the successful examiner, a task rendered easier by the freer legal methods in Russia. Porphyry Petrovitch was obviously to appear infected by Raskolnikov's psychology, a theme possible in itself, and, in this instance, thoroughly legitimate; but to suit our tastes it would have had to remain more in the background and not to detract from the essential action. This scene might constitute one of the surest arguments for the idea of Dostoevsky's "cruel talent." In the face of the purgatory to which this criminal is exposed, in itself only a particle of the "punishment," whoever doubts the validity of the novel's title (34) is more cruel than Dostoevsky himself.

The third and decisive interview with the examiner takes place in Raskolnikov's room, after he has confessed to Sonia and refused the cross she has offered. He asserts that he will go on struggling because he does not admit anyone's right to inflict punishment. In its legal aspect his position is not desperate, since his terror of the little man has proved ill-founded, and the police have another victim in their clutches. They cannot prove anything against him, and he will not tolerate any more torture from them. So he thinks. But things turn out differently. Porphyry suddenly changes his method. He stops rolling round the room, sits still and talks calmly and rationally. He has come to offer his adversary an explanation, indeed, to apologize to him. He realizes that he has carried his interrogation beyond the bounds of authority. He has been led away by abnormal passion, fully aware that his manner must have racked the neurotic youth, has done his utmost to intensify the torture. Raskolnikov must please not look on him as a monster and must believe in his repentance. He is going frankly and without joking to show how he became and was, indeed, bound to become suspicious.

Raskolnikov falters. Is that the truth? Is this a feint? has the man really changed?—" The thought that Porphyry Petrovitch considers him innocent begins to torture him."

The examiner talks at some length. Much that has already been said is repeated, not with the object of torturing, but in order to put the cards clearly and neatly on the table, as is fitting. It sounds different, it sounds very alluring, it is really relevant, and it is difficult not to listen.

DOSTOEVSKY

The essay is also introduced. No one has so thoroughly understood the essay. Not only its content; on that subject there can be differing opinions; that can be considered fantastic and absurd; but the, so-to-say, æsthetic side, the young man's audacity in writing such a thing, " the audacity of despair," the devotion, regardless of the consequences. That is how a competent amateur meets an artist on his own ground. Porphyry Petrovitch expands in this third interview. Without actually saying so he acknowledges his esteem for Raskolnikov and admits that he wants to " ingratiate " himself with him; and this discreet confession is no cheap confidence trick, he can prove his sincerity. Oh, not romanticism, nothing " Schilleresque." His position, his profession, his ball-like stomach debar him from that; it is merely a liking for, an understanding of the matter. If he had not this liking, would he find his way about in such a maze? Porphyry puts all his cards on the table, reveals how that blockhead of a Razumihin has helped the examination, how this bosom-friend has registered, as infallibly as a thermometer, every otherwise unnoticeable reaction of the suspect. Everything is plain-sailing now, and Porphyry amiably invites him to—confess!

Raskolnikov jumps up. He has not expected this, though he ought to have guessed it from the drift of the conversation. The æsthete has fooled the criminal, who was so interested in the speaker's manner that he forgot his anxiety. Now he is tearing at his chains and beginning to rave. But the examiner will not countenance that. Why should he? Surely we are reasonable, decent people. Of course, if at the moment it is not convenient to throw up the sponge, they will willingly wait a few days longer. He will not be unreasonably hurried, he can think things over calmly. But Porphyry can only urge him to note how uncommonly favourable is the moment for a voluntary confession (for someone else has pleaded guilty and no official charge has been preferred against the real culprit), and not to let it come to painful arrest. Porphyry Petrovitch can, with a clear conscience, answer for the conceivably extenuating circumstances and will hush up everything, even, of course, his own part in the story, " the whole psychology," so that the effect of the voluntary confession may not be lessened. The tone of this promise precludes any possible doubt. Porphyry develops. His peculiar faculty lends itself to the task of tackling such a person as Raskolnikov, and it is in his nature to be more interested in the means than in the end. A very clever person, this lawyer. There is something more than merely a murderer in this fellow. In sober words Porphyry sets out the entire problem of the novel, and it gains in simplicity. An absurd idea has driven the young student to this sorry pass. With his cleverness and talent he will strike a better idea, and that will extricate him from this sorry pass. It is no affair of an examining lawyer, particularly of such a sceptic with an obese belly, who actually is a finished man, to express himself on the subject of the better idea. All the same this much is certain; the so-called punishments of society are not to be compared to the pretty instruments which we prepare for ourselves. The advantages of official suffering are not to be underrated. The shamming Nikolay is an epicure. A best friend could recommend Raskolnikov no more excellent means than Siberia for eventually getting " into the open." Naturally an awkward moment, this abandoning of seclusion; but, as a matter of fact, he has already abandoned his underworld by virtue of his somewhat unusual procedure with the money-lender. In for a penny, in for a pound. Only to get out into the open! For what does it cost in the end? the ridiculous comfort of the underworld? the " disgrace?" Surely those are mere -isms. We know that, we students of the underworld. The main thing is: away with the underworld! Anything can be put up with if there is anywhere to go, anywhere reasonable. Perhaps it is Siberia. Moreover, the value of the Christian dogma must not be underrated. Porphyry almost envies the traveller. Perhaps in his heart of hearts he did envy him.

So much for the detective story. Its novelty is brilliant. Of the Sherlock Holmes film there is only just enough to maintain the tension. The criminal case has long became a pure work of art; the advantage of an artistic conception, which accepted a popular setting with the same readiness with which Dostoevsky accepted journalism, is obvious. Nothing is less popular than the events set forth. Dostoevsky steers clear of any romanticism, which might create a halo round the criminal and sensationalism on a melodramatic stage. Sensationalism is also only an -ism, and it is only behind this that the drama lies, and behind the drama the unmistakable moral. In the three scenes with the examiner the man Raskolnikov fares extremely badly. There is no glamour about him which might invite superficial sympathy; he is what the idea of the work makes him: " quivering creature." Only through the eyes of the lawyer will he be found not beneath contempt. Dostoevsky goes so far as to charge him with tolerating the innocent Nikolay's opportune hysteria, but wastes no words on it, either of apology or of accusation, because any consideration of this theme would degrade the discussion; the point does not arise because Raskolnikov would naturally never agree to someone else standing in his shoes, and at most discerns in it a fresh exaction of his adversary. The idea of being thought innocent leads to fresh torments.

In the meantime he widens the breach with the past and says good-bye to those who were once his own people. These melancholy scenes without words, melancholy as Volga melodies, have already begun before the conflict with the examiner has really started; they prove the unimportance of the duel. He talks of separation to his mother and sister at the very moment when Razumihin is unfolding before the two women plans for a new life—" Cut yourselves off from me if you love me, otherwise I shall have to hate you." Dounia, his brave, strong-minded sister, takes his abstruse words for lack of feeling and is revolted by her brother's egoism; and Razumihin, despite his love for Dounia, reproaches her lack of understanding. If she cannot see his " mental distraction " she must be feelingless herself. He hurries after Raskolnikov along the

SONIA

dark corridor. For a second they stand eye to eye, speechless—" Then Razumihin trembled. A terrible something stepped between them, some vague, gruesome, ghastly thought in the minds of both, understood by both. Razumihin became pale as death."

" Do you understand now? " asks Raskolnikov. He calls on his friend to go back to the others and quits the house.

It is also in such scenes that can be found relationship to the Schilleresque, reflexes of the mimicry of earlier times, when feeling had no part in the action. Attempts have been made to read something quite different into this scene (35). It is just the connexion between feeling and action which has fundamentally altered. The reality of the whole is so forceful that a mere nothing is able to support such obscurities. Without needing words, feeling envelops the tragedy, silent and proud, and it is much more our feeling than his which bursts through here. Why should it not be called sentimental?—indeed extremely sentimental and, if you like, Schilleresque; and though we may find fresh objections to this feeling, we may nevertheless be overwhelmed by emotion, just as we are overwhelmed by our sympathy for Werther, the other miscreant.

But Raskolnikov avoids giving way at this moment. By imposing on Razumihin a fresh obligation, he counters the indifference which disappointment at his own obstinate reserve threatens to engender in his friend; with the foresight of a man setting his house in order he entrusts his sister to Razumihin's care. Gently, as gently as he can, always master of himself, even when his nerves are on edge, he prepares his people for the blow, and with the refinement of good-breeding, with a delicacy which effaces his apparent egoism, he steers clear of any tenderness which his people might misinterpret at a later date. There is frequent contact between æstheticism and morality.

Raskolnikov goes to Sonia. She is out there, he will be out there too. It is natural to go to her. But is she far enough out there? That must be settled first. He

127

reflects calmly on his position. We are both out there, this is no time for idle words; the Schilleresque would be silly.

Sonia needs to say very little; he knows her previous history from her father's story in the tavern. The rest is obvious, and the future self-evident. First thrashed by her step-mother—No, no, she asserts—Very well! then on the streets, to fill papa's glass. Her trials on the streets; shouldering the burden of the little ones after her step-mother has gone; delicate shoulders, her fingers of death. Her fingers have always been like that, exclaims Sonia, and the people here, the stammering family of Kapernaumov, are good. But her step-mother has consumption, as every one knows, spits blood, as every one knows. Katerina Ivanovna will shortly die. Then it will be harder. The eldest child, the pretty Poletchka, will naturally go on the streets as soon as possible.—Stop, Sonia cries, not that!— She defends herself. That would be quite impossible, for: " God will not allow anything so terrible! "—God? dear me!—He torments her. It has to be, indeed, she is used to a great deal, and in spite of it she is glad of his visit. But why does he torment her even with God? He must be ill; perhaps mad, that accounts for his insane eyes. No, God will not allow that.

She replies with God to everything he says. He laughs and his laughter scares her. He can feel that the cup of her suffering is full. Then he bows down and kisses her foot. Now she really thinks him insane. But he only wanted to show her his veneration, for she suffers more than he, and never once complains, still replies with God. What good does it do her? That is a riddle. He has done this, that and the other, but knows, or at least imagines why. But she endures this filth in vain, does not save anyone by it, achieves nothing, cannot possibly dispel the curse on the family; her sacrifice is fruitless. Then why not plunge head-first into the water?

Oh, these thoughts are not new to her. She has often contemplated that solution but always rejected it on God's account. Raskolnikov shudders. Does she not notice the boundless filth of her streets? No, she does not seem to notice it. Perhaps she is mad?

Her eyes light up when he asks her if she often prays to God. He goes on questioning her and begins to think it is she who is insane: religious mania. There lies the Bible, the New Testament. Everything is clear. The Bible was given her by Lizaveta with whom all the local poor had dealings, this Lizaveta who chanced to come in when he was with the money-lender and whom he thereupon killed as well. Lizaveta—Sonia. In a moment he will be mad too, and then they will march to the madhouse together.

He lets her read the miracle of Lazarus, and the kinetic element in the story, the resurrection, works in him. For an æsthete who knows what a symbol is, such an awakening would be possible even to-day. Naturally it has nothing whatever to do with God, but only with the kinetic element.

Now he informs her that he is separating from his people, from every one, and wants to come to her; that she has crushed a life; even if it is only her own, it is a life all the same, and she cannot go on alone; and that he has done much the same, as she will learn later, and he too cannot go on alone. Alone both of them would go to the madhouse. Together they might save one another. Therefore away, anywhere, to a new life, new strength, new power, power over the quivering creature!

She does not know what he wants, understands only that he is in ecstasy, and threatened by madness, and that his words pierce her to the marrow. What will he say later? God will not forsake her.

He dispels her fantasy. You must fight, it is a duty; it is mere laziness, this idea that God saves people from sickness and the madhouse, restores to health a consumptive who spits blood and cannot look after herself, or feeds starving children; laziness! You have to fight. They will fight together.

This first long speech, particularly the beginning of it,

recalls the brothel scene in the *Letters from the Underworld*, where the underworldling foretells the future to the disconcerted prostitute in order to vent his torments on her. Raskolnikov also torments, consumed by torment, and has difficulty ·in overcoming the malicious tone of his forerunner. His sudden kneeling down before her suffering makes a great impression, in spite of his having already " paid honour " to his sister in letting her take a seat beside Sonia. The kneeling down is less an act of humiliation than a kind of ceremony of the outlaw.

It is just this scene, in relation to earlier work, which proves Dostoevsky's development. The improvement does not lie in the medium, for that mask-like dialectic of the *Letters from the Underworld* could not be surpassed; but in the different conception, the construction, above all in the pictorial reality. The thoughts of the murderer, the simple faith of the girl, all that is, at bottom, as simple as the Primitives, whilst in the *Letters from the Underworld* there is cunning subtlety. Dialectic would clog the ponderous march of the action. Life stands before us, born of a rhythm which needs no subtle details. The picture, once a movable easel-painting, has become a *fresco*. No passage of the work is so dramatic. Novel and epic vanish. The dialogue, Dostoevsky's born medium, achieves its purpose with the utmost economy. The words are chiselled and the dialogue is full of symbols (36).

We enjoy this scene, not only because it is a fitting vehicle for its content, but also because it is form in itself; there is not the excitement of the scenes with the examiner, it appeals to quite a different sense. We stand in superstitious awe before the symbolism which soothes us and prepares our minds for the new prospect which Dostoevsky reveals. The Bible passage, which has since been turned to account by many followers, becomes a parallel legend.

In the second scene in which Sonia learns of the murder, the drama of the action is intensified, but not the dramatic form; the latter is rather restrained. Again the artist's touch. The author avoids becoming theatrical even when

SONIA

the situation lends itself to such treatment. At the moment of confession, by a marvellous subtlety, Raskolnikov is once again at the scene of the murder. As the word is on the tip of his tongue he sees himself again lifting the axe out of the sling, and recognizes in Sonia's face the expression of the speechless Lizaveta.

But Sonia is not a Lizaveta. Once over the first terror, she seizes on the idea which was the motive of his coming to her, exalts it as though it were of her own creation: together! wherever he goes she will follow. To Siberia! anywhere! together! together!

She is at once in love with him. That is a novel situation; it seemed impossible to choose a variant which was not hackneyed. It is not because he climbs down to her that she loves him; such social humbug means nothing to her. To her, the fervent believer, the deed of murder is inconceivable. Every one else manages somehow, even mother and sister, friend and court of law. Sympathy with the murderer overcomes horror at the crime. Sonia cannot reconcile herself. The shock of the murder is like a blow from an axe, but since she is still alive she will from now on live for him alone, for him, the most unfortunate of living creatures. That is Sonia, the delicate Sonia, with her fingers of death and her frail body, thrashed by her mother, imposed on by her father, crushed by the street, and yet her life is fuller, healthier than any; hers is devotion to the common good. As a Christian? Undoubtedly she is a Christian, but her Christianity, like the symbolism of the drama, is beyond the reach of the common herd. Do not believe, if indeed you find such a thing possible! There is absolutely nothing to believe here, only eyes are necessary. You must live and must have reason for living. Pick up the reason where you find it. But if you have no reason, well, what then? There is no religious ecstasy about it, nothing is further from Sonia than to convert this unfortunate man. The very strength of Christ in her precludes imparting Him. To convert is to profane God; surely you cannot tread in another's footsteps even if you want to.

But how could he want to murder? Is a thing like that possible?

She muſt know tnat before she can help. Naturally, to her mind, money was the only possible motive: someone was ſtarving, either his mother, or his siſter, or he himself.

No, that was not the reason, he says, " a little irritably." It was not hunger, and he took no money, does not even know whether there is any money amongſt the buried objefts. He hid everything and has not been there since. Perhaps later, he laughs.

He cannot explain, for she would not underſtand, it was foolish to begin explaining.—No, she says, not foolish at all! ¨If only he had come before!—Does not her power speak out? She says the delicate creature could have guided him before. He only has to speak. If he puts it in the proper way she will underſtand all right, in her own way. He sets to with Napoleon, Toulon, Mont Blanc, but, she says timidly, she would rather have it " without examples."

Without examples! To tell it without examples. He knows well what that means. Has she in her timid simple-mindedness any notion of what she is depriving him by refusing the examples, him, the wavering æſthete? These two paltry words express all that can give woman superiority over man.

But Sonia feels it is disease. A man muſt be out of his mind to murder for the sake of such things as Mont Blanc, whatever they may be.

His irritation grows. He has not murdered at all, only killed a louse. Again there is no mention of the innocent Lizaveta. Sonia does not notice it. She acquiesces in eliminating the personal element, and, incidentally elimi-nates even more. Is any human being a louse?

The tower crumbles slowly. Firſt a crack here, then a crack there. It crumbles unceasingly. One piece tumbles after another. The frail girl succeeds where all the wise men of the world would have failed. He tries to save what is ſtill left, to check the fall of the wreckage, to recover the

FINALE

loft threads of inspiration. Napoleon lies amongft the
débris. He is not a Napoleon. You cease to be a Napoleon
the moment you ask yourself whether you are one, whether
a Napoleon would crawl under the bed to the red box; you
are at moft an æsthete, a louse, a louse crazy on beauty,
burfting with beauty. But is it not juft because you are
not eager to remain a louse that it is worth while doing
away with a ftupid money-lender?

She sees him under the spell of the devil, not the devil
of common parlance, but the real devil of mediæval pictures;
and yet she grips tightly the hands of this devil incarnate:
together! together! Strange the ftrength in her slender
fingers! He also speaks despondently of the devil, be it
only as a laft resort, as though to palm off the murder on
Satan. With that comes the final collapse; the wreckage is
complete.

What now? he asks groaning.

She jumps up. What now?

Then an amazing thing: as if inspired she utters the
word which Someone else addressed to the rotting corpse:
"Arise!" He gets up, goaded by her word, and asks
dejectedly what he is to do now. "Go at once," she
commands, "place yourself at the cross-roads, bow down
and kiss the earth you have defiled. Then bow before all
men in all the four quarters of the globe and say aloud: I
have killed. God will grant you new life."

As a token of the vow she wants to hang on him her
little wooden cross; he ftill will not take it. The laft
spasms. But wait, he ftammers, and breaks into a smile
as before. Perhaps later! and she adds, just like Porphyry
Petrovitch, yes, ftill wait calmly! She is indeed "inspired"
at his decision ftill to wait, because it muft surely come
gradually and because she realizes, as Porphyry Petrovitch
and even Svidrigailov, the sensualift, realize, firft of all he
muft get into the open.

Next day he returns and wants to surrender to the
police, but only "because perhaps it is more beneficial."
She hangs the cross on him and implores him to pray at

least once; he courteously agrees. " Even with an upright heart," he adds, like some elegant gentleman invited to join a drawing-room game.

In the Haymarket he saunters half in jest and mixes with the crowd. He is dizzy, and with good reason, for we are already near the police-station. In the middle of the square he remembers her command and kneels down, to the amusement of the crowd. But that proves nothing; an æsthetic reaction. Again he is fooled by the beautiful, though it soothes the nerves.

Nor does his self-denunciation at the police-station prove much. He makes his explanation, not to Porphyry Petrovitch, but to the insolent police-lieutenant with whom he has already once had a scene, before there was any charge against him. Some people prefer the butcher's blade to the surgeon's knife.

The novel ends at this point. Since Dostoevsky's novel form demands unity of place and time, it had to end in Petersburg. The curtain falls at the proper moment, for the judicial proceedings could not have equalled in interest the details which have been fully set out. Nevertheless, as in most of the greater novels, Dostoevsky has accorded an epilogue in which a glance is cast after the criminal. Raskolnikov did not formally repent even in Siberia, a fact from which ideologues have drawn all sorts of conclusions about Dostoevsky's thought - processes, philosophy and religion, instead of confining themselves to the poet's creation and, if need be, to the *katorga* ; for the most famous *katorga*-historian has himself told us that every one of its inmates disclaimed repentance without, on that account, becoming godless. An ending such as is expected would not have solved the problem and would have been a conventionalism. Raskolnikov was doubtless still as godless in the *katorga* as he was when he denounced himself; the long and the short of the many emotions which conduced to this step were the need to get into the open; whether that has ever led to true Christianity remains to be seen. All the same, it is a much more probable course than this game with Napoleon, Mont Blanc and Toulon. The examples were ultimately rejected. It is difficult to foresee how Christianity could have brought about conversion. There were too many factors at work in this brooding spirit which were opposed to any collective creed; the suppression of those factors might have robbed him of what was best in him, his spiritual resilience. Presumably he realized the value of discipline and made it his duty to discipline his unbridled impulses. Dostoevsky quite rightly infers that, because he renounced suicide, he may rise again. Even if there was nothing heroic about the incentive to denounce himself, it was evidently more potent than the temptation of the Neva, when on that evil evening he stood on the bridge. Moreover, in the first draft of the novel Raskolnikov ends in suicide; he shoots himself. A positive instinct withstood the temptation of such an extreme, though obvious, ending which in itself would have solved nothing. The will to a higher order of things, perhaps even an æsthetic feeling " without examples," urged him to go on living. Possibly the young man still cherished the desire for experiment. The path to Christianity is still a long way off.

If ever Raskolnikov recognized this goal he could only attain it by a roundabout route, just as he arrived only indirectly at self-denunciation. Not the weakness of Dostoevsky's religious sense, but his objectivity and his discretion restrained him from depicting a more rapid conversion. In the draft of the novel Dostoevsky observes at the end: " The last line; inscrutable are the paths whereon God finds man." He was right in ultimately striking out this last moralization.

If Raskolnikov ever trod the path which Dostoevsky had trodden before him, along which the poet dared not lead him, he had to thank Sonia for it. He was swayed, not by the Christian idea, but by this girl with the tender fingers and limited mind. She followed him to Siberia. After he had duly hated her for it, as he hated himself and every one else, his love for his " nurse," as he once called her in Petersburg, lay in the realm of the new order of things. She broke with her former life, despite the restraint which the *katorga* imposed on her, and, in the development of their relationship, was as unobtrusive as were her convictions.

The skilful treatment of this relationship is also admirable, though it did not occur to Dostoevsky immediately. In the first drafts of the novel the attraction between Raskolnikov and Sonia plays a considerable part. In the second draft Sonia writes a glowing letter: " I love you and will be your slave." It is suggested that one of her reasons for liking him is the recovery of her self-confidence which she owes to him. Dostoevsky adds, in parenthesis, that the letter must have an " artistic " effect. " Raskolnikov comes to her after this letter. His confession. She shrinks back, and he leaves her. Conflagration. Salvation. Hurrah! there is life! His despair, his sauntering about. He debates every point, looks after the three children. Dreams of fresh crimes, saves from death."

Nothing of that has reached the novel; such outpourings would have marred the action. However " artistic " the planned letter might have succeeded in being, it would still have been an unpardonable error. Any confession of love by Sonia would have been bound to belittle her and to detract from the chastity of her appearance. In the sketch of the conversation after his confession Sonia says of the murdered woman: " If she was a louse, why do you torment yourself about it? " The utilitarian note in this retort is scarcely in keeping with Sonia's nature. Dostoevsky has struck out of her speeches every suggestion of argumentation.

It is just the same with Raskolnikov. In the third draft Dostoevsky still considered a declaration of love necessary. Here is the sketch of a speech: " Why I have come to like you? because you are mine alone, because you are the only one left me. You are everything to me. My mother, my sister, all have become strangers and probably will never agree with me again. If I don't tell them everything, I can't be in unison with them any longer, and if I do tell them, they can't be. But, on the other hand, we two are equally cursed, and, therefore, our path is a common one, even if we are looking in different directions. You are my queen now, and my destiny, my life, my all——."

Raskolnikov could never have spoken like that, and it is beyond understanding how the obvious improvement could have escaped the notice of the Russian scholar, Glivenko, who annotated the drafts of *Crime and Punishment*. The suggestion that this difference between the drafts and the finished work indicates a hardening of the hero, and possibly of the poet, is beside the point.

Dostoevsky's restraint in depicting the attraction between Raskolnikov and Sonia and his scant reference to their future present many possibilities. The convict's love for Sonia may have become his guiding light, and may have turned eight abject years into eight lofty ones. He may have cherished it as fanatically as, previously, he had fastened on to his Napoleon idea; finally, Christianity may have been thrust upon him by force of contact, but then only because of the desire to share everything, including thoughts. Moreover, Sonia's thought was in no way a Protestantism to provoke the protest of the intellectual, but a mystery. For her companion's paradoxical way of thinking the mystery could not be simple enough.

In the epilogue Dostoevsky referred only to Christianity through contagion. Christian unity certainly seems more natural than the pagan unity of that Europe-weary painter who, on a distant isle, abandoned himself to love for a coloured native, and, through his love, went so far as to kneel with her, and mumble strange prayers.[1] To be sure, a very charming roof-garden story whose lyricism does not answer sceptical questions.

It is doubtful whether a Raskolnikov is deeply penetrated by the prayer and how long it will last, if indeed he himself lasts. (But—here the distinction from the roof-

[1] Gauguin, who went to Tahiti, and subsequently married a native.—Tr.

garden story—we are not concerned with this question, and in any case it has no importance for criticism of the novel.) Even if Christianity were only a bridge for the seeker, he does not need meanwhile to approach the death from which he has arisen.

Crime and Punishment is the tragedy of a superman, not of the, but of a particular one. From the action and final issue there is not a shadow of a doubt about Dostoevsky's attitude towards this Nietzschean phase. The novel covers a wider field than this phase, which has been dealt with *ad nauseam*. Raskolnikov's behaviour under the shadow of this fetish, from which later the German philosopher was to develop his creed, is not tragic but tragi-comic. The pith of the tragedy is the hero's æstheticism, and therewith a problem, which we are accustomed to take humorously, is treated with a seriousness worthy of its significance. Intimacy with all the incitements of beauty, which we are wont to call culture, does not stop us from robbing and murdering. The æsthetic behaviour of our time, which leads to over-refinement of natural impulses, to artistic atrophy, does not spring from a sense of unity, but from antagonism between human beings. The rise and decay of art in our time is the upshot, visible afar, of this unsocial cult.

In this *odi profanum* Dostoevsky, with astounding vision, recognized one of the most seductive poisons of the West against which Russia had to guard; and he has shown forcefully the other side of that ideal, and made a generalization befitting the dignity and range of the problem.

There is an abundance of living ideas in this first great epic. We as little think of enquiring how far the novel succeeded as, at the sight of a tilled field, of asking whether the soil is good or bad. We realize that the work was necessary, and that is everything. We can do a great deal with it, dig, build on it, or burrow. In any case the novel, whether good or bad, is much better than Dostoevsky wrote it, and that sort of thing is true only of great works. He not only leaves us to complete his work, but compels

EPISODES

us to. This impetus from the finite into the infinite is of the essence of the creation.

In *Crime and Punishment* also there are long-drawn passages. A few grimaces could be cut out of the tiring scenes with the ball-like Porphyry. Tedious is the turbulent funeral feaſt at Sonia's mother's, and the hiſtory of Luzhin, the jilted *fiancé*, and of his far too complicated intrigue againſt Sonia. Doſtoevsky needed to delay the main aſtion, but made too much of the intervening episodes. These episodes are always successful, it is true, not only in themselves, but also in carrying the main thread, even if only its atmosphere, which permeates every seſtion. A piece of this atmosphere, which we should like to see painted by Rembrandt, is the little heeded ſtreet scene with Sonia's crazy mother after the funeral feaſt, her ſtreet dance with the " noble " children, and her death on the pavement. Only in passages in *King Lear* can be found such swirling miſts, rent by shrieks.

Svidrigailov, the shrewd suicide, is involved in the main episode. Moreover, a fantaſtic number of people meet with violent deaths, three times as many as in any play of Shakespeare. This mass-dying passes unnoticed. During the whole period only one dead person, the money-lender, is aſtually seen, so rapidly is fresh sand shovelled into the arena.

Svidrigailov is something more. He would like to be a counterpart to Raskolnikov, not in the æſthetic, but in the sensual sense, and has to show what a less Schilleresque outsider ends in. He does not think of the underworld den, and therefore—this should be noted—misses the resurrection. The rendezvous with Dounia, Raskolnikov's courageous siſter, leads to a Wild-Weſt scene. He is determined to have this girl, whom he has desired for years, and for whom he has already moved heaven and earth. Her revolver does not make him flinch, in faſt it is a welcome titillation which, so he believes, simplifies matters. She fires, the bullet grazes him, and he lets her fire again. Is she hesitating? The brave Dounia really

139

wavers. How can she kill a man only two paces away! and she flings the weapon away, and trembling, implores mercy. Svidrigailov in a brief, very brief fit of generosity, of which he strongly recommends her to take prompt advantage, undertakes to let her go in safety. He would have preferred this shooting affair to have turned out differently. He was sensuously bored with life. He settled the matter for himself a few hours later, after scattering his fortune on all sides. These details (37) and the sensualist's fantastic dreams are disconcerting. This is one of the few passages in the work which betray hesitancy and hastiness. Similar passages still occur much later and often constitute transitions to works which follow them. Svidrigailov is a preparation for the atmosphere of *The Possessed*.

Crime and Punishment is the ripe fruit of the *katorga*. If there is still any doubt about the aim of the hero's resurrection, a doubt which perhaps the author dared not remove and which can only worry inquisitive people, there is certainly no doubt about the resurrection of Dostoevsky the poet. The burden of personal suffering was overcome.

In spite of that, many thinkers in Russia and Germany perceive in *Crime and Punishment* propaganda for scepticism, and there has even been idle chatter about satanism. It is not worth discussing. It is a perversion of facts to state that Dostoevsky wanted to identify himself with his unrepentant hero and to glorify this attitude towards murder. Posthumous envy has maliciously imputed to him his heroes' crimes; but even the most stupid of his enemies cannot want to impute the æsthete to him.

I called the impetus from the finite to the infinite the real creation, but this might give a false impression; the portrayal of the finite is the best thing in the work. It is not the profusion of ideas, not the profound nobility of his morality, not the getting-behind-things, but rather the thing itself which is essentially vital. *Crime and Punishment* introduces a new conception of reality. The canvas is broad and teeming with life. Every single figure appears in the living flesh in a way denied in Dostoevsky's earlier works, as well as in those of other poets. Flaubert's scenes are viewed through powerful inverted opera-glasses. His people seem far away, and consequently smaller, but every detail, every movement is precisely drawn. It is just this invariably consistent remoteness and diminution which we admire most, but we never get closer to these people, we do not want to get closer, because Flaubert's experiment succeeds. There is no experimentalism in *Crime and Punishment*; so it seems anyhow. Dostoevsky puts us right into the middle of his people, we are much closer to them than to people in real life, and consequently we discover characteristics which we scarcely notice in nature. These discoveries are apparently due to our intimate intercourse with the characters. Who would think of taking part in one of the many conversations in the *Education Sentimentale?* We are in close touch, not only with Raskolnikov, but with every super. Dostoevsky's art consists in steering us clear of confusion through this maze of events. His dramatic idea succeeds. The many figures, each with its personal note, its own language, its own mode of behaviour, are kept within bounds. In order to quicken the *tempo* Dostoevsky accepts the dramatic formula of unity of time and place, an innovation which makes considerable demands on the conception, and precludes many of the usual stop-gaps in novel-literature. The stupendous action runs its course within a few days, and the complicated psychological associations are portrayed almost exclusively by the dialogue; as little space is devoted to explanations, other than in dialogue, as to the stage-directions in a modern play. Here we have a novel-drama.

Reading gives us no idea of the difficulties of this form. Presumably even Dostoevsky did not notice them. Since, however, he was already engaged on *Crime and Punishment* in Siberia, it must have been many years before the form of the novel-drama matured; this assumption is to a certain extent borne out by the sketches for the work.

Analysis later on will give us a closer view of the

technique of the novel-drama. However, in choosing this form, Dostoevsky was not actuated by technical considerations. Another Aristotle might perceive in the novel-drama a revival of the *katharsis* which is at the root of Greek tragedy.

CHAPTER XI

When the greater part of *Crime and Punishment* was already published in the *Russian Messenger* Dostoevsky had to interrupt his work to write *The Gambler*. He was forced to take this step by the usurious contract with the publisher Stellovsky, to whom he had sold himself in a moment of great need. His misery had become acute in 1864 through the death of his brother. Michael left enormous debts and the bankrupt *Epoca*. If Dostoevsky had thought less of the family honour he could without difficulty have avoided this burden. On top of this he dragged along with him his stepson Pavel, the son of his first wife, an idler and a good-for-nothing. The final catastrophe of the *Epoca* increased the debt on bills to 25,000 roubles (38). I mention the amount to give the reader a notion of his real burdens. Stellovsky had reserved to himself the rights for a collected edition of the works so far published, and Dostoevsky had pledged himself to contribute into the bargain a novel, *The Gambler*, and to deliver it by the first of November 1866. His total remuneration amounted to 3000 roubles and the publisher had the right to take over all future collected editions without further payment if delivery of *The Gambler* were even a single day late.

Dostoevsky began to write the novel at the commencement of October, and within the month it was finished. This *tour de force* only succeeded with the aid of a stenographer who soon afterwards became Dostoevsky's second wife. He still found time during the month to fall in love. According to his wife's account they did not exert themselves to excess. As Madame Dostoevsky relates, a great deal of the time set apart for work was spent in conversation. At the beginning Dostoevsky dictated extempore. Then he took to preparing at night what had to be written on the morrow.

DOSTOEVSKY

The result was a shocker. Work was handicapped in all kinds of ways. The interruption of *Crime and Punishment* seems in itself an insuperable obstacle. How was it possible to detach his thoughts from the drama and turn them to the episodes in Roulettenburg? In other circumstances doubtless Dostoevsky would not have dreamt of making a novel out of this fleeting experience.

Dostoevsky was intimately acquainted with the subject of gambling. Incidentally the most violent of his attacks of gambling mania happened after the book was completed. Despite his personal experience, his study is not convincing, from which it might be argued that his convincing portrayal of other vices was not the result of personal experience, and that gambling was one of the unproductive vices. The subject is too limited. Dostoevsky himself set no great store by the novel and kept putting off beginning. "All the same it will be," he writes to an acquaintance, "quite a decent little novel, with, indeed, shadows of real characters." (39). He under-rated it. Shadows are not the only things in the book. There is a magnificent character in the old *babouchka*,[1] on whose Moscow bed of sickness her necessitous heirs in Roulettenburg are building fond hopes, and who suddenly swoops down on them, the very picture of health, and rapidly and permanently lays the demon of gambling. Even the picture of the gambler who wins is important— a study of nerves which it excites our nerves to read. It was only the novel which remained a shadow.

This feeble and insignificant work, a stop-gap in the widest meaning, was recently made use of in a biography (40). With true Russian lack of restraint Dostoevsky was for a time a prey to the demon of gambling and repeated attempts have been made to cast it in his teeth. The Roulettenburg episode, which was a mere drop in the ocean of his eventful life, has been painted as a large black blot which is to lend colour to the gloomy tone in which it is sought to portray him.

Dostoevsky has himself contributed to this misrepresen-

[1] Russian for grandmother.—Tr.

tation by his peculiarly reckless self-accusations which, instead of speaking, as they should, in his favour, have been taken literally. Some of our great men would cut a curious figure if all their incidental self-criticism were read in that way. Dostoevsky's generosity which knew no bounds, and his equally boundless lack of economy, an amazing inability to cope with figures, and above all, his material circumstances, which were nearly always straitened and particularly humiliating to him, lured him to dream of capturing wealth. There was no desire for luxurious living behind this, for he was extremely unpretentious and always lived moderately. He wanted money to avoid starvation. This dream, which was one of the poet's favourite themes, drove him to gamble. He did not seize on roulette as the drinker on the bottle. Doubtless he was unusually susceptible to the temptation and the demon bolted with him as soon as he gave it its head. Once at the table it was not an easy matter to get up again. No special aptitude drove him there; it was the natural outcome of pressing need. On the first two visits when he had of necessity to fill his purse, his luck was out of all proportion—to his misfortune. After his second marriage, when he was fleeing from his creditors, he was again in straitened circumstances, and the memory of his luck in Wiesbaden kindled hopes of escaping from this degrading position, an attempt which had been made a thousand times and always in vain, doubly fruitless for a man of such infinite energy. The temptation must have been so much the greater when he had once stopped producing and his energy was unable to find its natural outlet in writing. Dostoevsky cannot be reckoned a professional gambler. He was a *dilettante*, the most extreme of *dilettanti*. Gamblers gamble whether they need money or not; cards are the same to them as food and drink. Dostoevsky could have played every day in Russia, yet he scarcely ever touched a card except at a game of patience. Grossman's assertion that he had already played in Semipalatinsk is expressly contradicted by Baron Vrangel, the only authoritative witness of this period. And, once he had given it up, there was no longer any risk of temptation, even in gambling resorts. In Ems, where in the seventies he spent a great deal of time taking the cure and where in his time gambling was still openly carried on, he never entered a gambling-room. As his material circumstances became more or less tolerable he thought no more of such things.

That Dostoevsky was once or twice lured into sacrificing house-keeping money and, with his wife's consent, into pawning lace mantillas and silk clothes—sad! profoundly sad! In spite of that it is not right to make irrelevant deductions from these stirring facts. In a later work Dostoevsky once again turned to account his experiences in the gambling-room. The passion of Arkady, in *A Raw Youth*, distinctly shown as a transitory weakness and, as a matter of fact, overcome without difficulty, is a much truer picture of Dostoevsky. So far detractors of the poet have abstained from making use of this autobiographical material.

The Gambler is a literary *tour de force* rather than a creative work. The poet escaped with his young wife from the misery in Petersburg and on foreign soil attained the second stage in his ascent.

Raskolnikov emerges from the underworld and the underworld threatens him. Fear of the underworld drives him to the deed, as well as yearning for the glorification of his own beauty. He almost forces his way out of the gloom which surrounds him, but still cannot feel the warmth of the sun. A glimmer of light hovers over the murderer in the poverty-stricken room in which Sonia commands him to rise again from the dead. Where is he going? From one underworld into another? Or into the sun? Dostoevsky felt the urgency of this question. Everything depended on the next step. Had Dostoevsky been a lover of gloom his next work would have been the blackest of all, unadulterated demonry, the moral bankruptcy of a man who had been converted in vain. Raskolnikov's mere resistance to the temptation of the last expedient, the brightest note of the drama, is enlightening in itself. Resistance, however, is not enough; renunciation of negative is not the same as positive; the vague glimmer was not sunlight, and the shadow man craved for sunlight. He wanted to show the positive, to express the unconditional. Yes, not indeed by some roundabout route, but directly; goodness, simple and complete, goodness which cannot be corrupted, goodness not the outcome of deliberation but spontaneous as crime; that is, truth, simple and complete, the childlike impulse; above all, beauty, simple and complete, beauty without æstheticism, without examples; in a word, the good, the true, the beautiful of the dethroned Schiller, but seen from another angle. It had to appeal to people of to-day—that was the difficulty. The drama could not be set a thousand years ago; the stage could not be some enchanted castle gorgeously illuminated, or some specially adapted island. It had to be there in Petersburg, to-day, amongst Petersburg people, and the play had to grip like the murder story. That is what he had distinctly in mind in *The Idiot*. His aim was ambitious because the hero's qualities were not to be concealed but to be shown romantically; the Idiot was not to be " actually a decent fellow " but essentially a good man, that is, his goodness was to have a visible effect. That was perfectly clear to Dostoevsky before he began. He has expressed himself in detail on that subject (41). In his eyes the only " positively beautiful figure " of this world was Christ, so that the Idiot had to be convincingly like Christ. Christ was the " absolutely beautiful man." Everything else was merely a consequence of this attribute. Dostoevsky believed that Christ redeems mankind with his beauty, and this belief denotes his religion.

From Raskolnikov to Christ. Dostoevsky dared not portray the murderer's conversion to Christianity. His sense of reality forbade him; but if he had written of the expiation—and his omission to do so has been quite unjustifiably deplored—it would never have been a Christian expiation. Raskolnikov may perhaps learn to tolerate human beings, but he will never learn to love them. We are no less aware of Raskolnikov's limitations than was

DOSTOEVSKY

Dostoevsky; that such a man should want to be a Christ is a preposterous thought. The roof-garden pricks up its ears.

Dostoevsky noticed that the nearest thing to " positive beauty " in Christian literature was Don Quixote, but Cervantes had recourse to ridiculousness. " The reader feels sympathy with the beautiful figure which is the subject of mockery and which is not conscious of its value." Dickens also is said to have worked in this way, but he achieved much less; Victor Hugo even less still. To-day it would probably be altogether impossible to give the positive element directly. Dostoevsky was thus expressing an elementary doubt which no one can pass over. On that account, he adds, the novel will presumably be terribly tedious.

There is something of Christ in Prince Myshkin, there is the one essential quality, the only one which can be portrayed, a thing which hitherto seemed unportrayable: beauty of heart. Let us be cautious and say, not Christ's beauty of heart, but the possibility and manner of such beauty. The almost inconceivable difficulty lies in the portrayal of his intelligence. Can such a man be intelligent in the accepted modern sense? What is commonly understood by intellect is a form of reasoning specially adapted to the struggle for existence and to the exploitation of one's neighbour. For the Idiot such an intellect is out of the question, as it would undoubtedly disturb his beauty. But he must at least have an intellect fit for human intercourse. His thought must in some way or other be able to reach the sphere of others without becoming sullied, and thus some, even if only a temporary, limitation must be imposed on his intellect. A certain amount of ridiculousness is of course inevitable, but a mere fraction of Don Quixote's ridiculousness suffices, and caricature can be altogether avoided.

Though the hero needs a veil, it is not bound to be convertible into a halo at a moment's notice. That is just the crux. The outward attributes of saintliness are, amongst other things, church-going, meditation, and pose. Quite apart from any saintliness, what he needs is the Christ-mind, if we care so to describe the elevating influence on others. It would never do to make him utter pious reflections. Prayer is only effect, not cause, and what has to be shown is the growth of feeling which leads up to this. Christ pleaded but did not pray. What we love most in the Idiot is his untainted omniscience. Others, too, are in a certain measure endowed with this gift; children for instance. Grown-up people with the untaintedness of children look ridiculous; but grown-up people may lack experience for quite plausible reasons; and just as well as the child which knows nothing of sexual love, just as well as Dostoevsky's " little hero," they may feel love intuitively and the absence of physical experience may in itself conduce to intellectual alertness.

The plausible reason is the young prince's illness. He spent several years, just those years in which others are acquiring vital experience, in a little Swiss resort at the house of a nerve-specialist, cut off from the world of movement. There he came into contact only with children and lived through a kind of children's Sermon on the Mount. He seems to have recovered from his illness; it consisted of epileptic attacks which upset his memory. But he still does not feel quite safe from these fits. In this illness there is naturally the tradition of bygone literary usage, the fool who dared to utter forbidden truths and the tradition of Shakespearean and Schilleresque madness to which the world, far from being crazy, was actually a simple problem. We instinctively smell out this dodge at once and it calls up all kinds of objections. Was Christ ill? Although this is not definitely known and many a psychopathologist has smelled out this, that and the other, and perhaps attributes the whole of Christianity to a flaw in Christ's brain, although even in His lifetime many a merchant in the temple regarded the intruder as abnormal, the sceptic smiles derisively at an explanation which is really only a compromise. But it is not a compromise, and

Myshkin's illness is not a dodge. Anyhow the truth of that is not so easily discerned. Myshkin is wrecked on the rock of his illness. Is that necessary? More will be said.

Even the people in the novel smile sceptically. The idiot-*cliché* is always at hand. They do not trouble to hide it from him. However, he has a great deal of tact, is, moreover, an aristocrat, and does not consider it worth while specially stressing that such a thing as an idiot is out of the question, at all events in Doctor Schneider's opinion. A spoof idiot, a mock idiot, an idiot out of the novel-world would say: " I'll soon show you how! " and would make the whole company sit up with a few spirited phrases in a voice which gently betrays his warped soul. Prince Myshkin's soul is not warped and he does not babble sententiously. In spite of that he makes them sit up.

This novel is amongst the greatest. *Crime and Punishment* was a bold thrust, but boldness isolates it. Doubtless the work manages to control the huge subject-matter, but at times there is a visible strain in holding together an atmosphere constantly split by dazzling flashes of lightning. There is something of the roulette-player about it. Again and again he flings on the maximum. He wins. We utter a sigh of relief. Falteringly he gets up and mechanically sticks the money into his pocket. It was time.

The Idiot is a profounder work; the theme moves on a higher plane. It has its turbulent element and teems with anomalies; but at bottom it is simple and quiescent. Events are like events in our own lives; days go by as our own days go by; commonplace details lend colour to the plausibility. The marvel thrives in the midst of palpable commonplaces. A Christ is descended into the workaday world.

On analysis the figure of the hero seems to present a most thankless task. If individual facts are ignored, there is a temptation to think of him as a puritan of crabbed mentality, thoroughly un-European and old-fashioned; it would seem that a poet who toys with the demon of a Raskolnikov could only find a Christ-like being in some

wild hermitage; at most a Christ in the wilderness, wrestling
with the Devil and exposed to the lurid temptations of a
holy Antony; an emaciated Christ of the Middle Ages on
the knees of a broken-hearted *Pietà*. Nothing is more
remote from the gentle, intelligent kindness of this prince.
And yet Prince Myshkin has surely become one of the
most perfect of Dostoevsky's figures. There are weaknesses in the novel and it is far surpassed by the incomparably richer and more closely-woven texture of the
Karamazov story. If dramatic tension is a criterion *Crime
and Punishment* is of a higher order. But if one single
figure is to be considered representative of Dostoevsky,
that figure must be the Idiot. He, more than any, was
after the poet's own heart. In a subtle and detached way
the man Dostoevsky tends to be biassed against Raskolnikov. Myshkin, on the other hand, he loves and, strange
to say, his love perfects his objectivity. He regards him as
a child to whom nothing should be added and it might
almost be said that, on that account, in drawing him, he
abstained from his usual creative methods. No figure is
less subjected to psychological treatment; no figure is
conceived more poetically.

As in *Crime and Punishment* the action begins with the
first sentence. The hero appears at once together with
Rogozhin, his wild companion, the boyar with a knife in
his boot, a type who has not yet been seen on Dostoevsky's
stage, the pure Russian untouched by Western influences,
who does not need much scratching to reveal the Tartar.
It is impossible to bungle a Rogozhin like that, a character
entirely free of complications, free of inhibitions; he runs
automatically like a clock. But it is just this clearness and
wildness which was bound to jeopardize less clear characters.
That is where Dostoevsky proved his worth as a producer.
With the utmost ease and without a trace of effort he
overcame difficulties of this sort, insurmountable to others.
The figure of Myshkin is just as spontaneous. He suffers
nothing from the contrast and acquires no benefit from it.
The third principal character, Nastasya Filippovna, is only

mentioned at first and, familiar as we are with every side of the picture, we at once believe we scent some import from the West, an introduction on well-known lines. The eternal driveller Lebedyev, the official who travels with him in the railway-compartment, is suspicious. He chances to know everybody whom Myshkin and Rogozhin talk about. He chances to know Nastasya. A Western writer would avoid having recourse to such accidents. Dostoevsky brought them right into the limelight, and no one raises any objection. This instance is typical. Lebedyev, whom *littérateurs* would reject on the ground of irrelevancy, is the very acme of intrusiveness, is a fellow-traveller, not only at the beginning, but all the way through, a fellow eater, a perfect bluebottle, so intolerable that it would be impossible to exaggerate this characteristic. Lebedyev is not here by accident, for Lebedyev will be found everywhere where he has no business to be. That seems to be why God made him

Prince Myshkin goes to the general's. The scene in the waiting-room is still part of the exposition. That could be the beginning, particularly in drama. The prince chats to the servant, says he is a distant relative of the general's wife, and the servant mistakes the communicative visitor for a beggar and dares not announce him. They must wait for Ganya, the secretary. Very well, thinks Myshkin, he can easily wait, he has nothing else to do. He tells the servant about Switzerland and how he has witnessed an execution. There is no special *motif* in this effacement of social boundaries. This is Russia. One is not finikin, for it is of course in Myshkin's nature to have a long chat with a servant. The story of the execution is prominent. Remarkable! thinks the servant and asks, is it really like that abroad? Myshkin replies, you want to know whether I'm really a prince and a relative of the general's wife, don't you? Yes, you need have no qualms about announcing me.

This scene is as picturesque as a Vermeer interior.

Now for General Epanchin, the servant scene on a higher level. The general also mistakes Myshkin for a beggar and the prince notices it with a smile. It really does not need much intelligence to divine this thought. Anyone of us guesses it. Possibly we have all been in a similar situation, but no one has thought of expressing his feelings so harmlessly. The prince has lived long outside society, such thoughts interest him, and, he adds by way of inference, certain relationships between himself and the general would be difficult to establish. The general is thunderstruck. But nothing was further from Myshkin's mind than improving his position, it was merely a harmless remark which, incidentally, makes clear to us the poet's intention of giving the general a supernumerary part; he has nothing much more to say throughout the novel.

An idiot, the general decides, but inoffensive and not unpleasant, perhaps even quite useful in view of his fine handwriting. At all events they need not stand on any ceremony with him. Whilst Myshkin is engaged on the handwriting test, the general and Ganya weave their intrigue. Ganya is to marry the beautiful Nastasya so that Totsky, her wealthy seducer, may be freed from her toils and marry one of the general's daughters.

The prince listens calmly; why not, since he is in the room? He has good hearing and keen sight and knows how to co-ordinate his experiences. So the photograph Ganya has brought is of the Nastasya who was discussed in the train this morning. She is certainly beautiful. And this Ganya is to marry her? Well, I never! But this Ganya does not love her at all, rather he hates her because he is to be paid for the marriage, and that is really not quite the thing. Possibly he would love her without money, but he thinks he ought to prize the ridiculous money still more. What foolishness! As a matter of fact Ganya would rather marry Aglaia, the general's youngest daughter.

Myshkin sees through the whole intrigue, but is not particularly interested in it. People clearly attach considerable importance to that kind of thing, that is why they commit mean actions. What they do is not so much evil as useless.

DOSTOEVSKY

Prince Myshkin is led into the ladies' room. He enjoys the company of the general's wife and her three daughters and lets himself go. Naturally each of the girls wants to chaff him in her own way, lure him into talking in order to laugh at him. He notices it and obliges them; that is how it was with the children in Switzerland. They learn how he lived there; it was a kind of garden guarded by children. They laughed in the garden from sunrise to sunset. If he went out of the garden he saw an execution or met someone who had stood before the scaffold. He has absorbed these things. They constitute his very limited repertoire: laughter and execution. He can report on them with amazing precision, just because he has not had much experience and therefore fails to make the usual distinctions. Curious that the little Swiss incidents should occur to him just at this moment! There is the same sort of garden in the company of the general's wife and the three girls. All women are children.

A certain vagueness was essential to the introduction of the hero. In the course of this scene light is thrown on his past. The Idiot recounts his experiences intelligently, but in such a way that the symptoms of his idiocy, far from being repressed, are accentuated. In fact, in a subtle way, an obscure relationship is hinted at between Myshkin and fresh characters. There is a definite point of contact between them. The general's wife is more robust, it is true, but the women react just as spontaneously as the prince. You can have three grown-up daughters and an aberrant general for a husband, and still retain a garden-like simplicity; you can be a very astute girl and know precisely what is wanted of a beautiful woman, and still let every action be determined by a childlike incorruptibility. And so there are all kinds of people of the prince's type who, far from being ill, are actually healthier than the vain intriguers who give themselves airs. The general's wife has the essential features of the *babouchka* in *The Gambler*, except that she is a born princess, utterly devoid of feminine coyness. Hypocrisy and lies bore her. She calls a spade a spade, does not try to control herself, and does not need control; there is nothing sentimental about her. Her daughters idolize and mother her, charming creatures who have been fed on freedom. Dostoevsky characterizes them skilfully. Much could be said about Dostoevsky's portrayal of family features. Aglaia, the youngest, whom Ganya vainly runs after, is most like her mother and more than any has the spirit of the Idiot.

This is the foreground in which the lighter part of the novel is played. Here Myshkin would find the world as he pictures it. It is not granted him, in fact he himself does not grant it. He is drawn to the background, to the dark power of which the girls speak on looking at the photograph of Nastasya. His forced intervention between Ganya and Aglaia ends with the rebuff of Ganya; the prince calmly delivers it; Ganya, dumbfounded, does not forgive him. Myshkin is the victim of the first poison. Ganya, spurred by ambition, rages at the Idiot's imperturbability and is on the point of striking him. In the background are Ganya's parents, the retired dipsomaniac general, his tormented wife, his children and their appurtenances. That makes another half dozen people who, in a trice, appear in the flesh. Not one of these numerous characters is badly drawn.

Myshkin is settled in his quarters. Madame Ivolgin, wife of the retired general, takes lodgers. General Ivolgin is a perfect example of the degenerate toper. Drunkards before him are mere sketches. He has learned the art, the hallowed art of lying, lying as an end in itself, lying untarnished by the smirch of usefulness; the Arcadian lie. Marmeladov and his predecessors lied sentimentally, drank in order to lie, to forget; all their actions were coloured by the underworld, they were utterly wretched drunkards. General Ivolgin is the artist at lying. Lying lends wings to his existence, enchants him. He lies for the sake of beauty, is also an idiot aspiring, in his own fashion, to salvation through beauty. He lies in his sleep. Within a second of meeting Myshkin he has woven a highly romantic tale about the prince's father who was naturally his bosom friend. With the ingenuousness of a child he makes up a story he has just read in the newspaper as if it were an event in his own life, and is ready with an answer to every objection. Drunk as he is he goes with Myshkin to a grand house belonging to utter strangers, solely because it sounds so well to fling at the servant " General Ivolgin and Prince Myshkin "! And he leaves a message for the lady of the house, who is fortunately out, that he hopes she will get what she expressed a wish for on Thursday evening when listening to Chopin. Thereupon he admits he has mistaken the house.

At the same time thoroughly honourable, thinks Kolya the fourteen-year offspring of the general. It is accounted for by drink and a certain laxity.

The incidents are more closely related to the action than is usual. There is something of Shakespearean improbability about the Idiot and the inebriated fool; the fool conducts the Idiot to Nastasya, to his fate. At times the characters are only half real, and yet there is never any question about their reality.

The prince's disease lurks in many of the characters; there is a medley of idiocy. Even those who are supposed to be healthy and think they have charmed lives, who are either amused at or irritated by the Idiot, may catch the infection; spreading infection seems to be the prince's unconscious mission. Germs of childlike behaviour out of the Swiss garden float in the air. The infection is at work in the afternoon scene at the Ivolgin's when he catches his first glimpse of the omnipotent beauty, lets her mistake him for a servant, and submits to being struck in the face by Ganya. He sees through Nastasya and without any effort makes her at one moment raise her mask of embitterment. And just such a moment comes to Ganya, the pusher, who is overcome by the humility of the person he has insulted, apologizes, and speaks out for the first time. He confesses to the prince why he wants to marry Nastasya, " because of an inner urge," because with the 75,000 roubles which the marriage will bring him he wants to cut short Raskolnikov's path and realize his idea of power. Will Naſtasya consent, reflects Myshkin? But Ganya's idea has turned his head, he attaches little importance to Myshkin's sober reflection.

There are many more or less disguised children in this ſtory and the prince's idiocy ſtands less and less alone. Yet it alone illuminates. The afternoon at Ivolgin's is the prelude to the big scene in the evening at Naſtasya's when it has to be decided whether she will accept Ganya and release Totsky. The scene ends with the victory of Rogozhin who makes the biggeſt bid. He goes off with the booty. This audacious climax, worked up with the utmoſt care, brings the act to a conclusion.

Removed from its context this scene would be impossible. What woman would allow herself to be auctioneered in her own home? What sort of a man would put up with Ganya's insults? Naſtasya flings Rogozhin's packet of 100,000 roubles into the fire. It is to be Ganya's if he picks it out without gloves; on top of that the surprising inheritance which suddenly transforms the prince's pauperism into opulence; on top of that the prince's proposal of marriage to Naſtasya; in the meantime Rogozhin and his horde. All this happens in a few minutes. There is blood and thunder galore; the film work is in full swing.

And it all has to be like that, cannot possibly be otherwise, has psychological and even more solid foundations, ſtands before us as firm as a rock. Naſtasya, misused by that *bourgeois* epicure Totsky, a noble creature in every fibre of her being, much too ſtrong, too " idiotic," to let herself be dragged along some *bourgeois* path, has turned the tables; from humiliation not of her own making she has become the heroine capable of trampling on her persecutors, and it follows as a matter of course from her Schilleresque idiocy that the firſt person she has trampled on is herself. Ganya, the half-baked Raskolnikov, who descended in a towering rage to coarse brutalities, has the ιbsurd experience he wants, and his idea, which has long since been untenable, collapses. He almoſt becomes a respectable person. But the Idiot perceives another execution and leaps to the rescue. He is going to ſtop this one. He alone fully underſtands Naſtasya and he alone is not disconcerted by the lawful side of her action; but so much the more by the human side. Naked beauty is dragged to the scaffold; ſtill worse, drags itself, egged on by romanticism, by some obscure motive which Myshkin doubtless underſtands, of which he alone is quite free. He alone could bring salvation. At the decisive moment there is something lacking in him; were he able to work a miracle, even were it only the raising of his voice, he would be the saviour.

That cannot be. Why? Not perhaps, as some people believe, because any such action would be too ſtraightforward for Doſtoevsky the thinker, but because the little which is necessary to make Myshkin's attitude effectual would sound a false note; any sort of romanticism would be incompatible with the Idiot's nature. Inſtead of Schilleresque goodness Myshkin possesses something which does not exiſt in the whole of this *milieu*, something which muſt express itself gently.

The action outſtrips the psychological explanation. Doubtless the day, the crowded day which began with the arrival of Myshkin and Rogozhin, can end like that. We have rummaged around between gardens and doubtful haunts, between laughter and tears. Now it is night and the light of a torch is needed on these scenes of revelry. Doubtless every actor is worked up to concert-pitch, although that may be only the tinieſt spark of the demonry which animates the principal actors. Doubtless this day of days has brought in its train such a torrent of blows and ſtings as might make the insulted and injured rise up like a rebellious people. From early morning there has been such a hammering at the doors that we cannot wonder when they collapse with a crash.

As the tinkling sleighs bear off Rogozhin's horde and his loot we are faced with a heap of *débris*.

FIRST ACT

After this wild act Dostoevsky asserted that the first part would have no material effect, that it was only a prelude, would explain nothing, set no problems, and aimed solely at whetting the reader's appetite for more (42).

But that object, sufficient in itself, is not the whole content of the act. We have experienced a catastrophe and are in the midst of the action. Nastasya has cleared off with the wild Rogozhin. She was, of course, actuated by plausible motives; that fact is clear, not from her character with which we are, as yet, little familiar, but from the chance situation on that evening which was uncommonly favourable to hasty action. What is certain is that the unfortunate woman has plunged head over heels to her doom, for Rogozhin is utterly inadequate and her association with this licentious youth is sheer madness. Just as obvious is the prince's inability to restrain her. His courtship was too sudden and bore too clearly the stamp of a gift, even if that was not his furthest intention. But every gift was bound to be nothing but a deep humiliation to the unfortunate woman.

Thus a violent expedient as a temporary measure; that is what Dostoevsky meant by his criticism of the first act. The drama has led to a Gordian knot. How does it go on?

There follows a remarkable break in the action. The *tempo*, which at the end has reached a terrific speed, comes to a sudden stop, apparently clogged by the violent ending. The second act begins in the manner of an epilogue in order to make clearer the unavoidable break in the unity of place and time; it is intentionally cooled down, a manner typical of Dostoevsky's epilogues; even after the action has re-commenced he still partly retains the narrative. The working-up and climax of the first part are self-contained and come to an end. Dostoevsky's solutions never follow the path on which the tension has begun. His accumulated forces are hidden and, when they again come to light, lead at once to quite unexpected images which produce a new climax. Thereafter everything is brought together by some sudden and almost fortuitous stroke, and the synthesis is completed.

DOSTOEVSKY

We learn incidentally from behind the scenes what has
happened to Naſtasya and Rogozhin, and what was the
prince's attitude towards them; but it remains indiſtinct.
The prince follows them to Moscow. Thereafter he spends
a short time with Naſtasya. Naſtasya flees from Rogozhin
to the prince and entreats him desperately to save her from
her wild suitor. The prince acquiesces and, ready to share
life with her, yields to all her desires. She is to be freed
from her madness for self-deſtruction. But as soon as she
comes to her senses again she refuses his sacrifice and flees
back to Rogozhin. Rogozhin is nothing to her, less than
a lackey. She hates him and does her utmoſt to turn his
love of her into hatred, expecting from his hatred only an
easing of her torture. Myshkin alone could save her. But
if she ſtays with Myshkin he will go to pieces. That is
her *idée fixe*. She promises Rogozhin to marry him and at
the laſt moment rushes away from him; her pretence of
deceiving him with others is only a method of duping him.
The self-deſtruction runs its course and the Chriſt-man is
condemned to be a passive onlooker.

We have to infer all that. Much can be gleaned from
the conversation between Myshkin and Rogozhin when they
firſt meet again in Petersburg. It is only later when the
novel can be seen in its entirety that the need for this
break in the action is apparent. For the time being
Doſtoevsky's refusal to elucidate the moſt important
side of preceding events is somewhat disconcerting. May
a writer be so remiss as to push essential parts of the action
off the ſtage? The manner of portrayal scarcely does
juſtice to the importance of the events involved. We learn
of little more than the local movements of the principal
characters, and are alarmed at the baldness when Myshkin
declares he loves Naſtasya only from pity and is therefore
not Rogozhin's rival. Is there some laxity in the poet's
thought behind this hazy situation? Perhaps a laxity in
his sense of morality? Does not the Idiot blaspheme pity
or love or even Chriſt? What did Myshkin actually want
when he offered Naſtasya his hand? The modern sceptic

is promptly ready with two, at leaſt two, attacks: one on
pity as such, on every kind of pity as an unwarranted and
invariably unproduĉtive interference with the rights of his
neighbour. Perhaps it was juſt Myshkin who completed
Naſtasya's misfortune. But as a matter of faĉt that has
nothing to do with the matter for, juſt as easily as pity,
suffering could be denied. Surely the aim of pity here is
not morality or saintliness; rather it deepens the tragic
situation between two human beings. The second attack
is direĉted againſt the unproduĉtivity of Myshkin's pity.
It is queſtioned whether the Idiot is capable of helping
any woman; his reſtraint suggeſts physical incapacity, and
his right to have any influence over Naſtasya is conteſted
because the sensuality denied him is the only means whereby
he could be of any assiſtance to her. These attacks have
been repeatedly expressed in writing.

This attitude caſts an unfair refleĉtion on the author's
problem, for the prince's eroticism has nothing to do with
it. This will be discussed later in another situation in which
he plays the part of a lover. It is not the man but the
woman who is in queſtion now, and, as is clear from everything that has happened, her inhibitions are much more
important than his. If one wants to go so deeply into
physical faĉts as to talk of impotence, it is Naſtasya rather
than he who muſt be made the subjeĉt of this profound
psycho-analysis. We do not know what happened to her
in Moscow, not even whether she gave herself to Rogozhin,
and what licence she allowed out of pique to her other
lovers, other "lackeys"; we only surmise that neither
Rogozhin nor anyone else could juſtifiably boaſt of any
essential success and learn later, so far as Doſtoevsky found
it necessary to touch on these details, that aĉtually she
remained chaſte in spite of her licentious life. But even if
she had been the miſtress of Myshkin, Rogozhin, or even
Keller, it would not have helped her. The erotic side of
Myshkin is not in queſtion. What drew her to him, what
made her fix on Myshkin as an idol, was juſt the Idiot's
"incapacity," his purity, as becomes more and more evident

later on. She was not the sort of woman to whom a sexual outlet would have brought alleviation. What she had to give of erotic had, earlie_ on, fallen into the dirty paws of the insistent Totsky. Many women are incapable of overcoming the effect of the more or less mechanical defilement of their youth, and are thenceforward sexually dead. Disgust stifles desire. The female martyr prefers crucifixion to repetition.

Nastasya is the only valid feminine example of the insulted and injured who is equal in strength to the man from the underworld den, and the chain of her *katorga* will never be loosed. Possibly her dreams are as intense as were the underworldling's thoughts, perhaps she paints an impossibly bright picture of love and, at the zenith of her dreams, recognizes the loathsomeness of man; how could she then expect things to be better later in life. The morrow begins for her before the orgy.

She cannot rid herself of the consciousness of her inferiority. She plays the devil with her pursuers; the most adept prostitute is not in the same street. The less she values herself the more she indulges in rowdy revelry. She is ignorant of the purifying intoxication of a Grushenka. Her only salvation lies in the omniscient and undefiled Idiot. At times she gropes for him. Then she is terrified that the purity of his gaze in which she bathes might, for once, inflamed by her beauty, assume the turbid glow which she sees in the eyes of her admirers.

Is it necessary to dissertate on the prince's retarded puberty? A pupil of Freud would like to know how that showed itself in him. I cannot divulge it. Even thoroughly robust people are often late in maturing because other things occupy their minds. Dostoevsky is supposed to have been like that. The prince's puberty may have been slow in developing because a great deal was growing in him. He would certainly not be expected to devote special attention to sexual matters.

Since that was the inevitable course of events, Dostoevsky may have been right in staying in Petersburg and turning

SECOND ACT

away from Moscow where Myshkin was putting himself to fruitless trouble, Rogozhin was storming in vain, and Naśtasya was vainly wounding herself more and more deeply. Dośtoevsky frequently committed the artiśtic blunder of dropping incidents previously śtressed because he thought better of it. Had it not been for the immediate setting in type of *The Idiot* whilśt he was śtill working on it, the misleading dissonances would presumably have been avoided.

In the midśt of the Moscow confusion and of the fruitless torments of a lover out of pity, the Idiot suddenly has a vision of the *milieu* of the childlike women of which he had caught a glimpse on that long Petersburg day, and he writes to Aglaia the faltering letter which is delivered by Kolya, the imperturbable messenger; a sign of life in the form of the queśtion whether Aglaia is happy, signed, "Your brother, Prince Myshkin." It could not have been done more naïvely. With such people it does begin like that, not in the presence of the objeċt of one's love, but long afterwards when imagination has coloured the vision. Myshkin is not perturbed by the faċt that he has aċtually promised himself to another woman, and he cannot excuse himself by diśtinguishing between pity and love, for he only became conscious of this diśtinċtion later on. He even fails to notice that there was anything incorreċt in it, for possibly he was capable of loving two women at once. Myshkin's inśtinċt of self-preservation is juśt as developed as anyone else's, except that his intereśt is not so self-centred as is usual. He has desire, he is neither shadow nor abśtraċtion, but a human being who wants other human beings. This need is the decisive faċtor; hence his contentment with the company of inferior people, his accessibility to all and every one.

This ardent longing for human beings is in itself proof that erotic relationships are only one side of his intereśt. The letter is the aċtual beginning of the second aċt; it reaches its deśtination and is followed shortly by the writer. Firśt we have to accompany him on his irritating visit to

163

the family of the intolerable Lebedyev with whom he takes up his quarters, and then follows the long conversation with Rogozhin about the love-escapades in Moscow. This scene is the central point of the act which might well be called Myshkin and Rogozhin. It deals with nothing but them.

The recital of the events of the intervening period becomes an altogether secondary object of the scene. It is done in a masterly way. As usual in such instances Dostoevsky, far from concealing the artistic mechanism, actually acquires a psychological *motif* in placing a third something at the table. The exciting factor is not Rogozhin's story of his experiences with Nastasya but the way in which he tells it. The scene rapidly develops into a clandestine battle between narrator and listener. We are suddenly right in the middle of the drama and faced with the prince's stumbling-block, his pity. Ha, ha! thinks Rogozhin, pity like that is perhaps more potent than other people's love, and he has no idea of the truth of his words. The prince scents mistrust and is on his guard. He does not notice the third something at the table, which threatens to devour him, and he tries to see through the chaos. He gives Rogozhin to understand that it would be as well to leave Nastasya alone; Rogozhin can never be happy with her; she ought to be taken abroad, perhaps to some Swiss garden. Rogozhin is on the watch. Will not the compassionate prince also go abroad by chance? There he could practise his pity to his heart's content. Certainly only an accident has brought him to Petersburg almost at the same time as Nastasya.

Myshkin disregards his suspicion and makes an inoffensive reply. No, he will not accompany her abroad and is not here on her account, but he will look after her. He wants to do that as a brother. He wants to be a brother to Rogozhin too, that is his sole motive in dissuading him from marriage. A marriage preceded by so much torment can scarcely be a happy one.

Rogozhin notices how often the ideas of Nastasya and

the prince tally. Naſtasya had the idea of revenge too.
Really they are excellently matched. She has certainly
given him his full share of torment. Once when she threatened with Keller, he beat her till she was black and blue.
After that he neither ate nor drank for thirty-six hours to
make it up with her. She went to the theatre with the
others and he was ſtill sitting there when she came back.
She was bored. Hunger-ſtrike, she said, did not suit him,
for a lackey muſt take what he can, not ſtarve. She omitted
to lock her bedroom door merely to show her contempt.
The next day he was ſtill sitting there. At laſt she acquiesced
out of boredom, consented to the marriage, and later ran
off again. Now there is again a wedding in prospeᶜt.

Perhaps it will ſtill be all right, ſtammers Myshkin.

No, shrieks Rogozhin, angry at the words, it can never
be all right. You can't make a silk purse out of a sow's
ear. She hates him. She can as little get rid of her hatred
as he of his love. That can't be helped. Rogozhin has to
swallow her hatred of Totsky and the whole crowd. She
could not do anything else even if she wanted to. Possibly
she did want to, tried to love him, wanted to make him
better, even told him the ſtory of the Emperor at Canossa
and gave him hiſtory-books. She cannot do it, nor can he.

The prince in his attempts at persuading him is like a
child persuading a viper not to bite. He does not underſtand why Naſtasya always rushes back to Rogozhin if she
really hates him. She muſt have some motive. Probably
she is only aᶜting and her words about Rogozhin bᵉlie her
feelings. Marriage to a man she hated would be sheer
suicide; she might juſt as well cut her own throat.

And that is exaᶜtly what it is, nothing more or less
than a form of suicide; some do it one way, some another.
If she marries him, it is merely to kill herself. Perhaps
now even an Idiot like that will take in the situation.
Rogozhin boils. The third something at the table swells
and puffs itself up, becomes a dark cloud, and the prince's
brain reels. He plays mechanically with a knife. Rogozhin
fixes his gaze on the blade. Leave that alone! he says and

takes it away. Then he imparts the laſt bit of news, though even a blind man could see for himself that Naſtasya loves only one man, loves Myshkin as Rogozhin loves her, exactly as he loves her. She has told him aloud and quite diſtinctly. This one man is everything to her. For this one man she would let herself be torn to shreds; out of sheer love she does not go to him for fear of ruining him, prefers to let herself be murdered by Rogozhin. That too she has told him aloud and diſtinctly.

Myshkin again plays with the knife. A disease, he murmurs, a disease! And how funny, to cut pages with such a big knife, almoſt a garden knife. For the second time Rogozhin snatches the knife from him and flings it into the corner. There is a flash in the cloud like lightning.

It is clear that Myshkin is not great in this scene. He talks trivially, is completely at a loss, ſtutters, and plays with the knife. If he were really a Chriſt-man, he ought to be able to help, even if only with impressive words. He seems detached; there are no tears; in the middle of the conversation he cannot help smiling at the ſtrange picture of the father on the wall.

A Chriſt he is not. He is denied the miracle of liberating Naſtasya from her mad idea and of curing Rogozhin. He knows it and therefore does not attempt it. There is not much sense in grand words. Presumably Chriſt also did not utter the beautiful words attributed to Him. There was something in His being which spoke to men.

Myshkin's goodness may appear queſtionable to those who reckon in terms of reality. One person was annoyed that he often spoke gently without saying anything of particular significance. Myshkin's words were only a part of his make-up, and his make-up was only a part of his beauty; that had to be shown in words, and in words which at times were bound to be empty. Myshkin's beauty was his artlessness, although he underſtood everything. Compared to a miracle-worker that is not much; it is not much compared even to a mind actively engaged in every-

day affairs. It would not have occurred to him to found
charitable institutions, but he gave things mature consideration whether or not they concerned him. He was
timid, but interest in people whom he feared outweighed
everything. He could play with the knife, enjoy the cloud
over his head, even if it contained the lightning which was
bound to slay him. Undoubtedly he lacked power; that
is why he was considered deficient; and, in moments when
capacity to act was expected, he certainly seemed to be a
thorough idiot. Perhaps, however, appearances were against
him, as well as other people's habit of exploiting their
neighbours. Possibly he was shrewder than others in
perceiving the futility of exploitation. Perhaps his moments
were not like those of others, perhaps he lived them more
fully than the normal man and gave his life to it. He did
not spare himself. Whilst other invalids tend to become
fastidious, his defect conduced to benevolence. His
irrational devotion was beautiful, charmed people, and
disarmed them. Rogozhin did not know what to make
of him. None of Myshkin's words convinced him, he was
struck only by Myshkin's unassailable defencelessness.

The prince is oppressed by the cloud, he wants to go.
Rogozhin leaves him in peace. Between the devil and the
deep sea Myshkin plays unsuspectingly with the knife and
Rogozhin asks him whether he believes in God; another
guarded question. By way of answer the prince relates
his three stories. First, that of the pious and eminently
honourable Russian who did no one any harm but who
became infatuated with his friend's watch and could not
help cutting his bosom-friend's throat, after fittingly crossing
himself and praying to God for forgiveness. This story
amuses Rogozhin immensely and he laughs uproariously.
The second story tells of the soldier who for forty copecks
sold the prince a cross which was supposed to be of silver
but was obviously of tin. The prince promptly hung the
cross round his neck and the soldier went off and squandered
the money in drink. And this story also, in which there is
a good deal both of Myshkin and of Russia, must have

fascinated Rogozhin, for he asks Myshkin for the cross. The prince makes his commentary. The essence of religion, it muſt be underſtood, is not affected by practical things, neither by transgression nor by crime, and all atheiſts miss the point. This commentary shakes Rogozhin. Thereupon they exchange crosses and become brothers in the cross, and Rogozhin leads his brother to his aged mother and makes her bless the prince as if he were her own son. Rogozhin and Myshkin embrace. There is something of old-Russian icons in this scene.

The prince saunters through the town. It is hot. He is oppressed and dissatisfied with himself, with Rogozhin and with Naſtasya. What will be the end of it all? He knows the danger he has been exposed to to-day and that he is not yet clear of it. He is very near to a would-be murderer, one in whom he has roused thoughts of murder. It is this fact, not who is the object of the murder, which weighs heavily upon him. Suddenly a bright idea flashes across his mind, the same idea which amidſt his torments in Moscow spurred him to write the letter. Aglaia is with her parents in the country-house in Pavlovsk. Away to Aglaia!

In a second he is at the railway ſtation, has bought a ticket, and passed on to the platform. Then suddenly he turns back, quits the ſtation, and makes for Naſtasya'a house. This passage is obscure. He feels that an epileptic fit is imminent and is thus at the mercy of his inſtincts and incapable of reasoning. What does he want at Naſtasya's? Doſtoevsky cannot be accused of shirking the issue under cover of the epileptic ſtate, for Myshkin's disease is juſt as much a part of the ſtory as anything else. It is perfectly plausible to let his epilepsy deprive him of his will-power; that may be the Idiot's moſt natural condition.

There is a hint at wanton thought, but obviously he cannot expect satisfaction of his primitive inſtincts, for he is right in his surmise that Naſtasya is likewise in Pavlovsk, and so he only goes as far as her house and not to her. Of at leaſt one thing he is equally certain, that Rogozhin, who

SECOND ACT

has kept a close watch on him since he first set foot in Petersburg and whose glowing eyes have been following him all day long, will quite definitely not leave him alone on this path. He feels the eyes behind him at every step, and it may have been this serpent's gaze which stopped him boarding the train to Pavlovsk. Playing with the knife, then?—Yes, playing indeed, but no longer thoughtlessly and mechanically; at least a dangerous game, for, when Rogozhin actually is behind him, all the vows of his brother in the cross must seem a fraud and, despite his will, this rival becomes a thief. This Myshkin does not and, in fact, cannot fail to feel in spite of the confusion created in his mind by the conversation with Rogozhin. He wants to sin, at least to give that impression in order to add a fourth to his three stories of Russian piety. He wants to sin, as best he can; not for sin's sake, for it is not Nastasya who lures him; that he should become a victim of desiring Nastasya carnally and Aglaia spiritually is an inconceivable banality. No, he wants to sin in order to rid himself of the mist which separates him from Rogozhin, in order to bear his share of the pollution, in order to have done with the passive rôle to which his idiocy condemns him. It is no consolation to him that, short of a miracle, even a saviour could not have helped a Rogozhin or a Nastasya; even were he conscious of his purity, it would not help matters in the least.

Oppressed by his guilty thoughts the sinless sinner slinks back to his inn after his fruitless visit to Nastasya's house. The glowing eyes are in hiding in the dark passage. Seized by an epileptic fit just at the moment when Rogozhin's knife is pointed at him he falls and is thus saved from the murderer.

As is common knowledge Dostoevsky's epileptic attacks were preceded by moments of vision and ecstasy wherein he came close to the realization of all his desires and enjoyed the quintessence of his idea. In those moments he was conscious of supernatural powers (43). For the purpose of describing Myshkin's epileptic fits he took a page out of his own life and dramatized his experiences, thereby impressing with the stamp of truth the fortuitous attack which saves Myshkin. Myshkin believes that with the supernatural powers at his command he can save his deluded brother in the cross, and with his eyes wide open steps towards the knife.

The sick man quickly recovers and is taken to Pavlovsk to the fussy Lebedyev. Here we are in the foreground of the novel. Myshkin meets the Epanchins again. The garden laughs and promises a return to health.

There is another unexpected change in the method. The demoniacal element disappears or is assimilated into the background, where it hangs like a cloud behind the scenes; in the foreground is set a society novel in the grand style, in the centre of which is a gem, the faint beginning of a love-story: Myshkin and Aglaia.

The action is no longer set in relief. Compared to what has taken place little happens on the stage and it becomes less and less possible to consider events in terms of drama. The dialogue is certainly relevant, but there is such a variety of it that it is difficult to see the wood for the trees. But what the action loses in relief it gains in depth. There is comparatively little depth in previous happenings; it is now easier to understand why Dostoevsky called the first act a prelude. The idea underlying the novel looms nearer; there follows what might bluntly be called abstract action. The tension is altogether different. The tune is called by Dostoevsky's humour which reaches its climax in the social part of the novel. A moment ago abandoned to the darkness, we now let ourselves be led into the light and it seems quite natural.

The wife of general Epanchin, the *babouchka*, becomes a principal character. She fusses round her beloved Aglaia like a clucking hen. Aglaia, who cannot keep quiet, recites the ballad of the poor knight, into which, of course, a meaning is read by Kolya, that *enfant terrible* and *postillon d'amour*. The prince proves himself utterly gauche and never misses an opportunity of disappointing Aglaia; that

only serves to deepen her affection for him. His chivalry
is put to the first test by the coarse attack of the wild horde
surrounding Burdovsky, the alleged son of Myshkin's
benefactor. People swarm on to the scene. It happens
that Epanchin and his whole *entourage* are with the prince,
as well, naturally, as Lebedyev and family.

The horde starts a veritable orgy of blackmail. The
deceased Pavlishtchev paid for the prince's maintenance in
Switzerland and bequeathed him his considerable fortune.
Burdovsky imagines he is the wealthy man's illegitimate son
and contests Myshkin's claim; the rightful heir, he con-
tends, is the son of his own flesh and blood. Legally the
will is indisputable, but it would not be decent for a man
to enrich himself in such a way. If, however, his Serene
Highness the Prince does take possession of the inheritance,
at least he must first pay back the money which Pavlishtchev
withheld from his own son and spent on the prince's maintenance in Switzerland. The story is complicated and the
turbulent scene is dragged out. For the benefit of their
poor orphan his charming comrades have launched in some
low journal an attack on the prince which reeks of calumny
and ridicule. He is described as an offshoot of a decadent
race and class and as degenerate to the point of idiocy,
with the additional stigma of ridiculousness. There is
something of the Parisian *fin de siècle* about the story, and
the lousy comrades, whose methods and behaviour foreshadow The Possessed, are very true to type.

At the request of the general's wife the article is read
aloud. They are intensely interested to see how the prince
will defend himself against this outrageous attack. The
entire Epanchin family including Aglaia is waiting for the
knight to shut his visor and crush the gang into dust.
Not a bit of it. Myshkin is at first thrown into complete
confusion. The gang of blackmailers gets more and more
the upper hand and wallows in abuse; it is pitiable how
Myshkin keeps on urging them not to get excited, he, the
person insulted. The general's wife trembles with indignation at him. Aglaia is petrified. The prince is bewildered

by the presence of so many people. Were it not for that
he could cope with the situation, for he knows all the links
in the chain of this complicated story. If only they would
give him time everything could be explained and there
would be no more thought of insult. Of course, if things
really were as they suppose, suppose in all good faith, they
would be justified in ridiculing and despising him; therefore
he has no intention of feeling insulted. Of course they
are not rogues at all; on the contrary, it is they themselves
who are the victim of fraud. If only they would give him
time! Naturally it was not right to give publicity to such
abusive articles without precise information, above all not
right to insult the estimable dead, such as his father and
his foster-father, that splendid benefactor, but it is easy to
understand how such things come about. Mr Burdovsky
has accepted Mr Keller's assistance, and even this Lebedyev
has rushed to Mr Keller's aid, Lebedyev who invariably
behaves as if he were dying of love for the prince. Well,
he has only touched up the article. After all that is not
so bad, for it must have been fascinating to see his literary
efforts shine.

The entire Epanchin family look as though they were
saying, go for them or you're a coward! And every one of
the Epanchins is suffering torture because Myshkin still
has no intention of going for them. The youths, who are
mere sketches of characters in *The Possessed*, are triumphant.
You can fling us out, but that won't prove much!

No, it would not prove anything, says the Idiot. It
would be senseless. There is, for example, this Ippolit, a
half-fledged youth in the last stage of tuberculosis, who
foams in the most loathsome way. In a moment he is
going to invite the company to his funeral. How has an
invalid like that come to devote his last breath to such a
swindle? Only be patient, in a moment everything will be
clear. Excuse me, let us sit down, please sit down.

The prince explains the story, heedless of interruptions.
In Switzerland at Dr Schneider's there were people like
that who never wanted to listen when things were being

explained to them in a reasonable way, and you had to be extremely patient, but eventually, if they were not too ill, they became reasonable and listened all the same. Mr Burdovsky is obviously ill, for he is clearly speechless from sheer emotion. Well, that is just what has happened to Myshkin. You are overcome by excitement and you become an idiot.

Intolerable! the Epanchins are heard to mutter.

At last there is light. A pettifogging lawyer started the ball rolling. This pettifogger approached the prince who had just come into his fortune. The prince saw through the swindle but, to be on the safe side, instructed Ganya to investigate and at the same time allocated 10,000 roubles to Mr Burdovsky. That was the most his foster-father had paid for the Swiss garden. As it turned out, Mr Burdovsky was not the illegitimate son of his revered benefactor at all, but all the same he would stick to his promise of 10,000 roubles, for, as things were, Mr Burdovsky stood, so to speak, for a son and considered himself such.

Ganya steps forward and confirms everything down to the minutest detail. Burdovsky's accusation against his mother of an indiscretion with the revered benefactor is false. Here are the proofs.

The horde hangs its head, for the facts admit of no dispute. The consumptive Ippolit is the first to recover. If that is so, how dare the prince insult poor but decent people by offering alms? Thank you very much for it, extremely grateful, very obliging of you. The gang foams once again.

The prince is sad. He has acted bluntly, has been dragged into saying too much, and now of course it is impossible for poor Burdovsky to accept the 10,000 roubles. Moreover he ought never to have insinuated that Burdovsky was suffering from the same disease as he. You always do the wrong thing. He apologizes.

Then the *babouchka* lets forth, and a veritable thunder-storm breaks out over the gang, over the prince, over the assembled multitude, over the world out of joint. And this prince, this idiot will naturally go off to the gang to-morrow and try to make things up with them in order to lick the dust off their boots, in order to cajole them into accepting his 10,000 roubles.

" Shall you go, yes or no? "

" Yes, I shall go," he says.

She bursts into such a frenzy of anger that she almost lays violent hands on the consumptive Ippolit, which does not, of course, prevent her taking him into her arms a moment later. And finally Ippolit sums up the whole situation with the observation, " we are all of us absurdly good people! "

In this scene the Idiot comes very near to the lofty Symbol. In no other way could a modern Christ behave, in no other way could he calmly submit to the crown of mocking thorns and convert the mockers to a sense of the essential. Badness is invariably only relative. There is an element of badness in all of us, and the Christ-man has his full share; but behind it all there lies something good which only fails to function because of some inevitable mistake. And the bad can be removed, generally with great ease. If that succeeds, the evil has had its good effect. Incorrigibly bad people, professional rogues, are extremely rare. We are not absurdly good but absurdly stupid, absurdly little informed about the proper application of our powers. If only we could stand outside things, helping humanity would be child's play.

There is nothing metaphysical in the symbolism of this scene, a fact which lends it peculiar weight. We are forced to feel that something really new has happened to the Idiot; that there is no need to change our sinful nature in order to become better and that we need only to be more reflective. The Idiot never rids himself of his idiocy or adorns himself with a halo which our sense of the essential could not accept. Just a little reflection and you will find that not one of us is a rogue, neither you nor he nor I, but that we are all the victims of fraud; by whom or what is

THIRD ACT

beside the point. Modern scepticism charges us to resist fraud; so does religion. Naturally fraud cannot be eluded. To-morrow it will be the same thing over again, and the day after to-morrow we shall once more be reflecting. Love your enemies and bless those who curse you! His very simplicity works miracles, a simplicity devoid of primitive mannerism. He does not resort to some supernatural power, nor is he a deliverer in camel's hair; he is just one of ourselves, a modern man in modern clothes with modern thoughts. Disciples are already at hand. The horde, which a moment ago was persecuting him, now bows penitently. It is true that the consumptive viper suddenly declares his boundless hatred for "the Jesuit with the syrup-soul," but this venomous outburst is only a last and fruitless effort; it cannot quench love. To-morrow he will kiss his hands.

Exactly the same thing happens to the Epanchins; all their sacred notions are thrown into confusion. Aglaia behaves like Ippolit and threatens ardent hatred. After three days of quiet seclusion he is forbidden by her ever to set foot in her house again; and the comic hen of a mother rushes to him and says the same thing. Never will she give her daughter to such an idiot, in case he is cherishing any such hope.

No, murmurs the prince timidly, of course he would not dream of such a thing.

Never have serious matters been treated with such piquancy. We are a long way off the humorous stories of the Siberian and pre-Siberian periods. It might still be possible to talk of a comedy of situation but for the subtlety and reality of the humour which never becomes farcical. We are a long way off *Don Quixote* and are gradually approaching the " positive " of which the poet dreamt. The Idiot's beauty becomes more and more distinct, the humour a light to lift the mask. Even Keller, the boxer, is absurdly good. In an extremely comic dialogue there is an exposition of a boxer's cynicism. Keller, by his own greatness of soul, ruins the chance of the credit he has hoped for. His soul, he complains, is always magnificent in theory, but unfortunately in practice steals anything it can lay hands on. He actually wanted to confess, had prepared a whole "*Ragoût fin* of tears," and after the confession he thought it would be easy to mention a loan. A mean trick, isn't it?—and Myshkin replies in all seriousness that the meanness lies in the awkward coincidence of two thoughts and that that happens to him every day; that he has long been engaged on the problem of dual thought, and that he is extremely pleased to find Mr Keller travelling along the same path.

Is it not palpable that the humour sustains just those weak passages which might add fuel to the flame of our scepticism, and that the figure of the Idiot slowly becomes more real?

The general's wife, having talked herself out of her wrath, resolves to receive the prince again.

He is not allowed to, replies Myshkin on the defensive; Aglaia has forbidden him.

That provokes the temperamental *babouchka*. She is beside herself with joy and storms about the simpleton. Does he not understand that that is nothing more or less than a command to go to her ill-bred daughter at once? This ill-bred girl, true daughter of her mother, needs a court-fool and she will not so easily find another. Then she herself drags him into her house.

There is a big step forward in these two acts. We were suspicious at first because of the swing of the first act. From now onwards we recognize a highly dramatic structure as well as the novel's lyrical qualities. In the fourth act the lyricism gradually dies away and the demoniacal and cloudy mountain in the background comes again to the fore. But before the lyricism fades away it gives a charming touch. Myshkin regrets his unseemly behaviour, his backward mind, his quite unfitting existence. Aglaia jumps up. Why is he saying all that, saying it here, to these of all people? Not one of those present is worth his little finger, not one of them has either his intelligence or his heart. He is cleverer and nobler than any of them. It is a pity he distorts his character, has no pride.

" The poor knight! hurrah! " shouts Kolya.

The mother is horrified, every one is horrified, but Aglaia has tasted blood. For the rest she has not the slightest intention of marrying Myshkin. To marry such a ridiculous person is out of the question. Only look how he is standing there! Perhaps he would be good enough to look in the mirror. She would never marry such an object.

" But he has not even asked you! " suggests one of her sisters. And Myshkin swears he has not asked her.

" What? " thunders the indignant *babouchka*. And the prince asserts again, has again the honour most respectfully to assert that he has never dreamt of making her a proposal. Some rogue must have slandered him. He has never thought of having the honour, of contemplating such a thing. No, by all that's holy!

At the sight of his face Aglaia bursts into laughter; so do her sisters and the whole *entourage*; even the prince does himself the honour of laughing. Aglaia enquires of her mother whether she may be allowed to go for a stroll with the young man who has just rebuffed her. And arm-in-arm at that! Heavens, this man does not even know how to offer a lady his arm! Aglaia is the very essence of Russian maidenly charm.

But in the background there is the distinct roll of thunder. Nastasya is in Pavlovsk and, surrounded by dozens of worshippers, is leading a daring life which Rogozhin anxiously endures. At times she encroaches on the garden-world next door; for the sake of upsetting things, so it seems, though she believes it is to help matters. It comes to a street-brawl on the promenade at Pavlovsk. Nastasya again provokes a friend of the Epanchins whom she thinks a suitor of Aglaia, and makes him out to be a former lover of hers. A companion of the man assaulted intermeddles, gets struck with a riding-whip for his pains, and is on the point of retaliating; it is only with difficulty that Myshkin

DOSTOEVSKY

saves her from rough handling. A duel is in the air. Aglaia wonders how he would behave in a duel.

" Would you be frightened? "

" Yes, I should think so," suggests Myshkin, " very much so, in fact."

" A coward then? "

" Not actually a coward, for a man who is frightened and does not run away, is, I should say, not a coward."

" You would not run away then? "

" No, perhaps not."

He is amused. (A man who has faced Rogozhin's eyes is entitled to be amused.) Needless to say Dostoevsky would never think of obliging the reader with a parenthesis of this kind.

She orders him to buy a pistol at once. It has to be loaded in this way; first powder, then some felt which can be found anywhere, in a mattress for instance, then the bullet. Not the other way round! Do you understand?

He understands, that is to say it begins to dawn on him, although it is most unseemly, although actually he ought not to let it dawn on him. The beginning of the dawning is so wonderful that he would like to be on an island to think it all out. " With this thought alone he would have enough for a thousand years."

He looks at the girl as if she were miles away from him; he would like to touch her to convince himself.

It is the reader's as well as the Idiot's first experience of this. Is there in these scenes one word, one picture, one touch which has appeared before in the thousands of confession-scenes in the world's literature? Have the Frenchmen ever dreamt of such charm? Whatever has gone before was merely an ornament. If anywhere this purity were possible in the German, but who would guarantee it against becoming high-falutin or Schilleresque or insipid? Nowhere is Dostoevsky's pre-eminence more obvious than when he discards his psychology, which people like to consider an ethnographic peculiarity, and tackles the simplest themes. It is as if his wealth of experience had shrouded him in innumerable veils which it is no easy matter to tear aside. When you think you have reached the *sanctum*, yet another veil confronts you. In the end there is nothing left but the child, the greatest marvel of all.

After this Myshkin sits alone on the Epanchins' verandah. Aglaia comes along, pretends to be surprised, and presses into his hand a note making a rendezvous for the following day. To-morrow morning at seven o'clock on the green bench. In a P.S. he is ordered not to show the note to anyone. You have to foresee every eventuality in dealing with such a ridiculous person, even if you blush in doing it. In a second P.S. the green bench is again described precisely. It is too bad that all these precautions are necessary. He ought to be ashamed.

Aha! exclaims Myshkin. And how astonished she pretended to be at finding him on the verandah although she must have known, since she had the note in her hand. Aha! Aha!

A happy Idiot perambulates in the park and cries Aha! An Idiot also manages to laugh aloud in a dark park and laughingly to bump up against people. He runs into Mr Keller. Mr Keller offers his services as a second in life or death—Oh, friend Keller, really a duel?—Well, we know now how to load, first powder, then felt, then the bullet, not of course the other way round!—Friend Keller, let's drink champagne. The whole gang must be invited, this very night, as quickly as possible. *Au revoir!*

Naturally she is amused at him, Myshkin observes to himself, but that does not matter; on the contrary, it is quite in the order of things. She will laugh still more, and that will be far more splendid.

He runs into Rogozhin, the first time since the attempt at murder. Rogozhin has still not got over it and Myshkin fully understands why. It is bound to be so. Rogozhin harbours a grudge against him. Perhaps Rogozhin imagines he is still thinking of the knife-business. Perhaps Myshkin is thinking of it, but in quite another way, and Rogozhin absolutely must come along and drink champagne for at midnight his birthday begins. The knife-business had to come, and it is a good thing it did come, for if it had not Myshkin would have felt he had slandered Rogozhin in his thoughts. He knew everything beforehand on that stupid day, including what happened with the knife. He thought of it whilst they were exchanging crosses, even before his mother, for Rogozhin surely only made his mother bless him so as to keep his hand in check and to protect his brother in the cross. But if all that had only been imagination and Rogozhin had not by chance seized hold of the knife, how abject he would feel before him now!

His brother in the cross enlightens him about Nastasya. She wants to make a match between Myshkin and Aglaia. That is her object. That is the only reason why she is carrying on like this, weaving intrigues, even going to the length of writing to Aglaia. And she will agree to marry Rogozhin only when this other marriage comes off. There is to be a double-wedding on the same day.

" So I am dependent on you," laughs Rogozhin.

This idea oppresses the prince. Whenever he visualizes the unfortunate woman he finds it difficult to think of anything else. But he sinks depression in hope. It is the beginning of a new life and midnight is a birthday for every one. He succeeds in persuading his gloomy companion to accompany him.

The corks are already popping at Lebedyev's. The entire horde of proselytes has assembled, and the sight of this crowd gladdens the prince's heart. He would love to embrace the whole world including the comic General Ivolgin and even the ubiquitous Lebedyev. But thanks to Ippolit's reading aloud the birthday celebrations take an original turn.

The somewhat valueless confession of the eighteen-year-old consumptive which ends in his abortive attempt at suicide, a slice of the underworld den, is an arbitrary piece of incidental music. A secondary character, an all too easily insulted and injured person, who could readily be dispensed with, is forced into the limelight and is incapable of asserting himself, could not do so even if he had anything more profound to tell us. An extensive episode of this kind is out of place in the novel, and as a matter of fact Ippolit is wrong. An invalid is ennobled not by his illness but by the resistance he offers to it, and this immature viper is of no more interest to us than the rest of them. The fact that the company remains unmoved embitters him, and he wants to vent his spleen at this inopportune moment. Even a person at death's door ought to be tactful. Only very youthful romantics like Kolya worry whether the cap was left out intentionally or not. Dostoevsky may have intended to darken the prospect by this Schilleresque interlude and to recall to the prince some memory which is less destined for him than for us. The effect of this night of revelry is amusing. Myshkin hurries from this poisonous orgy to the park, and at seven o'clock Aglaia finds her lover asleep on the green bench. That is just like this ridiculous person, and it is also just like him to confess that he has been dreaming of Nastasya. But Aglaia wants to climb with him, wants to be equally ridiculous, and all her maidenly sensibility is to be silenced. In her own fashion she suggests eloping. But he is not to make any mistake about it, it is only because she wants him to show her the world. There are a hundred and one things she has not seen yet, a Gothic Cathedral, for instance, Rome, and Paris.

He perceives the child in her. She belongs amongst the children in the Swiss garden and is sacred to him: the figure of light which once in Moscow freed him from torment, at the mere thought of which he breathes more freely, something only to be contemplated in thought.

Only look at her, Idiot! we want to yell at him. There's the rub! If only their eyes should meet once in this indescribable scene, all our anxious hopes would be fulfilled. But she is chaste, this girl who wants to elope, who has long since had a Yes ready for the question which he does not think of putting. She will risk heaven-knows-what with her tongue, feign worldliness from sheer perversity, and yet when it comes to love matters she is a child. Though she says she knows everything, she misses the moment of catching one another's eyes, the moment which makes words unnecessary and would bring even this Idiot to her feet. She studiously avoids looking at him, so it is expressly stated, turns her glance aside, although once emotion so gets the upper hand that she has to check herself from sinking on his shoulder.

They talk of Nastasya and talk past one another. It never occurs to him that she might confuse his affection for the figure of light, the only real love, with the pity which drove him to Nastasya. She asks and he answers. Yes, he came for Nastasya's sake.

If it were his love of truth which moved him to this thoughtless confession, his honesty would be brutality. He thinks he is allowed to tell his figure of light that he has come for Nastasya's sake because his coming is a mere drop in the ocean of the life which belongs to her, because he is completely unable to grasp his endless feeling for Aglaia. Pity is more natural. He speaks to her of Nastasya in the casually familiar way in which he would speak to God of the unhappy woman, as if it were utterly impossible for him to be misunderstood. But she would not be a woman if her belief in him could endure such a thought. A modern Daphnis and Chloe in an epoch which mistrusts love and lets it die; a Russian Daphnis and Chloe, destined, as Russians, not to pastoral frolic but to struggle and pain.

He came, then, for Nastasya's sake; then he loves Nastasya! And suddenly there flashes across her mind the history of this unconscious prince who has lived with this horrible woman such and such time in Moscow and then somewhere else. She ran away from him and he ran after her and he did actually propose marriage to her, he to this woman! And she blurts out that she does not love him at all, not even a little bit.

He does not answer. Answer, you Idiot! No, what for, for she is right. Is it not enough that the one woman loves him? Must not one be crazy to love a person like him?

Ganya is her chosen one, she says maliciously, the Ganya out of the first act. It was here on this very bench that she promised herself to him.

Stop, not that! He knows better. It is impossible to know definitely whom she does love but there is no doubt about whom she cannot love.

It is just Ganya! Ganya if anyone! And she invents the story of the ordeal by fire which later was to be realized by a Vincent van Gogh.[1]

Of course he sees through the artifice and recovers his humour. How can you stick your hand into a burning candle out of doors? Did Ganya bring a candle with him for this express purpose? Besides, good old Ganya's fingers were right enough yesterday. Aha! Aha!

She surrenders, trembles with laughter. The leaves of the trees tremble too. In all seriousness she explains the psychology of her lie. If you want a deception to succeed you must intersperse improbabilities. But this time she has not quite hit the nail on the head; and he must have a good idea of why she recently recited Pushkin's *Poor Knight*.

Surely everything ought to be perfectly clear now. She can hardly go further than that, and again she asks, did he really come here for that woman's sake?

The Idiot stands by his statement. He really intended helping Nastasya, but—she can well form some idea of his baseness—he had no notion of how to set about helping her, no notion at all.

Her answer is tolerant. He does not know the object of his journey but at bottom loves the other woman, is that not so?

No, he does not love her, that is just the appalling part of it, he could never love, could never have loved her. The time spent with her was a perpetual torment because

---

[1] Van Gogh was in love with his cousin, but her father forbade him to see her. Thereupon he held his hand over a light and asked to be allowed to see her for as long as he held his hand in the flame.—Tr.

he always failed to rid the unhappy woman of her sense of guilt, and he was bound to fail because his heart is incapable of loving her. To be incapable of loving so unhappy a being!—If Aglaia only knew her whole life she would certainly feel pity.

But there he comes to a dead end. Aglaia is a woman now and cannot share things; warmth for another woman, call it what he will, is treason. Myshkin's pity is one of those opaque affairs she has had enough of. She has also had enough of the letters which this Naſtasya dares to write to her. She considers the woman's misfortune nothing more or less than jealousy, and if he feels disposed to sacrifice himself—it would suit him admirably—he may do so. Heavens! He is horrified at her harshness. Such a sacrifice, he suggeſts, is quite on the cards, if it had any sense at all and he were not positive that it would be useless and bring about the ruin of both of them. Anything unnatural is far removed from him. But is not this harshness also unnatural? Aglaia cannot be brutal.

Oh! but she can, has gone so far as to do monſtrous things, now more than ever—and she says the firſt thing that comes to her. And since the answer she expeĉts is naturally not forthcoming she goes off in a rage.

This negative result is, of course, not conclusive; it only indicates possibilities. The misunderſtanding can lead to a real difference if Aglaia does not overcome her mistruſt and brutality. They both fail in this scene; she because she is incapable of sacrificing one whit of her accumulated affeĉtion for the one man; he because of his lack of egoism. Daphnis and Chloe are ſtill unenlightened. Then the *babouchka* suddenly turns up and helps to ease the situation.

There is another arbitrary interlude to fill in the necessary pause; the ſtory of the roubles ſtolen and recovered, an elaborate variant of the earlier ſtory of the honeſt thief.

The difference between the two ſtories gives a good idea how far Doſtoevsky had already advanced. The ſtory

affords Lebedyev an opportunity of making the most of his
fidgety restlessness and brings the forgotten General Ivolgin
into the limelight. Dostoevsky has perfected his drunkard
type. He also has an opportunity of demonstrating in a
new and unusual manner his axiom of " our guilt towards
every one and for every one." We are convinced despite
our laughter. This first part of the act—if we wish to
adhere to this subdividing of the novel-drama—again has
a film-like ending. Perhaps it was daring to divulge
Nastasya's letters to Aglaia and thus to establish in writing
the unhappy woman's distracted state. Nastasya's utterances do not show her to advantage. We are gradually
approaching the tragic issue. In the darkness of the park
Nastasya flings herself at the prince's feet.

All this whirs past in a succession of rapid pictures,
not without confusing us at times. Some of the padding
betrays a hurried hand and could easily have been touched
up. Often it is only a matter of false punctuation. Dostoevsky's restless thirst for creation made episodes out of
commas and full-stops.

Many a hurriedly drawn secondary incident intensifies
the main *motif* to an unexpected degree. The more fortuitous the events which surround the prince, the more
carefully considered seems every feature of his conduct.
His action never comes into contact with the violent stage
which stands in bold relief. Dostoevsky wisely refrained
from yielding to the mood of the moment and improving
on Myshkin's behaviour even in the slightest degree. The
vision of the Christ - man before whom the penitent
Magdalene kneels would not be so stirring if his heart had
previously surrendered to his beloved's impetuosity.

The second part of the act has first to wind up the
episodes of the first part. At the instance of Myshkin
Lebedyev at last resolves to " recover " the pocket-book
stolen from him by General Ivolgin which the thief has
remorsefully returned to the place he took it from. The
general lies to his dying day. An extremely honest person,
remarks the prince.

DOSTOEVSKY

The Epanchins have decided on the engagement. It is true the eager Aglaia torments the prince to excess and becomes offensive if anyone makes the vaguest hint at the proposed marriage, but in the family dialect that signifies her resolve to let herself be quartered for Myshkin. It is decided to introduce the prince to the grand world, and to this end a *soirée* is held.

Aglaia prepares her prince. The people who are coming to-morrow are certainly rabble, every man-Jack of them, and it is part of her parents' vulgar make-up to be patronized by these dignitaries; but there it is, and you have to grin and bear it. She hopes he will entertain every one and carry on a good old discourse, say on the subject of the death penalty. She is reckoning, too, on his usual gesticulations and recommends the large Chinese vase in the drawing-room which has long awaited him.

Myshkin is delighted at her veiled gesture of solidarity. But eventually she really succeeds in putting the fear of society into him. Without a shadow of a doubt he will behave wildly, talk utter nonsense and, as sure as fate, knock down the Chinese vase. It would be best for him not to turn up, and then they would have a betrothal without a betrothed. At last they manage to agree. He promises not to open his mouth and to keep as far as possible from the vase. Aglaia suddenly becomes affectionate; he will not later bring up this unmannerliness against her? Now would be the moment. Her words are perfectly frank, she sees herself already married. Everything is as clear as daylight. Even he must grasp things, inexperienced as he is with women, and he has grasped them. Now he wants to talk. Oh, what is all this chatter to her! She has had enough of it. Chloe cries for her Daphnis.

A delicate situation. This time there is more ground for enquiry about physiological limitations. *Babouchka* expresses maternal solicitude and Myshkin is anxious about his illness. Is it not time to fetch the psycho-analyst?

No, in my opinion there is still not the slightest reason for doubting the prince's ability to generate a dozen children, and the limitation which no one, least of all Dostoevsky, has overlooked, needs no scientific explanation. If Dostoevsky, as a trustworthy realist, touches on the apprehensions of the general's wife, it is not in order to make her his mouthpiece. Nastasya's fate amply explains Myshkin's behaviour. Quite apart from his natural slowness, from his capacity for happiness at the mere prospect of happiness, and his anxiety first to prove himself worthy of his good fortune, quite apart from these factors, would he not have to renounce his attitude in the first act, indeed his attitude throughout if he now turned to love with the rapidity desired by Aglaia and impatient readers? But above all he has now been told three times that his union with Aglaia means the death of Nastasya, the third time by Nastasya herself in the very conversation in which she deprecates pity. How often may he have said it to himself? Is that not enough for an idiot?

And something else. Apart from Myshkin and Nastasya there are ties between Nastasya and Aglaia, direct as well as indirect. The entire letter-business is only introduced to emphasize the relationship between the two women and further to implicate Myshkin. Granted that the prince could succeed in reconciling himself with his conscience, can he, not as an idiot, not as a Christ-man but as a normally conscientious and reasonable person, tolerate the unsettled situation between the women which may at any moment lead to disaster? Would not even a person less conscientious than the prince desire to straighten things out? They must not be divided on such an important question, particularly in a union so essentially spiritual. Nastasya would be a menacing phantom even without her " dark power," a thorn of jealousy for the woman, a thorn of remorse for the man; such a lack of harmony suffices to wreck any marriage. The phantom must be rooted out by dragging it resolutely into the light of day. Myshkin's words about " the being which stands between them " leave no doubt of his intention. The marriage cannot be a success till the phantom is disposed of.

There can be no other interpretation, nothing points to any other limitation. Myshkin's love is no more a sexual problem than Raskolnikov's love for Sonia. The root of the relationship lies in both instances in the same region but at different depths. Sonia saves Raskolnikov with the " communion." Presumably she presented the convict with children after his release from the *katorga*. That is beside the point. Sonia, with her crucified body and her naked soul, is capable of living only on God, and of at once understanding and overcoming any limitation in Myshkin; she is even capable of a spiritual companionship with him. An Aglaia can never achieve that. Her pride forbids it, her aristocratic grace, her make-up, her beauty. The limitation is in her as in Nastasya, not in the Idiot. Her poor-knight-romance strikes none of Sonia's notes, and it is certain that Dostoevsky did not miss this point. He does not accept Aglaia any more than he accepts Raskolnikov, looks across at Aglaia as in a hostile camp, but looks with the benevolent eyes of a poet and lavishes on her all the charms of a world far removed from him. Between the lines can be read a certain prejudice against this care-free girl. The same reserve is noticeable as in *Crime and Punishment*. He somewhat exaggerates the foolish virgin; the flapper in Aglaia sometimes talks more childishly than necessary; and it is not by accident that the epilogue leaves her in the lurch.

In the conversation with the company Aglaia interrupts the prince at the first mention of Nastasya. She refuses to hear anything about her. All the shady factors are to be kept outside. No, Myshkin insists, that is just what they must talk about. She interrupts him again, " quite anxiously," and is glad to be called away. The phantom is still between them.

The love problem in *The Idiot* is chock-full of social tendencies. Aglaia takes part in the prince's dissertation at Epanchins' *soirée*. Whatever is still obscure in their relationship is explained on this evening. The *soirée* begins very pleasantly for every one and makes the Idiot unexpectedly happy. He would rather have stayed away and would have spent the usual evening with viper and restless proletarian. Now things are different. They receive graciously the interesting young man with the good name who sits discreetly on his chair, wears evening-dress like every one else, and keeps his mouth shut; they are well-pleased with the Epanchins' choice. Even the horrible old hag Byelokonskaya finds little fault with him. Myshkin gazes in admiration. This politeness, these well-chosen conventions, these fine manners, this breeding and caste of thought! He enjoys every moment and reads deep meanings into their phrases. For the first time he recognizes the advantage of an urbane education. In spite of their worldliness there is a natural modesty in these people which lends weight to their every phrase, every word, every glance. Myshkin is deeply ashamed of the almost hostile picture he had painted of them and feels he ought to apologize to every one.

For a time he sits glued to his chair in silent wonder, at a respectful distance from the Chinese vase. Still, such an experience is not to be ignored; the interest lies not in the originality of some guest or in the profound ideas expressed, although doubtless not a few would well repay careful thought. What is gratifying is the strange repetition of the Swiss garden, the last thing you expect in a city like this, amongst perverse and eternally wrangling people; a Swiss garden carried to a degree undreamt of in Switzerland at Dr Schneider's. Memory of a former seclusion amongst children! There is an end to seclusion now. The garden is not confined to the mountainous recesses of a foreign land. It is far greater and more fruitful here, in his beloved homeland, and the children have developed into worthy, mature, happy grown-ups who bring happiness in their train. And he is one of them.

One of the guests mentions Pavlishtchev, his foster-father, to whom he owes Switzerland and everything else. There is someone here who knew his revered benefactor; it turns out that this infinitely pleasant and kindly gentleman is a relative of his revered benefactor and, moreover, a relative of his benefactor's female cousin who brought up the youth whilst he was still a complete idiot.

He cannot contain himself any longer; silence would be a crime. Immense happiness loosens the dumb man's tongue. At last he can put into words his deep gratitude to his revered benefactor who died before his return. These worthy people are Pavlishtchev's deputies and he has to thank them all for their unforgettable kindness. He feels he ought to go down on his knees before the relative of the revered benefactor. But he is also deeply indebted to the others, to the entire venerable assembly, and since they allow him to share their thoughts he will open his heart to them. There have come to light things which, often as he has thought of them, he has never dared give breath to. They speak of an orthodox Russian's conversion to Roman Catholicism. How can that be? Our orthodox church and Rome! He ardently defends the orthodox church and rails at the teaching of the antichrist. His speech gathers momentum. The pomp of Western Christianity is a mockery of Christ. There is no longer faith there at all, only will to power. The Church of Rome is a continuation of Roman imperialism, a tyranny. The pope wields a sword. Where the sword holds sway reign lies and deception. Superstition is rife and breeds crime —His words thunder forth like a mountain torrent.— At the other end of this mockery stands atheism, at the end of atheism chaos, murder for the love of murder, the senseless, dissolution of all form, all beauty, nothingness.

This is an altogether different Myshkin. Aglaia and the Epanchins have never seen him like that. The *babouchka* does not understand what it is all about. Is this the shy and placid Idiot, the eccentric whose very eccentricity is his own bugbear? Is this the poor knight who snatches a glimpse of his lady and is prepared to be flayed for the privilege of staying by his figure of light? God alone knows whence this new Myshkin has suddenly descended! He has come not as reformer and counsellor of this stunted rabble, condemned to mete out justice in phrases. His maxim is deeds rather than words. There is virile thought and passion in this man who grips humanity.

Naturally not this company. The great world is not yet ripe for this conquering herald. He exaggerates, say some; we know all that, say others. What do we care about theology? And to start with he ought to pause for breath. But he would stifle if he could not have his say; possibly he was nearly stifling already; who knows whether this was not perhaps his only limitation? No, not theology! What seems theological in his iconoclasm has long since been *vieux jeu*. The rigid bureaucracy and stultification of religion has given birth to all sorts of offshoots. With atheism came socialism; not the social spirit of Christ which can be found in every peasant, but this damnable abstraction. Socialism without God, which mistakes science for religion, is also a product of the disrupted church; once again a doctrine of violence born of despair in order to substitute materialism for the lost faith; once again a crude struggle, destruction and dissolution.

He only has time to tell half his thoughts. The other half they will doubtless complete themselves, for every one, so he believes, thinks likewise. On that account we must stick together and together ward off the disruption which has long since poisoned the West. We still have our faith. Woe to us, woe to the world if we too lose it! If this disruption is imported amongst us our passion would carry it to the bitter end. If once one of us turns Catholic he promptly becomes a Jesuit, and of the worst type. If he becomes an atheist he cannot rest till he has forcibly exterminated God. Why that is so? Because our spiritual fervour turns every belief, even unbelief, into a religion.

Never has there been a clearer exposition of the Russian problem of to-day, half a century before the world noticed it. The words are those of a prophet.

The Epanchins' guests are perturbed and the young Aglaia stares vacantly. What is he driving at? A fresh cloud threatens the betrothal. The Idiot's field of vision

DOSTOEVSKY

is too vaſt to play the part of Daphnis; but he is not conscious of this obſtacle. He would bring too much rather than too little into their wedded life. It is not Naſtasya but a huge gulf which separates them. The Idiot has a mission.

Show Russia to the Russians, help them to delve! Show Russia to the world! Old Europe is tottering! We are ſtupid enough to submit to it, and an artificial leg makes more impression on us than a real one. The whole of Europe's aĉtivity depends on subſtitutes. The aim of its thought is division and again and again division. Every god is to be divided up into his component parts. This hollow culture will never produce a new cult and does not, in faĉt, need it, for it has already learnt to dispense with God. The resurreĉtion of humanity lies with the Russian Chriſt.

Myshkin expounds Russian thought. It needs no comment. Here we are concerned only with the validity of the Idiot's idea. At all events it is not less potent than the Napoleon idea of Raskolnikov.

The speaker has risen ecſtatically and ſtands like a prophet before the aſtonished assembly; and, like all confessors who get up, at the same moment he bumps againſt the sacred pedeſtal; the huge Chinese vase, the family pride, totters and falls, and the inevitable calamity descends upon them.

Doſtoevsky omits to emphasize the climax of the drama, the new tragic, tragi-comic symbol, the rising of the garden-man in contraſt to the underworld man to which, till now, his genius had attached itself. It is as if he had entirely failed to notice the vaſt panorama at which a century will ſtare itself blind. Myshkin sees nothing but the shattered pieces; even those, says Doſtoevsky, he scarcely sees, so terrible seem to him the inevitable consequences.

But the inevitable does not happen, the dreaded catastrophe fails to materialize. No one even insults him; unperturbed they colleĉt the pieces and smile out of

192

courtesy as if nothing had occurred. But, but, has he injured no one? All the same he felt as though he had been carried away by his words and had said things which here of all places he ought not to have said, forbidden things which were bound to wound, and the shattered vase surely bears testimony to the depth of the wound. No, the vase really was only an earthen pot, even for the *babouchka*, and not worth talking about; he can see that in Aglaia's eyes, in every one's eyes.

His good fortune dazzles him. He understands, believes he understands. His fear of bumping against something else is once again only an illusion, born of his pitiable pusillanimity. Arise! cries an inner voice, you, prince of an ancient stock, here you are amongst princes of your own land. They are the same as you, only more mature and worthier, and misunderstanding is impossible.

Thereon he laughs happily and the others chime in just as heartily. It really is a laughing matter! Is not dear Aglaia's foresight a laughing matter? He was to do this and refrain from doing that. Of course she thinks he is an idiot and that he does not know his way about. Oh, he knows all he needs to know. What he lacked was obviously only a knowledge of his own kind; now he will never be frightened of anything again.

He fulfils his duty with the poise of a well-born person. To each of the dignitaries he says a polite word, flatteries such as princes are accustomed to. Those who mistrust us are of little spirit. If only they were all here, all the insulted and injured, and could see how things are going on and hear what is being said! Can people who talk as they talk here be hard and pitiless and strangers to life?—You, prince, have recently, I know, done a noble work, and you, prince, who are said to ill-treat your peasants, have given them lands on top of freedom. You, prince, have saved an innocent man from Siberia, and you, venerable princess, have received a suffering man in Moscow like your own son.

Naturally that is not all quite right, but it might be so, and he depicts it as it is bound to be. They comment

DOSTOEVSKY

on him, but feel flattered all the same and smile; even Byelokonskaya cannot help feeling flattered, the horrible old hag who finds him impossible.

In vain they strive to calm him; he jumps up again distractedly. Oh, we will prove ourselves worthy of the good fortune of being princes and not be afraid of our ridiculousness. We must confess that we are all ridiculous. Whoever craves for beauty will never escape ridicule. We will not shirk the ultimate sacrifice of becoming servants of our people, will bring it our happiness, our beauty, for truly, only look at the skies, at a blade of grass, at a child, only peer into a loving eye—the world is beautiful!

He is overcome again, something collapses. This time it is he himself, the Idiot. He is seized by the fit which has threatened the whole evening. He utters a terrible cry and Aglaia catches him as he falls.

Thus ends Myshkin's entry into the great world; the simplest and most possible of all solutions. What young man has not done the same at some time or other: thought he could redeem the world and come crashing to earth?

The gloomy end draws near. The Idiot has been within an ace of freedom from dark influences. Dostoevsky has almost completely realized the " positive heroism " which hovered before him from the very beginning. In our time there is nothing more positive than this figure at this moment.

Why did not Dostoevsky remain true to the positive till the end? The Idiot is once and for all enshrouded in mental darkness. Was this last tragic turn obligatory? Does the idea, the development inevitably demand it? Or would some other *dénouement* be possible? Probably we cannot conceive any other ending, so convinced are we of Dostoevsky's solution; and yet there is disillusionment, whilst the ending of *Crime and Punishment* is absolutely convincing. Before we enter the enveloping night of the *finale* let us state that the ending was not determined exclusively by the theme but rather by the renunciation of the poet who had not yet reached maturity. A waft from

DOSTOEVSKY IN 1879

[*face p. 194*

the underworld still lingered round the bold optimist who a moment ago let his hero aspire to the stars. He has doubtless overcome what is ridiculous in the Idiot, and the previous scene, a quixotic background in which there is a certain grandeur, is an immortal achievement. Nevertheless Myshkin seems only to escape the comic in order to sink more deeply into the tragic. The rise, which is prepared at great length, is followed by a rapid fall. It is not the end in itself nor the manner of the end which is in question. Van Gogh's heroism is not alone not lessened by the outbreak of madness which led to suicide, but is actually accentuated by it. In the same way the Idiot's idea might remain completely undisturbed by his madness, even, in certain circumstances, enriched. The madness does not necessarily shut out his " idiocy." It is senseless to think of him enjoying good health or leading a contented life. To Dostoevsky, most Christian of all poets, such a thought would have been presumptuous, after the crucifixion of his prototype; this latter memory alone would have sufficed to deter him from a less tragic ending. If there is room for criticism at all, it might be levelled at the circumstances which lead up to the end; the Idiot fails, not because of his idea, but because of the clouds in the background which, relatively, are of secondary importance. But such a flaw in the conception would force us to regard Myshkin merely as an epileptic whose inspired vision would be bound to end in collapse. In any case this turn of events has clipped the wings of " positive heroism," even though it does not prevent us from whole-heartedly embracing the hero's idea and setting him up as an idol of our fondest worship.

Myshkin's worldly rôle is played out. About that the Epanchins are in no doubt, particularly the *babouchka*. Consequently—so says that part of the general's wife which is the *babouchka*—the rôle of betrothed and son-in-law is played out. And, as is her way, she emphasizes what she does not mean, solely to see what her little daughter will have to say about it. But Aglaia assumes the attitude that she has never given a serious thought to the prince and that she has considered the matter long since settled. Thereupon her mother flares up and feels like turning out the whole pack of them, including her little daughter, if only the Idiot can be retained.

"That's the kind of man he is," she says, and is promptly frightened at herself. But Aglaia is her daughter. She has done with worldly ambition which in any case was only veneer. This move succeeds. Myshkin has not spoken in vain. Even his illness does not matter. He will be restored to health. Aglaia belongs to him. There is only one obstacle: this woman Nastasya. She must be got rid of.

That is the flaw. Had this obstacle not barred Aglaia's path there would have been no tragic ending. The obstacle has been prepared with great pains and Myshkin's situation, which is obscure to Aglaia, though not to us, has been carefully retained. Aglaia may have attributed many a word and action of Myshkin, possibly even his illness, to contact with this demoniacal woman and, thus inflamed, she is now going to make a clean sweep. We know, of course, of her jealousy. In spite of all that the flaw remains. Dostoevsky was not a person to resort to small probabilities as a general rule. We miss the heart-to-heart talk between Myshkin and Aglaia such as cleared the air between Sonia and Raskolnikov. The resistance which the girl offers to Myshkin's one single unambiguous attempt before the *soirée* does not suffice. It is difficult to accept the fact that the prince's eloquence about communion with the people, Russia, Europe, should fail him when communion with the woman he loves is in question. If his love is to pale into insignificance before the grander tasks of the Christ-man, a thoroughly plausible hypothesis, perhaps even a necessity, this very factor would have to become a *motif* to round off the composition. Such a *motif* would have produced a more positive attitude in the hero at the end of his career, side by side with an equally tragic issue.

Instead of the heart-to-heart talk between Myshkin

and Aglaia there is a duel between the two women in the
presence of the prince and Rogozhin. This scene outrages
European sensibilities, outrages our sense of proportion.
Can an Aglaia talk like that and, at one fell swoop, scatter
to the winds everything her upbringing has endowed her
with? Whence does she derive her power? It is she who
fires the first shot. Her ferocity is saturated with a hatred
reminiscent of old sagas. It would not be asking more of
this tender pampered girl to make her tear off her clothes
and stand stark-naked before them. Dostoevsky certainly
made such an imputation possible, but in this instance he
justified himself. It was a bold stroke suddenly to release
the demon in her. There, dance!—and nothing seems
improbable in this wild woman, previously so naïve, who
now hurls herself at her almost defenceless victim in unbridled passion. The force of her fury bursts the bonds
of restraint; there is a touch of genius in her raving. She
discovers Nastasya's baseness, her depraved vanity in playing
fast and loose between Myshkin and Rogozhin merely in
order to play a heroic part, in order to magnify the scandal,
because she is in love with her own ignominy, with her
own underworld life. It is not by chance that these words
fall from Aglaia's lips; they seem to be the outcome of
protracted brooding of which she has said nothing to
Myshkin. Myshkin, on the other hand, has not dared to
broach the subject; he could have done little at this juncture.
We learn later why one day before the company she would
not allow discussion of Nastasya. It was already too late.
Amongst other things contributing to Aglaia's rebellion
was not only the hatred born of her jealousy but also the
healthy instinct of a true daughter of the *babouchka*, the
almost arrogant healthiness of the unspoiled aristocrat
to whom everything obscure about Nastasya was the un-
cleanliness of a lower-class person. Like a child in her
injustice she digs up every detail. Why did not the fallen
angel simply show the door to Totsky, her seducer, instead
of allowing herself to be kept for years? Why this comedy?
Very well, Totsky was a brute and did what he liked with

her. The simpleton would not have found things so easy
with any other woman. But why did she not once and for
all have done with him and with all the rest of them? Only
because she needed money, because the fallen angel clearly
wanted a soft bed to lie on. She had luxury on the brain,
a bit mad, flung one man's hundred thousand roubles into
the fire and, to make up for it, took double the amount
from the next. Why could this heroine not have worked
as a washerwoman and been honest?

Nastasya is at a loss before this bombardment of
questions, this onslaught, brutal in its frankness. Her
replies in self-defence are uneven and conventional; her
behaviour in her torment is more ladylike than that of her
wrathful aggressor. Myshkin notices her torment and
suffers and, naturally, that only eggs on the angry girl.
Yes, she does love Myshkin, admits it frankly, says why,
and blushes in doing so, and is loved by Myshkin in return,
that is as clear as daylight, and this *comédienne* knows that
perfectly well. The prince could never love such a woman.
He not alone does not love her, he hates her. He said so
himself. With this palpable lie, a lie worthy of a *babouchka*
at her best, Aglaia plays straight into the hands of her
opponent. She has driven it too far. Even a less soft-
hearted person could not have helped feeling pity. Nastasya
is at the end of her tether. If Myshkin really said that——
Yes, did he really say it? Her *noblesse* forbids her confront
them both, but there is no need to. No, it is not true.
Myshkin does not say such things, could not possibly have
said it, and rather the world go to the devil than the prince
corroborate a lie.

Nastasya recovers. The demon which she has let loose
not only on her idol, the prince, but on every one, runs
amok. Her game is even more audacious than Aglaia's.
If I want to, I will take your sweetheart from you even
now, I only need to wink for him to stay, and you will go
back to your mamma alone. She herself does not believe
in the success of this bold stroke, only let herself be carried
away in order to break through her den once again, in

order to die in beauty. Myshkin would never obey the command. But now it is her turn; she with her experience can play a shrewder game than this wrathful girl. Only pity will move the prince. Is he going to suffer this immense injustice? Is he going to stand by whilst she is treated as a prostitute; she for whose purity he has himself stood bail, she who, however compromised her reputation, has never surrendered her body since Totsky?

Were Myshkin conscious of his Paris rôle in this fantastic drama probably Nastasya's ingenuity would fail; the apple would inevitably fall to Aglaia. But Myshkin sees only the stricken being who stakes her life on a glance, and it would be infamous to begrudge her that. Aglaia cannot endure his one second of vacillation and rushes out. He wants to follow, but at that moment Nastasya loses consciousness.

This scene speeds on like the great scene of the first act. A kind of epilogue, whose sober account is soothing after these violent events, links up with the next scene. We learn without comment how women, even tender girls, expect brutality of a man at times, particularly towards others, and that even in the best society the suppression of brutality is held to be insulting and immoral. We learn of the truly Russian fate of the prince who quite by accident is going to marry Nastasya instead of Aglaia, thinks it quite " insignificant " both for Aglaia and for himself, and believes he could explain matters to her in two words if only she would let him. For, so he thinks, if he were not to marry Nastasya the poor madwoman would die, without a doubt. We learn that an idiot can love two women at the same time, and, the main thing, that he blames himself, and no one else, for this confused state of affairs, possibly with justification.

Then the curtain is drawn to reveal for the last time the white bride beneath her linen sheet on her couch of rest. Near her sit the two brothers in the cross, Rogozhin the murderer, and Myshkin, the idiot. It takes place in the gloomy house of Rogozhin where a while ago the prince had played with the knife. When yesterday the bride came here in her flight from her bridegroom they stepped softly upstairs lest anyone should notice them, and Nastasya put her finger to her lip to intimate to her lackey to go more softly in case the prince should come upon them before everything was over. This last picture of the living woman is unforgettable.

The brothers in the cross then prepare the resting-place they are going to share and lie down together. Myshkin's tears flow on to the face of the unconscious Rogozhin and he ceaselessly strokes his cheeks. That is how they were found next day. The prince had long since ceased to know whether what his hand was touching was a face or a blade of grass.

Dostoevsky pondered on the last part for a long time and then wrote it rapidly. He did not overlook the flaw. He has taken liberties, he confesses on the 7th October 1868 in a letter before the last part was written. On the 11th December he writes, in a letter to Maikov,[1] that the reader will be struck by the unexpected ending, but will, after little reflection, recognize the solution as the only one possible; the " end as end " he considers good. When the last part was already in the press there was the usual regret. " Very long drawn, written hurriedly, a failure," he writes on the 26th February 1869 to Strachov; but even if he is unable to defend the novel, the idea is good. It had only moderate public success, and Dostoevsky, accustomed to judge by the number of editions, considered it a failure. In his letters about 1870 he invariably talks of nothing but this unsuccessful novel. Later, in the year 1877, when his entire works except *The Brothers Karamazov* had been published, he set himself amongst those who considered *The Idiot* his best work (44).

We feel the same, up till the time, of course, of *The Brothers Karamazov*. It is true, there are earlier works which are more rounded, which have not the weak points

---

[1] Apollon Nikolaevitch Maikov, poet, 1821-1897, with whom Dostoevsky often corresponded.—Tr.

of *The Idiot*. *The Eternal Husband*, the novel which immediately followed it, is one of these, though it has not
the good points of *The Idiot*. Were the novel only a fragment, even that fragment of " positive heroism," only a
glimmer of that supernatural illumination would mean more
to our confused and obscure ideas than all that a novel-
writer, even a Dostoevsky, could create out of normal and
abnormal experiences. With his broken language, his
flaw, with all the shortcomings of which he can be accused,
he points into the beyond. In this novel also we have the
feeling, which Dostoevsky himself often sought to express,
that he has not put into concrete form everything, not
nearly everything which he saw. When in the midst of the
duel with Aglaia Nastasya is almost at her last gasp,
Dostoevsky suddenly interrupts the conversation in order
to draw our attention to the spiritual qualities of the defeated
woman. Nastasya, in spite of her utter shamelessness, is
far more shameful " than one would have thought," and
possesses " quite a considerable spiritual power and profundity." He suggests that perhaps the reading of novels
has turned her head, and so forth. He introduces arguments which would do justice to a Madame Bovary, introduces them at the end of the novel when we have already
long been familiar with Nastasya's nature, on which half
the novel turns, and when the consequences of her nature
begin to lead to the final climax of the drama. In the
midst of an amazing psychological concatenation such
banalities have the effect of trimmings by an alien hand, of
retouching by an amateur to whom one corner of the
picture is too bare. Such weaknesses would wreck a Balzac,
not to speak of a Flaubert. We pass over these things in
Dostoevsky as if from somewhere or other a withered leaf
had fallen on the page. We blow it away and go on reading.
The idea, what Dostoevsky calls his idea, becomes so
powerful, once he has set it in motion, that its progress
seems automatic.

Is the Idiot beautiful? Hardly in a traditional sense,
as little as we ourselves either are or can be in this sense;

but certainly as beautiful as is within the power of present-day man. One thing is certain: the Idiot's influence on us in his best moments is the influence of beauty; he neither terrifies nor lacerates, but elevates and purifies. It is certain that the redemption which he strives to bring to his neighbour lies only in the domain of his beauty, in his harmony which is not distorted by any peculiarity and is so remote that to us only an idiot can be a harmonious being. The pre-Karamazov Dostoevsky was incapable of picturing him otherwise and let him succumb.

Is the Idiot true? There is scarcely any doubt about it unless it is considered that his behaviour is the only lie, and truth everything else which is thought, said and done in the world. It is, of course, understood that this refers to his manner of living, thinking and acting, and not to himself. We do not know enough about him to draw any comparisons, and we should need to know much more of him than of others. Dostoevsky has left much of his life in the dark; doubtless he had to. His truth is not very important, I mean the truth he speaks. At times it seems mildly foolish and feeble. What renders him much more true and probable is his attempt to read what is relative in every truth, his unhesitating renunciation of all personal benefits from his limitation. This tendency could not be worked out conclusively, but Dostoevsky did so much towards it that we can say he was as true as is humanly possible. The hero of *The Idiot* is as true as Aglaia whom we could draw, as the *babouchka* whose voice we hear, as the drunkard and swindler Ivolgin. Dostoevsky makes him live without resorting to very clear-cut features. No other figure could be at home in so many masks. This hovering reality seems to me to be one of the outstanding features of the composition. Dostoevsky has succeeded in drawing the hero with thought alone, and has brought him nearer to us with thoughts than any other figure of the novel. After little reflection this kind of reality will be recognized as the only one worth attempting in this instance.

Is the Idiot good? You could reply to that as Dostoev-

sky replied to the Russian atheists who did not want to
know anything of Christ. Show me a better man to put
in His stead!—He was as good as was consistent with
remaining beautiful and true; as good as possible. The
limitations of these ideas need not be discussed here. With
the Karamazovs Dostoevsky has spared us the trouble.

The development of *The Idiot* can be traced from
numerous sketches amongst the literary remains. It is
surprising that the idea matured slowly over a long and
thoughtful period before the poet put pen to paper. The
problem was as carefully weighed as the writing down was
rapid. The notes for *Crime and Punishment* prove how
amazingly long was the period of gestation. The question
alone whether the novel was to be written in the I-form
was very carefully pondered; all kinds of æsthetic considerations were taken into account. One would have
expected a person like Dostoevsky to solve these problems
spontaneously. There is one sketch of the entire second
chapter of *Crime and Punishment* in the first person. The
growth of the idea of *The Idiot* covers an immense field.
There is no trace of the actual story at the beginning.
Amongst the plans mentioned by Brodsky for works which
never materialized there are sketches for a novel, *Mignon*,
and for a short story, *Spring-love*, on which Dostoevsky
must have been already engaged in 1859 in Siberia.
Brodsky rightly surmises that the latter formed the basis of
The Insulted and Injured. But both sketches, particularly
that for *Mignon*, contain the outlines of the female characters
in *The Idiot.* There is actually a scene in which someone
gets boxed on the ears. The sketch for *Mignon* belongs to
the year 1860 and may have been suggested by the Mignon
of *Wilhelm Meister.* The whole novel is gradually built
round this figure. In the first sketch of *The Idiot* the
decisive part is played by the rivalry between the disgraced
Mignon and the unnamed " heroine." Mignon becomes
Nastasya and the " heroine " Aglaia.

Sakulin has given a detailed commentary on the many
sketches for *The Idiot* which came to light posthumously.

DOSTOEVSKY

Apart from the rivalry of the two female characters there is nothing very definite at the beginning, and the hero of the novel does not attain his cardinal significance till very much later. The first sketches denote rather a complicated novel of intrigue of the French school. The centre of gravity lies for quite a long time in the two women. Of the male characters the son of General Ivolgin, from whom later Ganya evolved, is originally the principal. The Idiot appears quite early as an epileptic, eccentric and *enfant terrible*, but only gradually comes into the lime-light. It is not till what Sakulin calls the eighth plan that the Christ-man is suggested. Previously he is, if anything, precisely the opposite. It is difficult to grasp how from this " strong, proud and passionate nature," from this man of " boundless selfishness " the pure figure of the Idiot could be evolved. In the first plan the Idiot is driven by passion to commit crime. His love for Mignon is purely erotic. " He rapes Mignon at some opportunity or other, sets the house on fire, burns off one of his fingers at his cousin's request. The Idiot's passion is great, his craving for love ardent, his pride immoderate. From pride he wants to gain power over himself, to learn to master himself, and he gets pleasure from humiliations. People who do not know him laugh at him. Those who do, begin to fear him." After Raskolnikov Dostoevsky clearly had great difficulty in breaking away from that type. He had in mind at that time a second Raskolnikov, more sensual and naïve than the murderer, unrestrained by brooding, who abandoned himself to his unbridled nature. " Infinite idealism coupled with infinite sensuality " (in another place " infinite egoism " is mentioned) are his distinguishing features. A greater contrast with the figure as it was ultimately drawn is inconceivable. Many memories helped to free him from this conception, amongst others an historical incident of the time of Catherine II, the abortive uprising in favour of Prince John VI who, whilst still a child, was imprisoned by the daughter of Peter the Great when she ascended the throne in 1741, and spent many years in a cell of the fortress Schlüsselburg.

ORIGIN

In 1754 an officer named Mirovitch tried to free the prince and wanted to set him on the throne. The attempt failed and the pretender was killed. In the notebooks there is a sketch which is a free adaptation of this incident entitled *The Emperor*. Its subject is the development of a prince who, detained " under the earth " in solitary confinement, is at once thrown back on his imagination to create a picture of the world. Mirovitch, the young officer who wants to proclaim the prince emperor, is the first human creature with whom he is in close touch, and this leads to a deep-rooted friendship. The officer approaches the prince with awe, seeks to prepare him for his calling, and draws his attention to his blue blood and to the difference in their social standing. The prisoner replies: " If you are not my equal I do not want to be emperor." The mentor tells his pupil his idea of greatness. A man who wants great things must not shrink before force, not even before death. He kills a cat to inure the youth to the sight of blood. The prince shudders. If human beings have to die for him he is not going to be emperor. An underworld existence without sin and evil. It is illumined by a girl, the daughter of the commandant. She becomes the prince's betrothed and, in his imagination, the future empress. Mirovitch, who introduced her to the prince, grows jealous. The prisoner comes to learn life's contradictions. " Finally," so it goes in the sketch, "rebellion. The commandant stabs the emperor who dies exalted and sad."

In the same notebook there is the cursory plan of a short story entitled *The Sacred Fool*. The " fool " surrounds himself with orphans and has a peculiar partiality for old clothes, is laughed at for it, is drawn into quarrels through no fault of his own, and, on account of his wife who deceives and finally deserts him, becomes involved in a duel in which he risks his life without attacking his opponent.

Both the " emperor," particularly that existence detached from the world, a condition essential to a pure being, as well as the childlike existence of the " sacred fool," contains elements of resistance against the world of ideas of *Crime and Punishment*. It was nearly eight years before *The Idiot* was evolved from this pleasant Schilleresque romanticism.

It is the simple process of evolution which pleases us. The work was not a bolt from the blue. It was the outcome of a thousand incidents, trivial in themselves, newspaper-episodes, anecdotes, all adapted when the spirit moved to piece them together. The web was long in the weaving. The idea is free of any arbitrary element. The hero gradually climbs from step to step. The lowest step was full of commonplaces and scarcely contained a particle of the Idiot himself, but the faintest inspiration sufficed to render the hero ultimately capable of " becoming conscious of the highest synthesis of life." There is no metaphysical accompaniment to the work. Dostoevsky spoke firmly to his demon. This scene must be lighter, is written in the margin, that one more humorous, the other more tense. More warmth! More life! More careful thought! More effect! More sphinx! Instructions of that kind are frequently found in the manuscripts. This poet was like a puppet - maker in the creation of his characters. The spiritual qualities of one actor were grafted on to another. One would never believe that the money-grubbing Ganya originally had traits of the prince. Characters were split up and, much less frequently, one was turned into two, and there is no trace of the seams. Nothing in the Idiot betrays an original relationship to Raskolnikov. Nevertheless, there were advantages in this process of metamorphosis which would have been absent in any spontaneous creation. The Idiot's Christ-like insight into the desire for power, sensuality and other egoistic shortcomings of the world he lives in, a supernatural yet never improbable insight, is doubtless connected with the history of this composition which is full of surprises. Moreover the development of *The Idiot*, like that of every significant artistic creation, was an ethical process.

CHAPTER XII

What followed *The Idiot ?* Originally Dostoevsky wanted
to tackle at once a novel about atheism, " a gigantic novel."
In a letter to his niece dated 6th February 1869 he writes
from Florence, " I am deep in the plan for a gigantic
novel . . . the theme is atheism. (It is not an indictment
of the convictions which are to-day gaining ground, but
something quite different, a real piece of writing.) I must
of course read up the subject. I have already sketched out
wonderfully two or three important characters, amongst
others a Catholic enthusiast, a priest (in the manner of
St François Xavier)." He refers again to the novel in a
letter of 8th March of the same year to the same person.
He expects the work will take two years. In both letters
he stresses the fact that he can write it only in Russia and
must therefore let it stand over till his return home.

The need for a novel of considerable compass is com-
prehensible. If Dostoevsky was capable of thinking of
another work after *The Idiot* it had to be something gigantic
in order to get over the inconclusive ending of *The Idiot*,
perhaps also in order to hide from it. According to the
notes amongst the literary remains the novel was to portray
a man who suddenly loses all belief in God and is driven
to theological speculation. After trying all kinds of religions
and sects, mixing and disputing with recluses and monks
of every sort, he finds at last " the Russian Christ and the
Russian God."

The plan contains rough sketches for the religious
argument of *The Brothers Karamazov*. Dostoevsky created
the Idiot without any religious veneer, and it is to this fact
that the Christ-man owes his charm. He must have felt
it a duty to make up for this fortunate omission with
some kind of theory, but doubtless was soon convinced

that an abstract *motif* of that sort would lead nowhere.

There is no significance in this fleeting aberration. But almost simultaneously the outlines of another plan emerged for which the epithet gigantic does not seem too strong. Dostoevsky wanted to write *The Life of a Great Sinner* which was to be his *Credo*. The sketches and studies for this novel occupy a great deal of space in his notebooks. Whole portions are in *scenario* or almost finished, and there are so many connecting links for essential situations that the Russian scholar Komarovitch was able to undertake the " reconstruction " of a considerable part of the story. The thought in this part is perfectly clear. It is the story of an unusual man who decides to become a hero and, after many false starts, achieves what Dostoevsky considered a heroic existence. The decision is reached at the most probable age. A boy of ten who has grown up in the most evil surroundings, amidst vice and filth, resolves to rise above the world about him. His surroundings imbue him with an infinite contempt. People thoughtlessly follow their impulses, one of which is the need for society, and thus lose their independence. You must not be mixed up with them. There is only one relationship which is not degrading, that of master and servant. He wants to be master. Every means of power is to be acquired. A lame girl lives in the house. She loves him. He confesses to her his dream of becoming a king. Our thoughts turn to the dreamlike early life of the Idiot. The girl becomes the little king's first subject. He tests his power on her, torments her, commands her. The lame Katya prays to God. What is God? The question is asked for the first time. The boy's thoughts of God are like the feeling he has for everything that is not of his dream-world; the unknown disgusts him and he considers the girl's belief in the unknown merely rebellion. " I am God," he says impressively to Katya, and compels her to bow down to him. " If you follow me in everything I will love you."

The boy grows up, goes to school and suffers severely

for his illegitimate birth and his poverty; he suffers much humiliation. (A piece of undisguised autobiography.) The young man is lonely and abandons himself still more to his idea of power. A money-lender has already taught the boy the value of money. He resolves to accumulate wealth. With money you can be lord of the world. He denies himself everything, practises self-castigation, trains his body to endure pain, deliberately burns himself, and overcomes his innate fear. He does not fail to notice the narrowness of his ideal, for he has read the poets, loves them and knows of a heroism beyond all material possessions. He tries to scorn this knowledge; he scorns everything that stands in his path and finally becomes a criminal. Together with a " robber " named Kulikov he commits a murder. It is not discovered. On the contrary the young man is held in higher esteem; contrary to expectation he passes an examination brilliantly and leaves school with honour. As a student he and a former school-friend, Lambert, indulge in all sorts of dissipation. At the same time there is an episode with his father which could lead to a human relationship and to self-realization. Again the lure of morality is forcibly overcome by his hunger for power. The hero sinks lower and lower and finally perpetrates a fresh crime with the school-friend, the profanation and robbery of a sacred picture. That is how the first of the five big divisions of the novel was to end. In the second part the young criminal goes into a monastery and meets Tikhon Sadonsky, the future Starets Zossima of *The Brothers Karamazov*. The holy man gradually prevails over him, not by dint of pious sermons but by virtue of his naïve joy of living. All living things are good, violence is worthless. " It is base to live as a monk, a man must have children." So he must also have sin and crime. He torments himself enough with his sins and crimes. Torment is good for it leads to rehabilitation; therefore crime is good too. It can drive a man to humility.

The hero leaves the monastery with this idea of humility. From pride he becomes gentle and forbearing towards others, but beneath these new qualities is still hidden the old contempt for people, and he is more than ever swayed by the desire for power. Dostoevsky clearly had in mind giving his hero every opportunity for self-idolization before he made his last confession and attained God.

The work was to have portrayed a man's life from the cradle to the grave. Dostoevsky wanted incidentally to explain and set out in detail his own attitude towards the world and towards God, particularly his ideas on individualism. All his main works are nothing more or less than experimental portrayals of the development of his own *weltanschauung*. The normal subject of every novel, the portrayal of a continuous existence over an extended period, was new to Dostoevsky and compelled him to change his technique. On this occasion he did not resort to the novel-drama form, his own invention, which in previous works he had brought to an astonishing pitch of perfection. This book demanded epic breadth. Dostoevsky has expressed himself to himself on that point with characteristic bluntness. He writes in his notebook: " There is practically no use here for scenes full of effect and theatrical passages."

That is the reason, or at least one of the reasons, why the novel remained unwritten. The contemplative form did not suit him. We have reason to be pleased at that. Komarovitch differs and concludes that it denoted a failing in his development. In riveting his attention on Dostoevsky's drafts the idealogue failed to notice the works themselves. Dostoevsky's last word lies in *The Brothers Karamazov*. Confessions of faith can always be formulated. What matters in a work of art is practical application whereby we can live through the confession. " The unemotional relevancy " to which Dostoevsky, according to his own words, felt himself driven, would have put his most essential gifts out of action and would never have led to a work of the rank of *The Idiot* or *Crime and Punishment*, but rather to a work of memoirs such as *The House of the Dead*, a medley which, for all its qualities, would not have been vital to him at this juncture. It was not undeveloped ethical sense, as Komarovitch thinks, but a highly developed sense of economizing his energies which moved him not to write this book.

The sinner-novel was the conception on which Doŝtoev-sky founded all his later works and on which he had founded those of the main works already written. Moreover, the abandoning of his plan may have been due to the faĉt that large portions of the contemplated biography would have been a diluted repetition of *Crime and Punishment*. In the notes for *Crime and Punishment* the hero is described in precisely those words which were to charaĉterize the great sinner: "Pride, contempt for human beings, hunger for power."

> .   .   .   .   .   .

Doŝtoevsky felt a powerful urge to prove in some unambiguous way, so-to-speak in a ŝtruggle between man and man, his Chriŝtianity which had led to the legend in *The Idiot*. This exhauŝtive work was not to be written in Dresden. In order to fulfil the promise held out by *The Idiot* Doŝtoevsky had to breathe Russian air, to feel the pulse of the people, to be amongŝt those who shared his thoughts, those who were preparing to raise their voices in the same cause: the issue between individualism and universalism (45). But circumŝtances at home were ŝtill so difficult that to return was impossible, and he poŝtponed this large work and busied himself with small fry. The ŝtories of *The Eternal Husband* and *The Possessed* muŝt be considered in this category. He perceived in *The Eternal Husband* a cheap *genre*-piĉture of the *Gambler* type and found it, as he wrote to his niece, "disguŝting to be occupying oneself with such things" (46). Really what could be pleasing after *The Idiot*? Nevertheless of its kind the ŝtory is a maŝterpiece.

This time, more than ever, there were considerable possibilities of tragedy in the comedy, which is very far from being farcical.

Since Molière there is nothing novel in this situation.

DOSTOEVSKY

A *cocu* can never be cuckolded enough, although the action itself has not much to do with the truth, or otherwise, of this proposition. Velchaninov, a one-time dandy, now retired, once adored by women and feared by men, is on the point of becoming a hypochondriac. He is a prey to brooding; if only he had a better memory he would be admirably fitted to write melancholy memoirs. The gentleman with the crape appears. He turns up everywhere. Who is this man? He must have seen him before, has run up against him somewhere or other. Where was it? Who can remember every unpleasant person he has met? It was certainly unpleasant. For lack of a better occupation the weary dandy racks his memory for the man's name, although it is a matter of sheer indifference to him, and he thereby verges on a mental breakdown. He keeps on meeting the man. By degrees it turns out that the man with the crape is not so indifferent as appears, and that their frequent encounters are not accidental. Dostoevsky shows marked talent in gradually drawing them together, whilst the dandy's resistances go on growing. The man with the crape becomes a nightmare, a disease, and finally they are sitting opposite one another in Velchaninov's room, at three in the morning, of course. Now the fun really begins. They recognize one another. Nine years ago in a provincial town the dandy was on intimate terms with Pavel Pavlovitch, the man with the crape, and on still more intimate terms with the dolt's wife, and the crape round his hat is connected with his deceased wife.

What does the fellow want of me? Velchaninov asks himself.

Madame Bovary is dead, God bless her. What has the crape to do with him?

Only friendship! says Pavel Pavlovitch with sickly emotion; friendship and gratitude, for surely Velchaninov was at that time a friend of the family, and even if they had heard nothing from him after his departure the memory of him remained deeply impressed, more deeply impressed than the memory of Mr Bagontov, his successor, an equally intimate friend of the family. He also lives in Petersburg now, and the man with the crape has hunted him up for the sake of friendship and gratitude; sad to relate, without success, for Bagontov is ill in bed. But Velchaninov means more to the man with the crape because he was, so to speak, the first-born friend of the family. Velchaninov does not seem to be too well either, has fever. Liver-trouble? Oh, then you must look after yourself.

Velchaninov finds his visitor more communicative than before. He has some quite lively conversations with him. Apart from that he seems to have become addicted to drink.

Next morning the dandy has already gone to look for the man with the crape. In the meantime all kinds of ideas have occurred to him. His *liaison* with the deceased was by no means an unimportant episode in his career and, at the time, nine years ago, was a comparatively strong attachment. He had to make way for Bagontov. Her excuse was that she was *enceinte* and it was therefore imperative for him to clear off at once to avoid scandal. That was very unpleasant at the time. She died of consumption, dear me! A charming woman, in her own way, rather whimsical and capricious. Dostoevsky may have been thinking of his first wife.

Velchaninov discovers the man with the crape in his hotel in the act of thrashing a little girl of about eight. On the table there is a half-empty bottle of champagne. The girl is taken into an adjoining room and the visitor is greeted with warmth. Yes, he must admit, murmurs the man with the crape, since that event he does have a glassful occasionally, but only from grief. Yes, yesterday too, in fact every day, but only from grief. The little girl is Lisa, the daughter of the deceased, our daughter. Yes, the Lord blessed the deceased just eight or nine months after the departure of our trusted friend.

Velchaninov cannot believe his ears. Such a thing has never happened to him before. The child must come in at once. A fascinating child, the image of her mother, but more tender, of an extraordinary tenderness. The same blue eyes, only more sparkling. You can hardly refrain from taking the little thing in your arms. And this drunkard is neglecting the little creature, shamefully, that is quite evident. He beats the poor child. Can one stand by and allow such a thing? When he goes out he simply locks her in, the tender creature, and leaves her there for days together. The angel loves him into the bargain, and is frightened of the dandy, that is positive. She must not stay in this morass, not a day longer, not an hour.

With some difficulty the man with the crape is persuaded and the child's incomprehensible opposition is overcome. Lisa is taken to friends of Velchaninov in a suburb. She will be all right there. They do everything for her, but cannot still her yearning for her father, for he never comes to the house. The dandy is absorbed by his anxiety for Lisa. He goes to see her every day, thinks of nothing else. Lisa is not happy amongst these kind people. She felt better with the father who thrashed her, and finally she falls ill with pining. Pavel Pavlovitch does not come near, though Velchaninov does his utmost to make him. The wretched man is in a perpetual state of drunkenness. He promises whatever is asked, is always infernally polite, but boozing renders him quite incapable.

Lisa grows worse. The dandy storms with anxiety and rage, but it does not help. Pavel Pavlovitch respectfully accepts all the curses hurled at him and goes on drinking. The dandy aches to squash him like a fly. He could do it, would have the strength to, is physically his superior, and would have no scruples about it. Instead of that he sees himself forced to creep into the secret recesses of his accursed cuckold-soul. At times the man with the crape gets the upper hand. Actually he has long had the upper hand, but behaves as if he did not notice it and contents himself with a cunning grin. At times, half accidentally, he assumes a peremptory tone and becomes a different person. It only lasts a few seconds; that too can be attributed to his drunkenness. At such moments the dandy will do anything the other man demands, even, when asked, kisses his lips which reek of alcohol.

All in vain. Lisa dies. Velchaninov is heart-broken. It is the first time in his life that disaster has crossed his path. The drunkard is with difficulty persuaded to fetch the necessary papers. Lisa could not even be buried without going to him. The cuckold's revenge is complete.

The behaviour of the man with the crape is described with diabolical precision. There is no word about the drunkard's suppressed frenzy. Even such dolts can show themselves " quite sphinx-like " and become terrible in their impenetrable futility. Classical retribution with modern mechanism.

The husband's revenge is followed by the lover's revenge. A few weeks later the parties meet again. The man with the crape is reformed, has given up drinking and is wearing a brand-new suit. So you see the whole drinking business was only a means to an end. He proudly informs the dandy of his betrothal. Yes, he is going to marry again. Why not? *Après la pluie le beau temps.*

This new love has cleansed the feelings of the man with the crape. He feels towards the former friend of the family just as he felt nine years ago, when the elegant young man introduced an interesting note into the house, talks to him with the confident ease due to a widely travelled man of the world. And next day the man with the crape blushingly expresses a wish that his friend accompany him, just once, preferably this very day, to the house of the councillor with the eight daughters. As a favour!

Velchaninov cannot believe his ears. That is going a bit too far! Pavel Pavlovitch implores him. He is actuated partly by friendship, by the warm heart of the *cocu* which wants every one to share in its good fortune, partly by the superstitious fancy that the dandy will make a good impression. They will see what fine friends he has, and that will be very helpful.

Dostoevsky did not trouble to explain this improbable

reaction. The suddenness of this *volte-face* characterizes, not the thoughtlessness of the writer, but the primitive psychology of the eternal husband.

Finally the dandy consents and Pavel Pavlovitch anxiously supervises his toilet. No mother dressing her young daughter for a ball could be more attentive. They go to the country-house. The dandy's old sporting spirit is roused in the company of young people. In the twinkling of an eye he is once again cock of the walk and the crape is hanging at half-mast. The young girl whom Pavel Pavlovitch has hunted out, the youngest of the eight daughters, still a mere flapper, has not in her wildest dreams given a thought to the man with the crape, but has long been betrothed to an impudent youth *à la* Kolya Ivolgin. If it were not for that, Velchaninov might have had a chance. Pavel Pavlovitch is horrified at what he has started. A true *cocu* he fails to recognize the new and most threatening foe, but overrates the old one and insists on leaving at once together with Velchaninov. The dandy does not mind, for he really does not attach any importance to this fooling about with silly young girls and, moreover, does not feel well; a touch of the old liver trouble. But Pavel Pavlovitch is perspiring with anxiety; he positively must have a talk with his mortal enemy and accompanies him home. The dandy is feverish and in no mood for a protracted discourse. He wants to lie down, but the man with the crape insists on having his say. His prattle is interrupted by the entry of the youth who is secretly betrothed to the councillor's young daughter. With youthful *verve* he proceeds to expound the rights of humanity and demands the unwelcome suitor's withdrawal. Thereupon he takes formal leave. This scene is a witty contribution to the chapter of youth. It enables the eternal husband to recognize the dandy's relative innocence. Velchaninov had already been authorized to give him a rebuff, but wanted to spare him that. Great excitement about it. Pavel Pavlovitch always considered Velchaninov an ideal man; a man of the world who fascinates and lets himself be fascinated. Unfortunately he is getting a bit old now and suffers with his liver.

That is only too true. At times this liver trouble leads to extremely painful attacks which last for hours and give him the devil. Luckily Pavel Pavlovitch knows an excellent remedy. Hot plates on the pit of the stomach work wonders. I will show you! Immense attention is devoted to the man of the world; a plate-warming business is fixed up in the kitchen, they bustle about, there is a great to-do. After a short time the attack is really stopped. Before going to sleep Velchaninov thanks the philanthropist and asks him to stay the night with him. He cannot help feeling moved. Pavel Pavlovitch is far better than he. He is almost brought to confess by the cessation of the gastric pains.

Excellent! observes the plate-warmer and puts out the light.

Velchaninov's sleep is disturbed. He has confused dreams, gets up in the middle of the night, bumps in the darkness against Pavel Pavlovitch and puts his hand on a razor. There is a struggle and the man with the crape is overpowered. Next morning he is dismissed unceremoniously. The parties are quits. The story ought to end at this point.

The man with the crape leaves Petersburg without a bride. Two years later on a journey the dandy meets him at a railway-buffet, again with a woman, married. The temperamental lady promptly invites him to come and stay with them. Velchaninov sets the husband's mind at ease.—One would rather do without this episode in the form of an epilogue, a journalistic trimming.

In the analysis of the frustrated hero of the razor ideas are touched upon which reappear in connexion with the murder of old Karamazov. Otherwise the story reveals little, if anything, of Dostoevsky's thought at that time, and that is the only reproach which can be levelled at it. It has no chronological place.

.   .   .   .   .   .

In *The Possessed*, on the other hand, ideas with which

Dostoevsky's mind was occupied at the time are all tne more strikingly expressed. Dostoevsky states that the work involved far greater effort than *The Idiot*. He worked at least two years at it (47). When he had already finished a large portion he rearranged it and actually changed the principal character. For a long time he set great hopes on the novel and recognized its failing too late. It was to have been in a way supplementary to *The Idiot*. He wanted to retain the atmosphere, but could not formulate the great project to which Russia was essential, and therefore contented himself with a dialectical sequel. This attempt has no more to do with Myshkin's atmosphere than have the last words of the epilogue to *The Idiot*, in which the *babouchka*, on the occasion of a visit to the prince's asylum, gives vent to her anger with foreign countries. What is now presented is the diametric opposite, the negative reverse of *The Idiot*: the underworld. It is everything which is not Christ-man and therefore devil. Whilst the Christ-man was portrayed from the inside, the devils are treated from the outside. In spite of the complexity of the design nothing is more external than the diction of *The Possessed*. The positiveness of Dostoevsky's *weltanschauung* can be gauged by his inability to handle this negative theme.

The defect is due to his undisguised intention of making short work of the nihilists, of branding them either as ridiculous or as criminals. Dostoevsky repeatedly expresses that without compunction. "I lay great store by the work; I mean not its artistic but its tendentious side. I want to express certain thoughts, even if doing so renders it an artistic failure . . . thoughts, long stored in my head and in my heart, urge me to this. Even if it becomes nothing but a pamphlet, at least I shall express once all I have to say" (48). He hoped to finish the work soon and then to set about the "novel" with enjoyment, that is he differentiated quite definitely between *The Possessed* and literature. Madame Dostoevsky recounts the facts which were taken from real life, from actual events, and speaks of the great difficulties of the work. "A propaganda-novel," she adds, " was obviously incompatible with his creative spirit "—she might have said incompatible with the spirit of all creative literature, a fact which is self-evident; but not incompatible with his creative will. For, as we know, his will was not subject to any æsthetic dogma but concerned itself rather with destinies and ideas the representation of which might promote Russia's spiritual welfare. Subconsciously utilitarian factors played no part, but it seems that his creative impulse had constantly to be supplemented by the introduction of ideas. In the course of his development there was constant adjustment between emotional and intellectual forces, for example insignificant essays written at the same time as *The Brothers Karamazov*.

In writing *The Possessed* he forced himself to a duty. It was a form of purification on a higher plane than he had attempted in *The Insulted and Injured*. He turned a deaf ear to the claims of literature which he had satisfied in *Crime and Punishment* and *The Idiot*. A special motive drove him to a thoroughly definite attitude. What he had learnt at first hand about the activities of revolutionaries in Russia filled him with alarm and enhanced his sense of responsibility (49). He always believed that as an immature youth he himself had added fuel to the flame, and he felt he had not expiated this crime, despite all he had suffered for it. The seed of Petrachevsky and his associates had taken root. The upheaval with which they had toyed like children loomed nearer, seemed to have made gigantic strides since his journey. He did not overrate it by any means. If Karl Nötzel is right, Netchaev, the murderer of the student Ivanov, can be deemed the spiritual creator of bolshevism (50). Netchaev became Verhovensky, Ivanov became Shatov. In the studies for *The Possessed* Verhovensky is usually called Netchaev.

Again the prophet revealed the future. In *The Idiot* could be felt the vague shadows of forthcoming events. Details of the Russian revolution and scenes are depicted here which were to be played half a century later almost word for word as he has written them. Unless this visionary

was nothing but a mere spiritualistic medium, he must
have felt too anxious to be dabbling in æsthetic pastimes,
and his cry of horror alone sufficed him as a note of
warning. The new *katorga* which now held him enchained
increased his vision and enhanced his fears. Added to
this was the turmoil of the French Commune, and the
burning of Paris associated itself with the incendiarism of
Petersburg nihilists. Europe stood in flames before him.
Later in *A Raw Youth* he generalized this indelible impression.

Russians of to-day who contend that he was an enemy
of progress point particularly to the " pamphlet." They
can as little be blamed for their wrath as for his fear.
He foresaw the counter-attacks, but did not date them so
late. In so far as they were directed against the author of
The Possessed they were justified, because in this work he
deliberately renounced the poet's duty to perceive great
rather than small truths and not to overlook eternal for
the sake of ephemeral values—duties which Dostoevsky's
masterpieces fulfil ideally. The parable of the Lisbon
earthquake can be interpreted in various ways. Dostoevsky
saw only one interpretation. To the rest he was blind and
wanted to remain blind. However scorched he may have
been by the fire of the incendiaries he could never have
failed to notice that this was only part of a story, even if,
in founding *The Possessed* on it, he was actuated by noble
motives. Moreover the demoniacal element which the
title foreshadows could least of all be depicted with such a
limited outlook.

Dostoevsky showed a great deal, and even more can be
read into him, as Hans Prager has demonstrated in his
deeply thought-out work (51), but Dostoevsky failed to
raise what he showed to the level of a symbol. The
mechanism of the revolutionary apparatus, functioning far
from its centre in a provincial town, becomes strangely
vivid; here every act of despotism is bound to seem like
the convulsing of a headless trunk. As Nötzel says, the
idea of the revolutionaries is a moral aim beyond morality.

PAGE OF MS. OF *THE POSSESSED*

[face p. 220

STRUCTURE

Liberation from all moral codes becomes a moral requirement. This is the inalienable shadow, not the entire
subject of the work, and is supposed to be the main theme.
Is it intellectually exhausted? From their very symptoms
can be inferred how appallingly stupid are these revolutionaries and how untenable their ideas. One feels, and it has
been corroborated by scholars, that Dostoevsky was thinking
rather of his youthful participation in these things, of the
immature ideas of the Petrachevsky circle in the forties,
than of the situation about 1870. A literary work would
not have been concerned with this. The wider the net,
the more numerous the flaws. The subject-matter and its
treatment do not develop. The senselessness of these
murders and acts of incendiarism is scarcely above the level
of the crimes of some robber-band, particularly when it
is observed that Dostoevsky shows understanding of the
nihilist movement, both intellectually and intuitively. There
is something missing between his clear conception and the
action of the novel. The robber-band spoils it as a historical
document. In many other works Dostoevsky has urged
us not to consider murder as an isolated deed and not to
suppress the preamble and the sequel, or the moral dictum
that all are guilty for all. Every one except Dostoevsky
would have to be excused the sequel—it is too gloomy.
No realist, however, with the objectivity of a Balzac, to
whom Dostoevsky is far superior in hundreds of instances,
could suppress the preamble because he would thereby
jeopardize his own development; an æsthetic consideration,
it is true, about which the fanatic has no scruples.

At the same time there is no lack of profound attempts
at depicting the spiritual make-up of the evil-doers. The
letter to Katkov quoted in the notes is of assistance.
Dostoevsky explains the deed of the murderer Netchaev as
" accessory in the sphere of activity of another personality "
for which he invents Stavrogin. Netchaev-Verhovensky is
for him " half-humorous," so dependent does the fellow
seem on other people's ideas which he is incapable of
thinking out for himself, but which he executes with

narrow consistency. Is there a humorous vein in Verhovensky which would be a relief, were it the result, not of
the tendency of the pan-phlet, but of his dependence on
other people's opinions? It is at most the outcome of our
own reflections and not of the author's portrayal. There is
a great deal of chatter, ideas stream forth, and behind it all
is constantly the great and eternal question: "Can, must,
may one believe in God or not?" The manner in which it
is propounded by Shatov and Kirilov is unparalleled in its
grandeur. But big and little questions are one thing and
human beings another. Elsewhere Dostoevsky has always
avoided the error of separating thought and action; that
is one of the attributes of his greatness. Here he has
committed the error. Undoubtedly the reader can bridge
the gulf, but no author has a right to demand this; it
leads to over-emphasis, a thing which Dostoevsky quite
rightly loathed like the plague. The emotional factor ceases
to play any part.

The vast plans in the literary remains, the numerous
dialogues and stage-directions, afford ample material for
studying the psychology both of the poet and of his
characters. The choice he made from his sketches
adequately illustrates his indecision. On the other hand
his wisdom is obvious when plan and final composition
are compared. He utilized only the essential, compressed
unsparingly and sharpened the points till they cut like
diamonds. On this occasion certain brilliant passages in
the sketches have been cast aside without any attempt at
replacing them. Brodsky has pointed out quite credibly
that *The Possessed* cannot be understood without the
passages which Dostoevsky suppressed. Brodsky's careful
compilation is interesting, but naturally no supplementary
synthesis can bridge the gap in the work itself.

Characteristically Dostoevsky sought to conceal this
defect. He failed in his portrayal of the revolutionaries'
motives. On the other hand at the end of the novel he
introduced a piece of symbolism which is singularly effective.
Stepan Trofimovitch is glorified by the prophetic vision

which had already illumined the Idiot: fanatical revolutionaries like the Russians are possessed of the devil and must vent their passion till the last so that the rest of mankind may regain its health. Stepan Trofimovitch acquires this doctrine from a reading of the Apocalypse; a reactionary doctrine which irritates the bolshevists.

Throughout the novel there are passages and incidents selected from different periods and different places (52). The beginning and end are devoted to the " estimable " Stepan Trofimovitch, the senile and soft-hearted poet without poem, professor without chair. He imagines he has once played a part and that the stress of the times has driven him into this provincial hole. Actually, of course, it is the result of his own inadequacy and inhibitions. Moreover, he is a free-thinker, in moderation and good taste, and has learnt in Paris to touch the revolutionary element with gloved hands; a type of Gallicized Russian with whom Russian novels of the period have made us familiar; but he has his peculiarities. He is a timorous adorer of his benefactress, the elegant and wealthy Varvara Petrovna, a *babouchka* of some depth, who loves him, looks after him and maltreats him as best she can; but there seems to be something lacking in his life and he locks away his affection in his chaste heart. He would be a fine character for a short story around which to weave some idyll, a light companion picture to *The Friend of the Family*, but he is out of place in a novel about devils. Originally he was the hero of the novel, a hero without heroism, but in the course of revision he has had to relinquish more and more of his importance. The contrast between this worthy representative of the Schilleresque and his rank revolutionary of a son—why is this monster his son?—serves no useful purpose; it is like a pastel stuck into the middle of an oil painting. Strachov drew attention to this crude error and Dostoevsky admitted it (53). In a letter to Maikov he calls Stepan Trofimovitch " a figure of secondary importance " with whom the novel is not concerned, but that, nevertheless, his history is so closely bound up with the main events that he is bound to be the "corner-stone of the whole." This is a flagrant contradiction. Dostoevsky suggests that his end may be important. Stepan does in fact acquire a peculiar colour in his last wanderings. Varvara Petrovna, the queen of his heart, has broken with him. His son, the loathsome Verhovensky, has disgraced him and committed monstrous crimes. The society in which the *dilettante* believed, which he with his Western culture wanted to raise and, after his son had lit a torch, to save at all costs is destroyed. Everything he had set his heart on lies shattered. Thereupon this great child with the gloved hand wanders off into the blue. Our thoughts turn to Foma Fomitch's escapade in *The Friend of the Family*, but this time there is all the seriousness of a child in it. With forty roubles in his pocket, patent leather on his feet, and in a state of high fever he goes off into the wide world to find the blue flower.[1] Of course he finds it. The first thing he does is to run up against a cart to which a peculiarly interesting cow is tied. Charming people are sitting in the cart, obliging but a little inquisitive—" enfin le peuple." At the first stop he finds a lady with books, a Bible-seller, *charmante dame*. She promptly becomes a friend. He will never leave her. He becomes worse and the compassionate lady is obliged to remain with him and look after him. Touching Russia! They fix themselves up in a village inn and talk of the Bible, a most interesting book which in spite of Renan has a certain value, and he comes to his life-history in the middle of which stands his love for Varvara Petrovna, the queen of his heart. Naturally, it might have been anyone, for example a warm-hearted book-lover like her. He is promptly head over heels in love. The Bible-lady must read the Bible to him, and now comes the flood of light. First of all the story of the swine who were possessed of devils, " thereupon went mad," hurled themselves into the sea and ridded the world of their existence. This quotation from the Gospel according

[1] To seek " the blue flower " vaguely signifies the longings and ideals of the German Romantic school.—Tr.

to St. Luke serves as a motto at the beginning of the novel. And then they come to the no less appropriate passage in the Gospel of St. John about the rejection of the lukewarm and the praise of the hot and the cold: a passage which might stand as a motto for the whole of Dostoevsky's Russia.

Strange how confidently Dostoevsky relied on the effect of this passage. It was of the whole essence of him. His confidence in the novel, which he had begun with enthusiasm, dwindled more and more, and finally the whole work went against the grain; but the scene between Stepan Trofimovitch and the Bible-woman was absolutely positive to him. " I will guarantee none of the rest," he writes to a friend, " but this passage I will positively go bail for " (54). One can scarcely think of anything less pretentious. Stepan entirely omits to explain the Bible passages. " Vous comprendrez après," he stammers feverishly, " it excites me too much now . . . nous comprendrons ensemble." Dostoevsky simply relied on the effect of the Gospel. His own part in it had nothing to do with the matter.

Whilst Stepan is sinking rapidly, the queen of his heart appears on the scene like a thundercloud and with *babouchka*-like bluntness leads the old idiot into the Elysian fields.

The tenderness of this story stands in bold relief against the rugged background of *The Possessed*. That is the principal failing. The difference in the two styles is physically painful. Though this story is the best thing in it, the novel would actually gain by its omission. Moreover, Dostoevsky had originally set the Bible-reading in the well-known scene (which was suppressed) between Stavrogin and the holy Tikhon, to whom Stavrogin goes to make his confession. Possibly the Bible passages would not have been so effective in the original form, but they would certainly have helped to make Stavrogin more real and to bring him closer to us.

The events outlined in the sketches surpass in crudity all the *katorga*-stories and at times attain a fantastic grandeur.

DOSTOEVSKY

The scene between Verhovensky and Kirilov, the suicide by conviction who is to cover up the murder of Shatov, is crushing in its effect. The baldness of this spiritual frenzy far excels the most gloomy of Shakespeare's situations. The dehumanizing of Verhovensky proceeds like the mechanism of an adding-machine. " Will he shoot himself or not? " he calculates as he stands by Kirilov. If this Verhovensky were shown the lever of a machine to wipe out the world, he would operate it as a matter of course, on principle, because there is no sense in reflection. Then he would settle down hungrily to his dinner and drop four pieces of sugar into his tea, neither more nor less.

The drawing of Kirilov, this maniac of a theophobe whose suicide is a protest against God's world, is distinctly clever, as is also that of the noble Shatov who perceives the folly of the conspirators' actions, breaks away from them, and is accordingly murdered. The scenes between Shatov and his wife, who has returned home with her child by another man, are amongst Dostoevsky's supreme passages. There are many brilliant touches; it is only the murderers who do not shine. Verhovensky seems too artificial. Of course he is conceivable; he may represent the robot of a modern revolution. He could in certain circumstances be devilishly interesting, even estimable; but it is just these circumstances which ought to be shown and are lacking. The stage of this provincial town is too narrow for the roar of these wild beasts. The acoustics fail or some proportion is wrong. The most disturbing feature is the absence of a central point, or rather the vagueness of the central point contemplated in Stavrogin. The Possessed destroy not only the town but even the construction of the novel. Verhovensky is really the principal actor, but only his utter nihilism, completely dissociated from ideology, is in keeping with the atmosphere. According to the altered plan Stavrogin was to have been the hero. He is the paradoxical aristocrat of nihilism, son of a magnate, son of Stephan's beloved queen, secret husband of a poor idiot (the " lame girl " out of *The Life of a Great Sinner*), terror and idol of the town and,

PAGE OF MS. OF *THE POSSESSED*

[*face* p. *226*

in particular, of Lisaveta Nikolaevna, the most beautiful
and elegant girl in the province. This hero is a fiasco.
Nowhere but in a Russian provincial town is demonry
possible at so little cost: a good name, refined speech,
maltreatment of the plebs, factors which are normally
conditions precedent to a successful *bourgeois* career. The
atmosphere around Stavrogin teems with ethical and social
problems, but they are a part of Dostoevsky, and not of the
essence of his hero! When ultimately these problems
absorb him, there is such confusion of idea that the effect
is lost. Stavrogin secretly marries the idiot, apparently in
order to humiliate himself and to expiate erotic crimes,
perhaps also from pity. Dostoevsky's division of ideas
misled him into endowing the idiot with prophetic powers
whereby -the picture becomes unnecessarily complicated.
What is it that Stavrogin does? Strange act of self-humilia-
tion, to confine himself to a marriage ceremony behind the
scenes! Strange pity not to bother in the least about his
wife! It will be said that that is just the demoniacal element.
Then again the external feature in Stavrogin, his facial
display, is much more forcefully depicted than his action.
He publicly disowns his wife, thus humiliating her still
more, and his well-twisted words on this occasion verge on
infamy which—so it almost seems—the author overlooks.
When on another occasion he acknowledges his wife, he
seems once again only to be pandering to a whim with the
object of creating an impression on his listeners. He
pockets the blow from Shatov, he, the pugnacious Stavrogin
who has often killed an opponent and is probably foolhardy
enough to pick a quarrel with a dozen bears at once.
Shatov calmly walks up to him and strikes him in the face.
For a moment they are expecting Stavrogin to crush him
into powder. They are on tenterhooks. The reader has
to hold his breath. But the expected does not happen.
Stavrogin checks himself and puts his hands behind his
back. The strain of it is so immense that the " light of
his eyes fades."

Stavrogin commits the same deeds as the Idiot for

diametrically opposite reasons. Of the main motives which actuate him only love of sensation and vanity are at all clear. It seems as if Dostoevsky had had in mind a caricature of Prince Myshkin as a piece of self-mockery. Bits of Schiller have contributed to the caricature. The shocker element has a peculiarly unpleasant effect in the catastrophic atmosphere of the second part. The scene between Lisa and Stavrogin at Skvoroshniki on the morning after the fire is thin.

Dostoevsky unquestionably repudiated the hero. The suicide in itself says enough. Stavrogin is as nonchalant with the silk thread as in his other deeds. Nevertheless he was to be a tragic figure. Dostoevsky, according to his own words, pictured him as the typical Russian, endowed with considerable powers which he does not know how to turn to account. Only when such men are dominated by a great idea are their powers used to any purpose. Without that idea they become criminals.

To rescue himself from this negative attitude the hero would have had to seek the idea, as once Raskolnikov had done. Our sympathy might have been roused at his fruitless effort. Stavrogin does not seek and it is not certain whether he has ever sought. But even if this were so, the past, of which we are ignorant, would not suffice for the tragedy of the present. It is doubtful whether there is any consistency in Stavrogin. This *dilettante* is not a Russian, he has well-known Western characteristics. What is Russian in him is only an aimless exaggeration. The objects of the exaggeration are not revealed. Enthusiastic admirers have mentioned Hamlet. Certainly a Hamlet could be read into Stavrogin's mask, but his mask is not the only thing. Life and literature teem with Hamlet-masks which have nothing of Shakespeare about them.

No figure more urgently needs the working-out which is contained both in the sketches and in the suppressed chapters; no figure has been so cruelly cut about. The picture lacks more than the famous confession which, suppressed at the instigation of the editorial staff of the

THE HERO

Russian Messenger, and then voluntarily left out of the book-edition, has only led to misapprehension in our times. A close study of the notebooks will give a very clear idea of the hero's tragedy which the poet had in mind; but that is all. Even were the stirring confession and the extraordinarily profound conversations with Shatov to have been inserted in the final edition they would not have made the figure sufficiently real. Dostoevsky knew why he cut. In the above-mentioned letter to Katkov he intended to " portray this character by means not of discussions but of scenes and actions." In order to keep his promise he suppressed what would have constituted explanation but not action. He may even have prescribed the " sphinx-like " for Stavrogin, just as he had done previously for Myshkin. But we see here only a suspicious significance in the idea.

Dostoevsky's novel-drama form obviously spoilt the hero as well as the entire novel. He saw things on a stage rather than on paper. Like Ibsen in *Hedda Gabler*, he became irritating reading, though in certain circumstances admirable on the stage. We can assume that Dostoevsky had in his head some other idea of Stavrogin than he actually put on paper; but that is no consolation.

The very tendentiousness of the novel prevented its realization. He was not enough of an automaton for a pamphlet which he wanted to write hurriedly straight from his heart " even if it is an artistic failure." The poet in him unintentionally saved him from such a blasphemy. But whilst the patriot battled with his fears, revolts and warnings, the creator had long overcome the obstacle and was already dreaming of a new work which should eschew all ideas of propaganda. This new work spoiled *The Possessed*. The more intensely he thought of a loftier Stavrogin, the Ivan Karamazov, and of a loftier Tikhon and of all the other figures of the new work still enshrouded in half-light, the more incapable he became of raising the pamphlet to the level of a work of art. It cannot be said that the Karamazovs sprang from *The Possessed*, for the first idea of them can be traced further back, and their actions are suggested by a later work. They have nothing to do with the nihilism of *The Possessed*. Only the least successful of the principal figures reappears in the new work. Stavrogin and his band were a dangerous poison and Dostoevsky was well rid of them. We have reason not to regret the failure of the pamphleteer.

CHAPTER XIII

In July 1871 Doſtoevsky returned to Petersburg with his wife and child, and firſt of all finished *The Possessed*. He was fully occupied with it till well into the year 1872. He wrote nothing in the next few years. *A Raw Youth* did not begin to appear in the *Fatherland Annals* till 1875. From the extensive notes for the novel it may be assumed that he began not, as is generally supposed, in 1874 but earlier, and that he devoted two years or more to it. It is in any case difficult to determine the actual beginning of a work from its connexions with other writings. Biographers may be right in assuming that there was a pause in Doſtoevsky's literary production after his return home, but this can scarcely be reconciled with the journalism on which he became actively engaged when in 1872 he joined the ſtaff of the *Grajdanin* ; this subsequently led to the firſt *Journal of an Author*. Doſtoevsky doubtless needed the really well-paid position of editor in order to lighten his burden of debt and meet the ſtill numerous claims of his considerable family, but he relinquished the poſt scarcely a year later. From now on circumſtances improved, thanks to his wife's husbandry. In 1873 this energetic woman took over the private publication of new editions. The *Journal of an Author* also appeared in 1873 printed privately.

Many economic factors may have conduced to Doſtoevsky's extensive journaliſtic activity in those years, ſtill more the need to mix as directly as possible with the Russian world. This unsatisfied need had wrecked *The Possessed*, a fact which the poet had doubtless not overlooked. Such an experience would have moved a roof-garden poet to increase the diſtance between himself and the present. Had Doſtoevsky been compelled at that time to decide yes or no, he would probably have cast aside the poet and surrendered himself to journalism, and that, it is understood, would have been the decision of a poet. He could not hope to attain the desired reality by abstract thought alone. Thoughts had given him enough torture abroad. *The Possessed* was full of them. It was only by constant contact with Russia and Russian reality that he could find his way out of the blind-alley.

Enough is said in the near relationship between parts of the *Journal* and *The Brothers Karamazov*. It was of Dostoevsky's whole essence that consciously he attached little importance to this preparation whilst he felt his journalism in this last period to be an indispensable medium for his moral calling. His rôle as educationalist was both narrowed and expanded by his humility. He was his own best pupil and invariably received as much as he gave. The *Journal* completes the picture of the restless letter-writer to whom countless people turned with the most secret questions of conscience and requests for advice; he turned no one away unanswered. It was the weapon of the protector of helpless humanity who was soon to acquire powerful influence in all circles of the people.

The ideologue's crisis was not finally solved till *The Brothers Karamazov*. *A Raw Youth* came in between. It was meant as a test. In the *Journal* of January 1876, when the novel was finished, Dostoevsky called it "a first test." It was the work of his rebirth or, rather, of his rebearing. With painful labour a new life was revealed. This autobiography of a young man, essentially corresponding in parts to the life of the young Dostoevsky, can at first glance be recognized as an extract from *The Life of a Great Sinner*, which thus, in its unfinished state, became a setting for a new event of incomparably greater significance. The gulf between *Crime and Punishment* and *The Idiot* was bridged.

At the beginning Arkady Dolgoruky, the twenty-year old hero, talks about his illegitimate birth. He is the son of a serf and the landowner Versilov. Old Makar Dolgoruky, his mother's lawful husband, also a former serf of Versilov, an illiterate Bible-scholar, familiar with and a lover of all stories of the saints, had at the age of fifty married Sofya, the young servant, because her father, before he died, bequeathed her to him as a kind of legacy. Makar only did what he considered his duty. "Naturally he was respected by everyone but was none the less unbearable to all of them. That was to change only later when he began his life of a pilgrim. Then they recognized in him almost a saint or at least a great martyr." With this introduction by the young Arkady the novel promptly attains a concrete level which is lacking in *The Possessed* in spite of the author's immense efforts. Life is possible in this real atmosphere, we can feel at home, we are at once faced with the essential plot, the relationship of the son to the father, a fresh, quite simple and infinite problem. The appeal is to our deepmost feelings rather than to our reasoning. The story is told by the principal character himself, Arkady, a son of two fathers. What moves us is his tone rather than his story, another complicated canvas with countless figures and episodes. The tone is the decisive factor.

In *The Possessed*, as in *The Insulted and Injured*, the vagueness of the narrator, a merely subordinate figure living on the fringe of events, casts a shadow of doubt across the whole. Stavrogin would have been much more real if he himself had told us about his demon, for he would never have attempted to express himself exhaustively in a pamphlet. He might have written that sort of thing just as he wrote his confession, but that would have been his affair and not Dostoevsky's. The autobiographical form of *A Raw Youth* made the utmost demands on Dostoevsky; the beginning, in particular, needed careful handling. The illegitimate son talks of things which are generally kept quiet by the person concerned. Awkward effects are avoided because the form of Arkady's narration immediately serves to characterize the hero. The pretext is rather shallow. The Dolgorukys are a well-known family of princes. Naturally everyone who hears Arkady's name

asks, " Prince Dolgoruky? "   And each time Arkady is
compelled to reply, " No, simply Dolgoruky! " He used
sometimes to add as a joke, " son of the peasant Dolgoruky,
natural son of my former landowner, Versilov."   We
have an immediate picture of this pugnacious youth and a
good idea of the effect of the joke in Arkady's surroundings.
Versilov sent the youth to the best boarding-school in
Moscow.   Only children of the best families were taken at
Monsieur Touchard's.

When he grows up he resolves " to break with everything and only to live for his ' idea.' "   Then Versilov
summons him to Petersburg.   Arkady has seen his noble
father only two or three times.   At that time Versilov was
enjoying the glamour of his privileged class and Arkady
was still very young.   Versilov has now lost the last of his
property and is living with Arkady's mother and his sister,
Lisa, in straitened circumstances; that is, he does not
actually live with them, he still has his own good quarters
elsewhere, but he spends the daytime with them.   Presumably he will disappear again presently.   That is his
way, to appear and disappear.   He has often taken the
mother with him or has let her follow him somewhere
abroad.   They have always come together again.   Sofya,
the mother, has remained a simple, harmless creature; the
former peasant in her is obvious but she is a good, unspoiled soul, always in a state of anxiety.   She can never
have been very pretty.   Arkady racks his brains.   There
has been only one problem for him since he first began to
think: what is the matter with father?   Only one problem,
apart from his " idea " of course.   He has devoted immense
attention to this problem.   How came this excellent and
fastidious gentleman to be involved with a servant who was
not even pretty?   When they spoke of it once Versilov
admitted in his, as Arkady thinks, casual way, " with a
most detached and intelligent expression," that there was
never any romance between Sofya Andreyevna and himself,
but that everything " just happened."

That is a little too much, particularly for us who hear

the words only from the son, the outcome of the "just happened," and even so, miss their intonation. But be the tone what it may, it ought to have struck quite a different note to create a good impression on Arkady. This intelligent detachment is enough to make anyone wild, most of all a young man already exasperated.

Arkady spends the first four weeks with his people like a ferocious dog, feared by his mother and sister, tolerated smilingly by Versilov. Arkady wants to hate his father and he does hate him as a matter of reason, of duty. Versilov's behaviour towards him and his mother—his sister does not appear to exist for him—must be crass egoism. Only pure tyranny can have driven him to make the poor woman come to him time and again. " On revient toujours," he ventures, with his intelligent detachment, to explain to his son. Hence doubtless the idea of summoning Arkady to Petersburg. And when he now spends the day with his family, which is threatened with poverty, he scarcely gives a thought to cutting down his expenses. The manner in which he feigns not even normal consideration is astonishing. The son's hatred is unquestionably justified, as is the hatred of Lisa, of her bullied mother and of Makar Dolgoruky, the lawful husband wandering about the world as a pilgrim. To Arkady righteousness as well as a primitive sense of pride seem to demand it. Even the reader ought to feel it. What would society come to otherwise?

Versilov does not dispute the injustice, but behaves as if it were more interesting to talk of other things, and when he turns the subject in his casual way, everyone follows his lead, including Arkady. Yet those casual remarks are difficult to grasp. They are not exactly witty though probably few people have Versilov's intelligence. Arkady would soon see through witticisms for he is no fool either. Could anything possibly be more interesting than this paradoxical situation? The direction of these unusual happenings is obscure at first. Probably they are not where appearance and intelligent detachment lead us to suppose, not in that superman domain which misled a Raskolnikov.

Arkady feels his inability to control his hatred. He guesses what his father, out of decency, out of breeding, self-mockery or pride, is keeping concealed about his relationship with his mother; what he surmises would justify his father, but he is not satisfied and we watch the conflict in him. Once the conflict is over he will be a man.

That is the educational factor in the novel, though it is certainly not forced down our throats; in point of fact it is only after arduous reading that the educational trend becomes apparent. Arkady recounts his impressions hastily; precociously he discerns the viciousness of adults, and he is as haughty as the budding hero of the "sinner-novel" in his contempt for the whole lot of them. It is another of Dostoevsky's studies of childhood, portrayed by a mind which had matured since *The Little Hero*. Arkady is too proud to sentimentalize about his unhappy childhood. At bottom, so he says now, everything he suffered was only stupid and vulgar. The legacy of his youthful embitterment is defiance rather than tears at his father's cruelty; it frequently shows itself in intense anger. He recalls with indignation the Monsieur Touchard who made him brush clothes; with greater indignation the blockhead who allowed himself to brush them. He flares up at every provocation, there is a constant struggle to rid himself of that sense of "being a lackey" which marked his childhood. The mixture of peasant and aristocratic blood is well depicted. His contempt for form and the urge in him to throw his weight about are truly proletarian characteristics. If he does not succeed straightway he goes for his object like a bull at a gate; hence later on the wild scenes in the gambling club. He appears to inherit his father's intellectuality and generosity, the rhythm of his whole existence, though there is marked absence of the customary allusions to inherited characteristics. The psychological relationship is only gradually revealed. The current theory of an Oedipus-complex could, if necessary, be completely refuted for the very reason that everything in the work seems to point to it.

Arkady is almost indifferent to his mother. He still suffers under his sense of shame at her before M. Touchard. He is sorry for her, but pity does not conduce to intimacy. His main concern is his father, the conflict with his father, though in conversation with him his looks belie his words. We see both sides of the question. There is no reference to the problem vital to struggling youth. Since Turgenev's *Fathers and Children*, the *leitmotiv* of all young men has been the conflict of ideas between succeeding generations. No sex stories; they are beneath the young man's contempt. He is swayed by quite different desires. Only spiritual excess is worthy of consideration. Romanovitch, the only scholar who has dealt with *A Raw Youth*, has not remained uninfluenced by current platitudes. In his view the main *motif* of the novel is Versilov's mysterious passion for Katerina Nikolaevna Ahmakov in which he finds hidden " the secret of platonic eros." That is typical of the attitude of our time towards its greatest poet. This incident is the least significant of the whole work and it is singled out merely because of the belief that the secrets of our time cannot be revealed except in terms of erotic catchwords. Was Ophelia the problem of Hamlet? There is far more justification for believing so. The affair with Madame Ahmakov is only one of the many episodes in the story which illustrate moments of the hero's success.

In many German editions the book is entitled, A " Werdender."[1] One might say The " Werdenden," for not only the youth develops but also Versilov, the father, this impenetrable, unsociable lover of humanity. In this figure Dostoevsky has entirely succeeded in conveying what in his notes he described as sphinx-like, what in Stavrogin lead him into bypaths. Abstract construction rendered Stavrogin meaningless and thus his reserve seemed to be a trick. Versilov's reticence is of the very essence of his aristocratic soul. He can only stutteringly express his

---

[1] *i.e.*, One who is developing.

multifarious emotions and, as he˜dislikes ſtuttering, he
remains silent as long as possible. When he speaks everything around him is gradually warmed and illumined.
That very often happens contrary to his intention. Apart
from the intentional process of development the work
abounds in all kinds of experiences, as if the poet had been
ſtoring them up for years in order one day to indulge in a
riot of exuberant incident.

Father and son both have an " idea." The son's can
be formulated and he recites it with youthful dignity.
Arkady wants to be a Rothschild; his motive is the same
as the " great sinner's " whilſt ſtill a child and Raskolnikov's
when he murdered the moneylender. Money is the key to
everything, to revenge, to retribution, to power. It is an
idea well suited to a schoolboy who, like once the young
Doſtoevsky himself, had to save every farthing. Arkady
believes he is quite capable of leading an ascetic life which
alone, in his opinion, can lead to a Rothschild, and at
times the privation to which he subjeċts himself is sheer
torture. Up to this point everything is more or less in
accordance with the plan for the " sinner-novel." Thinking
of his idea soon carries him beyond the realm of material
indulgence, the more easily that he has not yet taſted of
these pleasures. Utilization of wealth leads to dissipation
and dissolution. Consciousness of wealth is the only real
gratification. You can do everything if you want to. The
loftieſt aim is renunciation. Acquire millions and billions,
not in order to live on the fat of the land, not in order to
do good, but in order to fling them away. That would be
the laſt trump. To become a Crœsus by your own efforts
and with the same effort to revert to beggary! Let others
jeer if they like. Prove to yourself in this way how irresiſt-
ible is the will. In short what really matters is to become a
Rothschild for your own sake, only for your own sake, juſt
as Raskolnikov only killed for his own sake, so as not to
feel himself a louse.

The father's idea has a far greater compass and is therefore less easy to define. It is only gradually and cautiously

revealed. Versilov guards it jealously; he would never dream of becoming conscious of it merely for the satisfaction of communicating it to others. The only fragments visible for the time being are those which Arkady attempts to understand. Arkady is puzzled. Everything he has so far learned about his father is repulsively unpleasant. Why is one not repelled? Is there apart from the Rothschild idea a self-love which is not degrading? At first both he and the reader are faced with nothing but questions. There seems to be some connexion between the two ideas. Perhaps the one is a continuation of the other on a higher plane.

The two ideas, their birth, development, conflict, these things in themselves constitute ample material for more than an average novel. We do not know whether Dostoevsky even thought of that. The work swarms with such themes. The greatest of all is the growing relationship between father and son.

Arkady is constantly assailed by fresh ideas. It is only by virtue of certain factors born of the self-love common to both his father and himself that he can tolerate Versilov in the circle of his illegitimate family. He is keenly alive to his father's brilliant rôle in the past. He has a vivid memory of every one of those rare meetings in his boyhood. After nine years he still remembers his father's every word, his captivating smiles, his smart appearance, even his coloured tie. Versilov spent a short time at Moscow and lived in the palace of his relatives and Arkady was taken there by his aunt Tatyana. Naturally that created an immense impression on the schoolboy who brushed clothes at Touchard's. As a matter of course Versilov scarcely noticed the brat. Next day the youth was allowed to go with auntie to an amateur performance at a private theatre. He had never been to a theatre before and it so happened that his father was playing the inspiring principal part. He joined enthusiastically in applauding the illustrious company. Everyone was full of admiration for Versilov.

The appearance of the father in all his charm associated with a first impression of the theatre, a huge event in the life of every child, was a brilliant idea on the part of the poet. The danger that Versilov's sphinx-like appearance might become theatrical is overcome by this bold stroke of bringing the hero on to the stage. Arkady recounts the theatre incident in the family circle in the presence of Versilov. It is the first amiable evening for weeks. Versilov has just this very day won his lawsuit against Prince Sergay and has come into a fortune. There is an end to the family's need. Like Dostoevsky himself when he had a few roubles in his pocket Versilov has brought home all sorts of delicacies from the most expensive shops. The timid mother breathes again and Lisa, his sister, is ordered to give up her foolish needlework. Versilov does not like to see young girls working. The only fly in the ointment is Arkady. He has finally made up his mind to leave his family in order to live only for his idea. Before doing so he wants to square accounts with Versilov. He would prefer to take his mother with him, wants rather belatedly to save her honour. The recounting of the theatre incident is part of the squaring-up. The more brilliant Versilov seemed then, the more wretched a figure he cuts to-day. But Arkady spins out his memories and almost forgets his object in recounting them. Even the bitter side of his childhood was sweetened by the boy's romantic yearning for his proud father. Arkady knows how to tell a story. His mother has not the least notion what has set his tongue wagging, but, scared as she is, she cherishes a hope that now everything is going to be put right. Tatyana, the brusque auntie, an old-maidish *babouchka* who idolizes Versilov, loves the mother tenderly and behaves as if she loathes the young man she has brought up, divines his intention and wants to shut him up. Versilov also sees what is coming but lets him talk on. "He must be allowed to talk so as to get it off his chest; the main thing for him is to get it off his chest." Arkady comes to his attempt at running away when, tormented by Touchard and yearning for Versilov, he could stand it no longer. He had told his companions about his grand father who lived in the palace and so splendidly played the part of the hero; a finer father than all their fathers put together. He could not explain why he was registered as the son of the former serf Dolgoruky though his father's name was Versilov, or why he was one day locked in a hole by Touchard, whose money had probably not arrived punctually, and was thus cut off from the other children. Auntie Tatyana looks daggers. Versilov would rather this part of the story were cut a bit shorter, if only for the mother's sake. "As a matter of fact, ce Touchard," he observes casually, "I remember him now, a little fidgetty fellow, recommended to me from very good quarters."

"Ce Touchard," Arkady continues, and now the fun begins. Oh, nothing further, nothing special in the least. Only don't be afraid! No one here is being blamed. He is only going to tell an anecdote in M. Touchard's favour, to amuse them. But that does not prevent him eventually offering his mother the alternatives, him or me. Thereupon, in a towering rage, he hurries to his " coffin " in the roof. There is a storm brewing in this sixth chapter. Dostoevsky is preparing its passage.

Every story about Versilov has added to Arkady's embitterment; like a detective he is on the track of every rumour. There is a question of love-affairs which Versilov has carried on regardless of Sofya. It is asserted that not so long ago he wanted to marry a young consumptive girl (a variant of the lame girl) who was passionately in love with him and came to grief over it. Arkady has even found out about his passion for Madame Ahmakov, the pretty young widow of the late General Ahmakov and daughter of old Prince Sokolsky, a friend of Versilov's, in whose house Arkady has been provisionally installed as paid secretary. The kind-hearted prince is fond of everyone, particularly of the young man, and tells him all sorts of stories. He learns more from Kraft, an episodic figure of the Petersburg student circle, in whose *milieu* there is a mild touch of *The Possessed*. Kraft hands Arkady a document of which no one has any knowledge ; had this document been in the hands of Versilov's opponent Versilov would probably have lost the law-suit which has just been decided in his favour. Arkady is to use his discretion with the document. Moreover, Kraft gives him details of the relationship with Madame Ahmakov which seriously implicate Versilov. It is here that we learn about her ominous letter, a film requisite which Dostoevsky quite harmlessly turned to account. Some years ago when the old prince upset his family by his apparent abnormalities his daughter suggested that he ought to be put under some sort of guardianship; this was written in a letter to a relative. Were the prince, who loves his daughter, to come by the letter there would be disaster, as he would probably cut her off. This letter also is in Arkady's possession; Arkady is going to return it to Katerina Nikolaevna whom he has not yet met, but he hesitates and this leads to endless intrigue.

Kraft is a calm person who always thinks to the point; he knows Versilov. Arkady thinks he ought to attach importance to Kraft's opinion of his father. Versilov is considered a peculiar and unscruplous person. His passion is quite capable of driving him to the lowest depths. Arkady has been told of a face-slapping affair. Some years ago abroad Versilov had an encounter with Prince Sergay and pocketed this public insult without a word. A hero wears a different complexion.

An hour after the scene in the family circle, when Arkady offered his mother a choice, Versilov climbs the steep steps to the " coffin " where takes place the first important discussion between them. Versilov comments on the scene downstairs in front of the mother, not with the concern of a father but with the acumen of a student of psychology. He has two criticisms to make. First he finds a lack of moderation; to have no sense of moderation is a serious failing. The paucity of result was out of all proportion to the volume of Arkady's palaver; and the effect was a little coarse. Secondly he has grievously misconceived his object. Arkady wanted to get in a blow at

his father. Good enough, quite " in the order of things! "
But actually he has succeeded only in hurting his mother's
feelings and that is naturally not in the order of things.
What attitude is a mother, particularly a Sofya, to adopt
towards such alternatives? As things are it seems it would
be for the general welfare if the young gentleman were to
go away, but only in such a way that mamma should be as
little as possible affected. That is to say she is really
suffering; and it would therefore be as well to laugh a bit
so that they might hear the laughter downstairs. That
would certainly help to comfort her. Simple people are
like that.

Versilov does not discuss Arkady's feelings. Everyone
has his feelings and must deal with them as he thinks fit,
but that ought to be done in private. Arkady is suffering
from the need of an audience. What induced him to tell
everybody at school about his illegitimate birth, whether
they were interested or not? Besides, what is he actually
complaining about? That he does not bear the name of
Versilov?

Oh, please, Arkady hastens to observe. That would
certainly be no honour.

Well then! replies Versilov. Besides, it is impossible
in Russia to marry a woman whose legal husband is still
alive. Arkady has only slandered his mother by hawking
the family history around.

Arkady feels choked. Since Versilov puts moderation
above everything, perhaps he will be able to curb even his
sudden outburst of love for his mother and get down to
things that matter.

Certainly! says Versilov, and the son begins his interrogation by broaching his father's guilt towards his mother.
What he actually wants to say is something quite different,
but words fail him. Besides, the digression about his
mother leads to his object. How is it that in twenty years
Versilov's fond love has not been capable of ridding his
mother of her peasant prejudices? She has remained
exactly what she was. Of course she was morally above

him, is above him even to-day—excuse me!—far above him, but spiritually she is dead. "Only Versilov is alive. The others are only permitted the honour of vegetating in his proximity if they nourish him with their force and living sap."

Once again his blow strikes only his mother. Just as once, when she had visited him at boarding-school, her shabby clothing had been a source of shame to him, so to-day her lack of education is a source of bitter disappointment. It would be easy for Versilov to reproach his son, but he refrains. In Arkady's thought there is too much of his own thought. Arkady has found something dark which Versilov himself would like to illuminate. It is true, there is something deathlike in his mother, possibly in every woman. It is certainly remarkable, so remarkable that it can be made an object neither of attack nor of defence. Versilov has not the least desire to exonerate himself by referring to this darkness in Sofya, but at bottom that is not what Arkady is aiming at, is it? He wants not to accuse but to enquire, really to enquire? Arkady presses for an explanation which no other father would tolerate; surely even his mother must have been living at some time or other and have been a woman and have had something lovable about her. Whereupon Versilov retorts, No, perhaps she has never been a woman.

Such a discussion is possible only between this father and this son, between whom there are no ties in the social sense, for Arkady owes his father nothing. But this unusual absence of social relationship is not in itself sufficient to overcome the reader's revulsion, on the contrary it enhances it for it stresses the inversion of relationships which are the mainstay of society. All the same there is no suggestion of cynicism, a favourite *motif* to-day; hence our revulsion is held in check. We gradually feel the son's independence of the father, and the father's thoroughly unsentimental detachment towards his son seems to us strange and unconventional rather than repulsive. The situation thrills us because what is here a chance relationship might happen between any father and son. There is something fundamental in this detachment to which other persons similarly situated do not give voice. The youth's artlessness makes discussion easier. Only a virgin mind could talk so unabashedly about eroticism. Though he has no personal experience he knows that eroticism is part of life and is the binding link between man and woman; it is man's task to mould woman into a human being. Versilov, so reckons Arkady, has not succeeded in that. His mother has not become a human being. Versilov only amused himself with a serf, like the Petersburg gentlemen when they visit their estates. What is incomprehensible is his subsequent behaviour. Of course he let her down for he was in no mind to make a human being of her; it is notorious that he did not bother much about her. Why did he always come back, why is he sitting there now?

Dostoevsky did not make his task an easy one. Arkady is again and again faced with Versilov's casualness in dealing with this question. Every word, every gesture shows the intelligent detachment which Arkady loathes. The readiness with which Versilov condescends to reply probably denotes only scorn and contempt.

Not much comes of the conversation although both Arkady and we ourselves are listening intently. It is necessary to get used to Versilov's mannerisms. The calm manner in which Arkady listens is in itself " lackey like," and he is only awaiting a favourable opportunity to dismiss Versilov with some coarse remark. What can he do to him except be rude?

But at bottom he is disconcerted by every reference of Versilov to his " silent marriage." What was the idea? This man whose manner towards his mother is so casual dares to speak of the " generosity of men " and asserts that " if marriage depended on women only, not a single one would last." Arkady trembles.

Versilov does not notice it. He is not seeking to incriminate Sofya. She is the purest and best woman he

has ever met. " Humility, forbearance, patience, submissiveness, and at the same time strength, yes, real strength."

Arkady finds the praise of his mother even harder to
bear. Versilov has no intention of being sarcastic in his
eulogy, but it is just this detachment which irritates Arkady.
You do not speak like that of your wife, least of all before
your son, unless Versilov is identifying himself with him.
And by what right does he identify himself with Arkady?

Versilov expresses himself with a kind of gratification
on the subject of " the real strength." " So far as convictions or what they call convictions are concerned—
because for real convictions there is naturally a complete
lack of hypotheses—that is for anything they consider
sacred, they will let themselves be tortured."

That is beyond detachment. Arkady feels this, as well
as the degradation that somewhere in his unconscious he
understands his father, perhaps even approves of his
behaviour.

" And now tell me yourself," continues Versilov, " do
I look like a torturer? "

Arkady has to check himself from nodding assent. His
lackey-soul which delighted in brushing other people's
clothes wants to nod. He sits there on tenterhooks.

" On that account," observes Versilov, " I also preferred
to keep silence and not only because it was easier. I confess
I do not regret it."

He does not regret. Is it possible to carry mockery
further? What does he not regret?

" In this way everything worked automatically on broad
and humane lines, towards which I cannot say I have
personally contributed." And as if divining Arkady's
thoughts, " in parenthesis I would observe that she never
believed in my humanity because for some vague reason
she suspected me and therefore was always trembling.
But in spite of trembling she has never yielded to culture."

That is the reply to Arkady's reproaches. His mother
was left in her lifeless state for humanity's sake. After a
while Versilov remarks: " There is something we don't

understand there." Who are we?—we men, we lords of creation, we intellectuals, we gentlemen from Petersburg, we guardians of humanity.

But actually this We disarms Arkady. He can do nothing but stammer stupidities and rude remarks which Versilov is humane enough to ignore.

" Listen, my young fellow," he says once, " I have put up with a good deal from you, as from a spoilt son; this time we'll let it pass."

The spoilt son is flabbergasted.

It is the most audacious of Dostoevsky's dialogues and, like all his dialogues, belongs more to the drama than to the novel, a little too terse for reading, depending, as it does, on gesture and vocal inflection. We read it too quickly and miss what lies behind it. It is possible, of course, to see Versilov otherwise than through the eyes of his mistrustful son who in this scene is driven to extreme misunderstanding of his father. Because Versilov knows the price of truth he is as little capable as Myshkin of concealing it. We are too rarely in a position to force our way to truth through lies. In the smiling detachment with which Versilov talks of his youthful folly we can perceive, more easily than Arkady, an attitude in which there is little, if anything, of the lustful squire. He did not surely come " just like that " to the unattractive servant and induce her to break her faith. This man has perhaps been everything possible in his relationships with women and it has certainly not always been he who received. Perhaps he did not even want to receive. He dares to say so. The motives for his romantic explanation are so obscure that Versilov's words are bound to increase Arkady's suspicion. The father knows that and therefore—such is the logic of a man supremely humble—again casually talks of humanity, and his presumption in so doing only makes his position more obscure.

They come to old Makar Dolgoruky. Versilov characterizes the peculiar saint with the same detachment. Makar is one of those about whom " we " are never quite certain. The mother is also one of them, people who have their own strength and who would not change if you talked to them all their lives. All the same it is worth while talking to them.

He wept on Makar's shoulder, jeers Arkady, who at the right moment recollects having heard something of that sort.

Yes, that is true, declares Versilov. As a matter of fact at such moving moments you do act, more to yourself than to anyone else. And strange to say you mean it quite sincerely all the same. Queer, isn't it? You believe everything you say and do, sob sincerely and somehow play the hypocrite in spite of it. Has that never happened to Arkady?

Arkady is again perplexed. That sort of thing has often happened to him. If this man is a fraud everything is fraud.

Versilov adheres to the subject of old Dolgoruky. You can learn from people like that, from the way they tell their stories and from their sobriety in matters which call for sober handling, in money matters for instance. The people have powers we do not dream of. At the time this affair happened there were many youthful ideas about humanity and there was an urge towards the people. However, the execution of such beautiful ideas is not so simple.

It is certainly not simple. Versilov has said a great deal with those few incidental words. Arkady might understand, indeed there is an inward agitation which drives him to understanding. But where would the hatred remain? This is all too new and the old ideas with which he came here will not surrender. He has heard too much about this man. Is not Versilov perhaps saying all that in order to whitewash himself? Why does he bother? Why does he want to win him over? Is there not perhaps some new game behind it all? Arkady's suspicions lead him into believing that Versilov knows something about Madame Ahmakov's letter and presumes it to be in Arkady's possession, and all his cunning is being directed towards obtaining the letter by a trick. Versilov tells him so to his face. Perhaps you have to be the prince's secretary to spy on his daughter.

Versilov gets up bored. Strange how much hatred there is in such youth. Merry youths are wont to be kind-hearted. How you can be deceived. Strange! We listen even if Arkady does not. The humanity of the jesting Versilov is becoming more palpable. Is there perhaps really love of mankind behind it all, love of mankind to the point of fanaticism? Possibly marrying a servant is only a means of getting nearer to the people. Suddenly the *motif* of *The Idiot* rings louder, even if it is only to remain an accompaniment. There may be a relationship to Myshkin in this father who lets his son show him the door and is no more than surprised and concerned about it, whom others can insult with impunity. We do not yet know to what degree and do not dare believe in the unbelievable.

Later on Arkady begins to hear what he did not want to listen to in his father's presence and doubts whether his crude defence was justified. Already next day he feels himself, at least formally, so far in accord with his father that he hits on the mad idea of challenging the young Prince Seryasha who struck his father in Ems. There is scarcely one principal work of Dostoevsky in which there does not figure, even if it never materializes, the duel which was a requisite of every *bourgeois* novel of the time. Naturally Arkady's trouble only leads to a new humiliation in which Madame Ahmakov is involved. He has seen her for a few minutes at her father's, the old prince's, and has been promptly struck by her beauty; perhaps not only by her beauty but also by seeing in the flesh a person who had long occupied his mind. This is the woman who has turned a deaf ear to his father, for whom his father is supposed to have committed crimes. Naturally the youth falls in love at first sight and dashes out. A lightning scene. Later he sees this beautiful woman without being seen by her. Quite by accident he overhears behind the curtain at Auntie Tatyana's a conversation in which Madame Ahmakov admits her fear that Arkady may be Versilov's spy. An unforeseen turn of events causes Arkady to rush forward. He showers reproaches on the proud woman who is frightened of him. Naturally she thinks he has intentionally been eavesdropping, and Tatyana wants to thrash him. Suspicion is allayed by his youthful impetuosity. They have to laugh at him. Oh, only you wait, you proud woman, he thinks, and fumbles for the letter he has sewn into the lining of his coat, the letter she fears and for which she would give a kingdom. If you only knew what I have on me!

Of course, he has not the least intention of making improper use of it, but it tickles his fancy to picture her face.

This scene essentially modifies his thoughts on his father. He is angry with the proud woman for having been so short with him and takes his father's side. Perhaps the letter ought to be given to Versilov so that he may fling it at the feet of her, his enemy.

In the next few days he has the opportunity of expressing his opinion about Versilov's actions which completely shatter his hatred. These actions permit Dostoevsky to indulge his fancy for episodes and to complicate the design. He seizes every opportunity of throwing sidelights on Versilov's character and then gives every auxiliary figure its own history, speech and behaviour. One of these episodes turns on the poor Olya Onissimovna and her mother, a widow, who, like once Raskolnikov's mother and sister, come to Petersburg and are reduced to penury. They set their hopes on a rich merchant who owed money to the widow's late husband. The merchant, far from paying, makes an unpleasant proposal to the pretty Olya. At the end of their tether Olya seeks a position as governess. A pleasant lady calls in answer to her advertisement and her house turns out to be a brothel from which Olya only escapes by violence. Versilov, by attempting to help the poor woman, creates the third act of this interlude. His smiles and delicacy are misunderstood. Olya is under the shadow of her recent experiences and, fearing that the smiling benefactor is tarred with the same brush as the merchant and the pleasant lady, flings the money back at him in front of Arkady. In a fit of hysteria she hangs herself. Arkady also has suspected his father and is ashamed at his mistake. Versilov's benevolence surpasses the usual bounds. His casualness is a mask to conceal his pensive mind. Every day, every hour is brimful of experience and yet one never comes to the end. It is impossible to take one's part sufficiently unseriously. The object of the interlude is accomplished, but the episode has resulted in a novel within a novel.

Versilov behaves just as unpretentiously in his own affair. Arkady has handed him the document, not Madame Ahmakov's ominous letter, but the paper which might have led to a different verdict in the lawsuit. Versilov promptly renounces this large inheritance in favour of the very Prince Sergay who years ago slapped his face. The best thing about this generous action is that it is accomplished without 'pedestal.' Arkady is delighted when he learns about it and hastens to the old prince who in his obtuse kindness rather fears than esteems Versilov. Everyone does. Arkady tries to convert everyone to Versilov. At the old prince's he comes to know Prince Sergay on whose head Versilov has heaped coals of fire.

Sergay is an improved edition of the fickle weakling of a prince in *The Insulted and Injured*. He plays here a similar part, more extensive and profound. Arkady makes friends with him. Sergay lives with a rich relative whose house Lisa, Arkady's sister, frequents, and he knows Lisa. There are relationships between Lisa and Prince Sergay which Arkady fails to notice. Lisa is an improved edition of the fiancée in *The Insulted and Injured*. Arkady and Lisa come to know one another better. She takes her mother's part. Womanliness gives her a certain superiority; a faint semblance of the silent motherliness of the mother. Arkady and Lisa discuss their parents. These short youthful outpourings contain the tenderest touches of the novel. Arkady's relationship to Lisa is such as a young man without a sister might imagine brotherly love. Lisa also bears a resemblance to Raskolnikov's sister, with more grace and charm, or, rather, Dostoevsky has learnt to draw such characters more delicately. For the sake of saying something Lisa talks about the owner of the house where Prince Sergay lives.

"Do you know what?" says Arkady, "hang her house and her too."

"No, she's an excellent person!"

"Maybe, for all I care, we're excellent people too. Look what a glorious day it is! And how pretty you look to-day, Lisa! . . ."

They talk about the girl who hanged herself, how terrible it must be to die in gloom like that. Lisa is afraid of death though mamma says that is a sin.

"Tell me, Arkady, do you know mother well?"

"Still only a little, Lisa, very little!"

"If you only knew what a splendid person she is! You first have to understand her extremely well."

"But you too," says Arkady, "I haven't known you till now, and now I do really know you. I have come to know you in a second. You may be frightened of death, Lisa, but all the same you're proud and fearless, better than I, far better than I! I'm frightfully fond of you, Lisa. Ah, Lisa, let death come when it must but till then— life, life! let us be sorry for that unhappy girl, but let us bless life all the same. No? No? Lisa, I have an idea! I suppose you know that Versilov has renounced the inheritance? You don't know my soul, Lisa, don't know what that man has meant to me."

"Why ever shouldn't I know! I know everything."

"You know everything? Well, that's just like you, you are clever, cleverer than Vassin. You and mamma, you have piercing eyes, I should say glance, not eyes. I'm talking drivel!—I'm bad in many ways, Lisa."

"You want looking after, that's all."

THE ANECDOTE

" Then look after me, Lisa! how delightful it is to look at you to-day. Where did you get your eyes from, where did you buy them, how much did you pay for them?— Lisa, I've never had a friend and I consider friendship nonsense, but friendship with you wouldn't be nonsense at all . . . Now then, Lisa, tell me frankly, have you been laughing at me or not for the last month? "

" Oh, you're so funny, you're awfully funny, Arkady. But do you know who else has been laughing at you? Mamma has. ' Such a queer customer! ' she whispered to me. ' Oh my, what a queer customer! ' You sit looking on and think we were frightened of you! . . ."

" Ah, Lisa, if only we could be longer on earth! "

" What, what did you say? "

" I didn't say anything."

" You're looking at me——"

" Yes, and you're looking at me. I'm looking at you and I love you."

That is the end of the first part, a first act of wide range. The work is divided into three such parts, of which the second is the climax. Arkady had at that time carried out his resolution, left the house and taken a room at some official's, but rarely stays there. He spends most of his time with his new friend, Sergay. His heart is with Versilov and he yearns to express his feelings again. But he is pig-headed, cannot make up his mind to go to him and is up to all kinds of mischief. His father comes to his lodging. One evening he is sitting at Arkady's table talking to the landlord. Arkady's eyes light up as he comes in. Thank goodness the ridiculous official is there. Now the fun begins.

Now the fun begins. The ridiculous official tells the ludicrous story of the huge stone. He has already told it to Versilov whilst he was waiting and Versilov encourages him to repeat it. The official revels in telling stories but is always afraid of being interrupted, for generally people are not very eager to hear them. The story of the stone is his star turn. From time immemorial the stone has lain in the middle of the road. As his majesty drove past one day he grew vexed and ordered it to be removed. That was more easily said than done; it was no ordinary stone but a good old boulder weighing thousands of pounds. Well, there were several ways of doing it; it was a matter of finding the right way. The Englishmen demanded fifteen thousand roubles and, if it were broken up, ten thousand, perhaps even twelve thousand, but at least ten thousand.

Arkady is indignant. Now they have come together at last and in steps this ridiculous official with his eternal story. But Versilov casts a surreptitious glance at him. He must let the poor devil have his run. The glance betrays so much compassion for the ridiculous official and, above all, so much tenderness that Arkady actually listens to the fellow with relish. He has never been so successful with his story. If he falters, Versilov discreetly comes to his assistance; when he makes an artistic pause to give his listeners time to be amazed, Versilov throws in an appropriate " just think of that! " or " Aha! " and pretends to be frightfully interested.—A Russian workman who has not the faintest notion of mechanism or machines boldly asserts that he will remove this pebble within twenty-four hours and he is not going to charge fifteen, not even ten thousand roubles, but merely a hundred. How? And he actually does it, just a workman whom they all ridiculed. Next day the stone has vanished. Do you know how he did it? Well, guess then!

Versilov, who knows the story of old, makes an effort to guess and the ridiculous official spreads his tail and really feels triumphant at his solution. Then his wife calls him away. When the two, who are aching to speak to one another, are at last left alone they discuss the anecdote. The joke is that the stone did not really disappear at all. It is still in the same place to this day; the good man has confused this story with another one. From this anecdote conversation drifts to anecdotes generally, how such a man

comes to telling stories, what he thinks about it and what
his object is, the psychology, so to speak, of the anecdotist.
You cannot help thinking this somewhat irrelevant, but
Versilov accepts it for what it is worth. Arkady also has
an anecdote, the one about Tchernyshev. He has often
told it. In fact you rather enjoy it. Versilov also knows
the anecdote about Tchernyshev, and then follows an
historical survey of the Russian anecdote. Arkady tells of
another pock-marked official who lodges in the same house
and who invariably interrupts with irrelevancies whenever
the ridiculous landlord wants to tell a story. Where did
that happen? Why? When? He drives it to such a pitch
that the landlord dances attendance on him merely for the
sake of gossiping. Yes, that is the other kind, suggests
Versilov. The first is the chatterbox who wants to fabricate.
You become impatient with him. The other is the prosaic
fellow, the man without a heart. You can do nothing
whatever with him. " Just let him invent a bit," recommends Versilov. " It's harmless amusement. Let him
invent as much as he likes. In the first place that shows
your delicacy and, secondly, they'll return it by letting you
invent; two birds with one stone."

Thus everything they were dying to say to one another
comes out in the course of this chatter. Yet it is a heart to
heart talk. Versilov suddenly notices the time, he must be
off. Arkady shows him downstairs. Versilov curses the
awkward stairway and Arkady observes that the cursing is
meant to prevent something else happening. Besides, he
will find his way all right now, Arkady must not catch
cold. " Merci, adieu! "

But Arkady does not go back and suddenly words
burst forth as if of their own accord.

" I knew for certain that you would come."

" And I knew that you knew. Thank you very much,
my boy." They reach the hall.—" We were already at
the front door and I was still following him. He was just
going to open the door when a gust of air put out my
candle. Suddenly I gripped his hand, for it was pitch-

dark. He quivered but said nothing. I bent over his hand and kissed it greedily, kissed it again and again."

Such passages take our breath away with their lyricism. The wild dramatist who seeks to set his novel in high-relief, the raving drunkard who can never pile up enough of blood-curdling incident attains the pinnacle of his creation with an aery nothing. The whole of Dostoevsky's idea, everything that can be said of his idea lies in this anecdote story.

This anecdote story contains everything. Even if we ignore its purpose, which is delightfully achieved, and its humour, there still remains its greatest charm: reality. Despite the absence of action the scene stands vividly before us. We are conscious of their deepest emotion, their every word and glance. Unreality becomes tangible. Every father and son must intuitively feel their intimacy. Sentiment between father and son may and should attain the highest purity. The pedagogical element is apparent. This father, who teaches and learns, and this son, who gives and receives, are one. Out of the fruitful atmosphere of communion is evolved the profundity of this educational novel, the only novel of our times which has any significance for fathers and sons. Here at last the natural father is legitimized; we recognize his as the only justifiable method. That he deserves the name of father is only because he is content to let his son rail at fatherhood, at all authority, and because his tolerance is the result not of the sense of duty of a father who is his son's " friend," but of a natural interest in life, in every life. He never is but becomes, wants to become a father. The development of youth is part of his own development. He is, in a word, a loving human being. That is neither an honour nor an obligation but a mystery.

That is why Dostoevsky let this youth be born out of wedlock. The abnormal situation rendered easier justification of his ideal. (In themselves all children are at first natural and most of them remain so despite all palaver on the subject, although it would never have occurred to

Dostoevsky to concern himself with such trifles. His creative impulse carried him beyond that.) It is almost better not to insist on rights and duties if the mystery is not experienced.

The scene in the hall alters only the inner relationship. Arkady quite naturally attempts to profit by it. Since he has a father now he expects something of him. What shall I do? he asks Versilov, and Versilov shirks the issue, too conscious of the futility of attempting to inculcate a moral code, too imbued with reverence for their mutual love. Of what use would it be? Of course he willingly answers questions, but the conversation invariably slips into abstractions and although they touch on problems of deep moral and religious significance, there is an atmosphere of the official telling his anecdote. The essentials remain in the background. If Arkady wants an anchorage he need only keep the Ten Commandments. Love of God and the orthodox faith are also to be recommended. And when the youth misconstrues the tone and flares up, declaring by way of reaction that he is an atheist, his father does not take up the gauntlet. Well, even atheism has its advantages. Atheists can be exemplary pillars of the fatherland. And love of your neighbour? Certainly, also an excellent precept, though it may be a shade overdone. You can really only love your neighbour by holding your nose, don't you think so? At bottom you love only the humanity you create for yourself, in other words, yourself. Arkady pricks up his ears. Yes, my boy, that's all I know about it, I wasn't consulted at the Creation. I've been occupied on these matters for ages and get no further. There are question marks everywhere. Perhaps you can help me from time to time.

This father prefers appearing unmoral to committing the stupidity of trying to stifle with platitudes the desires of growing people. As Arkady keeps on pressing for something positive, Versilov cautiously counsels him to regard love of your neighbour as an attempt at setting up an intimate relationship with the person you happen to be with at the moment. The advice is not meant to be a hint, it is Versilov's first allusion to his own line of conduct which is formulated in the third part. Versilov promptly criticizes his own advice ironically. In his humble opinion that sort of thing can at any rate do no harm. Moreover an occupation, such as architecture or jurisprudence, or to specialize in any way whatever has a soothing effect.

Arkady is hurt by the mockery of his sphinx-like father who sees through his attempt at trapping him in " prosaic even if good sentiments." If his father were really to express the expected sentiments, this true son of Versilov would soon grow out of his childlike veneration. It does not help matters, you must learn by experience, and a father has to take to heart that silence suits a man better than words, wise as they may be.

Versilov adheres firmly to that although and just because the youth's present mode of life would benefit by paternal solicitude. Arkady has put his " idea " aside and for the time being contents himself with more worldly pleasures. Friendship with the empty-headed Prince Sergay leads him astray. He squanders the money Sergay lends him, indulges himself and endeavours to ape his father, at least externally. Sergay introduces him to clubs where Arkady gambles without any special passion, fully conscious that this is only a phase; he could give up all this luxury at any moment. Possibly his indulgence is only a form of challenge to his father. That does not prevent Sergay from gradually feeling the strain, that is the social, not the financial strain; for since the prince wants to be just and to return Versilov a portion of the fortune, the monetary demands of his naïve friend do not cause him any special concern. The foolish young fop considers Arkady his social inferior, and Arkady is weak enough to want to force himself into Sergay's aristocratic circle just because he feels their resentment at his intrusion. But Sergay has, or thinks he has, other reasons for an unfriendly attitude, and Arkady, failing to understand the sudden outbursts of the man he loves, swallows them as mere whims. Sergay has a run of bad luck. A financial cataſtrophe looms in the diſtance.

Versilov pretends not to notice Arkady's changed manner of living and confines himself to trying to influence the prince, a procedure which Sergay will not tolerate. His inferior mentality fails to perceive in Versilov's reflections anything but idle phrases. He soon forgets Versilov's generosity and once again sees in him the social inferior whose face he has once slapped. Father and son are tarred with the same brush. Sergay feels juſtified in coarsely assuming that Arkady is aware of his *liaison* with Lisa, and is accepting his money for tolerating it. The youth does not foresee the ſtorm that is brewing. The unscrupulous prince's motives are completely foreign to him. The scenes with the moneylender Stebelkov ought to prepare him, but his head is too full of fine things. Arkady is happy. He is in close intercourse with Katerina Nikolaevna, the woman of his heart. His love for his father, who had preceded him in the beautiful woman's affections, plays a part which is possibly a decisive factor in his secret joy in a new and priceless "anecdote" under whose influence sense of communion with him is deepened. It is the firſt love of a youth, free of carnal desire, and its tenderness removes whatever might sully the beauty of the double *motif*. He thinks he can talk to the woman he adores like one ſtudent to another, and he opens his heart to her. She tolerates it smilingly and lets him have a peep at her heart; what he thinks he sees there fills him with delight. She becomes the acme of perfection and completely overshadows his idea. It is far more splendid to capture human beings than to chase after ideas. Versilov's hint has fallen on fruitful soil. There is a confession. He is roused by the proud woman's admission that her dealings with him were actuated by a desire to get at the root of his supposed espionage; she was always in terror of the ominous letter. She counted on his "impulsiveness" and on her power over men to entice the secret from him. But in his long conversations with her, when they talked enthusiaſtically about Russia, he suspected her duplicity and, deeply as he was moved by contact with the " immeasurable beauty,"— he loves such words—yet it was painful for him to feel at the same time " the inquisitorial serpent " in his ideal. The words rattle out and make an impression on the listener. She indulges in self-accusation. This confidence far exceeds his wildest dreams. The most he hoped for was spiritual confidence, and when she informs him that she is betrothed to Baron Büring, he remains unstirred by any selfish impulse. All that worries him is whether this baron is worthy of her immeasurableness, a thing which he naturally doubts. In order to comfort the woman he adores and because he is ashamed of not having given up the letter long ago, he tells a white lie to the effect that the letter was in Kraft's possession and was burnt by him before his eyes;. and he decides to cut the letter out of the lining that very evening and destroy it. She is so affected by the exciting conversation that she entirely loses sight of her original objective.

This scene is full of life, but does not nearly come up to the anecdote dialogue. In spite of its importance to the novel it obviously meant very much less to the poet than the conversations between father and son which, in themselves, are not vital links in the chain of events. Doubtless here too Arkady is expressing his feelings, but there is not the same feeling behind the words. Madame Ahmakov does not get her due. She appears to us more as an object of Arkady's estimation than as a reality in herself. She is, of course, meant to be seen from this aspect both by Arkady as well as Versilov, and therefore here, as elsewhere, the hero has to lead the discussion; but Dostoevsky generally gave more reality even to many of his less important characters. Katerina Nikolaevna's pride ill-suits her fear of intrigue and of the youth's attacks. Does she remember the dangers to which the possibly less platonic father exposed her? It is rather feeble, and she seems to strike a purely conventional note in deciding to terminate the close intercourse with Arkady. It is also striking how easily Arkady takes it. There ought to have been some definite indications. Doſtoevsky in his haſtiness omitted them. Even in the subsequent conversation between Arkady and Versilov on the subjeâ of Madame Ahmakov, in which the youth relates his experience, the novel element preponderates and there is far too little noticeable of the woman's dual relationship to father and son. Still, how could anyone depiâ this dual rôle without in some way falling short? Doſtoevsky did not see Katerina Nikolaevna diſtinâly enough. Moreover, possibly the situation could not have been developed without some detailed erotic exposition, and in connexion with Arkady the poet would have found erotic problems awkward. But if he was to have been content with the son's mimicry of the father towards Katerina Nikolaevna, a brilliant *motif* without any eroticism, she ought to have disappeared at this junâure. Inſtead she becomes the subsidiary centre of the aâion. The poet was led aſtray by the noveliſt, a faâ which caused considerable damage to this part of the work.

Now Arkady tumbles to earth. He has to pay dearly for having been the temporary acquaintance of these ariſtocrats. It is a brilliant sequel to *The Gambler*. The gold which has been showered upon him is of no benefit. Society punishes the intruder. Sergay rails againſt the father and flings the ignominy of Arkady's siſter in the face of the unsuspeâing youth. Does he not know that she is with child by him?

What does Arkady do? Does he hurl himself at the brute? Not a bit of it! He ſtares open-eyed like a child, unable to grasp things. Pain recalls his youth and brings a child's bitter tears to his eyes. The prince recognizes his miſtake and apologizes, but Arkady does not answer and hurries to Lisa.

Now for a revised chapter out of *The Insulted and Injured*. Lisa believes in the prince. She thinks he may be weak but he is not wicked, and in her delusion she will not let herself be undeceived. Sergay affords a glimpse of himself and confesses meanness after meanness. He lacks the power to build afresh. She has to put up with her mother's fanaticism. She is not a Sonia, he still less a Raskolnikov. Her brother wants to help the drowning man and is himself sucked into the whirlpool.

This chapter is a jumble. Anna Andreyevna, Arkady's half-sister, one of Versilov's two legitimate children of a former marriage, wants to marry the old prince; a thoroughly fantastic idea. She and Katerina Nikolaevna, the prince's daughter, are at daggers drawn and Arkady is dragged into their intrigues. Versilov writes to Madame Ahmakov that the ominous letter which she dreads was not burnt, as Arkady asserted, and was never in the hands of Kraft, but that it will recoil on her if she continues to chase after a youth who is still in his teens. To add insult to injury he writes similarly to Baron Büring, her betrothed. We are not told of Versilov's motives. Was he actuated by jealousy? Of whom? Of Büring, of Arkady perhaps? It is surprising that Dostoevsky leaves us in the dark. The father's main concern is for the youth who has thus been enmeshed. Versilov's misunderstanding of Katerina Nikolaevna is constantly indicated, but his experiences with her are far too shadowy. If he is seeking to protect his son, how can he at the same time call him a liar and a deceiver? The demon in Versilov seems too vague to be grasped. The worst feature is that we have not even breathing space. *Motifs* topple over one another and, like poor Arkady himself, we are chased from one to the other.

It is he who suffers the consequences of his father's mania; blows rain down on him from every side. He is despised by his " ideal " and nearly thrashed by Büring. He still wants to help Sergay. The prince has committed forgeries and only a great deal of money will enable him to escape from the toils of his extortioners. As it happens there is no escape for him, a fact of which Arkady is well aware. Arkady chooses the gambling hell as a means of escape merely for the sake of doping himself. A variant of *The Gambler*. In Roulettenburg the outsider gambles luckily in order to help the woman he adores in vain and she repays him by flinging the bank-notes in his face. In *A Raw Youth* this fanatic devotion is rewarded with an insane affront. In this scene there is a masterly drawing of the prince; a last glimmer of social snobbery, a mere quiver of the dying class-consciousness—in theory already dead—spurs him to shake off the man who is his social inferior. This time Arkady suffers the most cruel of all humiliations. Innocent as he is, he is searched for the stolen money and flung into the street. This repetition of the *motif* heightens the restlessness of the chapter. Dostoevsky, in the first gambling scene, has already hinted at the second, but his intention of preparing us is lost sight of in the turmoil of events. The reader is at the end of his tether, and at the end of the chapter is as stupefied as the maltreated hero himself.

Immediately after this passage, which would ruin a play, the author pursues the *motif* further. After the club scene Arkady runs like a wild animal through the Petersburg streets. What shall I do by way of revenge? Whenever he wants to rest for a moment he is driven on by some fresh and intolerable bitterness. Thief! thunders in his ears. And is he not really a thief, in his own eyes at least, even if not to the scoundrels who have robbed him? Has he not robbed himself of his life, his soul? His " idea " flashes through his mind, this stagnant, long since rejected Rothschild-idea which, despite its minuteness, stands before his eyes as something heroic and spurs him afresh. Nice asceticism, this living between your hairdresser and your tailor! nice power you gain at a gambling-table! The idea was conceived by a whipper-snapper, but a miserable wretch has been false to it. Everything he ever thought of profaned! Past, present, future shattered at one fell swoop! He would like to put an end to himself. And the madness of feeling a kind of satisfaction in this disgrace! They have recognized his lackey-blood, just as Monsieur Touchard recognized it at the accursed school, and the lackey now wants to humiliate himself still further, wants to wallow in ignominy and drag with him into the vortex everything within reach. The tendency to crime somewhere between the underworld den and Raskolnikov. What shall I destroy? What havoc can I wreak? In the course of his nocturnal wandering through the deserted streets he runs across a large woodyard. That's it! If he could climb over the wall he could set the yard on fire; it would blaze up instantaneously in this cold weather. He is a good gymnast and the climb would be as easy as winking. But when he is nearly at the top he falls, strikes the back of his head, and has only strength enough to creep into the corner of a gateway. He is lulled to sleep by the deep chimes of bells. It is the bell of the red church of St. Nicholas in Moscow, opposite Touchard's school. He dreams of his mother's visit when she brought him the horrible peasant's bread and gave him the copeks wrapped in a peasant's scarf, that scarf he chanced to find again later and then always took to bed with him. He dreams of the tenderness with which he used to think in bed of his poverty-stricken mother, and her trembling life, and how he was thrashed by the big schoolboy Lambert when he burst into tears and could not help crying for his mother. The active youth belongs to his father, the dreamy boy to his mother.

He wakes up because someone is really thrashing him. He is half frozen and someone is trying to restore him to life. Unbelievable as it may seem, the someone is the schoolfriend who used to thrash him.

" Lambert! " cries Arkady.

" Who are you? " asks the fuddled Lambert in amazement.

" Dolgoruky! "

" What Dolgoruky? "

And promptly there comes from the half conscious youth the hundred times repeated answer: " simply Dolgoruky."

In Lambert is introduced a new episodic character and with him a new chain of intrigues. The schoolfriend drags the sick youth to his home where he hands him over to his Alphonsine, a French girl whom Dostoevsky makes speak

MAKAR

his appalling French. This Alphonsine with her lapdog is
a comic figure in an earlier manner. Arkady takes to his
heels and drags himself home to his mother. He learns
that his innocence has been established at the club and that
Sergay has given himself into the hands of the law. Then
he is stricken with fever and becomes seriously ill. So ends
the second part.

. . . . . .

In the middle of the third part stands Makar Dolgoruky,
the pilgrim, Arkady's lawful father. After his return to
life the sick youth finds the aged man with the terrible
white beard. The introduction of Makar into Arkady's
autobiography at once assures this character of a fitting
atmosphere. Arkady is still in a half-stupor and imagines
he is being born again. Of course this idea promptly
becomes the subject of mockery and annoyance. Aha,
re-birth, something new! Re-birth is part and parcel of
every decent convalescence. So, on with re-birth!

Again the reader's scepticism is anticipated by that of
the hero. Arkady begins his re-birth with lively vexation
at everything which breathes, at his mother, who is devoted
in her attention to him, at Lisa, because she is occupied
with her own affairs, at Auntie Tatyana, because she no
longer curses him, at the infernal sunspot on the wall
because it always appears at the same hour. He hates all
and everything, and prefers to keep to himself. He swears
to himself that as soon as he can crawl again he will be up
and away.

In the next room is the old invalid with the huge white
beard. He has long been sitting bolt upright on Mother's
footstool before the bed. They gaze at one another for a
while and the old man laughs softly. Arkady defines
laughter and Dostoevsky again anticipates any objection on
the ground of irrelevancy by making Arkady generalize on
the subject of laughter. Quite a thesis on laughter! Without
knowing it we become familiar with Makar who has nothing
to do with this tirade.

There follows a long conversation between the old man,

who is quitting life, and the youth, who is just entering into it. Naturally Arkady promptly recognizes the visitor and is pleased with the inoffensiveness of the old man whose silvery hair adds to his dignity without pandering to his vanity. He is not as Arkady imagined him. Truth is stranger than fiction! Arkady had pictured his pilgrim-father as backward and lifeless as his mother, incapable of progressing, cherishing piety as a substitute for thought. But the pilgrim has seen all sorts of things. Many things cross your path if you wander day in day out. Wandering is beautiful. Every day with nature brings a new mystery. Nature abounds in strange secrets.

Arkady acts up to his principles and interrogates this father too, according to the rules of the game. That nature-business is extremely strange. This substitution does not, then, prevent a certain lively participation in affairs. Presumably it is only so many words. That remains to be seen. What do you think of science, Makar Dolgoruky? Arkady expects the usual clerical poison. But the old man has no such thought. If he were to meddle in science he would become proud, which would serve no useful purpose, for if science is something lofty, there is no need for arrogance. (Lap it up, young man!) But to nibble at it a bit is certainly not a sin. And he tells the story of the microscope. All his stories have a humorous point which he himself seems to miss. That is just what pleases in the old man; there is something of the beyond in him, it has to do with his age. His is the fever of old age and Arkady's the fever of youth. Fever drives both of them to gossip and thus they come together. There can be much to tie an old man to a young man—Makar always says young man. It is the reader, not Arkady, who notes that. There is already much in common between the two generations, Arkady and Versilov. Now the third generation is going to be added. That is the fundamental *motif* of the third part, in fact of the entire work; a very significant point. Dostoevsky is also a pilgrim who seems to miss the points of his stories.

MAKAR

Naturally Makar is to be the advocate of God—so thinks Arkady, as well as the reader; Arkady less than the reader because he is in actual contact with this real being; the reader because roof-garden tricks make him suspicious of reality. A roof-garden writer would fool all expectations and make Makar the opposite of a pious person, would make him some Tolstoy with a beard and abundance of wisdom, at bottom an enemy of religion or, at all events, of the church, and pious in spite of it and so forth. No, Makar is an orthodox pilgrim like hundreds of others, one who was formerly a serf. There is no duplicity in him. Platitudes, says Arkady who does not mince matters even before Makar. The old man has adopted the language of the pious, makes use of " high-flown " *clichés* and does not mind dragging in the name of God, for He is behind science as well. Like everyone of his type he carries on a sort of propaganda for the orthodox creed. If he does not become insufferable, it lies in the simple fact that piety does not necessarily deprive a Russian peasant, who has been wandering for years, of his natural cunning, his natural good-heartedness, his natural servility. Ecclesiastical flourishes lend to the old man's dignity an ornament which he would never lay aside. But we can remove it if we feel like it. Then there would still remain a human being, a pilgrim. Pilgrimage is the mark of this, as well as of every right thinking person, so thinks the poet and the orthodox Dostoevsky.

In the conversations with the doctor pilgrimage is entirely divested of clerical flavour. The doctor suggests that it was not religion but the love of a nomadic life which drove Makar to wander, and his disease is nothing more nor less than restlessness. The impetuous Arkady, who considers this an insult, promptly jumps down the doctor's throat. It is we who are tramps rather than this old man. There is more stability in him than in all of us put together and the whole medical crew are not worth his little finger.

" How do you find him? " asks Auntie Tatyana who is

always irritated by this precocious boor. " God bless him! "
says Makar. " He is wide-awake all right! "

Versilov's guilt in driving from hearth and home the
old man whom he had robbed has been partly expiated by
this vagabondage which has become a blessing in disguise.
It is by this roundabout route that the question of God is
really brought to the fore. It is the doctor who leads the
discussion, the main characters are only listeners. The
doctor stands for the atheist. This foreign word translated
into Makar's Russian becomes not godless but restless,
also a vagabond. In the course of his journeyings Makar
has run up against all kinds of people, great and small,
stupid and learned, but not godless. And the doctor
cannot be godless because he is a merry fellow. " A merry
fellow cannot be godless."

In his simple way the old man expresses the last thought
of the Idiot and carries it a stage further. People who
think themselves godless only grow weary; the more they
take from outside, even the most bitter enjoyment, the
more weary they grow. They appease themselves with the
" sweetness of books " and go on hungering. " The more
there is reasoning, the greater their weariness. They all go
to ruin and praise their ruin." But everyone always seeks
again for something to bow down to. " For a man who
bows down to nothing could never bear the burden of
himself."

This fundamental idea is illustrated by Makar's charming pilgrim story of the rich merchant in the city of Afimevsk.
He was a drunkard and a brute who caused much evil in
his arrogance, but he subsequently adopted the child of the
debtor he had injured, and finally married his widow.
(Another marriage from humility beyond love.) He has
the boy decently educated and loves him as his own son.
But the delicate child falls ill and cannot rid itself of fear of
the former tyrant. Once when he carelessly smashes a
lamp he rushes off through the garden. He is stopped
outside by a child who is carrying a hedgehog in a basket.
He has never seen anything like that. " Oh, give me the

little hedgehog!" Then he hears the voice of the tyrant pursuing him. The child presses his little fists to his breast, rushes into the river and is drowned. The merchant sends for the teacher who knows how to paint. He is to paint the story of the child on a grand scale, just as he painted pictures in the tavern, but finer if possible. The basket with the hedgehog is to be in the picture and above the whole the celestial hosts are to be shown coming to meet the child. The teacher does not think the hosts quite suitable. A ray of light would be better which, so to speak, the boy approaches. That would be finer. He paints the ray of light, as well as the hedgehog in the basket. The picture is a great success but, though the merchant is proud of it, it does not help him. Nothing helps him, neither his marriage nor the building of a church by way of expiation, nor his multifarious institutions and benefactions; nor the birth of a child, for it promptly falls ill and dies in spite of the greatest of all doctors from Moscow at a cost of eight hundred roubles. Thereupon the merchant abandons everything, transfers all his property to his wife and wanders off. He is supposed to be a pilgrim to this day.

A Russian counterpart to Flaubert's *St. Julien*, except that the profounder thought behind Dostoevsky's story in its association with the entire work yields more than merely æsthetic pleasure; we are sometimes ashamed that we descend to mere æsthetic pleasure.

Makar, in the course of his many wanderings, has never found a person like that, who bows down to nothing, for everyone always goes on seeking. " If such a man has abjured God he bows down to some idol, a wooden or golden or an imaginary one. They are all idolaters but not godless." But Makar has heard of really godless people and thinks there must be such people somewhere.

" There are such people," Versilov suddenly observes, " and there are bound to be such people." And Arkady whole-heartedly agrees: " Yes, there must be such people."

We listen attentively. Old Makar has touched on Versilov's secret. Is he a godless person like that? There is a touch of *The Possessed* in this scene. Is this "idea" with which Arkady agrees impetuously, really Versilov's? Certainly not! Versilov's ideas cannot be destructive. We shall hear more of this later.

The room in which Makar calmly awaits his last journey is like a port in a turbulent storm of events. Peace reigns here. Even auntie's caustic harshness becomes transfigured. Here is told the story of the priceless court scene with her cook whom she had beaten, and here Arkady finds beauty and what he calls the sublime, something he had looked for in vain amongst the aristocrats. You can always shelter here if out yonder the sea is too rough. All the inmates of this house do that; even Versilov, another kind of pilgrim, who seeks and fails to find a substitute for Makar's talisman. Each in his own way. Father and son again find themselves in the harmony of this venerable anecdote. Their common worship of the old man's beauty binds them more closely. Only Lisa wants to break away. It is a fine idea that it is just she, the sufferer, who strives to contradict. Makar has to do penance for Sergay. The persistence of her love for her lost lover absorbs her so fully that she has no patience for anything else, and she is the only person who disturbs the harmony of Makar's retreat.

The reader also escapes here, where literature pursues its quiet course, whilst outside there is a veritable storm of action worthy of a thriller. There is development of the detective story with Lambert, the gamble with Arkady's ominous letter. One cannot help feeling that the Lambert business is pure padding. Its sole interest is the opportunity it offers to show up the youth's platonic worship. Dostoevsky makes him virile in his drunkenness, during which he plays with the idea that Lambert can help to win Katerina Nikolaevna for him by means of the letter. This scene is admirably worked out. Lambert wants to persuade him that Madame Ahmakov loves him too and will willingly accept him. Arkady jumps at the idea, but his common-sense tells him that it is vile and absurd. The viler, the better.

THE SEDUCTION

" Are you worse then than anyone else? " asks Lambert, " you are good-looking, well-educated."

" Yes," he whispers in his drunkenness, " good-looking and educated."

" You are always well-dressed."

" Yes, always well-dressed."

" And you're a decent fellow."

" Yes, a decent fellow."

This dialogue embodies the youth's carnal dream. Steeped in drunkenness, with Lambert's aid he loses his ideal: women are infamous.

Retribution follows swiftly. Just as he returns to the retreat old Makar dies. But it is Versilov and not the young sinner who is most moved. The event loosens his tongue. At a moment when Arkady least expects it he learns of his father's " idea."

As is inevitable, the long-awaited explanation is somewhat disappointing, not to Arkady but to the reader. Our impatience is itself partly to blame for the disappointment. There is not and cannot be a simple formula for all this person's riddles. Dostoevsky is also partly to blame; at all events we think so although the writer's mistake shows some of his most amiable characteristics. The intractable idealist has never yet dared to speak out so candidly.

Versilov admits he is a vagabond. His entire life has been a series of questionings and wanderings, and he has chased after the shadow and missed the substance. When he forgot Arkady and left his mother, it was to have been for longer, possibly for ever, for he felt that something else had a greater claim on him. It happened to be an important moment in the history of Europe. That drew him away.

Revolutionary, nihilist, thinks Arkady. Off to Europe to be in a plot; clear as daylight! He ought to have come to that conclusion long ago.

No, not that! Not nihilism, nothing spectacular. It would be wrong to censure such things and the noble people who wanted them, but Versilov was not one of them. On the contrary he belongs rather to the die-hard reaction-aries, because he cherishes the old, which in that particular moment in European history began to perish. It was 1870, the year of the outbreak of war. Two great nations, great European nations, flew at one another's throat. For us, Arkady, that is no joke, not merely a subject of drawing-room conversation. For us that is not some newspaper stunt or diplomatic show. At that time there was not one European in Europe. That was the trouble. It was only in Russia that a clique of aristocrats, intellectual aristocrats, were thinking like Europeans. Moreover Versilov considers Russia, not Europe, to be the real home of the European. The Frenchman, the Englishman or the German can only serve humanity if they remain utterly and entirely French, English, or German. That is their misfortune. Only the Russian is capable of " being most Russian when he is most European." What we call that? Well, the name is beside the point. Shall we call it " Russian melancholy "? You could find something else in it, but invariably something to do with the feelings; anyhow something unique which enables the Russian to be a German amongst Germans, a Frenchman amongst Frenchmen, and an Englishman amongst Englishmen. You can also call it freedom, for anyone who belongs to the Russian *élite* is freer than any European. And something more than that, he foreknows the future man.

Arkady listens very attentively. A new notion of the aristocrat dawns on him, something loftier than this term has ever conveyed to him before, and he is vexed at having entertained the thought of nihilism. That war oppressed people like Versilov, was bound to oppress them more than anyone else. That war was " Europe's death knell " and they were driving towards a burial. They drove on as if to an endless burial. It was not the bloodshed which was terrible, nor was it the burning of the Tuileries; it was neither the war in itself nor the stupid burning in itself; it was the idea of the consequences. That war began war without end. The burning of the palace was the beginning of the burning of all palaces. The downfall of everything we cherished, the downfall of Europe began.

But the Russian European—" My dear, I tell you that, in the vain hope that you will understand the whole of this fantasy "—the Russian European dreamt of a Golden Age.

At this moment Versilov wears the anxious look of the ridiculous official telling the story of the stone. Will he be interrupted and asked where and how? Will he be allowed to go on fabricating?

Of course Golden Age is just a name like Russian melancholy and freedom. You do not absolutely need to think of Claude Lorraine's picture in Dresden, although that remarkable Frenchman has depicted " the all-embracing sun " admirably. The connexion between Lorraine's thoughts and events of the moment, which are far removed from the Kingdom of God, is rather far-fetched, so that Versilov could hardly take exception to Arkady's laughter.

But Arkady is not laughing. Another might, but not he. Why not Arkady? Because Arkady is a youth. Arkady understands that especially when darkness begins to set in, people's thoughts turn to the sun. Arkady, the son of Versilov, understands everything in the realm of a setting sun. That may be fantastic, bold to a degree, but we will accept it. The only danger is that boldness fail at the last moment. The slightest disturbance of the story would be disastrous. Arkady is anxiously waiting to catch an empty phrase. Makar could be forgiven his *clichés* because he carried them on his back, in his knapsack. A roof-garden platitude from Versilov, the thinker, would be intolerable. What, for instance, does Versilov mean by the Kingdom of God? Arkady has been told that he played the apostle out there abroad and talked at length about the right creed. To the youth that has always seemed the worst feature of all. Vicious tongues assert that he wore the chains of a penitent under his coat and proclaimed God. The interrogation reaches a decisive point.

Versilov does not shirk the issue. Such men do not shirk, even when their whole life is at stake.—Well then,

there were not exactly chains and no great speeches, for
out there there was no one to listen to them; otherwise of
course, who knows! It is true that at the time he would
have been capable of all sorts of speeches and has in fact
done things which to some people may seem like penitent's
chains. Indeed, because people failed to see what he saw,
this burial, this endless burial, because they failed to catch
the knell which drummed in his ears, he would have talked
himself blue and borne heaven knows what gigantic chains.
If they had seen it, if their stopped-up ears had heard that
terrible din, do you not suppose that everyone would have
raised a cry like the Jews before the walls of Jerusalem?
Surely that war and the burning of Paris were also only
abbreviations and symbols. It was not he who did the
proclaiming. What could he have proclaimed? It was the
others. And it was not God who was proclaimed but the
dethronement of God. You were not there so you must
take all that for granted. I actually went through it.

The dethronement of God—because some emperor or
other was being hounded out? Nonsense! Because a few
hundred thousands were being massacred? That has
happened hundreds of times in the history of the world
and God has remained God. But how it happened: the
bloody unravelling of externals and at the same time the
so-called scientific, that is to say mechanical unravelling of
profundities—was that vast coincidence token enough?
Decent onlookers were angered by the dethronement, not
because of the thing itself but because of the way it was
carried out. Only the method was in question. Why
shouldn't you hit on the idea of dethroning God? That
was possible in Russia too. We had atheists like everyone
else. " What appalled in this European dethronement was
its smugness."

That is a new phraseology. Makar, the Russian pilgrim,
speaks of restless people. The Russian European, the
aristocrat, speaks of smug vulgarians. He is dumbfounded
by the mechanical nature of this dethronement. One day
the *bourgeois* in Europe wakes up and God has vanished.

VERSILOV

He goes to his office as usual and ponders on his digestion. Many of them hiss God off the stage like a bad actor. Most of them do not even hiss, it would be a waste of time and energy. People in the West call that logic. Even their logic, even their sense of reality have something of vulgar smugness in them.

" Then did you believe so fervently in God? " asks Arkady mistrustfully.

Now for the explanation of that answer to old Makar, that there must be godless people. This last bold climax is illuminating. Versilov suggests that whether you believe or not is perhaps not really important, for who can reply with certainty if he is asked to give a definite yes or no to every article of faith? The belief which the Europeans, say, if you like, the smug *bourgeois* in Europe, lost was everything, was God, and if you lose that, if God all of a sudden completely and entirely disappears, the loss must naturally be noticed. That is not a matter of feelings, it is a very real thing. For if you notice the loss, you will be set on finding a substitute. It will always be a hard task for the European vagabond from Russia to believe in the ultimate abandonment of God, but he can picture it. Very well, humanity loses God and belief in immortality. Love of the Almighty is at an end. The great all-embracing sun vanishes and mankind stands alone. Well, what next? Will men then not turn to account just their solitude, their orphanage? When God, who has befriended them for centuries, finally vanishes, will it not come naturally to them to snuggle into one another for the sake of their own warmth? And what happens to the masses' former love for the Almighty? An immense torrent is set loose. Versilov could never imagine people narrow-minded and smug, and accordingly assumes that this torrent, which once spent itself in the skies, would change its course, and that people would love their neighbour and the earth and every blade of grass as once they loved God. This insight into their earth-bound existence would enable them to embrace life with so much the greater tenderness. " They would see nature with new eyes as a lover his beloved." Since there is no longer any Father in Heaven, every child will call every adult father. And thus they will overcome their sorrow that God is dead. From the love of God there will arise the love of all things.

A new melody though not a new thought. The thought may be as old as God himself, and thousands may have conceived it in one form or another. We are not concerned with that. What is new is the construction on which everything depends, this dramatic thought-process. The rhythm is new. The note it strikes is not the note of *The Possessed*. There there is only destruction after the downfall of faith. Stavrogin knows merely the alternatives, faith or decline, and if modern civilization renders faith impossible, it is better to consume everything in fire; that is why Stavrogin says Verhovensky is right. After Christ comes the "dead machine." If this no longer affords sufficient nourishment to the starving, "people will fling their sucklings into the flames or devour them " (55). The manner in which Stavrogin treats Verhovensky in itself indicates the first and final argument against the theory of devouring. It is not for nothing that Stavrogin is a prince in the draft of *The Possessed* which explains the problem more clearly than is done in the book itself. The aristocrat cannot be reconciled with the smug destroyer, even if he countenances his logic. Versilov, a close relative of Stavrogin, is proud of his nobility which he seeks to make the mark of distinction of a sect, sworn enemy of smugness; a way of escape for the decaying good European. This good European cannot obliterate Renan and Darwin and Malthus and has no thought of doing so. His nobility does not call for blind resistance to reasoned thought or for the simplicity of Makar, the peasant, to whom science is too lofty; but for understanding born of knowledge. Christianity made ethics easier for us. If Christianity collapses we shall certainly not burn any sucklings. On the contrary, we shall do more than was done before, shall by sheer force of our nobility weave a Golden Age, *car tel*

est notre plaisir. So that the fall of God might be a benefit.
There are and are bound to be such godless people.

Of course, that's all imagination, fantasy, adds Versilov
with a derisive smile, but all the same, was the idea of God
less fantastic, and is not the idea of a humanity without
God fantastic to the point of absurdity?

The thought is worthy of an " idiot." Versilov continues the idea of nobility at the point where Myshkin's
jumping up upset the pedestal. Arkady is again ready to
fall at his father's feet. Arkady is not smug. The schoolboy wants again to ask, what am I to do then?

The romantic edifice promptly totters. You cannot
acquire ethics from beauty; that is just the tragedy. All
the Raskolnikovs and Stavrogins are wrecked on that rock.
You have to be an " idiot " to avoid being wrecked. The
father might just as well ask the son, what shall I do?
We do not know, no one knows. You can't stop the burial.
Stand still, raise your hat and, if the spirit moves you, weep!

The father tells what he has done. One must be
content with the loneliness which he recently recommended.
At that time he intended to make at least one person happy.

" A bookish thought," suggests Arkady.

Perhaps it was and perhaps it was not. Were it only
out of a book, it would concern only someone in the
abstract. But everyone has one, at least one person who is
not abstract to him, and it would be really quite reasonable
to make it everybody's duty to render at least one single
person happy; just as, in view of the deforestation of
Russia, it would be a good thing to compel every peasant
to plant at least one tree during his lifetime. " Incidentally
one tree is rather little. You might demand one tree for
every year."

Old Makar might have thought that out; he would
have said it without irony as a practical peasant.

Versilov cannot say it like that for to him the one
concrete being was Arkady's mother, the woman whom he
had once seduced because of some vague, if not impure
impulse, a thought out of a book; the woman who slavishly

loves him, whom up to the present he has vainly tried to set free. To make this one woman, only one woman, happy, to rid her of her inherited dread of the stranger who is still a landowner to her, of her shame at her rough peasant's fingers, to be in complete harmony with this one woman: paltry task! gigantic, superhuman task, suited— he knows it only too well—to stamp the whole tree-idea as sheer nonsense.

He sent for Sofya to come abroad, wanted to take Arkady to himself and just at that moment his passion for Katerina Nikolaevna intervened; the reverse side of golden freedom. A vagabond's love cannot be controlled. Only passionate beings resist the logic which enslaves, but their dreams cost them dearly. He struggles against the passion, hits on the idea of marrying the consumptive imbecile and asks Sofya for her permission. The invalid's death thwarts his purpose. Instead of Arkady he takes the imbecile's illegitimate child and brings it up. Sofya is led to suspect he is the father. He endures this unrighteous slander. Vagabonds will not be controlled.

Is this behaviour sufficient incentive for his fantastic idea? Versilov overcame his passion for Madame Ahmakov who at that time was frightened of him. It is said he conquered himself by means of monastic discipline and not alone ceased to desire Katerina Nikolaevna but actually hated her. Why, asks Arkady—and we feel the same— did he not return to the mother of his child instead of taking that child of a stranger? Was his love for Sofya really sincere? Arkady's power of comprehension is put to a hard test. He only manages to steer clear of this obscure incident by recollecting Madame Ahmakov's words that Versilov was an " abstract being " and " a shade ridiculous." These phrases throw light on Versilov as well as on the poet and also on the Idiot, and almost completely disarm criticism. Perhaps Versilov actually loved no one but Sofya and believed in his love. Thus his craving for expiation found return to Sofya too transparent, too personal, too selfish, and the marriage with the imbecile was to have

been one of the penitent's chains. Perhaps he was torn by
pity for the imbecile who loved him to distraction (like the
lame girl her Stavrogin). We cannot penetrate this abstract
humanity. Possibly latent in it is a necessary tribute to a
sublimated value, for a time concealed, which in Versilov's
idea attains its climax. In his early youth Dostoevsky loved
that idea passionately, then hated it equally for years, gibed
at it to the utmost, and brought the whole of his psychological knowledge to bear against it, yet fortunately was
never able to root it out. I mean the " Schilleresque." It
does not help us. In Dostoevsky's inability to rid himself
of Schiller we must recognize one of the surest guarantees
of his optimism. That becomes still clearer in *The Brothers
Karamazov.*

The turn the action takes towards the end of the work
is to prove how untenable is Versilov's abstraction. It
succeeds only too well. The vagabond is once again at the
crossroads. Makar is dead. There is now nothing to
prevent Versilov legitimizing his association with Sofya and
arranging his life as a lawful paterfamilias. Once again he
fails, this last time more than ever. The solemnity of old
Makar's funeral day spurs him to loosen his tongue before
the assembled mourners. He " splits himself up " into the
sensible, composed Versilov and the senseless " double,"
and it is in the nature of his abstract humanity to perceive
the division in himself and to warn the others. The shadow
of the underworldling is cast across the scene. A little
wooden icon is lying in front of him, a relic which Makar
always carried with him and bequeathed to this vagabond
of another order. The symbol is obvious. " Do you know,
Sonia! " he says to the terrified Sofya (calling her now by
the pet-name of the beloved of Raskolnikov, that other
penitent, whose penance remains in the mist), " I have now,
in this very moment, this very second, an overwhelming
desire to fling the thing against the stove, there against the
edge. It would promptly split in two, just in two, neither
more nor less."

The little room from which Makar has departed has

loſt its peacefulness. Versilov wants to go wandering abroad again. The vagabond cannot endure the warm ſtove. It is not because she is not his angel, not because he ccnsiders her an enemy, that he wants to leave her. How could she be an enemy? She is his angel, and he will come back again like laſt time, as always. And in a sudden fit of fury he grabs the icon and flings it againſt the ſtove. As he foresaw, the wooden image breaks in two.

" Don't take that for a symbol, Sonia. I have not smashed it because it was Makar's legacy, I have only smashed it for the sake of smashing. I shall come back to you all the same, to you, my laſt angel. Or, if you like, take it as a symbol, for that's what it muſt have been! "

He leaves them aghaſt. The breath of the abſtraĉt which troubles the scene does not hinder the reality of the demoniac impulse; we are relieved that even in this laſt moment Doſtoevsky was not led aſtray by some roof-garden mannerism, and did the man juſtice. Quite apart from Versilov's hidden motives everyone has in like circum-ſtances felt the senseless contradiĉtions of the double in himself and has been tempted—not solely through fear of the haven—to ſteer the boat once again on to the high seas, even were sacred heirlooms and the boat itself to founder in the process.

That is what threatens the vagabond. Arkady eaves-drops and overhears his conversation with Katerina Niko-laevna. These eavesdropping scenes are disagreeable features of the autobiographical form. Fresh complications are involved in seeking to make them plausible, although they cannot in the nature of things be convincing.

This conversation is complementary to the discussion between Madame Ahmakov and Arkady, but does not make her any more real. Versilov's passion, an unnecessary *motif*, remains vague. We are to be convinced how far he is enslaved; but it goes againſt the grain. There is some-thing wrong here. Her almoſt love of Versilov is an evil omen. The entire scene does not get beyond the almoſt, and therefore it is queſtionable whether Arkady's eavesdropping can possibly rouse him to the point of bitterness towards his innocent seductress which his subsequent action indicates.

This time it is the son who wants to free the father from the woman's toils, a last arabesque; unfortunately only an arabesque. Arkady's love for his father outweighs all other feelings. We believe that of him; we would believe it still more readily without this scene. The novellesque entanglements render the depths of the action banal.

Arkady's attempt at saving his father throws him once again into the hands of Lambert, and once again he is drugged with champagne. This time his drunkenness only gives vent to his hatred. He confesses that he was moved by jealousy as well as love for his father. The psychology would have had to be carried much further to make this confusion of feelings credible and purposeful. Dostoevsky has no more time, he is hurrying towards the end. In his intoxication Arkady hatches with Lambert the filthy plot of setting a trap for Katerina Nikolaevna. They will demand money and something else from her in exchange for the ominous letter which Arkady still—how long!—carries in the lining of his coat. And Lambert, who is only thinking of the money, undertakes that she will agree to the something else. Versilov will be behind the curtain like a spying Othello, and when he sees that she is prepared to stoop to any vileness, even to the " something else," disgust will unquestionably cure him, at long last, of his passion. The drunken man falls asleep at Lambert's. Next morning he is full of remorse and dissociates himself from these intrigues; but it is too late. Lambert has stolen the ominous letter whilst he was asleep. Arkady is unaware of this fact and to-day he is at last going to give back the letter, unconditionally of course.

A few film-scenes bring the book to an end. The first turns round the old prince. For some incomprehensible reason Anna Andreyevna, Arkady's half-sister, clings to the insane project of marrying the old man and thinks she can only accomplish this by separating the prince and her arch-enemy, his daughter. She hopes to achieve this by means of the letter which Lambert wants to sell to the other side. She implores Arkady's aid in vain. The old prince acquiesces in everything. He grows more and more like the hero of the Siberian comic-story, *Uncle's Dream*, without losing our sympathy; the most moving figure of the whole work. He does not want to know about the intrigue which is being woven around him. Only peace, peace at any price! Moreover he mistrusts everyone who comes near him because, though he loves them all, he cannot remember who is who. Only the ridiculous official, Arkady's land-lord, is an abomination; he mistakes him for a disguised governor of a lunatic asylum, to which he is to be taken.

The youth does his best for his old prince, as well as for Versilov, Katerina Nikolaevna and her enemy. He wants a general reconciliation, he wants to embrace the whole world. He succeeds in the noisy final scene, a real shocker, in preventing his father becoming murderer and suicide. Versilov does nothing worse than wound himself, but the vagabond thereby becomes anchored to his haven. An exception to the rule; there are no corpses.

> . . . . . .

This network of intrigue provokes criticism. Whilst it progresses one feels the shattering bumps of a badly sprung carriage on an interminable journey. It would almost seem as though Dostoevsky had been ashamed of the actual theme of the work, that finest of all themes, and had therefore disguised it in a cloak of curtains, espionage and ominous letters. At the conclusion he serves up intrigues galore lest we imagine that something real has happened. This mass of episodes is painful. His arbitrary methods amount almost to destruction. What is it all for? Is the gulf between this work and the roof-garden to be made physically real? Pain at the weaknesses of the work is not a roof-garden feeling. The development overcomes our pain. The power of the symbol outweighs every other consideration and forces us to accept even the weaknesses of the work as parts of the symbols, and to content our-

DEVELOPMENT

selves in the knowledge that every irrelevant chain of stories is an accompaniment to the essential development. That glowing undercurrent, of which we spoke at the beginning, gleams throughout the entire work. Even if the whole novel is only an anecdote, we have the same experience as have Versilov and Arkady during the anecdote. The chatter only serves to enliven the silence, and we sit with Dostoevsky at the table, gaze at one another and, when the gust of air puts out the candle, fumble for his hand to kiss greedily. The mystery of father-son, son-father pierces the ominous chaos like the thought of God which again and again dispels the logic of smug vulgarians totting up figures. This atmosphere of confusion renders impossible a glimpse of the future; that is its function. What has happened to Arkady's and Versilov's ideas? They also are part of the anecdote. Live, live, and all ideas are destined some day or other to be flung by their creator against the edge of the stove, not because they are worthless but because smashing is also part of development.

A Raw Youth is " a first test." In the epilogue this autobiography of a hero of a " chance family " is deemed to be only " material for a later work of art." To a writer who, far from confining his interest to storytelling, is really concerned about the present, nothing remains nowadays but to sit guessing in chaos and to blunder. " But when the violent conflict of the day is over and the future dawns, some future artist will discover beautiful forms for the portrayal of bygone disorder and chaos." We shall see. We have seen the fruit of that age-long yearning for an epic which was unsuited to the poet's genius. The continuity which he planned with his *Life of a Great Sinner* he spread over three characters of equal restlessness; Arkady, Versilov, and Makar; youth, manhood and old age. A fantastic undertaking, simple as the continuous action of primitive paintings. Arkady, Versilov, Makar, three sharply defined types, as clearly distinguished as later the three Karamazov brothers, are mysteriously identical in their great development and restless pilgrimage. Was

DOSTOEVSKY

Dostoevsky aware of this similarity? It may be assumed so since he sought to disguise this fact by giving each a marked individuality. What other object could be served by this illusory scaffolding round a brilliant façade? The idea may also have sprung unconsciously from the plan of the " sinner "-novel which was deeply rooted in him. Truth probably lies mid-way between the two.

The development has as a further object a summing up of his entire works. Unquestionably the novel often fails in economy. No other work is so arbitrarily diffuse, at all events relatively, for other works against which this charge might be levelled, for example *The Possessed*, lack so definite a central idea and become therefore subject to such arbitrary treatment. Works with just such a central theme, such as *Crime and Punishment* and *The Idiot*, are far less confused. One weakness is peculiar only to *A Raw Youth*, the careless repetition of *motifs*. All the same it is just *A Raw Youth* which is symptomatic of a vast and incomparable attempt at economy. It owed its origin exclusively to the need for establishing order. The order which Dostoevsky sought could not be exhaustively dealt with in the novel in question. This " first test " constituted a huge survey, an expression of the poet's accumulated experiences. Every work containing evolutionary elements, from *The Double* onwards, was carefully sifted, tested as to its durability and, where necessary, equipped with fresh supports. Whilst the casual repetition of the *motifs* of *A Raw Youth* are at times disconcerting, the recapitulation of parts of the work only inspires admiration, strengthens our belief in the validity of those parts and intensifies our enjoyment. For not only does he allude to the *motifs* or their echoes, but he also makes corrections and additions which are destined to show up each earlier work in a stronger light.

This procedure is unique. We have to thank *A Raw Youth* for enlightenment on matters and ideas in *The Idiot* of which at the time we were in doubt. Versilov stands in Myshkin's place and replies in his stead to our questions. He also has a place beside Stavrogin. Versilov benefits by

DEVELOPMENT

certain characteristics which in the draft of *The Possessed* were given to the "prince"; the suppression of these in the final draft did serious damage to the figure of Stavrogin. Arkady and Versilov both help Raskolnikov, and Raskolnikov, in his turn, enlightens us about the youth in instances where the rapidity of the action makes it difficult for us to follow. Now we know more definitely what we are to think of Raskolnikov's æstheticism and Myshkin's nobility, and why the memoir-writer from the "underworld den" left us still a trace of heaven.

The dry skeleton of *The Insulted and Injured* is clothed with flesh; the insulted no longer indulge in sentimental groans but actually begin to praise life.

A strange result is that the work, though in itself leaving much to be desired, adds force to previous works. Such a paltry jest as the dream of the prince who is to be married attains a new significance. Uncle no longer capers about like some puppet on a provincial stage but becomes real.

This effect is not peculiar to *A Raw Youth* only, but it is unusually obvious in this novel. That quality of interpenetration and mutual completion noticeable in all Dostoevsky's works is specially stressed here; a result due to his unique personality. Both before and since many novelists have made a cycle of their works, actuated by a desire to intensify and generalize. One man concentrated on social categories, another grouped his ideas in the form of a history of a family; an inessential interplay of names. Most of the things to which our times have given birth are mere records. Whilst the card index conquers lands and peoples and the genealogical tree branches out in all directions the writer remains where he is and does not shift. Dostoevsky circled round his one object. He was like the painter who, in the mountain at the gates of his native city, found sufficient inspiration for the whole of his life.[1] If necessary he would have managed with a plate of apples, possibly apples of soap or wax. He roamed about, bustled

---

[1] Mont Ste Victoire near Aix-en-Provence, where Cézanne was born, figures in much of his work.—Tr.

around, absorbed a thousand and one impressions in order
to paint the mountain at the gates of the city, nothing but
the mountain, the mountain again and again. When the
sinner struggled with God, the mountain grew and gained
in shape. When the revolutionary was dragged to the
scaffold, the mountain pulled faces. When the chains of
the *katorga* clanked, the mountain began to whisper. At
the burning of the Tuileries the mountain thundered and
preached to the clouds.

Dostoevsky's Mont Ste Victoire was man, the great
sinner. He was already seeking for man when he was
writing, or wanted to write, novels like anyone else, let
himself be misled by ambition and had not yet distinguished
between literature of the squirearchy and the new word.
Writing was no special vocation, it was the result of a
common human function: writing meant development. In
a late notebook there is the sentence: " Man does not
actually live through his whole life, he only invents." It
may be assumed that the consciousness of development
began to penetrate Dostoevsky when, in the *katorga*, he
felt his rôle as teacher and pupil, and that in the Dresden
period, of which the woes and raptures resound again in
Versilov's idea, his understanding took a definite step
forwards. The sketches for the " sinner "-novel and *The
Possessed* were the first dubious outcomes of this progress.
In the conception of them the artist's creative impulse was
forcibly suppressed. The preacher of ethics supplanted the
apostle of beauty and development became ideological; the
most perilous stage in his career. Dostoevsky perceived
the danger and, after his return home, stopped writing for
a time. Again life streamed through the clogged channels
and he fixed his liberated gaze on the mountain. The
weaknesses of *A Raw Youth* were a safety valve. Dostoevsky
often noted in the margin of his drafts that there must be
plenty of action. The notes were to restrain him from
coming too close to the mountain and thus fixing its outline
too rigidly. The impulse to romance, previously stifled,
was now given free rein lest the idea be lost. Conscious

and unconscious thought played hide and seek round the mountain. The episodes had one other function. They were to conceal the depths of the problem and to counterbalance the poet's exceptional vision, to help to hold the reader's interest. Finally, profoundly as we may be moved by this triune vagabondage, glad as we may be at the childlikeness in Arkady's dreams, willingly as we may accept the mystery of the relationship between father and son, the entire work still remains only a first test, a ledge on the final climb of both Dostoevsky and ourselves.

CHAPTER XIV

APART from journalism there is nothing between *A Raw Youth* and *The Brothers Karamazov* except the short story, *A Gentle Spirit*. A usurer marries a client who is down and out; the marriage is unhappy; she realizes her husband's love only at the moment of committing suicide; a last touching contribution to the chapter of the insulted and injured. *A Raw Youth* remains the immediate prelude to the work of his prime. In *The Brothers Karamazov* the theme is again the relationship between father and son. But the relationship is from a negative viewpoint. This time it deals with the hatred of the children for the parent. In his defence at the end of the book the shrewd lawyer raises the legitimacy of the father, portrayed in *A Raw Youth*, to the level of a moral requirement which, if not satisfied, demands retribution. That is what the advocate says. Dostoevsky has more to say.

Apart from Dmitri who threatens to kill his father, apart from Ivan, the second brother, who plays with the idea of patricide and thereby comes to grief, there is Alyosha. The threatening darkness is rent asunder at the sound of this name and we are looking into the blue sky. The murder of the father is accomplished by the fourth son, the illegitimate one; not a " natural " son like Arkady, but an infamous bastard, a lackey by birth rather than in his own imagination.

Concurrent with the story of the father and his sons there runs an intermediate theme, the main *motif* of the mature Dostoevsky, the legitimacy of the Father in Heaven. Even in this last stage he adheres to the rule of making the action of one work the background of the next. In this instance it leads to an unforeseen widening of the panorama. A gigantic stage is disclosed. From the little room of old

REALITY

Makar, in which Arkady and his people shelter themselves from the storm of the world outside, springs the white monastery beyond the town, the Mecca of countless pilgrims from all parts of Russia, who day in day out set out for the hermitage of the great Zossima. Makar may have been of those who came to seek the blessing of the saint. We ourselves now enter the sanctuary and come to know the very essence of Makar.

As Makar to Zossima, as the Petersburg backroom to the radiant monastery, so is the entire novel to the earlier " first test." The monastery is a world in itself and the town in the vicinity is another no less familiar to us. We peer into every nook and cranny of the monastery and the hermitage, get a glimpse of the secluded cell of the wild monk Ferapont and gaze on the town with its lanes and alleys, its fenced-in gardens, its market place and its peasants, are given a precise picture of the Karamazov home and its neighbourhood. A slightly gradient path leads from the town to the monastery.

A great deal more is shown in this novel. The town, with the white monastery at its gates, appears before us like a picture we pass every day. In the picture are the incidents. Its symbolism is not tendentious. At the end we know only too well that the path leads not only from the world into the monastery, but also from the monastery into the world; it is particularly the latter route we are to remember, as the holy Zossima impresses upon us. This broad canvas affords ample space, and the demand on our emotion and understanding is thereby more easily satisfied than in *A Raw Youth*, not to mention *The Possessed*. Is the theme greater? It is difficult to surpass the profundity of the ideas in *A Raw Youth*. It is due to the reality of *The Brothers Karamazov* if we have no hesitation in placing it far higher than all other works put together. Dostoevsky's idea is one thing, his reality another. Often the two things run together unbridled in zig-zag course. His insatiable thirst for life entailed many subsidiary stories which often bear little relation to the main theme. Dostoevsky overcame that in *The Brothers Karamazov* as far as he could without imposing too narrow a limit on himself. He did not dispense with the episode or his diffusion, but these things were no longer irrelevant. The episodes here were more than ever twigs and branches of a tree, and the expansion of the canvas, which the lengthy passages effected was welcome, if not actually essential.

In the centre is the Laocoon group of the father and the sons interlaced with devils. They all crave for what Arkady recognized as the only *raison d'être* : life, life above everything! Dostoevsky wanted the hero to be Alyosha, the youngest son, whom the snakes have scarcely touched, and he drew him with all his love of youth. Dmitri becomes the mainstay of the action, Ivan of the tragedy. But actually this entire Russian family stands for all Russia.

Old Karamazov is the most violent and debased; he is an epitome of all that is bestial in the genus man. Amongst other things he embodies the foolish characteristics of drunken liars in earlier novels, and, like all the principal characters of the later works, he has his prototypes; but none of them give any inkling of his repulsiveness. This monster, more unlike Dostoevsky than any of his characters, is the most real of all the Karamazovs. Dostoevsky took special pains in drawing him. The rapid sketches of other characters which sufficed, particularly for intellectual types, would have failed in this instance. Dostoevsky's deep study has resulted in an amazing figure. The straight-forwardness of the type rendered his task easier. There is nothing of the double in the old man; he might have been drawn by any contemporary novelist. So much the more astonishing is his superiority; he stands quite alone amongst the sensual monsters of world-literature, an autocrat, a king in depravity. The types which preceded him in Western literature were mere forerunners. Balzac and Zola, in depicting excesses, were satisfied with pictures of partial insanity, which scarcely outvie the desires of normal types. Their work is essentially an eroticism of situation. *Nana*, and whatever else Zola imagined in the guise of his *bête*

THE OLD MAN

humaine, Mirabeau's erotic " supplices," whether they take place in the East or West, Wedekind's burlesques, paint viciousness, and interest only the literary clique. In such a dissection the writer can introduce only little of the personal element, a fact which at times, in Wedekind's drama for example, leads to a curious medley, since sentimentality and cynicism always lie side by side there. In Strindberg the sexual element is involuntarily detached, and on that account the tragi-comic effect is heightened. The tragedy lies not in Strindberg's drama but in himself, this son of a servant, who had in him nothing of the spirit of *A Raw Youth,* and since he spontaneously abandoned himself to his obsession, his fate casts a convincing shadow across the whole of his work. Moreover, child of a time which was already experiencing Dostoevsky, he was able to use Dostoevsky's psychology as a model.

Old Karamazov would have called all these writers *dilettanti.* He has no scruples and is deeply conscious of the usefulness of his amorality. He swallows life like brandy. Sex is the sum and substance of his entire activity. He can never have enough. Whenever the spiritual element enters it narrows his capacity for enjoyment; at most it ought to serve the development of his sexual cunning. He carries that a long way. He does not need to go to Paris or Naples. Nature is inexhaustible. Every town, every hamlet teems with opportunities; of every woman, whatever her age or rank, of the " barefooted " who know nothing of silk and satin, you can create a heaven if only you go about it in the proper way—and what a heaven! " There have never been ugly women for me," he says proudly. Even the filthy village idiot, called Smerdyatchaya, the stinking one, who spends the night in a ditch amongst nettles, is not to be sneered at if you imbue her with the proper spirit.

Those are the words of an artist to whom his craft is everything. The object does not count. I paint a Helen of every wench I meet. The maniacal lust devours every humane feeling and is a law unto itself. Art for art's sake.

" He stands on his voluptuousness as if it were of stone,"
Ivan says of him, and it is difficult to say whether there is
not a touch of envy in the boundless contempt which the
monster inspires in the distracted thinker.

The old man is strong, stronger than all his sons put
together, a monument of filth. Get on with it, think if
you like, pray, curse, go into a monastery, yet you're only
scallywags " with the milk of children in your veins instead
of blood." An inviolable power rages in the old man's
blood, keeps his old body and brain supple, eggs him on,
makes him cunning, makes him cock of the walk. You
must be rich so that when you get too old to excite young
women naturally you can lure them with money and
" dainties." The idea of the great sinner becomes clothed
in flesh and blood. The old man deceives everyone,
particularly his own sons, has deceived two women into
their graves. Smerdyakov, his epileptic cook, was the
outcome of his ' affair with Smerdyatchaya. Is it not
possible to deceive even heaven? Probably there is no
heaven. God is also only an invention of mere milk-sops
and only fools are taken in by this priestly mumbo-jumbo.
Alyosha, poor boy, must not be allowed to fall into their
clutches. What comes after life really does not matter,
and his dear sons need not put themselves to the trouble of
prayers for the dead. If a man makes the most of his life
he has no time for anything else. All the same it is strange
how many people seem to be of a different opinion, not
only idiots. Do you really believe or do you only pretend
to? You ought to try to get at the bottom of that. Sometimes he has an inspiration in the middle of his brandy.
Tell me, Ivan, is there a God? No, says Ivan. Alyosha?
Alyosha says yes. Naturally, what else could he say, he,
the novice! Smerdyakov also has to have his say and
explains with subtlety that there is no God. The old man
becomes irritated at this fruitless waste of energy. Think
of the mass of gold and silver in the monastery alone!
Ivan, who at times gives breath to a dry Shavian humour,
hints that if religion were removed the existence of his

father as well as his tastes would become questionable. Without God men would not be tolerant enough; without God there would be no culture and no brandy. Quite right! says the old man and calls himself an ass. He has had a dark foreboding of something of that sort for a long time. So the monks must be left alone. But for decency's sake and once again quite seriously, is there a God behind all that, yes or no? Is there immortality? " Just a little, the faintest, for all I care? "

Again Ivan denies and Alyosha affirms. Probably Ivan is right, sighs the old man. He reckons with sympathy and antipathy. It is quite definite that Ivan does not believe. The old man takes that for illwill. Everyone ought to believe really, but particularly Ivan, Ivan above everyone. As far as he himself is concerned lack of time excuses him. In any case there is scarcely time to settle the most urgent affairs. But that Ivan fellow who has nothing to do does not even believe in girls. He loves nothing and nobody, a queer fellow! Where does a man like that come from? You have to be careful of Dmitri. Dmitri loses control of himself when he is roused, it would be best to push him off to America for a year or two, if only for Grushenka's sake, but, naturally, without Grushenka. You start squabbling with Dmitri, that's bad! You may run about for weeks with a black eye, a laughing-stock to the girls. Dmitri is a scoundrel. But the other fellow is sinister. In spite of everything the old man has, at bottom, more in common with the religious Alyosha than with the sinister Ivan. You can understand Alyosha, you need not be frightened of him. He believes Ivan capable of anything. You do not feel comfortable sleeping under the same roof as a fellow like that. But probably Alyosha is wrong with his yes and Ivan has hit the mark with his no. People like that are always right.

The psychology of the old man is not complicated and he tries hard not to make it complicated. The more simply you tackle things which other people think important, the more angry they become. Perhaps he is not quite so simple as he makes out; perhaps beneath the surface are all sorts of complications fostered by old age but concealed by his buffoonery. When the obscure things attempt to come to the surface he laughs, or tries to make light of them with his filthy tittering. Tittering is part of his make-up. When at night he has dismissed Grigory, the old servant, and Smerdyakov, the cook, who have to sleep in the outhouse, he trails his tittering through the dark house and waits for Grushenka. Is she coming or not, this beauty of beauties? The envelope with the 3000 roubles is in readiness. And dainties into the bargain, he titters. Whether she will come is more important than the existence of God and nearly as negative; nearly, not quite. Somewhere in the desert, thinks the subtle Smerdyakov, there may perhaps be two persons who can believe thus in God and command the mountain to glide into the sea, whereupon the said mountain will not fail to perform its allotted task. Two persons are not much, and where are they? Grushenka at least you can see. The odds are on her.

The old man is a gambler and has endowed all his sons, including Smerdyakov, with the spirit of gambling, apart from other vices. He carries it further than they, even with his ugly face which bears traces of maltreatment. A dozen times he stands in front of the mirror, arranges his red silk scarf and calculates. It is possible that with this face Grushenka is lost once and for all and is rushing to his rival, the younger man. But he has never been so handsome as to entice a Grushenka. It is possible that just the opposite will happen, out of sheer perversity, when she learns to whom he owes the bruises! Pity, he titters. Who knows, with women! This creature always makes me think of the old Dutch toper, particularly when his leering face, with its wrinkles and furrowed brows and baggy eyes, grins in the mirror. We can imagine the sire of the Karamazov's as one of Rembrandt's favourite models. On the night of the murder he has dressed himself up in honour of the vainly awaited Grushenka. He wears a coloured silk

THE LAST PORTRAIT OF DOSTOEVSKY

Taken in 1880, six months before his death

[*face p. 294*

dressing-gown tied with a silken cord. Golden studs
glitter in the D..tch linen. Thus he stands in the brightly
illuminated open window and peers into the darkness. To
his first-born who comes to look inside for the very woman
whom the old man believes he hears outside, this dressed-
up scarecrow must seem like a phantom from another
world.

Their father's depravity has been the cause of much
suffering to the three sons. He has never troubled about
them. Like Arkady, they were brought up in some distant
spot, far apart. They happened to be cared for by relatives.
Only now all three have returned home. Alyosha lives as
a novice in the monastery into which, with his beloved
Zossima's permission, he wants to enter permanently. He
wears the cowl without a vow. He was drawn here by his
wish to see his mother's grave. The eldest, Dmitri, a
short while ago an officer, son of the first marriage, came,
by force of circumstances, to settle his inheritance with his
fraudulent father and has taken a room in the town. Only
Ivan stays as a guest in the house.

The sons scarcely knew their father till recently and
his depravity is therefore brought home to them all the
more forcefully. There can be no greater humiliation to
Ivan and Dmitri than to be descended from this creature;
particularly to Ivan. They do not mention it. Each of
them observes with gnashing teeth, this is your father, this
monster who, to satisfy his voluptuousness, openly prostitutes himself at every opportunity. Realization of this fact
puts the finishing touch to Ivan's doctrine which fights shy
of God and man. Dmitri vents his fury without restraint,
provoked by his father's mad passion for Grushenka. The
monster must be put to death. Alyosha alone does not
hate his father because hatred is not in his nature. But
far from suffering any the less on that account, he may
suffer even more than the others, for he is the only person
whom the old man pretends to love. This horrible situation
is set out in the extensive first act. The action begins in
the monastery. Dmitri has agreed with his father to have

DOSTOEVSKY

out in front of Zossima their dispute about the inheritance
from his mother. Besides the sons various relatives and
friends of the family are present. Fyodor Pavlovitch turns
the affair into a farce. His shameful buffoonery is doubly
infamous in this venerable *milieu* which everyone, even the
unbelieving Ivan, treats with the utmost reverence. With
his cheap jokes he mocks everything which bars his path,
including Zossima himself, and plays the sentimental drunkard; all for the sake of not having to pay Ivan. Instead of
discussing the legal position he reveals Dmitri's secret in
the most brutal way, how he was betrothed to Katerina
Ivanovna and left her in the lurch on Grushenka's account.
Dmitri is at his wit's end. Nothing but the sanctity of the
place restrains him.

The scene in the house between the drunken father and
his two sons, Ivan and Alyosha, carries the situation a step
further. The old man relates how once, in order to purge
Alyosha's mother of her mysticism, he took her miracle-
working icon from the wall and spat on it before her eyes.
His mother, beside herself, wanted to fall on him but only
succeeded in clasping her hands and suddenly sank to the
ground as if struck by lightning. The drunkard has
scarcely ended when Alyosha trembles like a leaf, clasps
his hands and faints. The old man calls for water. Ivan
is to sprinkle water in the boy's face, quickly. That is
how they brought his mother round too, just like that.
Alyosha has collapsed because of his mother, because of
the *klikuscha*,[1] his dear mother.

" I believe his mother was my mother too, do you
understand! " says Ivan, his face distorted.

No, the drunkard does not understand.

" What do you mean, your mother too? " he mumbles
stupidly. " What do you mean? What mother are you
talking of? "

He pulls himself together and gradually it dawns on
him. The devil! The *klikuscha* is Ivan's mother too; he
had quite forgotten that.

[1] Russian. A woman possessed with the devil.—TR.

STRUCTURE

At that moment Dmitri bursts in expecting to find Grushenka here and the old man is badly knocked about. It had to be. Ivan and Alyosha intervene and the old man only escapes by the skin of his teeth. Later on Ivan suggests to Alyosha that the old man was very nearly done for.

" God forbid! "

" Forbid? why? " mumbles Ivan. " One insect will devour the other and it will serve them both right."

When Alyosha shudders Ivan observes casually that of course he will stop that sort of thing in future, but at the moment he has a headache.

Alyosha sits at his father's bedside. The old man's first word on recovering is about Ivan. What is Ivan saying? What is he doing? Where is he? As if it were Ivan and not Dmitri who had knocked him about, another allusion to his greater enemy.

Alyosha finds Ivan sitting outside and expresses his deep anxiety about Dmitri and their father. Possibly one day they will find their father murdered. Ivan's allusion to the insects also troubles him. Has any one man the right to determine whether or not another man shall live?

Such questions, suggests Ivan, are decided naturally, not as a matter of right or worthiness. Moreover everyone has the right to desire what he will.

" But surely not another man's death! "

" Why not even death ultimately? Why be bothered if all men live like that and ultimately are incapable of living in any other way? "

Ivan reveals himself so casually that he scarcely seems serious. He asks Alyosha with a smile whether he considers him capable of murdering the old man.

" What are you thinking of, Ivan? I have never for one moment entertained such a thought. I don't think Dmitri would do such a thing either."

Ivan accepts that with a nonchalant smile. He will always protect the old man. " All the same I retain complete liberty of desire in any given instance."

297

A main thread of the action is prepared. The fact that, for the first time since their separation, the brothers meet in the atmosphere of their father is peculiarly favourable to the dramatic course of events. Their father inspires them to say things which help to explain the situation, particularly their relationship to one another. In so far as Alyosha is an intermediary in all or nearly all the relationships, he is the hero. He alone has anything in common with his father. He alone is mediator between the hostile elements, Dmitri and Ivan, between the hostile women, Katerina and Grushenka, who widen the gulf between the two brothers; he is mediator in the town whenever he is called upon, and, finally, between town and monastery, his most difficult task, which casts a symbolic light on everything else.

Since the action involves members of the same family who, either directly or through Alyosha, are in constant contact with one another and bound together by a varied but all the same perceptible blood-relationship, this complicated structure appears simpler and more compact than most other works.

The two main female characters, counterparts of the two hostile brothers, each have a double relationship with different members of the family; Grushenka with the father and Dmitri; Katerina with Dmitri and Ivan; to a point also the third woman, Lisa Hohlakov, with Alyosha and Ivan. All these cross-currents stir up the main stream of the action which remains within the family and finally drags in the illegitimate son also. Alyosha, the only innocent one, is at the end quite alone on the scene.

In addition some thirty subsidiary characters appear like a huge orchestra with every conceivable instrument. Yet this vast canvas entirely avoids the confusion of characters which troubled the reader of *A Raw Youth* right to the end. In spite of the digressions the huge central structure remains undisturbed. In our memory even the extensive story of Zossima curves round the main theme. Dostoevsky makes use of a kind of revolving stage which does good service to this novel-drama with its numerous threads of action. One could imagine two storeys; on the lower the large revolving stage where the scenes change and the *tempo* is gradually quickened; on the upper the white monastery with hermitage and cell. Surrounding all this, the wood. This arrangement makes for unity of place. During the greater part the eye falls again and again on the peaceful white walls. Then, when Alyosha has renounced this tranquil spot, the monastery is veiled in darkness and completely vanishes into the swirling clouds whilst the action moves at full speed below. When peace reigns again this white sunny stonework has become a large grey building which serves a different purpose. So it remains till the end. Unity of time is rigidly adhered to until the indispensable interlude between the night of the murder and the court scene. In the centre of the family sits the old man enthroned on a slightly raised dais; in front of him, to the right and left, Ivan and Dmitri, the two blood-relations, enemies of their father and of one another; a glowing triangle. In front of them, a long way in front, Alyosha; at the wing on Ivan's side stands Smerdyakov, and behind him, Rakitin; at the wing on Dmitri's side, Grushenka.

The Karamazov demon in Ivan, the Westerner, has taken an intellectual turn. The old man's tittering materialism has led his son to the vague abode of his " Euclidean reasoning " into which he wants to inveigle Alyosha. These two brothers present a curious freak of nature, for they have nothing in common in their attitude, yet they must have resembled one another in tone of voice, even in appearance; they had the same mother. Both steer clear of unchastity, Alyosha because of his purity, Ivan because of the thinker's need to conserve his energy for the building of his vague abode, or, as a last resort, because of his weakness. At times Ivan's restraint has the effect of the unchastity of a eunuch. " Such men are not human beings but whirling sand," says the old man who knows the world. Ivan's vague abode has to become a misanthropic dwelling of abstraction, an underworld den with ivory walls. He is still building it and will never dwell there permanently. He lacks the strength for solitude. He wants fellow-dwellers, would like Alyosha to join him, persuades himself that Alyosha is exposed to danger in the monastery garden and belongs to him. Failing Alyosha he will be content with more modest lodgers. He pretends to be maturer than he actually is. Alyosha thinks he sees through him and attributes his immaturity to his youthfulness. He does not realize his brother's weakness. Ivan oscillates between Stavrogin and Versilov. Versilov's ideas about love of mankind, which you can attain only by holding your nose, and about the most precious burial-grounds in Europe recur word for word, but an Ivan is not actuated by the motive of a Versilov. His behaviour towards Katerina is only partly dictated by Versilov's humanity. To him Katya's self-torment in her love for Dmitri is one of those unfathomable convictions for which, as Versilov said, women will let themselves be crucified, but behind Ivan's intellect, which sees that at its true worth, there is none of Versilov's warmth—hence the tendency to the unreal and to unbelief, two weaknesses which Dostoevsky considered inter-related. In his opinion they constitute the breeding ground of Russian anarchy (56). The wise Zossima says to Ivan: "For the moment you are acting in desperation when you write newspaper-articles and discourse in society without even believing in your own arguments." It is true that Ivan is tormented, but the newspaper articles and society have claims on him. Desperation will not drive him to any decision. His thought-out rationalism surpasses that of the father he despises who wanted to purge his *klikuscha* of mysticism. Since in his opinion morality rests solely on belief in immortality and since he does not believe in immortality he arrives at the axiom that "everything is permissible," a dictum which finds adherents. All the same it would be sullying his fingers to pursue this theory in practice. He contents himself with retaining complete liberty of desire in this inſtance. Ivan is the perfeſt Hamlet-type of a new age, unsuccessfull; attempted by Doſtoevsky in Stavrogin. The sphinxlike, heroic pose is dropped. We are in direſt contaſt with Ivan's philosophy. We see him ſtruggle for it and around it and become a martyr to it. He is the tragic figure in the book. Doſtoevsky succeeds in creating the tragedy exclusively by means of a few definite incidents in this thinker's life and does not have recourse to the chance fate of a man debarred from taking an aſtive part in life. His passivity makes him the hidden mainspring of the aſtion. The long discussion between Ivan and Alyosha, which introduces Ivan into the foreground, begins casually and is thoroughly Russian. They have been here together for nearly three months and have scarcely spoken a word. They have met only on a few fleeting occasions in Moscow. Ivan wants to go away shortly; it crossed his mind that it would be pleasant to know his brother before leaving and to bid him good-bye. What are we talking about? The old man and Dmitri, or love for that romantic young woman Katerina? A decent fellow does not discuss personalities. Well then, about God! Or shall we begin with the devil? We know Doſtoevsky's method of ſtressing the serious by making it sound slightly comic.

There is naïveté in Ivan's unbelief. Pity, which seems to have been the foundation of his vague abode, lends a human touch to his thought. Why is there so much torment in this world of God? Humanity suffers and is so senselessly organized that its suffering only increases. Ivan wants to unroll before Alyosha the whole piſture of humanity's suffering, a mere bagatelle for a young Russian. But for the sake of brevity he will speak of only a tenth part of humanity, only of the suffering of children. Why do children have to suffer? There may be juſtice in the torments of adults, for they have eaten of the apple, are omniscient, and therefore have become " like God." But the little ones have not yet eaten. " Do you love little children, Alyosha? " The tempter does not need to ask, often enough he has seen Alyosha in the company of children. He himself loves children; a murderer himself can love them. If there were only children, Christ's command would be a mere trifle, though they were ugly and smelt.

Ivan has made a fine collection of the tortures of children. One suspects he has had someone else's assistance. Dostoevsky, the child-worshipper, has had a hand in it. Ivan unpacks the usual parcel, then more spicy things.

What's the idea? groans Alyosha, flushed like some dreaming youth. What for? So that we may recognize the rational arrangement of the world and the harmony towards which we are moving.

Then follow choicer stories. Ivan talks with feverish rapidity. None of these things have been invented, they are gospel truth. Everything appeared in the newspapers giving date and place (57); the story of the foolish Albert in Switzerland, the swine-herd who was not even allowed to eat husks and was bound to become a murderer; repented shortly before his execution, to the moral satisfaction of the whole of Geneva, began to praise God and the universal harmony and was beheaded with a last word of praise on his lips; the story of the five-year old girl whom her parents, worthy people, tortured to death in the most refined way; that of the little boy who, for the amusement of the general, was torn to pieces by hounds.

He dips more and more deeply into his fiendish basket. Shall I stop, Alyosha? No, quiver Alyosha's lips. At last this gentle novice in the monk's cowl is so deeply moved that he too could kill the monster who devours children.

Ivan laughs. Just fancy, a little monk like that!

Alyosha pulls himself together. He has said something stupid. Everything is senseless, observes Ivan, striving to introduce sense is only misrepresenting facts. "Listen! If everyone has to suffer in order to pay the price of eternal harmony, then please tell me what that has to do with little children! Why are they also only manure to fertilize the soil for someone else's future harmony?"

Ivan grows. He puts the children aside, embraces "all

the tears of mankind with which the earth is soaked from its surface down to its very core." He is so swayed by the spirit of rebellion that he forgets his usual dialecticism; his abstract thought is shattered and he is faced with the burning question, " What is it all for? If eternal harmony comes all the same at the end of all this horror, then I can do without it, for it can never atone for its millions and thousands of millions of senseless sacrifices. I don't want to see the mother embrace the torturer of her son in Christian forgiveness, the sight would disgust me." The harmony is not worth one single tear of the tortured child which beats its breast with its little fist and prays to its beloved God—of what use is vengeance to me, what good to me are the hellish torments of the torturer, how can hell ever make amends?—and where is the harmony if there is still a hell? He will not sing in chorus, " righteous art Thou, O Lord, for Thy ways are made manifest! " He will sing neither to-day nor on the day of judgment. And therefore he returns his " ticket of admission." It is not God he rejects. God is man's greatest invention. But he rejects God's world. As an honourable man he cannot accept it.

" That is rebellion! " stammers Alyosha.

Then Ivan puts the simple question, " assume that you had to erect the edifice of human destiny with the ultimate object of making everyone happy and of creating at last an atmosphere of peace and goodwill, but that to this end you had inevitably to torture to death one single tiny being— would you undertake it? tell me, and don't lie! " And Alyosha replies as his pure mind was bound to reply, " No, I would not undertake it."

" And can you believe," Ivan asks further, " that the people for whom you are building will agree to accept their good fortune at the price of that drop of blood so un- righteously spilt? "

And again Alyosha replies, " No I cannot believe it."

In *The Possessed* this vital question has been broached by Dostoevsky far more searchingly, but he has never lent the hopeless question such force of obvious simplicity. There is nothing of the negative in this fiery rebel. It is not his reasoning alone which rebels and accuses. Neither could Versilov have reproached him with being a smug controversialist nor Shatov have spoken of a lackey mind.

It is magnificent that the novice offers no resistance to the torch of Ivan's rebellion, but naturally he soon retorts in the only way possible to a disciple of Zossima and mentions Christ. The edifice has been built up on Him. That is no answer to Ivan's accusation. It is not Christ he has doubted. The fate and works of Christ are only a further confirmation, and Ivan recounts his story of the Grand Inquisitor. In the sixteenth century when the Spanish Inquisition is burning its victims by scores, Christ comes to earth again, this time wrapt in silence. The people recognize Him at once. The Grand Inquisitor also recognizes Him and has Him arrested at the gates of Seville cathedral. Christ is led to prison. At night the Grand Inquisitor visits Him and the church settles accounts with its idol. Christ has blundered. It was not His humanity and the freedom which He brought, or thought to bring, which could help man born rebellious. In allowing them to act according to their own dictates He has only increased their torment. Christ's failure arose in the wilderness when the great spirit approached Him in order, so the books say, to tempt Him, and put the three questions to Him. It was then that the greatest miracle happened. It was within the mighty tempter's power to give those questions form and substance. Christ has doubtless weighed up the three questions, for he was a god and superior to the fearful spirit and refrained from turning the stones into bread. Man does not live by bread alone. Thus He decreed. The first, most terrible of blunders, for man must have bread before he can obey commands and be virtuous. Christ behaved like a god amongst gods, not with the benevolence which humanity needs. He thought only of the chosen, not of the millions and thousands of millions of feeble ones. But to the church the millions are also dear. He scorned the miracle, scorned unconditional worship, scorned the surest means, the secret. Fortunately He went and the church was able to retrieve His failure. From love of humanity it subsequently accepted the command of the great spirit in the wilderness. Christ has burdened the servants of the church with the torture of lying in His name. They have invented miracle, worship and the secret, and thereby corrected what could be corrected. Now He has come back. What does He want? To destroy what in fifteen hundred years has been built up with great pains? It cannot be allowed. If anyone deserves burning at the stake, it is He, this spirit returned to earth. To-morrow He will be burned.

The " poem " which the cynic Ivan calls senseless stuff deals exhaustively with whatever reproach an orthodox Russian, and not only an orthodox one, can level at the Catholic Church, and not only at the Catholic Church. Dostoevsky has often expressed that Rome serves not Christ but the devil; but never in a form so picturesque, dignified, and full of tragic grandeur.

Dostoevsky took the outline of the Grand Inquisitor from the father-and-son drama of Schiller whose problems so obsessed him in his youth that he overlooked the occasional shortcomings of Schiller's fiery portrayal. The connexion between the two scenes, to which Bodisco has recently drawn attention, is not confined to the theme (58). The few words of the Inquisitor in Don Carlos contain elements of the fanaticism of Dostoevsky's figure. The Russian retains the stern manner which has grandeur in Schiller's drama too, but shrouds the figure in a veil of tragic demonry. The icy power of the ecclesiastic crumbles before Christ's dignity. The Saviour appears in place of the feeble king who completely breaks down in the final scene of *Don Carlos*. This exchange of personages permits the inner action, which Schiller omitted, to be worked out with a masterliness which has no counterpart in the domain of Philip and his son. One would never expect the majesty of these scenes from the creator of the Karamazovs. It is only the Grand Inquisitor who speaks. Christ listens in silence to all his accusations. He has nothing to add to the word with which He went to the cross. When the old man has finished Christ steps up to him without a word and kisses him. " And, listen, the old Inquisitor's lips quiver. He goes to the door of the vaulted prison and says: Go! and come never again! "

Thus even the mature Dostoevsky was still in close communion with the god of his youth. There is also other evidence of that (59).

Dostoevsky has not meted out to Schiller the kind of purification which Van Gogh accorded Millet. It could never be said that Dostoevsky's was a simplification, or that he divested it of the sentimental. His restitution of Schiller goes deeper and enriches him in every sense. It is not by a categorically different interpretation that he exalts the same material by more modern methods. Rather the *motif*— and here the distinction from the Van Gogh-Millet parallel —is widened in the spirit of the model, and from the feeble king arises a radiant god.

The immensity of this achievement can scarcely be appreciated at first sight. Schiller's ideas are carried much further, his play is seen in a new light and becomes capable of interpreting the greatest problem of our age. In the Grand Inquisitor new forces are gathered of which the author of *Don Carlos* had no inkling. With the parable of the stones and bread rigid Catholicism becomes the main-stay of mass-religion of our days which, with the slogan of universal equality, deprives man of everything irrational and thereby seeks to impose on him a far more terrible tyranny. Socialism creeps into the deserted bed of the worldly church and a hundred funeral pyres flame up afresh. The old dignitary of Seville repeats in different words the creed of *The Possessed*.

Our habitual disdain of Schiller is silenced at the thought of this venerable connexion with Dostoevsky. It did not exist before Dostoevsky. In his speech on Pushkin, his public swan-song, Schiller shines, between Cervantes and

THE GRAND INQUISITOR

Shakespeare, as one of the three brilliant ſtars in the heavens of European literature. That none of us will agree to that does not matter. We suddenly recognize that what with a shrug we are wont to call Schiller's mentality and to dismiss as *vieux jeu*, was ſtill a living force in this Russian, and therefore ſtill lives in so far as Doſtoevsky may be deemed a living force amongſt us. He lives not only in Doſtoevsky's gratitude but throughout his work. It is ſtrange that Doſtoevsky noticed something we had missed, and that we Germans have to thank him for the revelation.

Doſtoevsky found in Schiller neither form nor theme, but inspiration. He continued *Don Carlos*, a faćt which is of greater significance to the analysis of his work than any other association. What little is traceable of French or even Russian influence is confined to his early work. In one form or another he has introduced the German poet at every ſtage and has finally erećted a noble monument in his memory.

The Inquisitor scene is not the only connexion of the Karamazovs with Schiller. Here the elećtive affinity encroaches direćtly on the subſtance as once in *The Insulted and Injured*. But the Schilleresque is so often encountered in the novel that we have to assume it is meant to serve as local colouring. Even old Karamazov does not escape its influence. He compares himself to old Moor. Ivan has less than the others of this family trait and has recourse to it more as an artiſtic veneer; not always with such a happy result as in his poem. When at Madame Holakov's Ivan's feelings towards Katerina are touched upon, the German quotation from his lips only renders feebler a scene already feeble. Alyosha is expressly aſtonished at finding his brother on the track of Schiller. Probably this is a preparation for the far more ſtriking connexion with the Grand Inquisitor.

After Ivan's recital there follows a true Doſtoevsky touch. Ivan perceives that his attempt to lure Alyosha into his abode has miscarried. Persuasion was in vain, he remains alone. Alyosha grieves for his brother whose laſt resort is realization of the senselessness of everything and the dictum, everything is permissible. What will become of Ivan?

" You have finished with me?" asks Ivan of his brother. Alyosha steps up to him and kisses him on the mouth, softly and silently.

" That's plagiarism!" laughs Ivan.

. . . . . .

Dmitri is the born Schiller type. Ivan is the Franz Moor of whom Schiller says in his preface, " vice is revealed here together with all its inner machinery. It makes powerless abstractions of Franz' confused conscience, reduces the guide of feeling to a mere shadow, and jestingly brushes aside the serious voice of religion. Whoever goes to those lengths (a distinction which we do not envy him), that is, of refining his reason at the cost of his feeling, to him the holy is no longer holy, to him humanity and God mean nothing—both worlds are as nothing in his eyes."

And Dmitri is Karl Moor of whom it is said, " a spirit whom the most depraved vice attracts only for the sake of the greatness which depends on it; for the sake of the power which it claims; for the sake of the dangers which accompany it. A remarkable and important being, equipped with every faculty necessary for becoming either a Brutus or a Catiline, according to the trend of the faculty. Unfortunate chains of circumstances determine the latter and he arrives at the former only at the end of an immense complication. False notions of activity and influence, abundance of vitality which burst through the barrier of every law were naturally bound to come to grief in everyday surroundings, and to these enthusiastic dreams of greatness and action only bitterness against the unideal world had to be added to give the rare Don Quixote whom in the robber Moor we abhor and love, admire and pity."

We do not hesitate for a moment in our sympathy between Ivan and Dmitri. We should all have forgiven him, even if he had killed his father in the wild scene at the beginning. He could never commit Smerdyakov's crime. If we imagine Dmitri as the slayer of his father, the distinction between manslaughter and murder can no longer be the subject of a legal quibble. Dmitri cannot commit any treacherous or humiliating act. Like many of Dostoevsky's liars he lies for the sake of appearance, from laziness, caprice, shame and arrogance, as a drunkard, as a poet, just as every decent, living person must lie, but not from avarice. Straightforward vulgarity is conceivable, but not premeditated meanness. That side of his father is quite foreign to him. Not the father's filth. In his blood rages the same eagerness for debauchery, but it is only a means to an end, an outlet for his craving for excitement, not, as in the old man, his sole *raison d'être*. As an officer he has learnt only how to die for honour, and he wants to live. His thirst for life has afforded him time to find his level. Everything bubbles over in him, particularly his generosity. His excesses are only miscarried generosity. His depravity is a figment of his imagination; he lacks the necessary burrowing instinct of his father. His demon storms heavenwards. Hell would attract him merely as a giddy abyss to plunge into head first if he happened to be oppressed by some action he thought dishonourable. A robust soldier, fit for any hardship—if only there were hardships!—of boyish sensitiveness. He is the oldest in years but in essence the youngest of the brothers.

His robberlike disorderliness surpasses, if possible, the utter slovenliness of his father who is actuated by greed. The old man finds in his slovenliness a fitting subject for cynical buffoonery. Dmitri suffers under his disorderliness, wants to hide it, and in trying to escape it goes from bad to worse. Nevertheless he feels the infamy of his existence and acquiesces in the contempt of Ivan who calls him and his father insects. Ivan is restrained, has an orderly mind, polish. In spite of that Dmitri would not be Ivan if he could; that is just what he cannot forgive himself. He wants something different. To charge through the crowd on a wild steed! Come along, brother! Up and fight the dragon! All the dragons in the world! Then the knight is arrested and forced to take off his soiled shirt before the eyes of everybody. At that moment he would not mind murdering three fathers.

In spite of all his disorderliness there is apparent a quite definite, distinguishing vein which regulates his inner life, even if it does not curb his superficial self; indeed it necessitates a certain licence in his bohemianism. This vein is so marked that we can immediately gauge what his reactions will be in given circumstances. He pursues his course, whether or not it is to his advantage, whether or not it pleases others with whom he comes into contact. Just that feature might be called his order or disorder. His emotion is not difficult to comprehend. Not one of the Karamazovs, not even Alyosha possesses such transparent, such unswerving feeling. Such a character points to a poet. He is a poet, though a poem by him is inconceivable. An illiterate poet! Dostoevsky accompanies his entry with several poetical quotations. Schiller's lines sound curious in his mouth. There is a touch of mockery in it which is to excuse his presumption in quoting. He has not the slightest notion of form, does not even know how Zossima ought to be addressed, and he is always hoping that his emotion will carry him through. Schiller has to speak for him. Schiller is his mouthpiece.

In Ivan there are poetical possibilities and he seizes on poetical expression to render his philosophy more persuasive. Like Raskolnikov he writes spirited essays for the newspapers, probably also for his own edification, but does not want to be considered a writer at any price. He is as arrogant and misanthropic as the hero of the "sinner"-novel who actually stooped to humility in order to stimulate his arrogance. He knows quite well how to address Zossima and displays profound reverence. He has as little desire to be considered compassionate as literary. Pity is only means to an end.

Dmitri abandons himself. Be embraced, millions! His disorderliness is a form of love of humanity. Alyosha, let us love one another. It may be Katya, it may be Grushenka, it's all the same, only love, so fervently that our miserable ego dissolves with all its dross. Dmitri does not write poetry, he invents; he can only live if he invents and he strains every nerve to attain this bliss, if only for a second. No rationalism mars his ecstasy. His nobility bursts through all the dross; he will not sacrifice one atom of his belief, even at the price of his existence. I am vulgar, filthy, depraved and victim of every possible temptation, but all that is only a stupid and irritating trifle. At bottom I am good, believe me, good, not from any merit, but from the way I'm made; I cannot be different. I love the beautiful. Yes, how can I make that credible, I, a man living in filth? Still, that's all it is, nothing but that. It is perfectly clear to me that I should be a miserable fool to want anything different. I see it in Grushenka too. There is something beautiful in her too, a movement, a line, goodness knows, something in her face and in her little toe. No, it's nothing to do with her body. I say that, I who burn for her body, who would sell my salvation for a night with her. Yes, I say that. It has so little to do with the body that if she gave herself to me and said, " don't touch me," I not alone would not, but could not touch her. I would sit next her and talk to her. I could talk to her all my life. I hate what is ugly. I say that, the most ugly of all, but I can't help it. A man could be so repulsive to me that I could kill him. If I were to see a man intentionally ugly and wantonly jeering at beauty, I could kill him, even if he were my father, because plague must be rooted out. Of course, nobody ought to kill. If it came to the point I probably shouldn't do it all the same. Let plague flourish for all I care! Who knows what good it may do!

Dmitri is Dostoevsky's masterpiece, though almost improvized. There are bits of Ivan in many earlier characters; the type already appears in *The Double*. Alyosha is foreshadowed in *The Idiot*; his forerunner helps us to understand him and also helped Dostoevsky. Dmitri is as surprising as is old Karamazov. He too is not quite without prototypes. Rogozhin, Myshkin's brother in the cross, has certain preparatory characteristics, notably his impulsive vehemence, but nothing of the latent poet. Rogozhin was up to that time the most real of Dostoevsky's characters. This boyar with the knife in his boot was by no means a phantom. We have already seen that he arose spontaneously. Compare him to Dmitri and he becomes a fleeting sketch, a shadowy impression, effective only in outline, a profile. Dmitri is shown in the same bold profile and at the same time in three dimensions. He is rounded off in the same way as old Karamazov. Even the central figures of *The Idiot* and *Crime and Punishment* have not the same reality. It is only when the degree of reality in the drawing of Dmitri has been grasped that the drawing of Ivan can be appreciated. Strange how one supports the other, although they never meet alone. There is never a duologue between them—what would they have to say to one another?—but despite that we glance from one to the other. The drawing of Ivan takes longer and does not attain its object till the end of the novel, whilst we understand Dmitri's rhythm in the first half hour. The active type of a Dmitri has a deeper appeal than the restrained type of an Ivan, though ultimately that is no special criterion. What moves us in Dmitri is his humanity rather than his success as a living character. The *chiaroscuro* atmosphere surrounds both of them.

The two women who determine Dmitri's fate constitute a counterpart to Aglaia and Nastasya, but they are different both in nature and appearance. Katerina hails from the realm of Aglaia, behaves similarly, but has none of her tomboy charm. She is more like Madame Ahmakov. Grushenka has had the same sort of experience as Nastasya, but gets over it. She does not belong to the obscure realm of the insulted and injured, but on a throne which is later prepared for her. She is as much a surprise amongst Dostoevsky's women as Dmitri, her born mate, amongst the men. All these figures, including Lisa and her loquacious mamma, the episodic Madame Hohlakov, point to Dostoevsky's maturity in character drawing. Compared to her successor Madame Ahmakov almost ceases to appear real. If Katya had been drawn with the least partiality on the part of the author she would promptly have sunk into the abyss where she really belongs, and would have lost her really womanly touch. It is Dmitri who relates what has happened before the story begins, how this proud girl called on the light-headed lieutenant and asked him for money to save her father who had embezzled regimental funds and was threatening to shoot himself. Dmitri "confesses" this in his first intimate conversation with Alyosha, which assures the relationship between the two brothers. The confession is essential, for the significance of the scene with Katya depends on its being narrated by the participant. Dostoevsky had to make his hero, of whom we know little at this juncture, reveal both himself and Katerina in the manner in which he recounted this affair. That is one of those hundreds of problems with which Dostoevsky's path was strewn and which we accept without any notion of the difficulties, insuperable to any other man. If the tone is suitable, everything is all right; but the art lies precisely in pitching the tone in such a way that in the money-business any pride or certainly any vagueness of attitude in Dmitri is avoided and the proper impression conveyed. If that does not succeed naturally, it does not succeed at all.

Dmitri had a second's great discomfort. It turned out all right eventually, but there was the second. When this proud, unapproachable, beautiful girl, who had already treated him like dirt, suddenly stood before him in his room, still unapproachable, for she only took this bold step for her father's sake, he hesitated for a moment. Incidentally it involved all that remained of his inheritance, but that was not the reason. The remainder of his inheritance in the shape of a 5000 rouble note lay in a book, in a dictionary, and was only waiting to go the way of all the other notes. Something else restrained him in that second. He was tempted to play a trick on this unapproachable beauty. He confesses everything to Alyosha, calls himself a vile insect. Katerina had never been more beautiful than at that moment, quite unapproachably beautiful, and naturally he ought to have reached out at once for the dictionary. But just because she was so unapproachable and he was a vile insect, despised by her, of course, despite her anxiety, he was suddenly seized by a kind of madness, he itched now at this very moment to do something quite unexpected and to act, not as Dmitri Karamazov, but as some sort of shopkeeper, and in the charming tone of a merchant to offer, confidentially, obligingly, not the absolutely necessary four or five thousand roubles, but say two hundred little roubles because, it goes without saying, a right-minded person does not fling his money to the winds. That did not last long. He removed the note from the dictionary, slipped it into an envelope, and with a courteous bow handed it to her.

" She trembled, stared at me rigidly for a second, then turned terribly pale, white as a sheet and suddenly—also without a word, all the same not precipitately but thus— she gently knelt down right in front of me, made a deep, deep bow and touched the floor with her forehead. Not like a schoolgirl, no, but like a Russian! When she had run off—do you know, I was wearing my sword and I wrenched it from its scabbard and was going to stab myself. Why, I don't know, and it would of course have been frightfully stupid, probably exaltation. Do you understand that a man can kill himself from exaltation, a certain kind of exaltation? All the same I didn't stab myself, I only kissed the blade and pushed it back into the scabbard— which incidentally I need not have mentioned now."

Is this exalted person who kisses his sword a Russian supposed to be living fifty years ago, or is he perhaps some Theodor Körner?[1]

The beautiful woman goes to Moscow, inherits an

[1] A German poet whose death in the War of Liberation of 1813 secured immortality for his literary work. His volume, *Schwert und Leier*, has furnished the example.—TR.

unexpected fortune, and becomes fabulously rich. One day a letter arrives for Dmitri " which pierced him to the core." The proud Katya offers to be his wife. She is content to be his chattel, the carpet beneath his feet, and so forth. He becomes engaged to her, but has to remain in the garrison town, and as Ivan happens to be in Moscow he sends him to her. Ivan falls in love with her, but she stands by Dmitri. Of course, asserts Dmitri, she loves only her own noble-mindedness. Moreover he has had to promise her to give up his dissolute life, for she naturally wants to save him. But he cannot change his skin and is going into the back-alley to Grushenka. Everything is useless. He no longer belongs to her, nor she to him. What use to her is such a man as he? Ivan who hates him because of her senseless intention would be a hundred times worthier. Now she is here in the town, and Alyosha is to go and say good-bye to her for him. A man who goes to Grushenka cannot be her betrothed. That is perfectly clear.

Alyosha tries to talk him over. He does not consider Katya's behaviour senseless. He thoroughly understands her loving a man like Dmitri. Alyosha misunderstands her and thereby shows that in his sympathy he is on our side. He certainly does not know Katerina's mind which deep down resents Dmitri's generosity and is more suited to Ivan; above all Alyosha has no notion that Dmitri's consideration for her at that time was a gift too lavish and too unexpected, a gift which flung her too deeply into the mud.

Then Dmitri confesses his passion for Grushenka. Everything Alyosha has been told about it fits in. If Grushenka is willing he will marry her to-morrow. But she does not want to yet. " Perhaps later " she laughs. For three nights he wooed her, the three nights in Mokroe. The gipsies fiddled, everyone danced, Mokroe was swimming in champagne. He paid for the three nights with someone else's money, squandered thousands and succeeded only in making her laugh at him all the more. It was only her foot he was allowed to kiss, her little toe. She is said to have belonged to many men, the laſt of them an old merchant who taught her about money-matters. So it is said. She laughs. Now his father is on her tracks, everybody is. Perhaps his father will get her because he has money. If you ask her she says neither yes nor no, but only laughs. He will be her slave, will fan the *samovar* for her lovers, will clean her lovers' galoshes.

This is similar to Rogozhin's abandonment. In the three nights at Mokroe there is a repetition of the silver tinkling of the troikas when the boyar rushed off with his prey and his horde. In contraſt to the pure and noble Katerina, Grushenka is introduced only as from the back-alley, a cat-like, cruel whore, a figure out of the inferno. Poor Alyosha's eyes burn when he hears her mentioned.

But something weighs more heavily upon Dmitri than all that. Those three nights were celebrated at Katerina's expense. She gave him three thousand roubles to take to the provincial capital; and he took them to Mokroe inſtead. If he is to plunge headfirſt to the devil he does not want to carry that burden of guilt with him. Juſt because there were once money matters between him and her he muſt return her those three thousand roubles.

That is his confession. He makes no mention of the one faƈtor which torments him moſt. He did not squander the whole three thousand roubles in Mokroe; he retained half as an iron ration. He will need it when Grushenka at laſt says yes. If you have no money Grushenka laughs at you. And he will go off with her the moment she agrees. That is why he is not touching this secret money which he carries at his breaſt. This gamble, which little suits him, ſtrikes him as the worſt feature, for it turns a whim into villainy and makes him a pickpocket. He is suffering under it. Of course he could have made a clean breaſt of it and obtained Katerina's forgiveness, even if she had known of the misappropriation.—I have squandered half of it, there, take what's left!—It would not have been so bad, particularly if it had been done at once on the day following the Mokroe affair. She knows with whom she has to deal. Now it is growing worse every day. The wallet with the money at his breast burns him. He cannot make up his mind to confess this to Alyosha. At a later date it leads to his undoing.

The wallet plays the same part as the letter sewn into Arkady's coat. But here there is psychological subtlety in the use of such expedients. The ominous factor is no longer resorted to arbitrarily, as in *A Raw Youth*, it only plays a limited part, mainly when it is most effective, and then it animates the inner action. Dmitri's primitive simplicity counters any objection.

The obligation to return the money becomes absolutely imperative at the moment when he does and, in fact, has to break off his engagement. Where is it to come from? His swindler of a father owes him much more. Smerdyakov has told him that three thousand roubles are lying ready in expectation of this very Grushenka.

This intricate money question concealed a danger which the poet, acquainted with such matters, might quite possibly have underrated. Money matters need careful handling and the Schilleresque romanticism of the hero, who kisses his sword in exaltation and yet appropriates money, was liable to give an awkward touch. Dmitri, who despises money, is driven into a quandary, enough to cramp the style of any warrior. His feelings for Katerina, his unbridled passion for Grushenka, and his jealousy of his father present a paradoxical situation. There are monetary complications involved in all these relationships.

We cannot discern the slightest contradiction in Dmitri's mentality, either before or after the murder; far less, indeed, after the murder, even if he is deemed to be the perpetrator. In this conversation, on the other hand, there are pitfalls in every word. Dostoevsky avoids them. Dmitri, in breathless haste, does not falter for a moment. It is rather Alyosha who is flat and colourless in this scene. His answers are merely catchwords to his brother. The chief actor in the scene absorbs our entire interest.

Dmitri clings to Alyosha. Only a miracle, the famous

miracle which every gambler expects, can save him, and Alyosha's offer to collect a part of the money by putting together the brothers' savings passes unheeded. The obvious course is too involved for such natures. Better to make a journey for the money to-morrow without any definite prospects. Alyosha is to go at once to his father. In one and the same breath he pins his faith to his father and fears lest he find Grushenka there.

And if that were so? If Grushenka were to go there? asks Alyosha.

That is part of the plot, not of the creative work.

Then I shall kill him! slips from Dmitri's lips.

It is not quite certain from Alyosha's answer how far he takes his brother seriously, but Dmitri completes his threat. Neither money nor jealousy would drive him so far, only disgust. The sight of them together, the old man's face, his double chin, his shameless laughter, might be too loathesome. Yes, that's when it might happen. We see the *motif*. Money and jealousy, torment as they are to him, are nevertheless not the fundamental incentives. The anomaly of ugliness next to beauty would be intolerable. He would never do Grushenka an injury. The utmost embitterment would never make him think of such a thing as that. She is beautiful. But the old man is a violation of nature. Loathing outweighs every other feeling. Even were Dmitri not craving for Grushenka the monster would have to be crushed. Not a word about patricide. In the face of his disgust any feeling between father and son is impossible.

After his fruitless attempt with the old man Alyosha betakes himself with a heavy heart to Katya to deliver her betrothed's message of farewell and finds Grushenka with her. The drama expands from another side. There is again thoroughly dramatic treatment in the duel between the two women. The drawing of the characters lies exclusively in the dialogue; the whole scene covers five or six pages and, with its far richer content, is even simpler and shorter than the analogous scene in *The Idiot* between

THE WOMEN

Nastasya, Aglaia and Myshkin, which may similarly be called dramatic.

The one-sided behaviour of the two women is worthy of men engaged in business matters. Katerina does not believe that their interests are incompatible. She has already had a talk with Grushenka before Alyosha's arrival; a very amiable chat with strokings and kisses and chocolate; and the kitten has purred affectionately. The affair with Dmitri was, so to speak, only an escapade, a diversion so as to forget someone else, the Polish officer. He had seduced the foolish girl, years ago. Katya understands. The message of farewell is not so serious as Alyosha makes out. This wild-cat, who is surrounded by all sorts of horrors, has only to be approached in the proper way, and we know how to do that—Katya makes the thoroughly womanly mistake of assuming Dmitri's faithlessness to be merely a machination of Grushenka and thus Alyosha's mission now seems unnecessary to her. She makes a second mistake in counting her chickens in this game with the kitten which was interrupted a moment ago. Not only a tactical error but a lack of tact. Her tolerance for Grushenka's exciting past and her exaggerated affection are not quite genuine. By means of emphatic gratitude she attempts to fix a promise which has not yet been given but might perhaps be given in other circumstances. She overrates herself and underrates the kitten. Her limitations become obvious. In her manner of summing-up Grushenka there is something of the condescension of the fine lady, and she lacks the necessary consideration in front of Alyosha. She ought never to have apprised him, without further ado, of Grushenka's secret hope that her Pole would return and that she would be re-united with him. With this indiscretion she commits a double injury; she divulges an apparently sincere confession, tries to explain her rival's renunciation, and thereby cheapens the effect of Grushenka's generosity.

Perhaps a little too much enthusiasm! thinks Alyosha.

Suddenly the cat shows her claws. The part which is

forced on her in Alyosha's presence displeases her. For you may take it hers is a hateful character, a heart which changes with the weather, and she has a wretched memory into the bargain. Perhaps to-morrow she will listen to poor Dmitri, and what then?

Katya stammers some conventional phrase to put things right. The cat arches its back and slinks to one side. She suddenly asks for the dear young lady's little hand. The young lady has kissed her hand three times. A Grushenka ought to kiss her hand at least three hundred times in return, ought she not? She takes hold of the noble hand, lifts it to her lips, and suddenly lets go. No, she has changed her mind; and she laughs her soft childish laugh.

Katya is stunned. What? What? And Grushenka, in the sweetest voice, bids her guard the memory of kissing her hand as a souvenir and a token of gratitude for the chocolate. Dmitri will be right royally amused at it—and she gazes at Katya " fixedly." Her confusion interests her. Katya cannot contain herself. She lets fly the usual words of abuse. Then Grushenka also becomes excited and Alyosha has difficulty in separating them. Grushenka departs in laughter.

Again and again on such occasions we ask ourselves how it is the poet has not dramatized such scenes. A stupid question!

The same night Alyosha gives a detailed report to his brother who has waited in the open. Dmitri is at first taken aback, then the Schilleresque hero bursts into up-roarious laughter. He is overjoyed at Grushenka, this infernal goddess of impudence. Yes, Katya is right, she ought to be thrashed, throttled, led to the scaffold, but before that happens he must run over there quickly to embrace her.

It is not difficult to recognize how much more closely Dmitri and Grushenka belong together, and that the sort of motives which encouraged the cat to show her claws also played their part to a certain degree in Dmitri's attitude towards the proud beauty. This touch is important.

THE WOMEN

In Dmitri's romanticism there is an indispensable fund of healthy realism which Katya's romanticism evokes.

That does not prevent Dmitri being thoroughly convinced of Katya's sincerity. In her own way she is just as sincere in her utterances as he. We all talk. " Let them invent," was said in *A Raw Youth*. But our sympathy depends on the tone in which things are said. Dmitri might fling himself on his sword for Katya, but could not live with her. Alyosha has already said that, though Mitya would always love her, he would not always be happy with her. In the scene at the Hohlakov's he astutely recognizes that she belongs to Ivan. She will not admit that herself till the end of the novel, after someone else has expiated her self-laceration. She has something of Ivan's artifice, but far more stamina. Her intellect is totally unable to cope with the tasks which pride imposes on her, and her maltreated feeling leads to affectation. She wants to surrender her beauty, just as Ivan very soon arrives at surrendering his intellect, and fails to perceive that there will then be nothing left. If she were not beautiful scarcely any attention would be paid her. Her prejudices are less firmly rooted than her beauty, far less firmly than the wall surrounding Ivan from whose battlements he calls Grushenka a beast and his brother an insect. She ought to have thought in exactly the same way. What restrains her is the same digression as leads Ivan to arrogance: literature, but in a cheaper edition. Her generosity depends on artificial tension. It is impossible to know whether later in life she might not become a kind of Madame Hohlakov.

Dmitri's break with her is now final. Alyosha's report has spurred his desire for Grushenka. Katya is the pure, Grushenka the impure; now he is going to plunge head over heels into the abyss. The primitive urge of his desire is animal, purely animal, undermines, so believes this primitive knight, all his former life, and makes him in the end a common highwayman. That is the worst feature. He is not leaping naked into the abyss, but with a wallet full of stolen roubles round his neck. Look, he says to

Alyosha, and thumps his breast where the wallet is hanging,
here lurks the abject knavery compared to which everything
else I have done is mere child's play! He is within an ace
of a full confession. Were it not night perhaps he would
confess. But confession is impossible. This wretched
money business is too petty compared to the torment in
his mind. We too could scarcely endure it. If this fact
were divulged now, Dmitri's exaggeration, although artistic-
ally well-founded, would be too obvious and methodical.
This consideration, which is absent in the *Raw Youth*
parallel, is convincing in this instance, and therefore the
consequences of Dmitri's omission, far from appearing as
the premeditated mechanism of the detective story, actually
link up and expand the human tragedy.

The brothers part. One hastens to the town, the other
ascends the dark path to the monastery, heavily oppressed.

.   .   .   .   .   .

The big wheel turns and the light is cast on the youngest
Karamazov. The stage is promptly filled with people. In
this way Alyosha is distinguished from the others, he is
never alone. He is either encircled by the monastery or by
children. He also pays frequent visits to his father, or sits
silently as mediator between the brothers. If the poet
wants to bring him into the limelight children cry around
him, or pious monks with their cowls brush past him.
Even then he is still an intermediary in another sense, a
creature midway between heaven and earth who is not
affected by the increasing reality which serves the other
characters in good stead. He seems to belong to an entirely
different world. He has not been touched by the power to
portray of this old Rembrandt who gives life to the other
Karamazovs. Nordic robustness would be alien to his
hovering movement. He is of different substance, so to
speak, not of substance at all. If there were only this
Rembrandt, if only the storm which sweeps aside the more
gentle creative method and rushes us into the drama were
able to open our eyes, we should miss the significance of
Alyosha and thereby miss, in the battle of heaven and earth,

the angel to whom Dostoevsky devoted his last word. Every one of us is exposed to that danger at the first reading. We are as little able to accept, in the midst of this tragedy, the completely untragic being who meanders amongst devils as amongst flowers, as Alyosha was able to restrain one brother from the back-alley and the other from hell. His gentle word fades away in the hurricane. Possibly he is untrue. An admirer of Rembrandt, accustomed to his tragic grandeur, would experience much the same when suddenly confronted with Raphael. That situation more or less corresponds to the impression at first reading. Wolynsky, in his brilliant study, likens Alyosha to a figure by Fra Angelico (60). Perhaps this alluring picture is a little too slight for Alyosha's spiritual and intellectual possibilities, but it indicates the seraphic predestination of the novice who, like the monk of San Marco, does not flee into God's garden out of remorse or expiation after a struggle with the world, does not need first to be converted, but spontaneously chooses his path. He is born for the monastery (not just for this monastery outside the town, which his Zossima bids him quit, perhaps not for any particular monastery at all), not so as to fast there and castigate himself like the gloomy monk Ferapont, but in order to extol God and His heavenly host. If it is permissible to describe him in the world of pictures one would prefer to add to Fra Angelico's sweetness the freer space which a Piero della Francesca animated with grander figures. We shall always be somewhere in the vicinity of Tuscan design.

Tuscany in this most Russian of Russian works! Whereupon every Russian will answer, why not? The European is surprised because he fails to appreciate the ubiquity of Dostoevsky's spiritual home. Russia extends from Byzantium to the Arctic and connects these two poles with a curve across Asia. The Western half of this continent bears the little European peninsula, like the head of a giant body a face with mobile features. The heart lies in Russia, a long way off. This heart is capable of many emotions. It could be thought of as the source of all emotion of which, till now, only a minute part has seen the light of day. Russia has never produced a plastic art and in painting never progressed beyond primitive icons, could, in fact had to stop at that because it contemplates the picture from a religious and not from an æsthetic viewpoint, because its belief was in no need of ostentatious development through a worldly church. Dostoevsky's thoughts about church and God have almost a geological foundation.

This people, subjugated by no civilization, most susceptible to spiritual approach, this people which, as Dostoevsky said, alone can produce the future European, which like no other suffers, weeps and prays, like no other sings, plays and dances, which bears such names as Alyosha, whose language possesses Romance euphony and is admirably suited to penetrative psychology, which has produced overnight the only significant literature of our times, at least as collective creation, surely this people must also possess that depth of emotion which has inspired individualistic Europe to the works of its great masters. To be capable of understanding instinctively the spirit of a Claude Lorraine, to grasp spontaneously a value essential and long since lost to most Europeans, is not a peculiarity of Dostoevsky, who was detached from art, but a Russian characteristic.

Alyosha is just as representative of that Russia as are Dmitri, Ivan and old Karamazov. Cheek by jowl with this infernal voluptuousness there thrives in the Russian an intense chastity. Intense chastity—something beyond the normal conception, almost inconceivable, particularly to the Protestant. Our lukewarm nonconformity cannot associate any exaltation with virtue without promptly visualizing fanatical ascetics, not a Fra Angelico but some berserker. Alyosha's chastity is part of his charming nature and knows nothing negative. He happens to develop differently from his neighbours who are haunted by lusts, but considers himself also a Karamazov whom the devil will lay hands on very shortly. There he is mistaken. The devil may leap on his shoulder, cling to him like a garment, another kind

of monk's cowl, but he could never get right inside him.
He might kill him, although the youth is tenacious and
agile, far from an emaciated ascetic; he is rather a Tobias,
fair, fresh-cheeked, in one hand the fish as his journey's
ration, the other hand clasped in the angel's, pressing
vigorously onwards. If the devil succeeds in killing him
it is only by accident and without sin.

He can be recognized as a younger brother of the Idiot,
though without his convenient limitations, illness and
ridiculousness, which the realist felt he needed in his
representation of the " positive hero." Nor is he a hero.
There is none of Myshkin's peculiarity, nor is there anything particularly tragic or romantic about him. At times
he is almost prosaic in his realism. He is not a Christ-man.
No one would want to nail him to a cross. He is universally
loved, not as Myshkin for whom love was born of varying
degrees of resentment, but in complete and overwhelming
devotion. There has never been a figure more lovable or
beloved. Dostoevsky was less ambitious with Alyosha than
with Myshkin. Alyosha could never be a counterpart to
Rogozhin's brother in the cross. Myshkin stands out
incomparably greater in the atmosphere of a smaller world.
Alyosha, despite his realism, has more of a loftier world in
himself. There are wings concealed beneath his comic
monk's cowl which, although a source of amusement to
Lisa, does not prevent him scaling fences. He could only
play a supernumerary part in the drama on Golgotha, for
instance that of an angel hovering round the cross, catching
the holy blood in a chalice. Then he would not smile
seraphically but remain a serious and matter-of-fact spectator.

Alyosha is a living legend. Everything in him reminiscent of Italy's narrative painters is part of the legend. " An
early lover of humanity," suggests Dostoevsky. Indeed he
is very early and will always remain early. Wolynsky considered him the ideal type of Russian youth because Russian
youth is concerned not with metaphysics " but with love of
humanity, warm-blooded and reverential, with a tendency
to reality." That may be. Dostoevsky has told us about

other Russian youths too, and still we believe it. The naturalness and spontaneity of Alyosha's tender love is apparent also in the Arkadys, even in the Raskolnikovs and every other sinner. In Alyosha it appears for once quite purely. We are dumbfounded at seeing a poet of our own times creating an angel, at that a representative angel, not in the abstract, but in a highly Russian manner. Intercourse with supernatural beings of this kind comes so naturally to the creator of the Karamazovs that he is able to retain a light conversational tone, even his humour. Alyosha's relationship with Lisa is a delicate picture. Lisa is in fits of laughter at the angel. An incorrigible, spoilt child, cheerful in spite of her illness, a relative of Aglaia, she has the impudence to desire Alyosha as a husband; and since his Zossima has recommended him to marry, he does not raise the slightest objection and kisses her on the lips. That is how it should be. From her room Lisa cries out to her mother who is talking to Alyosha about Ivan, "Mamma, don't spoil him!" Wolynsky suggests that Alyosha would be disillusioned in such a marriage. That is improbable. Naturally such a droll marriage would never materialize. What does that matter? Lisa deliberately squeezes her finger in the door for the sake of a fresh sensation. The bruised nail will disappear and then they will laugh again. No woman will ever be captivated by the angel, no woman ever disillusioned. No Aglaia-Nastasya drama will ever be played around him and it would be banal to introduce the factors which rendered Myshkin's fitness for marriage doubtful. If ever Lisa marries some Ivan or other, who more than adequately satisfies her childish need for pain, there will be a breath of Alyosha beside her, drying her tears. Nevertheless Alyosha also is liable to disillusionment. When, at the death of his beloved Zossima, there is the totally unexpected odour from the corpse and revolt amongst the two parties in the monastery, the novice quivers with pain at ugliness and bursts into tears. Dostoevsky could not have brought us back to earth in any other way in our dreams about

Alyosha without destroying them. Here Rembrandt approximates to Fra Angelico and heavenly smiles are crowned by those of the earth. There is a humour we scarcely dare to admit in these details of the odour-affair, in the sniffing of the monks, their concealed or open sneering, and Alyosha has his temptation. We forgive the poet the long, extremely long Zossima-epistle which enabled him to turn to account his studies of the monastery, forgive him willingly because of the subsequent history of the holy man who did not remain unavenged. For once Alyosha is embittered; there has been no miracle. Ivan's sermons go in at one ear and out at the other, and are interesting to Alyosha only as evidence of his brother's condition. No discourse can turn him from God; a campaign against his Zossima would be fruitless. But when the odour of the corpse drives the youth from the monastery into the wood and the tempter Rakitin, a spurious Ivan, appears before him and reads in his face the " promotion " of Zossima, then the woeful novice repeats Ivan's words almost mechanically and now he too will not accept God's world. This variant opens up all sorts of possibilities of a pagan beauty worship, a worship common to all the Karamazovs, to all, even the most Christian of Dostoevsky's heroes. It is almost a pity that Dostoevsky did not make more use of the opportunity of revealing the deepest and most miraculous source of his religion. Ugliness crushes Alyosha. He is ready now to go into the back-alley. Grushenka is planning an orgy and hops on the novice's lap. She has long wanted to " devour " him, and Rakitin is to be royally rewarded if he brings her his catch. But fortune smiles on angels and children. Grushenka naturally disguises herself. Alyosha finds her not nearly so terrible. She is much the same to-day as a few days ago with Katya, and if you only understand her there is nothing to be frightened at; a woman like any other, a sister. It is not Katya but Alyosha who knows how to handle her. Satan will have to whistle.

Grushenka's mood for the great act in Mokroe is also developed in this scene. Alyosha has stirred her heart and now she tells him too the story of her Pole which the young lady did not understand yesterday. She only disguised herself from desire, anger and shame; Nastasya's *motif*. Now she is being called by her former lover. His carriage will arrive at any moment to take her to Mokroe. He is a widower now and wants to marry her. He will open his eyes wide. The little meagre girl has grown into a flowering beauty who knows the ways of the world. He will be presented to a Grushenka who will make his eyes drop out of their sockets. And then when he is ablaze she will show him the door. Or, tell me, Alyosha, shall I forgive him?

"You have already forgiven him," smiles Alyosha. Whilst Grushenka is speeding to her Pole in Mokroe, Alyosha hurries to the monastery. It is not only because he has escaped from the back-alley safe and sound that he is driven to the dead man's bier. He could not say what urges him to run more and more quickly. Probably it has something to do with Zossima's instruction to go into the world instead of eventually becoming a monk; an instruction which has remained incomprehensible to him to this day. He is only now beginning to understand.

Dostoevsky intimates Alyosha's transformation, his presentiment of his mission and, at the same time, the intensifying of the humanity in the angel with a symbolism of which even Southern church imagery is incapable. All the windows in this chamber of the dead have been opened. Consequently, observes Alyosha to himself, the odour must have grown stronger. Already the scandal appears to be only a memory to him. Father Paissy is monotonously reading the Gospel and is just at the marriage of Cana. The youth falls into a trance and dreams of a marriage of Cana in which both he and his Zossima take part. They experience the first miracle, the great, blessed miracle of joy. Then Alyosha steps out into the night, into the open air. "It was as if the stillness of the earth were blending with the stillness of heaven and the mystery of the earth became one with the mystery of the stars." Alyosha stands

still and listens. " Suddenly, as if struck, he flings himself
to the earth, embraces it, kisses it weeping and sobbing,
soaks it with his tears and swears in ecstasy to love it for
ever." Thus it is just the scandal, the absence of miracle
which have led him to a miracle, to a miracle undreamt of
by any Grand Inquisitor. He belongs to the earth. Now
he has the strength to obey his Zossima and to exchange
the monastery for the world.

The legend is completed. As in the story of the Grand
Inquisitor one vaguely feels the development of some
earlier theme, except that there is no continuation of Schiller
and the development does not spring from a " poem."
That may be the reason why it is impossible to recognize
any source of inspiration. Only one single person has had
the reverence and the genius to catch the rhythm and to
compose a psalm in trembling words on the mystery of
heaven and earth.

Berdyaev, in his profound work on Dostoevsky's
weltanschauung and religion, pointed to the lack of renaissance and humanism (as a historical conception) in the
history of Russia, and recognized in this defect not only a
necessary consequence of the geographical and social conditions of his homeland, but, above all, the expression of
Russian mentality (61). He rightly considers this defect
advantageous since it enabled people like Dostoevsky more
easily to find a jumping-off ground for a new Christian
confession and to devote themselves unconditionally to every
struggle of the conscience. Perhaps Europe also once
grasped the question of God with Russian intensity. That
is a long time ago. To-day there is no possibility of comparison. We must admit that one of our greatest riddles
about Russia is that the very minds which we have to
thank for the most recent revelations about modern man,
possibly even about the man of to-morrow, are those in
which the conflict around Christianity rages most tur-
bulently.

Alyosha, like every Karamazov and every Russian, has
a share in the great question. To the Russian mind his

share is modest. Yet there is some special feature in him which seems to me to be some dreamlike and precious substitute for the denied renaissance.

. . . . . .

The only principal character who has neither forerunner nor preparatory features is Smerdyakov, the bastard. He is one of those characters, by no means scarce in Dostoevsky's work, who suffer from his own illness, epilepsy. That external feature is all he has in common with other figures. His relationship to the family is only touched on in the preface in the form of a rumour. Neither the brothers nor the old man ever refer to it. Smerdyakov is a servant and belongs to the backstairs with the other servant, old Grigory. He serves with dignity and subtlety. No one would think him the son of the filthy imbecile. Despite his poverty he is painfully clean, decked out and neat, boots polished and well-kempt. Similarly his mind and his old-fashioned phraseology are symbols of *bourgeois* respectability. A mask. You could imagine him masquerading in the cowl of a venetian pall bearer with eye-slits in the mask. Even Ivan's superior intellect cannot penetrate the mask. Incidentally he pretends only to exist as Ivan's shadow and behaves as a satellite of this heterodox philosopher. When the fancy takes him he plays with his master and torments him to madness.

He first comes to the fore after the Grand Inquisitor scene. This sequence is important. After Ivan's failure with Alyosha he meets Smerdyakov who is all the more readily at his service. You can do anything with me, says the concealed smile, I am your lackey, your vessel which warily catches every drop you deign to let fall. Every particle of your poison soaks in and I give a daily rub-up to your axiom, everything is permissible.

Ivan loathes this creature. What on earth has moved him to waste one word on this abortion? He secretly caught himself feeling perverted pleasure in speaking to the fellow and noticed how the pedant devoured every word—as if he had some secret vice in common with him.

SMERDYAKOV

To-day after leaving Alyosha this ruminant is more repug-
nant than ever. He wants to shake him off, to fling a
word of abuse at him and go his way but, as usual, he
stops. The devoted monster's screwed-up eye winks
imperceptibly; knew at once you'd stay all the same, sure
to have something highly interesting to tell me. Ivan
wants to shriek at him, but, contrary to expectation, quite
different words fall amiably and gently from his lips.
Whether his father has gone to bed yet?—He does not
know how he comes to ask so absurd a question. A moment
ago he had not given it a thought. And how does he
manage to speak gently?

"It pleases him to sleep," replies Smerdyakov slowly
and his eye winks, knew all the same you'd begin. Note
that, you were the first! And he contentedly changes his
position from one foot to the other.

An equivocal conversation ensues in which, as in all
conversations between these two, one speaks with his
mouth and the other with his eyes. At times Smerdyakov
also makes use of his polished boots in order to reflect his
pedantic self-satisfaction. He expounds with sighs his unpleasant situation between the old gentleman and his
respected eldest son. The old gentleman is angrily enquiring for the lady and Mr Dmitri is himself enquiring
for the lady. The one wants to have the said lady in the
house and behaves as if someone could help to bring it
about. And the other side of the picture is the respected
son threatening to crush you like a louse if the said lady
enters the house.—Slowly and minutely he explains his
foreboding of some crime. If Dmitri and the old gentleman meet at night, something will happen. Therefore he
advises Ivan to go off to-morrow to a small place in the
vicinity where his father wants something attended to.
He speaks as if he does not notice his own contradiction;
his half-closed eye belies his words. Ivan wants to break
away, fear of this loathesome creature—for fear it certainly
is—is sheer nonsense, but he makes no move, goes on
listening, mysteriously curious how the fellow is going to

develop his assumptions.—Sad to relate, Mr Dmitri knows the signal, the tap on the window which will promptly make the old man open it at night. How Dmitri got to know of the signal? Well, of course, one could not help feeling Mr Dmitri ought to be told. From fear of course, fear of Mr Dmitri's dreadful temper. What other reason do you suppose there would be for telling him? Naturally only to prove to Mr Dmitri the devotion and servility of his servant, otherwise he might be suspicious. All the same Mr Dmitri is not going to be allowed in so far as it is possible to watch him and ſtop him. But suppose one had a fit, what then? That happens, you know. To-morrow, precisely to-morrow he is going to have a fit, and one which will laſt a long time, possibly three days.

It ſtands to reason that no epileptic can foretell a fit, certainly not its duration, and it follows that he has no intention of asserting that as a fact. So it is really absurd to ſtay even five minutes with this creature. In spite of that Ivan asks " then you can pretend to have a fit? " He wants to know what is at the bottom of all this ſtupidity.

Yes, that is also possible, comes the answer, and there would be nothing wrong in it if it were done from fear, apart from the fact that everything is permissible. If the fit came now, it would be impossible to keep a watch. But then Grigory would be there, suggeſts Ivan impatiently. Certainly, replies Smerdyakov, theoretically Grigory's exiſt-ence cannot be denied. In practice however the non-exiſtence of Grigory would once again be proved, in as much as he has gout and juſt to-morrow is going to be rubbed with alcohol and then, as is well known, he will be dead-drunk, for all the alcohol that is not outside him he puts inside him and that is why you cannot count on Grigory.

Does it not sound as though this fellow were plotting it all out for to-morrow? And what is his object in all this gossip?—Well, smiles the creature inoffensively, what is the object of keeping it quiet?—His twinkling eye suddenly seems quite close as if under a magnifying glass. Ivan is seized by a fit of anger. But what for? Nonsense, it's all nonsense! Dmitri will never seriously do the old man any harm. To begin with, Grushenka will not come, so Dmitri will have no pretext.

But at every objection the busy Smerdyakov drags up at least three retorts. There are certain people you can never rely on, people like that lady and that gentleman. And Ivan, who has recently witnessed the thrashing business, must also be aware of that. Then there is the money-business on top of it. Mr Dmitri needs money.

Ivan interrupts. How dares the lackey say such a thing! Dmitri would never commit a crime for the sake of money.—But Mr Dmitri does need money, a great deal of money, and there is the danger that if the said lady wanted and only deigned to beckon with her little finger, the old gentleman would promptly make over to her not only the three thousand roubles but his entire fortune. And then neither Mr Dmitri nor Mr Ivan nor their little brother would inherit a brass farthing. But if the old gentleman departed this life, each of the respected sons would come into at the very least forty thousand roubles. But Mr Dmitri knows all that and it must be regarded as dangerous.

Ivan finds it difficult to keep still. Then that's the reason why the fellow advises him to go away to-morrow despite all that may then happen. Smerdyakov winks knowingly and with impertinent familiarity happens to gaze straight into Ivan's eyes. Yes, that is absolutely correct. At the appropriate moment he adds that he is, of course, only giving this advice from sympathy for Mr Ivan. It were better to go away than to be present at such an affair. A gigantic idiot or a gigantic villain! thinks Ivan and gets up. For a moment Smerdyakov turns his head away in terror. Ivan laughs. Nonsense! It is inconceivable that the fellow is playing with him, is up to some infernal machination. He is only an idiot talking rubbish from sheer fear. Let him have his fear.

" I shall go to Moscow to-morrow! " he says suddenly.

DOSTOEVSKY

Not to the little spot in the vicinity, but right away to Moscow.

Smerdyakov hastens to assure him that that is the best thing he can do, for they can always send a telegram to Moscow and " upset " him.

Again Ivan is taken aback. Surely the creature's fear ought to be greater once his protector has gone away. Suddenly the fellow is still only a lackey, a dog awaiting his master's order. What the master does is good.

Ivan goes off in laughter and enters the house in laughter. His laughter would seem strange to anyone seeing his face. In fact he could not himself have said what happened to him at that moment.

In *The Idiot* the consumptive Ippolit, in the course of his story on the prince's birthday, tells of a beetle like a reptile which ran about his room and paralyzed him with horror and disgust. The worst was when the animal moved forwards in long regular twists. Only that reptile could have been Smerdyakov's forerunner.

Next morning Ivan does actually go away. The old man is glad to be rid of him; now nothing prevents Grushenka coming tapping at the window. He imagines Ivan's departure will encourage her. Probably she was only waiting for Ivan to disappear. His ease is disturbed by the news of his cook's epileptic fit. He has been in the cellar, unconscious and foaming at the mouth; the doctor declares the attack to be serious. The old man has to go without his accustomed fish-soup. In the evening he is informed of a second disaster. Old Grigory has caught cold and has had to go to bed, completely lame.

Dostoevsky interrupted the action at this point and inserted the part devoted to Zossima. The break was necessary to give the reader breathing space and to gather the threads of the action. He also needed this part both for the protrayal of Alyosha and for consolidating the tendency of his second storey. The white monastery was to be not merely decorative but, like the glory over El Greco's Entombment of Count Orgaz, the earthly action with an ætherial canopy. It was easier for the painter because association with heaven of the earthly factor, a legendary ceremony, could be deemed an accepted fact, whereas the poet had to create the association from an action thoroughly unsuited to the purpose. Such obvious agreement between upper and lower picture, as in Greco's painting, was bound to be denied the creator of the Kara-mazovs. His struggle around this is scarcely appreciated by the reader intent on continuation of the action; it is quite natural to go on reading with friendly condescension— *in magnis voluisse sat est.* As we are not concerned here with fostering detective desires, it is worth while pausing for a moment, especially since a large part of the novel is involved, the sixth and seventh of the twelve books, and we cannot skip them without further ado. If we had been told in advance of the symbolism which Dostoevsky intended employing, we should have had grave doubts of its feasibility. It is sometimes advisable to ask ourselves the question before we proceed with the given answer. Dostoev-sky was forced to digress and made use of episodes. I mention only one here. In Zossima's life-story there is reference to a murderer who, like the hero of the " sinner "-novel, remains undetected. He confesses his crime to the young Zossima and is gradually persuaded by him at the risk of his life to make a public confession of his guilt. Since he has gained universal esteem and respect in an otherwise exemplary life, no one believes him, and he dies without suffering any punishment except the torment of his own conscience. This story, a parallel to that of Makar about the tyrant who ended as a pilgrim, is an inversion of the judicial error in *The Brothers Karamazov,* but points the same moral: conscience inflicts greater punishment than any court of law. That is Zossima's fundamental tenet. His teachings reveal the ultimate depths of Dostoevsky's theophily and theology. Zossima invariably possesses con-siderable personal dignity, is extraordinarily wise and far superior to the inflexibly intellectual Grand Inquisitor, his theoretical counterpart. He nearly always overcomes clerical formality by means of pure humanity. In his posthumous teachings we encounter the same simplicity as, in his lifetime, he introduced into his discussions of eternal questions, never as an insistent giver but always ready to receive. That affords a living glamour to the figure consecrated by death. Love of God is love of life. Alyosha imitates his teacher literally when in the starry night he embraces the earth with sobs. In this embrace the relationship between upper and lower storey becomes overpowering and dramatic, immediately before the white monastery disappears.

.   .   .   .   .   .

The long interval enables Dostoevsky to recommence the action with the central character. Without this pause, particularly immediately after the scene between Ivan and Smerdyakov, the incentive to Dmitri's action, his monetary need, would not be forceful enough and we should not so readily appreciate the drama. Dostoevsky can now pick up the thread without difficulty. Dmitri's excitement is developed in three stages. With every turn of the wheel there is a new *milieu*, complete in every detail, into which Dmitri penetrates in ever increasing *tempo*. First the old merchant in the large house who rebuffs his every effusion with the stereotyped answer, "we don't handle such business." To be rid of him he recommends him to go to the peasant Lyagavy who is interested in old Karamazov's woodlands and is staying just on the spot, a few miles from here, at the priest's. Dmitri thanks him effusively for his advice, manages to borrow money for horses and tears off. Naturally, the priest is not at home. Dmitri hurries after him and finds him, but the peasant is not with him. He was there, but is now in the woods, at the forester's. The little father takes Dmitri there. They find the forester and the peasant with him. But Lyagavy is not in a fit state for business, he is sleeping out his drunkenness. Dmitri moves heaven and earth to bring him round. Finally fatigue overcomes him and he oversleeps, for the next day the peasant has drunk himself incapable again and is firmly convinced that Dmitri is a

BEFORE THE DEED

rogue who has once cheated him. Finally Dmitri grasps that his efforts are useless. He will never rake up the three thousand roubles and meantime Grushenka may go to the old man. A passing driver takes him to the next post-station. There he pulls himself together, fixes on a new idea and races back to the town to Madame Hohlakov, the third stage. Lisa's mother gives him a cordial reception, without harping on the early hour of his visit. We are human beings and above such things. In fact she had expected him. He was bound to come to her, this very day, she knew it. Cautiously he tries to dam the flood of her words.—Please, we know already. He is not the first we have helped. Whether he knows her married cousin? He had lost everything too and the waves enveloped him. She persuaded him to start a stud-farm. Do you know anything about horse-breeding?

Dmitri bursts out with his request and is surprised not to receive a rebuff. Yes, she will give him something, and not only three thousand. She will save him. Dmitri is in his seventh heaven. He will willingly listen to her if only she will save him from disgrace and despair, from suicide. But he does not need more than the fateful three thousand. Three thousand in exchange for boundless gratitude and excellent security.

" What do you think of gold mines? " she asks.

Gold mines?—of course he has not thought of them. But she has thought of them for him. Every time she has seen him it was quite definite, he must go to the gold mines. She has already decided that from his gait. Perhaps he doubts whether it is possible to judge a man from his gait. That is reality. After this corpse business in the monastery, with the fiasco of the miracle, we are all for reality, and the three thousand he is groaning for are as good as in his pocket. Only, off to the gold mines, at top speed!

These three stages were invented by a connoisseur whose mistress was necessity and who did not flinch at her caprices. The fantastic fabrications of people at their wits' ends were his food for years. He made several desperate fool's errands and from the pinnacle of his dream sank deeper and deeper into misery. A man like that knows how to create tension and is not insensible to the involuntary comedy entailed.

After the third attempt Dmitri gives it up. Let Katya think him a swindler, it cannot be helped. Only one course lies open, to take Grushenka and escape, away, as far as possible. His passion for Grushenka is the only inducement left.

Then begins another chase. Grushenka is supposed to be with the merchant with whom she has business relations. But she has only been there a moment. Back to her house! She is not there either. He flings himself at the feet of the servant in the kitchen. For Christ's sake where is she? The servant says she does not know. Lies and deceit, of course! Where can she be? Naturally with the old man!

There is nothing left of Dmitri except feet. As he leaves the kitchen he catches sight of the glittering brass pestle. He snatches it mechanically and tears out. He hears cries of terror behind him. He races to the house and leaps over the fence. If I find her with him! No, she's not the one to be punished! It's this monster, this infernal monster!

The night is dark. Dmitri creeps up to the window and peers at the old man. To judge by his face, she is not there. Dostoevsky astutely recognized that the result of this would be to increase the furious man's frenzy. If the two were together, there would be an end. His nerves are so on edge that any violent end would be a blessing to him. Possibly it will not come to that and he will be forced to sober down and to eke out his accursed existence. A new sensation, " an absurd vexation," overcomes him. Unable to bear his hesitation he gives the signal—rap—rap—rap!

The old man inside starts and opens the window.

" Grushenka, is that you? "

She is not with him. There is no longer any doubt about it. The new sensation gnaws at him.

THE DEED

"Where are you?" comes a whisper from the window, "my darling, my little angel!"

The old man appears, dressed up to the nines, leans out of the window, bends to one side and shows his profile, his flabby double chin, his hook nose, his spongy lips, his lascivious pig's eyes—Oh, the monster!

"Wait!" whispers the old man, "I'll open the door." Dmitri, no longer conscious of his actions, rips out the pestle.

— — — —

These dashes are those of Dostoevsky, the novelist. Their employment is questionable. He did not want to dispense with the tension. Immediately afterwards is written, "'yet God was protecting me,' Dmitri observed later." Whoever believes these words, knows definitely. Dmitri chose the more natural of the two courses open to him and ran away whilst the old man went to the front-door. It was scarcely a matter of choice. The deed hung on a thread. Some external factor, a mere accident prevented it. Possibly terror at his nearness to it frightened him away. God protected him. This nearness excuses Dostoevsky for not having made the question quite clear at once. What lies behind those dashes concerns the judicial and not the moral part of the novel, and since the further action depends on contrast between justice and morality, a popular writer could not renounce the mystery.

Dmitri rushes away and disaster overtakes him in the garden. Old Grigory has heard him. The light shining through the open window, the shadow of the fleeting figure—so what has long been feared has come to pass. "Parricide!" he yells in a shrill voice and grabs at the fugitive who is on the point of climbing over the fence. In wild fury Dmitri lashes out with the pestle. A blow was bound to come, no matter who the victim. He leaps back into the garden to see what damage he has done. The old man is lying lifeless in a pool of blood. Dmitri mechanically pulls out his handkerchief and mechanically wipes the old man's head. He cannot stem the flow of blood, there is nothing more to be done here.

"You have crossed my path, old man! then lie there!"

He hastens to Grushenka's house and learns from the terrified cook that the lady has gone to Mokroe to her officer.

"What sort of an officer?" he bellows. The house trembles.

"The Polish officer! the former one, the Pole!"

He lets fall his blood-stained hands. The former one!

Fury will not help now. This is quite a different proposition. The old merchant was a mere nothing, so was that drunken lout in the hut, so was the lady with the gold mines. Even his father at the window, even poor old Grigory were mere nothings. It is the former one. "He gazed at him, this monster, and horror made his blood run cold." Now he knows everything. Grushenka told him of the Pole, he was blind not to see the danger. Dmitri suddenly ceases to be a murderous tyrant and becomes a young boy, "a quiet and lovable boy" (as once the raw youth after his great blow), and Fenya, the old servant, recovers from her fright and tells him everything, even Grushenka's last greeting to him and her message that she loved him for one short hour.

By degrees he pulls himself together. Dostoevsky indicates Dmitri's dark goal without a single word of explanation. We feel as Dmitri feels. His rage has spent itself and will never recur. There is death in his soul. He leaves Fenya and goes casually to an acquaintance with whom he has pledged his pistol-case, his last pawnable possession. The man notices the blood-stains. Been fighting? It would not be the first time. How awful the fellow looks!

Dear me! blood! observes Dmitri in front of the mirror. That must be removed. He gratefully accepts Mr Perhotin's kind offer to let him have a wash and, in the meantime, puts on the table a packet of bank-notes which he was holding in his hand. His manner is so casual that momentarily the pedantic Perhotin has no thought of anything wrong. But we are taken aback. Whence all that money? Our thoughts revert to the dashes and make us doubt Mitya's reference to merciful God, for we are not yet aware of the little wallet at his breast. No one knows about it. The detective story begins. Dmitri opened the wallet on his way to Perhotin, for what was the object of keeping it now? He needed money to redeem his pistols.

Mr Perhotin sends his servant into the next shop to change the money. At the mention of the provision shop Dmitri recalls the night with Grushenka at Mokroe. It was in that shop he bought provisions for the orgy. " Hi! young fellow! tell the provision merchant to get a hamper ready, the same stuff as before, so many bottles of champagne and everything the same as before! We're going to Mokroe. Come with us, Perhotin! "

He is already in the throes of intoxication. It was that night in Mokroe she gave him the short hour of love—oh, only to kiss her little foot. Why not another night like that? Even were it only a momentary glimpse before he is flung headlong into Hades!

Perhotin is not in the mood to " pay homage to the queen," and cannot make head or tail of " golden-haired Phœbus " and all these concoctions, and prefers his game of billiards. Nor does he care what the madman is going to do with the pistol. A mad night and then, finished, the end of all these fellows. Perhotin is not a nursemaid; on the other hand he keeps a close eye on the provision merchant and checks the account to a farthing.

As Dmitri gets into his troika, old Fenya comes running up to him. Surely he will not do any harm to the lady and to her former lover!—No, Mitya is not going to harm another soul.

He talks to the driver on the way. " Whip up, Andrey, whip up. Andrey, are you a driver or not, eh? "

Well, of course, says Andrey, of course he is a driver.

Well then, he can drive, knows that you have to move aside and let others pass—— " Andrey, don't run over anyone! . . . but if you have run over anyone, then away with you! "

Yes, says Andrey, many a one drives blindly on, thinks neither of man nor beast, driving straight ahead.

" Straight to hell! " interjects Dmitri. " Andrey, you simple soul, tell me, is Dmitri Karamazov driving straight to hell or not, what do you think? Whip up the left one! "

Andrey whips up the left one and tells how hell groaned when Christ went straight there from the cross and set all sinners free. It groaned a good deal, for now it had nothing more to roast. But God comforted hell, saying there would soon be some more coming there and it would have quite enough to do. But as for Mr Dmitri he is only a little child, so he always seems.

" And you forgive me, Andrey? . . . No, for every one, you alone for every one, this very moment, here on the way, do you forgive me for every one? Speak, you simple heart? "

Andrey mumbles something, astounded at this confused discussion, and Dmitri prays whilst the troika tears along, prays like one demented. He entreats God to be merciful, for he loves Him. If He sends him to hell, he will love Him in hell too. One thing only, to be allowed to love Grushenka, to love her till the end, only till the morning. The nearer they approach, the more ardently Mitya prays. " Whip up, Andrey, whip up! " He is not worried about the former lover. He is not jealous of anyone in the world. Blood has been spilt and vanity has followed the blood into nothingness. The nearer they approach, the less violent grows Dmitri's torment about his right to her. Let her go with her former lover. He will bless him, will be his brother. He will give out only love, give, give. " Whip up, Andrey, whip up! " The village is already in sight, the inn with the light in the window. So they are still up. The troika flies along. Dmitri has lost the sense of his body, he is only conscious of their speed. Once arrived he comes to earth again and asks the landlord what is happening. Is she merry? How is the other man? Is he flinging money about? Speak! aha, listen, Trifon!

He gives his orders. Fetch the gipsies, music! Rope in all the girls, the whole village must dance! Two hundred roubles for the chorus!

Grushenka is horrified at his entry. She is sitting by a fat little man, her former lover. Nastasya's Totsky has turned into a little Pole. He has a friend with him, a tall Pole. At the table are two of Dmitri's acquaintances from the town, Maximov, an insignificant-looking sponger, a variant of Lebyadkin in *The Idiot*, though inoffensive, and the blond Kalganov, a youth. Mitya gazes at Grushenka. He may look at her, may sit down by her, may even talk to her. She frightened of him? If she only knew! Not frighten her, not frighten anyone, make way. Only to be with her a few hours till the morning!

He speaks with difficulty and is promptly upset. His nerves are giving out. Grushenka understands, he does not mean any harm. But he should be merry now, don't weep, be merry! A blessing that he has come, because things have not been too merry so far. There is no reason for tears, not the slightest.

She stresses that, but he fails to understand. He only understands that she is not angry with him. There is still warmth, the world is not yet swallowed up, it is still good and beautiful, has never been so good and beautiful. Even the little *pan*, her former lover, is good and beautiful, though he does smoke a hookah and has a belly. Why shouldn't he? Does that make him any the less a noble Pole, good and beautiful? Irritating that he behaves so stupidly, but who knows what his reasons may be? And the other *pan* seems a bit supercilious; if he were to get up he would hit his head on the ceiling. What does that matter? What's that to us? She has forgiven him, she is not angry. Fetch the champagne! Trifon, look sharp!

The first part of the evening, whilst the two Poles are present, is thoroughly flat, banal intentionally, as well as in exposition. The two Poles are not treated sympathetically.

DOSTOEVSKY

Dostoevsky is less tolerant than Mitya. Grushenka's disillusionment with her former seducer who led her away
with his melancholy sing-song, is supposed to be vast, but
remains unformed. Dostoevsky's desire not to distract
attention caused him to neglect this detail. To drown the
tedium they play a game and the Poles are caught cheating.
Dmitri turns them out and then the orgy begins.

The Russian invasion of the European stage has made
us familiar with this kind of revelry. Just as the painter of
Flemish fairs has portrayed the bacchanalia of his country,
as Watteau and Lancret the French version, so Dostoevsky
has done it in words. The difference in period can be
disregarded. The typical Russian revel is so childlike that
it transcends our conception of orgy. It is true that there
is complete abandonment for the revels spread " right
across the whole earth," but in this general embrace indulgence of individual desires is precluded. Drunkenness is
part of the game. Dostoevsky heads the chapter " frenzy."
" I want to get drunk," cries Grushenka. " Be off, be
merry, tell them to dance, let them all enjoy themselves,
even the cats and dogs." And when the wine begins to
take effect and they stagger about, the childlikeness, in
which there can be nothing ugly, becomes more apparent
than ever.

It is not unintentionally that Dostoevsky makes one of
the participants introduce a different note. Maximov, the
old gourmand who never misses an orgy, wants a special
titbit and tries to cadge from Mitya in order to coax
Maryushka.

" Hang it all! " laughs Dmitri. " But to the devil with
it all, wait a bit! first let's drink! " Only a person as
ridiculous as Maximov could think of such things. Just
as little unintentional was Dostoevsky's characterization of
the blond Kalganov, the handsome youth who laughs,
drinks and sleeps, whose flaxen hair Grushenka strokes,
who thinks as little as she of the kiss she gives him. Amidst
all this revelry there is a vague touch of Alyosha in the
young man.

FRENZY

But Mitya drowns all his joys and sorrows. Time speeds on. Reality is a thousand times more wonderful than he had hoped on the way here. God has heard his prayer for he can love till the end. With every glance at Grushenka his bliss increases tenfold. Grushenka belongs to him, her falcon, has never belonged to anyone else, will always belong only to her falcon. Dmitri trembles. Only to live now, now that it is worth while; now you could turn over a new leaf. He saw all that in his beloved before, knew it was necessary only to remove the ſtupid reſtraint. She is the light he has sought in his darkness.—Go away and shoot yourself?

Mitya, what are you ſtaring at? Mitya, my falcon, drink!—He laughs, lifts the glass with its golden wine and has to force his eyes to close and smile to avoid the sight of the old man's accursed blood at the fence. For a moment he creeps out into the darkness to breathe—what is the matter? What is it then? Surely to die is nonsense! Can a man who experiences this be damned? Perhaps the old man is not dead after all? And if he is dead, cannot God, the omnipotent, bring him back to life? God, the omnipotent, has managed to drive away one phantom, one which seemed much more terrible, the former lover. The monſter became ridiculous and will never return. Cannot the other be driven away too? If only it were possible, if only God, the omnipotent, could drive away this second phantom, this blood!

And again Dmitri prays like one demented. " God bring back to life the dead man at the fence! God, my God, remove this terrible cup from me! "

His prayer clearly indicates which burden of torment oppresses and which does not. The misleading dashes have already disappeared for the reader who can see through this simple creature. Concealment of the murder of his father is inconceivable at such a moment. Even if he thought lightly of killing a noxious inseɕt—which would be imputing too much to a man who has nothing of Raskolnikov about him—he could not be moved to such a prayer whilſt

345

he had on his conscience a murder he had desired and accomplished. Beside this overwhelming emotion the question whence the money came is paltry. If at this juncture we still have the courage to criticize, we might deplore the omission to deal with that question and reproach the poet for having set us an inadmissible riddle, but that would in no way stifle our enjoyment.

This orgy really succeeds in stretching right across the earth. The composition works miracles. Grushenka, this infernal woman from the back-alley, this wild-beast, grows to a legendary grandeur—not only for Dmitri whom bliss makes almost diffident, and with good reason, not only for the inebriated chorus which to-morrow will sing another tune, but for all of us who gaze on this ribaldry from a distance. Grushenka is queen of all the earth and beyond. Something indescribable is happening. The buoyant, rollicking mirth of the dancers and singers and drinkers carries their mutual love to immense heights. Every emptied glass is a sacrifice at the altar of their passion. Champagne streams down every throat, glitters through every eye, bubbles in the very air, and the general intoxication increases the intoxication of the queen. Grushenka is drunk. It is impossible to picture a woman so inebriated without a shudder of disgust or without oneself being a drunken brute. There is nothing animal in Grushenka, in fact her drunkenness purifies her. She stands as a symbol of all that is childlike in Russian orgy. She fascinates, but by no means charms away her drunken merriment, laughs and reels, and her words become more and more incoherent. The more her ecstasy grows the more distinctly is revealed the child unsullied by depravity, of whom the conversation with Alyosha gave us an inkling. A child—that is not a preconceived notion but absolute reality; child in so far as a grown-up woman can be a child. The child in her is inspired by her falcon in whom she realizes the lover she has dreamt of, who is the cause of her blessing the disillusionment she has suffered. She is herself amazed at her transformation. How has it come about? " Just think

of it, Mitya, my falcon, I have grown good. No, tell me,
all of you, come here, all of you, I want to ask you just one
thing, why am I so good? I am good, very good. Well,
then, why am I so good?"

The beauty of this passage illustrates Dostoevsky's
brilliance. There is something in it similar to, though
incomparably greater than, the anecdote scene in *A Raw
Youth*. How could stammered words translated, perhaps
coarsely translated, have so rhythmical an effect? We fail
to grasp it because we stare, as if hypnotized, at the two or
three lines which carry us to the climax, and attribute the
brilliance to them, whereas in reality these lines are themselves the result of the brilliance. Amazing how details are
spontaneously introduced at such moments! One might
search for the word amongst hundreds, mould each tone—
modulate it, as Cézanne said. Dostoevsky is primarily
concerned with the structure; never, if one may use the
expression, with the laying on of the paint. That is why
he is so easily translatable. Who knows what more is in
the original? Russian literary critics have accused him of
writing badly; they may or may not be right, but they
have failed to deal with his essential quality. Dostoevsky
does not violate the language, as happened in Germany in
the age of naturalism and still happens in this age of tele-
graphic writing. He has recourse neither to exaggerated
interjections nor to vernacular, but accepts the obvious and
perfectly natural language. The novel-drama carries us so
far that words are scarcely needed at the decisive moment.
Here he has imperceptibly worked up the effect he desires
so that Grushenka can now move us in any way she wishes.
" I want to dance! " she cries. " Let them all come and
see how I can dance, how beautifully I dance! "

She whips out her white cambric handkerchief which
she wants to wave in her *kazachyok*,[1] " holds the corner of
it in two fingers of her right hand." The effect of such a
precise detail at the appropriate moment suffices. The
chorus arrange themselves. Maximov, the vivacious little

[1] Russian—Cossack dance.—Tr.

pig, rushes up and hops about on his aged legs. Stop, you foolish fellow! Pay attention! The queen is going to dance a *solo*. She has already begun to sway, her mouth half open, her head bent back, a *bayadère*, a beloved of Bacchus. Then she stops, falters, and lifts her finger with all the circumspection of a drunkard.

"I'm weak, excuse me—too weak—I can't—it's my fault!" She whispers and bows in every direction. The chorus titters. "Had a drop too much, the fine lady!" And Maximov nods to the girls and points to the queen. "Little bit exhilarated."

Comedy worthy of Mozart! He also could have ventured to represent a queen dancing in her cups.

The revels grow apace, the chorus breaks into song, the girls dance in wild frenzy. Grushenka is weary and lets Mitya carry her behind the curtain. Now the falcon is overcome by desire. She implores him not to touch her; she is his for ever, but not now, not here, and Mitya promptly becomes nothing but calm adoration. Grushenka whispers, "Away from here, far away, begin a new life, a beautiful life—anywhere where you can dig, sow, build, always together."

Mitya groans. Dawn is breaking. Confession about the blood is on the tip of his tongue, but he cannot bring it over him. He confesses only the theft, the accursed money. She laughs. The young lady's money? Well, that can easily be given back. Grushenka has plenty, more than enough, and everything is his. Only away, quickly!

Yes, away! he murmurs. Siberia!

Why Siberia? But why not Siberia? If he wants to go to Siberia she will follow him. There is snow there, snow is beautiful. You can drive there. The trot of horses and the jingling bells!

There really has been the sound of jingling bells some-where, or was it the clinking of glasses or the delirious song of the chorus? Grushenka falls asleep and dreams of a distant journey through the far-off shimmering snow, safe in her Mitya's arms. The sudden quietness wakens her.

FRENZY

All of a sudden the chorus is silent, everything is veiled in silence. Not a sound in the house which a moment ago shook with tumultuous din. Mitya bends over his beloved and notices she is staring fixedly beyond him at the curtain. A strange face peers in it at them. They have come to arrest Lieutenant Karamazov. Mitya utters a cry.

There is no connecting link in this transformation. People appear on the scene like dolls with glass eyes. No wonder Dmitri stares. Parricide! someone shouts. Dmitri frowns. He has heard that cry before. And his father too? But how? But why not his father? It might quite well have been. He still feels his clenched fist round the pestle as the face appeared at the window. But no, it cannot be, not his father, there is something wrong there, it was Grigory, the old man at the fence. For God's sake what has happened to Grigory?

No, Grigory is alive. That scatters the threatening clouds. So he is not a murderer, so the cup of bitterness has passed him by. The Almighty has worked the miracle. Lord, I thank you! No, gentlemen, I have had nothing to do with my father. I wanted to, but God was protecting me. Innocent I am not, but I have not done it. Grushenka, God has saved me, I am not a murderer!

Grushenka is transformed; in her submissiveness she flings herself at the feet of his pursuers. She is the only guilty one. He committed the murder for her sake. She drove him to it by tormenting him.

The note of passion which was originally intended for Raskolnikov's companion fits in here quite well. Sonia's Christian note would be disturbing. She is not in the least horrified at the thought of the crime; she is firmly convinced of it; in fact after all that has preceded it she is bound to be convinced. Her love for her falcon is, if anything, greater, for he has struck down a creature for her sake. If there was still any hesitation before this stranger, Dmitri, if the outburst of love for Mitya was connected with her painful disillusionment at her former love and could be deemed part of the orgy or one of her gifts as queen, now everything is swept aside. Her one and only impulse is, together! The spiritual union which Sonya offered the murderer and which had to become the subject of a protracted development, is here attained at once by an elementary sense of kinship, and she enfolds Dmitri in her protecting wings. Judge us both together! But the wing of protection is futile, for it tends to incriminate her beloved. Do what you like with him, I shall stand by him!

Consciousness of this enables Dmitri to approach the purgatory of the interrogation with a light heart. Grigory is alive and Grushenka is his. Nothing else matters.

Allow me, gentlemen, we shall soon settle this silly misunderstanding. Do not think ill of it, because peculiar circumstances surround the deed. You are bound to consider me the guilty one. Yes, there are funny things in the world. Now pay attention! In ten minutes everything will be settled and you will know exactly how matters stand. You will be quite amused. Only let me explain!

He knows the chief of police, the examining lawyer, and the public prosecutor, he has met these gentlemen on various occasions. They are all inoffensive and highly respectable people. Gentlemen, we shall have a good laugh to-day. We shall shriek with laughter.

It turns out that things cannot be done quite so quickly. To Dmitri, of course, everything is perfectly simple, for it was not he, that is understood; enough said. But for the others there are certain difficulties. The fact remains that the old man has been killed, that is quite clear, and someone must have killed him, of course. The only person seen near the house at the time of the murder is sitting here now. He behaved afterwards in a particularly strange manner, just like a man who had committed such a crime, and before the deed he had behaved like a man intending to commit such a crime. That is common knowledge all over the town. In addition, it seems he needed three thousand roubles, and just three thousand roubles were stolen by the murderer. Yesterday evening he had not a farthing in his pocket and an hour later he possessed a bundle of bank-notes. Presumably the murder was committed with this brass pestle and he had fetched the weapon from such and such a place; without, so he asserts in his simplicity, having any definite intention.

All this proceeds slowly and in an orderly manner, whilst he talks of his feelings for Grushenka, about which no one has asked him, or protests his joy that Grigory is still alive, a matter which is totally irrelevant and were better not mentioned, for it so happens that the old servant is the one witness whose evidence is likely to be dangerous. You must admit, Dmitri Fyodorovitch, that all this is a strange coincidence.

Yes, he must admit that. Write it down clearly and neatly. They ask him if he suspects anyone, Smerdyakov for example, the epileptic cook, who at the time lay in bed so ill that the doctor still fears for his life.—Smerdyakov? Mitya has thought of that evil fellow; a possibility, were it not for his fit. But even without his fit the scallywag would not have been capable of it, far too cowardly and weak as a chicken. Smerdyakov can be counted out of it. —Anyone else?—No, but what has that to do with him? Surely that is the affair of you gentlemen. It is a riddle to him too, but one thing is positive, it was not he and they cannot demand of him to surrender his head for the lack of someone better. The matter is obviously not so simple as these gentlemen imagine and nothing will be achieved by this inquisition about trifles. It is a well-known fact that this is their usual procedure, legal quibbles about trifles, that is why so many innocents are sentenced. What did the man eat and drink yesterday evening! All written down neatly. That writing down is enough in itself to make a man nervous. And then suddenly they say, it's you and no one else!—Gentlemen, I will not take offence, for you do your best, you are victims of your ridiculous system. Would you like to write that down too?

The authorities cannot help smiling. Is this and that and the other really so irrelevant? Yes, replies Dmitri irritably, thoroughly irrelevant. It is a matter of feelings, not of cunning man-traps.

No one has ever resorted to so modest a defence. Typical *dilettante*. That fits in, too, for where could a lieutenant like him, so infinitely light-hearted, have learnt the tricks of the expert criminal?

Dmitri begins to fidget. He is asked why he needed the three thousand roubles which he sought so eagerly for a few days. How does that concern the gentlemen? That is a purely private matter. Well, then, I don't care, to settle a debt, a debt of honour. No, don't write that down! Kindly write down, he refuses to answer!—He also refuses to answer the decisive question where the money came from. They may do what they please with him, he is not going to reveal to all the world the disgrace of this breach of trust. Thereupon the prosecutor is obliged to warn him of the consequences of his refusal. It would be so simple to answer the question and to explain everything in a word, and he has already promised.

Would not even a best friend arrive at painful suspicions if this point were still not cleared up? Surely he must see that. The danger is considerable.

He sees it quite clearly, sees everything quite clearly, but stands by his refusal.—Not even some indication of the motives which prompt him to silence?—Yes, that he will grant them, as they press for it. Behind his refusal is disgrace, disgrace far greater than the murder and robbery of his father.

They show him the paper which was found on the floor near the murdered man, a large envelope bearing an inscription in his father's hand. He sees light. Only one person knew of that envelope; he must be the murderer. So it is Smerdyakov after all; he was the only one who knew the signal, the only one who knew what lay under the pillow. Go off and arrest the fellow at once! He is the murderer, and nobody else!

All the same, suggests the examining lawyer cautiously, there is one other person who knew about the signal and the envelope. You must not forget him.

INTERROGATION

Mitya ſtares. The danger grows immense. These are not honourable people, they do not consider him an honourable man, they are enemies, miserable enemies at that. They force him to take off every ſtitch of clothing, take it away from him and search the lining for the reſt of the ſtolen money, for only half of it has been found on him. He has to take off his socks and show his crumpled big toe. And his clothes are not returned to him for they are pieces of evidence and have to go to the court. Were it not for Kalganov he would have nothing to put on. Kalganov gets no thanks. The trousers are too long and he can hardly button the coat. They have disfigured him, the rabble! (Would a real murderer dare to think of such a thing?)

And now he has to proſtitute himself utterly, for he muſt escape from this noose somehow. Prosecutor and examining lawyer prick up their ears.

Now follows the moſt fantaſtic of all his fabrications, the ſtory of the wallet. Is that the whole of his secret? Prosecutor and examining lawyer exchange glances. The fellow is carrying it too far. Why then were the fifteen hundred roubles such a disgrace in face of all that is at ſtake? Surely, if anything was blameworthy, it was the appropriation of the three thousand, not the division of it. If he took the money from his betrothed it nevertheless remained in the family.

Dmitri is shocked. The men of honour make no diſtinction between lightheadedness and pickpocketry. Perhaps the gentlemen see nothing wrong in the motive: deceiving his betrothed in order to win his beloved. But the gentlemen have no further use for moral delicacies and Mitya has surrendered his secret to no purpose. He might juſt as well have told it to the brick walls. He liſtens apathetically to the interrogation of the witnesses. Only when Grushenka appears does he wake up. She caſts a glance at him. Be calm, my falcon! Mitya jumps up. " I call God to witness that I am innocent of my father's blood! "

DOSTOEVSKY

She goes to the icon in the corner, crosses herself and offers fervent thanks to Heaven. Then she turns to the lawyer and calls on him to believe what Dmitri has said. That man would not lie against his conscience. Her brief appearance is dignified and gives Mitya encouragement. She is the only person from his world. Before he is conducted to the town he tells the two representatives of authority that creatures like him need such blows to bring them to reason. " I accept the torment and the disgrace, for I want to suffer and thus grow better. . . . I accept the punishment, not because I killed him, but because I wanted to kill him. . . . All the same I shall fight you for my life and I warn you of that in advance." He apologizes for his unseemly words during the interrogation. A great deal was still not clear to him before. Now he is going to be arrested and so he wants to offer them his hand for a final farewell. Naturally they do not take his hand so chivalrously proffered, and the young examining lawyer with the fine rings says all that can be said in such a situation, and wishes him the best of luck.

The authorities do not shine in this process, but are good, humdrum citizens. We are in the provinces, not in Petersburg where Raskolnikov was faced with a crafty bloodhound. Porphyry Petrovitch, with his *flair*, would have scented the innocent, would have accepted Dmitri's naïve assertion that it was not a matter of " trifles," even though they stood out in bold relief, but of " feelings," and would have followed the advice of rousing Smerdyakov from his fit.

More important than the details of the interrogation which Dostoevsky, the amateur criminologist, was unwilling to dispense with, is the chivalrous man's protest which can be read between the lines of the interrogation. To the prosecutor used to normal cases these ebullitions of conscience are merely fantastic chatter. Behind Dmitri stands Dostoevsky, the validity of whose feelings some would even to-day like to contest. But the latent protest in itself is chivalrous, just and conciliatory. Prosecutor and

THE CHORUS

lawyer do not behave ridiculously, but as fits the circumstances. Their mistake is the result of their scrupulous
adherence to legal procedure. There is a higher law above
lawyer and accused.

.   .   .   .   .

The poet is forced by the novel-drama form to skip the
interval between the long night in Mokroe and the court
process. For that reason he introduces an interlude in the
same way as after the fifth book which ends with Ivan's
departure. He also needs it for the transition from the
tone, in which Dmitri's interrogation is conducted, to the
completely different tone of the three interrogations to
which Ivan subjects Smerdyakov. Alyosha is once again
mediator, but this time the scene is not set in the monastery.
In the place of the glory stands the law-court with its prison,
and thus it remains till the final act, where it occupies the
entire stage. But now Alyosha has a different *entourage*.
The scene is filled with a host of schoolboys with bright
eyes. Kolya is their leader. Kolya Krassotkin has all the
attributes of a leader. He has not attained that position
as a matter of course. So long as his deeds lay wrapped in
darkness he suffered from being the youngest and smallest
of all and was laughed at by the clique, till one day he
happened to drop a remark that for a wager he was prepared
to lie down on the railway track and let an express run over
him. To shut him up once and for all they agreed and the
wager won him his position. He is a kindly being, affable
with the boys, tolerant of the weaknesses of his fellow-
creatures, but averse to every kind of sentimentality. The
exaggerated love of his mother, Krassotkin's widow, who is
terrified what he will do next, jars on his nerves. He has
all the matter-of-factness of Kolya Ivolgin, free of prejudices;
a revolutionary, intent on the task of raising the standard
of the clique, of keeping the masters within bounds, and of
not tolerating any meanness. He is as capable of imbuing
animals as human beings with respect. At a nod from him
Perezvon, his mongrel, rolls on its back and pretends to
be dead.

The only one who, for a short time, was at loggerheads with Kolya was Ilyusha, son of the " wisp of tow." Ilyusha once stuck a penknife into Kolya's leg. That is why he came to grief.

Kolya is interested in Mr Karamazov. This young man is always in the company of the schoolboys, although he really has other things to do, for very shortly his brother's tedious case is going to be heard. The young man does not seem to trouble much about it, holds discussions with them, accompanies the boys to Ilyusha's sickbed, seems one of the feeble sort. Alyosha has sent a message that he would be delighted to know Mr Krassotkin. Kolya is not accustomed to let himself be invited to public receptions and will himself decide when he wants Mr Karamazov to approach him. And he whistles to his dog. " Ici, Perezvon! "

We have had a hasty glimpse of these boys in a previous chapter when Alyosha, passing through the town, became mixed up in the stoning affray. Smurov and the rest of them were letting fly at the impudent young Ilyusha who had mortally insulted them. Alyosha felt sorry for him up against so many, and received no thanks for his interference. Ilyusha flung a few stones at him and, as he approached, bit his finger. That led to the visit to his father, the so-called wisp of tow, a captain who has come down in the world, one of the genus insulted and injured, remotely related to General Ivolgin. Dmitri has had a public scene with him which led to the nickname of wisp of tow, and Ilyusha wanted to exact revenge for his father on Dmitri's brother.

We have forgotten the scene we read cursorily, hence the apparent abruptness of the boys' appearance. But this scene is so dramatic that we are convinced.

Therein lies the superiority over the first great interlude, in which Zossima was the central figure. In the Zossima chapters there was abundance of wisdom, mysticism and symbolism, but what they lacked our sense of touch, particularly our impatient sense of touch of to-day, will not forgo at any price. At times there is complete absence of aǩion. Not because they are quiet and played in an atmosphere opposed to preceding events, by no means. This difference in atmosphere was at the time as necessary and welcome as now. What we objeǩed to was the way the difference was portrayed; it did not ǩand out in bold relief. The quietude of the monaǩery did not suffice to calm the ǩorm which preceded it, and Alyosha's rôle in those surroundings, however beautifully it developed, however perfeǩ its symbolism, did not always compensate for the heterogeneity of the manner of presentation. On the other hand the interlude with Kolya and his companions is, like Grushenka's drunkenness, ǩimulating as dawn breaking over the foreǩ after a wild night. There are two essential improvements: the connexion with Alyosha, although much less tangible than Alyosha's relationship to the monaǩery, convinces spontaneously because it reveals the moǩ natural charaǩeriǩic of the novice, his youth reǩrained by the shadow of the monaǩery. But more effeǩive ǩill is an unexpeǩed relationship of the interlude to the night in Mokroe.

When Ilyusha had recovered he had broken with all his companions because they had poked fun at him since his father's escapade about the wisp of tow with the tangled red hair. The relationship of the boy to his father is a parallel, on a smaller scale, to that of Arkady and Versilov. The captain is also publicly insulted, pockets the insult, and does not fight a duel. At the time Ilyusha resolved that when he was grown-up he would fling the insulter a challenge; he would knock the miserable fellow down, brandish his sword over him and, at the very laǩ moment, spare his life. So much for you!—Such had been his thoughts as he ǩood in the ditch and he and the other boys flung ǩones at one another. Since he had had to lie in bed he had thought of nothing but his dog Zhutchka whom he had loǩ one unlucky day. Alyosha had reconciled the boys and gradually prevailed on each one of them to come to the sick-bed. They came every day and were kind to the invalid. Only Kolya abǩained. Mass sympathy did not appeal to him. Kolya went his own way, liked to make himself and Perezvon popular at the weekly market, studied the people, and drove the market-women crazy. " The people are not to be underrated," he said to Smurov, whose parents had forbidden him speak to him. " Our power is derived from the people, but if some boorish ruffian is stupid in his heart you can quite cheerfully knock him about a bit." Kolya acts as a counterpoise to the poet's transcendentalism.

Kolya had fallen out with Ilyusha, his former intimate, on account of the dog business. A wicked person had advised Ilyusha to give Zhutchka, by way of a change in food, a piece of bread spiked with needles. Ilyusha had done so. You may chase a goose under a moving cart, but to feed a dog on needles is vile. The dog had whined and never been seen again. Naturally Ilyusha was full of remorse and thought day and night of his prank. Nevertheless Kolya considered he deserved severe punishment and threw him over. That hurt the boy grievously, first the loss of Zhutchka whom he naturally thought dead, secondly the loss of Kolya, his best friend, for it was not an everyday occurrence for a boy in a higher class to consort with one in a lower. That did not, of course, prevent the small boy letting Kolya know at the next opportunity that from now on he was going to feed all dogs with spiked bread.

All this and a great deal more is discussed at Alyosha's first meeting with Kolya. Kolya expounds his views on pedagogy, particularly on the supposed value of the classical languages, as well as his views on Russia, Voltaire and atheism, which he whole-heartedly accepts; in short, all that a thirteen-year-old boy has in his noddle. At the same time he is not free of anxiety lest Alyosha think him a swanker, whilst in reality he is concerned only with creating a serious friendship which might possibly be advantageous even to Mr Karamazov on account of their common interest in education of the people. They go together to Ilyusha and there is reconciliation. At the appropriate moment Kolya calls to his dog, " Ici, Perezvon! " and Ilyusha is

enraptured at the sight of his Zhutchka he thought dead.
Then he is not . murderer after all. Kolya makes the dog
perform all sorts of tricks. To fill his cup of happiness he
presents the invalid with the brass cannon.

In this tragedy the children constitute a moving chorus
which is strangely unconnected with the actual drama. It
is a self-contained world with a law unto itself, calmly
pursuing its course, weeping and laughing. But the
chorus unconsciously plays a part, and it is just this very
unconsciousness which enhances the effect. The ingenuous
devotion of the schoolboys with their chorus-leader in their
midst vindicates the falcon behind bolt and bar, and ridicules
the officials to whom feelings mean nothing

The air teems with momentous feelings, small, great,
ridiculous, diseased, strong, poisonous, holy feelings, and
Alyosha, the busy bee, takes his fill, flitting from one to
the other. The schoolboy chorus is the outermost circle
around the drama. Madame Hohlakov, the great childish
child with her twaddle about modern legal procedure,
forms the link between this boyish chorus and the court.
In Lisa, her little daughter, there is a fidgety child which
would like to become a little devil, and her fidgeting
betrays the nervousness of someone else. She asserts that
she can peacefully consume her pineapple compot in the
face of other people's tortures.

The originator of this theory also has his feelings on
the matter. He sits next to Smerdyakov and institutes an
enquiry about what happened on the evening in question
and how the epileptic fit and the rest of it could have been
foreseen. Smerdyakov no longer takes the same interest
in his personal appearance, he is in hospital and has come
down in the world; therefore he polishes his feelings all
the more attentively and enjoys his visitor's feelings, relishes
them like a pineapple compot. He does not dwell long
on Ivan's questions, for the learned doctors are thoroughly
conversant with the circumstances of the fit, have submitted
him to constant examination; even an uneducated man
could probably judge his state of health. On the other

hand, in his own subtle way, he expounds who is the guilty one in this murder business. If you tell an honoured son that this, that and the other will happen if he leaves the house of his honoured father and goes off, and if the honoured son goes off all the same, precisely as was recommended to him, then it does not seem vitally important who actually delivered the blow, especially if the said honoured son has illuminated things with his doctrine of the freedom of feeling, and thus the gentleman who goes off is the real murderer because, though he could have prevented it, he merely used someone else as his tool.

Ivan has to sit and listen to that. Why does he listen? Why does he not jump up? Why does he ask, instead, what interest he could possibly have had in the old man's death?

Smerdyakov was expecting that question, a comic question from such a clever man, a man it was always a pleasure to talk to. And the inheritance? Forty thousand, is that nothing then?

It was you! cries Ivan. He cries out in rage, more for the sake of silencing the brute than because he really thinks him the murderer.

The brute smiles. You haven't had enough by a long chalk!—If that were so it would certainly be of little practical value to Mr Ivan. First, Mr Ivan would be still further incriminated and the higher authorities would be bound to notice it, because those enjoyable conversations preceded the event, and even if Mr Ivan were not to reach Siberia on the strength of it, all the same people in society would likewise notice what would be most unpleasant for Mr Ivan. Secondly—and this secondly is drawled out slowly; if Smerdyakov were wearing polished boots instead of hospital shoes and were not forced by weakness to remain seated, he would now be shifting from one foot to the other and watching his reflection in his boots—secondly, financially it would be highly disadvantageous, for if Mr Dmitri had in effect killed their respected procreator and were presumably, as a result, to be sentenced, he would be dispossessed of his nobility and fortune, and his share of the money would fall to the other two sons, that is, forty would turn into sixty.

Smerdyakov smiles. Why don't you hit me? Curious that the proud gentleman shows positively no sign of being outraged and has not the least thought of hitting him. It is true that, since the abolition of serfdom, whipping has been prohibited, but noble gentlemen can always make an exception for the sake of protecting their privileged interests, even in the enlightened French Republic. Only a very progressive and clever gentleman would abstain from mediæval usage and refrain from making a useless row. Such is the clever gentleman who also refrains from suggesting to the examining lawyer the possibility of a feigned epileptic attack, and there he is right, for the lawyer would not have given it a moment's serious consideration. What man wanting to feign an attack would himself make a preliminary announcement—to the victim's own son at that? Since the gentleman has not mentioned it the lackey has also not mentioned those enjoyable conversations prior to the event.

He will denounce him this very day, says Ivan as he leaves. His thoughts are in complete turmoil. Did I will the murder? Yes, the insect must be exterminated from off the face of the earth. Did I count on that when I went away? Did I take him seriously at the time? No, I laughed at him, laughed quite loudly. Ivan's thoughts turn to his laughter, he still feels the ensuing cramp in his jaws. No, everything was very different. Only one thing did not occur to him, that this creature could act independently. No, one would never have thought him capable of the deed. That is the devastating error. And if Smerdyakov really did it, what then? If he did not do it it can still be called an accident or levity or carelessness. But is he really the criminal? Is it he? or is it not?—No, he is only pretending so as to torment me, he certainly would not give himself away. Pleasure cannot be carried to the point of self-destruction.

He goes to Katya, makes a clean breast of everything to his beloved. She shows him a letter Mitya wrote her when he was drunk the evening before the deed. In it he writes that to-morrow he is going to move heaven and earth to find the money; if he fails he will smash his father's head in. Patricide rather than her contempt.

Obviously the man who wrote that was capable of anything, ready to do anything. That letter, with its mathematically precise details black on white, is conclusive evidence in conjunction with all the other factors. Ivan breathes again. It cannot be Smerdyakov. For the time being he finds comfort in these facts.

The threads have gradually become interwoven, and now we are accompanying Alyosha into the prison. In the dark cell emotion bursts forth afresh. Torment has not broken the falcon, he rises higher than ever. Ivan is caught, little Lisa is caught, Katya and the entire world are in a net; only Dmitri is free. The prison only accentuates his emotion. At last he can meditate in peace, unencumbered by foolish and ephemeral inspirations. No one has any idea what a blessing that is.

Alyosha is surprised. Is there then nothing more to be done? To-morrow is the great day. Has he prepared his defence? Has he an answer to all these enquiries? Has everything been agreed with his counsel?

Listen, Alyosha, of course that is all very important in its way, but the main thing is: I am. Do you understand? In spite of everything, I am. You cannot deprive me of that. " Whatever chains you forge for me, I am still alive, I still see the sun. And even if I don't see it, I know all the same that it is there."

But to-morrow? insists Alyosha.—Well, to-morrow will be like any other day, a paltry day, a dark day. Naturally the lawyers and doctors will do their best. What do they know of guilt? Each is guilty for all and for everything. What someone else did I almost did myself. It's all the same in the long run.

Dmitri has developed in these few weeks. At the same

time he is still the same primitive being, of uncouth speech
and blustering mien. The great lawyer from Petersburg is
nothing more than a cunning scoundrel. Not for one
moment does he believe in his client's innocence, but to-
morrow he is going to prove it as surely as twice two make
four. And Rakitin is going to write a short article about
the whole affair, from the standpoint of environment with
a sprinkling of socialism, and it is to be shown that it was
Ivan's accursed duty and obligation and, in a certain
measure, a natural law to put an end to the old man.—
Only one thing: Grushenka! Are convicts allowed to
marry?

He has not the slightest doubt that he will be convicted.
That will be as it may. But Grushenka cannot go with
him to the mines. It will be hard without her.

They talk of everything on which the prisoner has
meditated. God has been supplanted by chemistry. Reverence is done with. This overthrow of God, of which
Rakitin is quite positive, weighs more heavily upon him
than what will be to-morrow's verdict of the jury, for from
now onwards, so at least it is asserted by Rakitin and
company, all fine feelings are only the convulsing of little
nerve-ends. When a lofty idea crosses the mind it is one
of those little nerve-ends kicking and sprawling in the
brain, that is all it is, and, in the same way, when you
commit some cowardly or scoundrelly action, it is only
another of those little nerve-ends convulsing. Oh, Alyosha,
that is all nonsense of course, but how about Grushenka?

Dostoevsky's argument is never so effective as when he
relies, as in this passage, on the tone alone. The intention
behind this conversation is obvious, more than obvious.
The pretext for returning to this old theme is almost forcibly
introduced. The tone disarms criticism. Were the whole
of European science with its chemistry substituted for
Rakitin it would be confronted with: all nonsense, of
course!

Mitya has something to ask Alyosha, something to do
with Ivan. Ivan stands much higher than either of them,

but cannot join in this discussion because he also believes in the little nerve-end theory. Alyosha is to decide. It is a very important question, and Alyosha is to keep his eyes in check, for Dmitri will be guided by what his eyes say. What does Alyosha think of America? Brother Ivan and Grushenka have planned his emigration. Hold your eyes in check, Alyosha! don't say anything yet, listen first! The escape has been well prepared. Everything is going splendidly. It costs a great deal, but Ivan is finding the money. Ivan is doing his utmost although he believes Mitya guilty. America is not beautiful, but Siberia without Grushenka—how could he endure it? Ivan says convicts are not allowed to marry. You may as well bash your head in if Grushenka is not with you in the mines. Alyosha, think of it, perhaps twenty years without Grushenka!

He looks anxiously at his brother, and Alyosha holds his eyes in check. Ivan says you can do things more worthwhile in America than under the earth in Siberia; of course he is right. But there is something else that the learned gentlemen with the little nerve-ends consider nonsense. Alyosha understands it. There is a hymn which suddenly breaks off on a stupid note. No, Alyosha, don't say anything yet, wait till to-morrow. The hymn is good, divinely good, but Mitya is only a human being. Undoubtedly you ought to be capable of going on till the end, and in America there are lots of scoundrels. Yes, you ought to. God pointed out a way and shortly before the cross you turned about. Don't speak yet, Alyosha, wait till to-morrow.

Alyosha ponders. The hymn rings in his ears, resounds through the narrow cell, expands the walls, raises the roof. Again Mitya asks, may convicts marry?

Time presses, they have to part. Alyosha asks whether Ivan really thinks his brother guilty. Mitya laughs bitterly. He wanted to ask him, but let it slide, for ultimately it was useless, you could see it at once from his eyes. Alyosha is already at the door. Mitya holds him tightly. For a second they can hear the beat of their hearts.

" Alyosha, tell me the whole truth. Do you believe that I am the murderer or not? "

Alyosha quivers under his brother's burden which sets his whole life in question. He bursts out breathlessly that he has never for one moment believed him guilty, and he raises his hand in token of oath.

Dmitri opens his lips for whispered thanks as if he had just escaped a fit of fainting. He leaves him with the words, " Go, love Ivan! "

This is the realization of the dream which began in *The Idiot* and stopped abruptly. It is a matter of indifference whether Dmitri escapes or not. He will do so and is right. As Alyosha later replies in answer to a fresh question, it would not be in Mitya's nature to let himself be crucified in his innocence. The turning back before the cross is not the flaw in *The Idiot*, but rather a practical matter and, in addition, a question of taste. The continuation of the hymn would be literature. Dostoevsky differentiates definitely between the two questions. Only on the evening in prison, before Alyosha has acknowledged his belief in his brother's innocence, does Mitya actually place in his brother's hands the decision whether he shall escape or not, but even then he demands that the answer be postponed. Afterwards, in the so-called epilogue, when Alyosha has already acquiesced in the plan of escape, Dmitri says the escape had been resolved on quite apart from Alyosha. Mitya's " feelings " are not called into question by this remark. If that were the question he would really let himself be crucified, with enraptured laughter and a blunt oath on his lips. We have heard what is essential. It is not a diseased outsider with a peculiar past who can be capable of singing the hymn and of shouldering the guilt of every one, but a full-blooded being.

That is the elevation of the son on the right. He frees himself from the coils of the Laocoön-group. Alyosha goes to Ivan. Ivan also asks him and Alyosha breaks through Ivan's armour with one word. The document with which Katya sought to calm the man who thirsted for lies has

DOSTOEVSKY

long since lost its effect, and from the few words which are let fall in the presence of Katya it transpires that she too does not regard the letter as conclusive evidence, but inclines to Ivan's opinion in the matter of who is guilty. Whether Dmitri is the murderer is of as little importance to her hatred as to Grushenka's love. When to-morrow as a witness she brings about his ruin she will only be satisfying her desire for revenge. If she saves him it will be only for the sake of punishing him. A ray of light is cast upon Ivan's relationship to her. The canker has already poisoned his love as well, and to-morrow, after the verdict, he is going to break with Katya.

Alyosha calmly and definitely declares Dmitri innocent and to Ivan's impatient question, who else then could be the murderer, Alyosha answers, " You yourself know who! "

" Do you mean that fabrication about the insane epileptic? Do you mean Smerdyakov? "

" You yourself know who."

" But who then, who? " shrieks Ivan.

Alyosha trembles, but the hymn is still in him and fortifies him.

" I know only one thing, it was not you who killed our father! "

Ivan needs time before he can smile again. Alyosha sees through him. He sees through all the terrible torments of conscience, as if some strange power had opened his eyes. " It is not you who killed him, that is where you are mistaken, you are not the murderer, listen, not you! God has sent me to tell you."

Alyosha's strength at this moment is extraordinary. The strange power has accorded him the right to absolve from sin. His announcement leaves Ivan petrified. He hears, not the solace of the words, but the knowledge behind them. For a second he imagines Alyosha has witnessed his nocturnal hallucinations and is impelled to ask whether he has seen " him." Alyosha does not know to whom he refers, and Ivan succeeds in mastering his overwrought nerves. He has no use for prophets and celestial emissaries.

THE EMISSARY

Once again he retreats into his shell. This short scene boldly pierces Ivan's darkness. "Think of me and my words!" vainly cries the emissary.

Ivan once more goes to Smerdyakov for a last interrogation. Teacher and pupil have exchanged places and a third something is present, also a feeling. Love has never been portrayed so passionately as in the Karamazovs, love of God, of life, of mankind, of woman. Never has hatred been depicted in such terrible colour as in this scene, hatred between men, that is, rationalized hatred which pulverizes the body and crushes the brain. Strindberg has created a literature of sex hatred and no one will follow in his wake. It was the outcome of his fate and of the essence of his peculiar genius. In the ordinary course of events some mitigation must result from sexual antagonism. We know that nature is like that. Dostoevsky has not suppressed this conditionality in his portrayals of sex hatred. At bottom it is all child's play beside the feeling between Ivan and Smerdyakov. Hatred between man and woman only renders their inequality greater. But those two become more similar, lose all social distinctions and vent their hatred in similar ways. They are two similarly constructed machines. They are both nearly at the end of their tether. Their bodies are like tattered rags hanging from a brain functioning at full pressure. In the end they are like cocks in the last round of which there is nothing left but beaks; as they cannot see their opponent any longer they hack blindly at the air. But Smerdyakov, the stronger hater, has suffered most because no other interest dilutes the poison. The teachings of Ivan which disintegrate the teacher are to the pupil nothing more or less than froth, a label, a bit of literature. He has done with dressing-up. Hatred has born this creature; already in the womb of his mother, Smerdyatchaya, he had stormed at everything connected with his procreator; his is the hatred of the bastard, of the downtrodden lackey, the hatred of generations of bastards and lackeys, not legendary but extremely personal, all accumulated in one single being.

367

Whilst Ivan, the intellectual, shrivels up, the other man grows beyond himself. Hatred endows him with spiritual dignity and seems to objectify the crime. Murder, a last resort in sex conflicts, has become only a secondary factor, ultimately merely a decorative pretext on which in reality the action of hatred is constructed. The very ashes of Smerdyakov will attempt to lacerate the Karamazovs.

He puts his cards on the table. Of course he killed the old man, he observes parenthetically, and Ivan is still hoping, hypnotized by the weary, monotonous voice. Smerdyakov is surprised. Did the gentleman then ever doubt of it? That has surely all been settled long ago. What's the good of pretending? God, how tedious! Can't we change the subject?

As Ivan requires proof Smerdyakov slowly pulls up his trousers and reveals a long white stocking. You must now take off the garter and then put your hand into the stocking. He pulls out a packet of papers and puts the three thousand roubles on the table. The reality of this gesture is dazzling.

Ivan smiles—this stocking and the paper packet hauled out of it, highly amusing! So it was not Dmitri after all —and there is at once a last glimmer of hope. Perhaps they were accomplices, at least in the deed. With this last hope of the bartering intellectual Ivan descends into the lowest depths.

" No, only together with you! " replies Smerdyakov dryly.

Ivan listens to his story. Curious how cleverly the fellow has worked everything out, this creature they thought such a fool. Ivan does not miss the merest trifle, the trifles are the titbits; he exhibits a kind of relish in the story, the relish of the expert. To see them together at the table no one would ever guess they were enemies. Smerdyakov tells his story simply and lucidly. It was really not difficult, we only needed a little luck; but one expects that. Our plan was well laid. When they come to Dmitri's escape through the garden Ivan again feels a gleam of hope. Smerdyakov winks; yes, that's what every one believes;

that's just our luck, and that's why our little brother will be found guilty to-morrow. You know that as well as I. It was a good idea to disguise oneself like that, an excellent idea. Plain as a pikestaff; he the tool, Ivan the brains.

The intellectual whimpers, grows smaller and smaller. Smerdyakov is surprised how quickly a man like that throws up the sponge.

And now?

Smerdyakov pushes the money over to him—if you please! Then you give the money back?—Of course, for it has nothing to do with the matter. We didn't murder for the sake of money, we did it to exterminate the insects. And then Ivan ought to have something solid in his hands. For the rest, it's a pity!

Ivan pulls himself together and takes the money. That will go to the court to-morrow. To-morrow he will denounce both of them, himself and the other man. Smerdyakov remains quite calm. That too has been foreseen. There will not be any denunciation, he is too finicking about trifles, he is the son of the gentleman who has passed over; of all the children he is the most closely related to the late departed.

The *virtuoso*, Smerdyakov, has saved up this identification with the insect till the last. And still another titbit; even if from a whim you choose the famous path of purification, circumstances will be against you, for the three thousand roubles are certainly not evidence. Do you know the numbers of the old man's notes? Are you reckoning on producing the stocking in court? Doubtless you are thinking Smerdyakov cannot avoid being examined? That is where you will again be sadly disappointed.

Later Ivan is sitting in his room and again his nocturnal visitor, the Gentleman, appears. The previous conversation is continued in the diction of Ivan, and its inevitable deductions are put to the test. The bankruptcy of the conscience is followed by the collapse of the thinker. The whole question of God which, since Ivan was first capable of thought, has tormented—no, not tormented, that is just his torment — has only occupied his mind as a

connoisseur and amateur who regards God as an interesting object: all this futile *dilettanteism* the Gentleman lets
pass by in confused anecdotes. He is a sponger who
must have lived in intimacy with Ivan. Ivan has a wet
cloth round his head to cool his heated brow and tries
to pin down this enigmatic vision. Does his visitor exist
or not? Of course he does not, for science is as little
tolerant of gentlemen who enter at night without opening
the door as of emissaries and prophets. All the same it
is impossible to shut your eyes to the extraordinary
reality of this Gentleman in his shabby elegance. He talks
loudly and distinctly enough considering he is a mirage;
moreover he is much older than Ivan, a little over fifty, and
must have a past. Only one thing gives him away, he reads
Ivan's thoughts. This rationalist clings to that. So the
Gentleman must be an hallucination in spite of his striped
trousers. There is a spice of bitterness in this reflection,
for what the Gentleman gives breath to are neither Ivan's
cleverest nor noblest thoughts. It is true that there are
quite good thoughts amongst them, but mainly the banal
beginnings, cultivated with difficulty, things of which you
are ashamed later on. Let us remember Zossima's opinion
of the conversational gifts of the thinker. Ivan is not a
Kirilov, not a fanatic to the bitter end, but rather a gifted
littérateur who may have a stroke of literary luck; ambition
is the motive of his thought. A successful banker would
scarcely recall with pleasure the days of his clerkdom.
Ivan resents what the apparition says rather than his
presence. He suffers torture. The Gentleman dishes
everything up again, things long since finished with, just
the things which are intolerable at the moment. The
devil himself could not turn the argument into more
cunning channels. The sponger has resorted to all the
tricks of the trade, banalities which might be all very well
in the company of susceptible ladies.

No, groans Ivan, he was not that sort of a lackey.
His mind could never have produced such a creature.
But if the Gentleman is not a fabrication of Ivan's brain—

a stomach disorder, as Dickens would have said—what is he then? So he is Satan after all?

The Gentleman knows how to handle his man, seems to have learnt that from Smerdyakov. Each time Ivan is on the point of believing in the reality of his visitor a word is let drop which confirms his identity. The Gentleman is Satan and a reflected Ivan at one and the same time.

This is the final and most appalling variant of *The Double*, that early work which, in its turn, was misunderstood and not quite understood by the author himself, a work that reached beyond the bounds of literature and pointed to Dostoevsky's goal in the nebulous distance. His development has attained the goal and justified the audacious stroke of his youthful ambition. Doubtless this application of the *alter ego* idea is only the last word of a picturesque, uncommonly artistic structure, and should not be unjustly isolated. All the same we have here an apotheosis of that idea. The shadow of a sublime figure encounters Golyadkin resurrected. The greatest scene in German literature is intermixed in this dual conversation of Ivan with his *alter ego*. The tragedy of Dostoevsky's collapsing hero is ennobled by the *Faust*-like element, long since a silent accompaniment in this growing work, far more concealed than the Schilleresque, foreign to Dostoevsky's form, but at least just as familiar to his creative thoughts, indeed to his whole urge to confession. But the old *Faust* scene receives new vehicles of expression and fresh perspectives.

Finally the Gentleman strikes Ivan's most sensitive spot. We learn this afterwards from the subsequent conversation with Alyosha who brings the news of Smerdyakov's end. With his usual tact, coupled with the boldest flight of intuition, Dostoevsky has set the decisive climax of the Mephistopheles scene behind the scenes, and thereby made it possible to introduce a final contact with Alyosha. What will happen to-morrow? smiles the Gentleman. Great purification of Mr Superman, eh? Who is that laughing? Great gesture before the assembled public, and the ladies, the grateful audience of the drawing-room philosopher, will be quite beside themselves with rapture. In the end we will grant ourselves a beautiful exit. Raskolnikov kneels in the market-place and confesses. But we are on the watch for that, we retain even in this critical moment still enough common sense and, before kneeling down, quickly place a handkerchief on the ground so as not to soil our trousers. In the deepmost recesses of this superman's soul there lingers the comforting certainty of a satisfactory ending to the performance, for there is certainly no risk.

Ivan finally loses control of himself and flings his tea-glass at the wall, another Luther.

Alyosha comes in. The moment Ivan learns of the suicide of the only witness who could have lent reality to his dream he promptly concludes that he foresaw this probability all the time. Smerdyakov's hatred transcends his corpse. Impossible to invent a more devastating revenge. The cord with which he hangs himself drags Ivan to Golyadkin's fate. The whole gang have got what they asked for. The bastard is quits with all three of them as well as with himself.

.   .   .   .   .   .

The day of the trial. Again the huge criminal apparatus. The stage is full to overflowing. There is a certain mistrust as to the outcome. What is it going to be? The case is elucidated in detail and no public discussion, whatever the results, could enhance the emotional upheaval which we have witnessed in close touch with the person concerned. The twelfth and last book is on a more modest scale which is determined by the disparity between publicity and intimacy. We notice this difference particularly at the beginning of the trial. With the swarms of people at the end of the work Dostoevsky obviously wanted to create an architectonic counterpart to the populous prelude in the monastery. He may also have been prompted by interest in the newly organized Russian jury-system.

If we once learn to appreciate the conditions governing this action our admiration for the poet is increased. The subject-matter compels him to adapt himself with amazing flexibility to a task which superficially would seem more closely connected with a French novel. It is only when the complicated mechanism is in full swing that the engineer lets go, accelerates hundreds of wheels, and a new drama is set in motion.

First, the examination of less important witnesses; dry humour, picturesque arabesques, quite free, quite matter-of-fact. The humour is not caricature and does not give undue prominence to any particular person; it permeates the glittering dust of the grey room. The reader takes his stand amongst the throng of spectators in the background and watches the coming and going of the figures before him. Dostoevsky is also in the crowd, discussing the matter with his neighbour. The innate realist cannot help suddenly introducing an *I* as reporter. It could easily have been dispensed with, and indicates the poet's intention of giving as light a touch as possible. What people are doing or not doing in court must be irrelevant. Even the accused in his box feels that. The whole atmosphere is charged, almost against the poet's will. Things are going well for the fellow in the box. Katya and Grushenka have given favourable evidence; Katya has even told of her begging expedition on her father's behalf. At the back there in the crowd they are nudging one another. Doubtless there was more in it than the lieutenant's deep bow, they think; and the accused writhes under this imputation. Grushenka tears the young lady to shreds. Then Ivan appears. The crowd is suddenly still. In front the little men at the long table all at once look awry. Dmitri sits bolt upright; he knows all Ivan can say. This scion of the house of Karamazov, all in all the rottenest fruit, is finished. Have done with him! And yet no sooner does he appear than our eyes are glued on him, our ears are agog for his insane words. This weakest of the scions of the house of Karamazov has shouldered the heaviest burden. We can see this divinely suffering being with the poet's eyes. He has interesting information to impart, he murmurs. Every one listens, every one seems to know what he is going to say, and the only question is whether he will say it and, if so, how.

His head sinks, he waits a few seconds. No, he has nothing special to say. Again the wheels begin to rotate. Go on, quickly, quickly! That sort of thing has to be done quickly. The president puts the usual questions. Ivan answers in duty bound. He feels ill, may he please retire? and he turns and goes slowly out. Suddenly he turns back again, smiles and makes some reference to *sarafan* and peasant-girl. " If I want to jump up, I shall, and if I don't want to, I shan't! " That is, it's some folk story.

The wheels stop. The president looks stern. The dust stands still in the sun.

Suddenly Ivan drags out the packet of money. Such and such. Smerdyakov and he. " Who wouldn't desire his father's death? "

There has been too much to-do about this phrase. It has to be heard within earshot of the wheels. It is the last word, on this side, of a man from beyond. Only don't pretend . . . at bottom we would all like to do it.

At the long table there is a wagging of heads on laced robes. In the box there is turmoil.

" Have you any witnesses? "

With the answer to that question reason is bound to collapse. Yes, he has witnesses, two in fact. One is dangling on a rope; the other one, a Gentleman, is sitting over there under the table in tight-fitting striped trousers.

He is raving. He begins to shriek. Katya shrieks and produces Dmitri's letter. Grushenka shrieks, Dmitri shrieks. The mechanism breaks down. Pause.

They repair the mechanism. It is off again. There are a few less people in the court. Reason reigns again and weighs matters logically. The prosecutor proves his case up to the hilt, and counsel for the defence does likewise. Whilst the jury deliberates the crowd moves backwards and forwards. Then reason triumphs and Dmitri is sentenced to hard labour in Siberia.

Subsequently in the epilogue there is another inquisition,

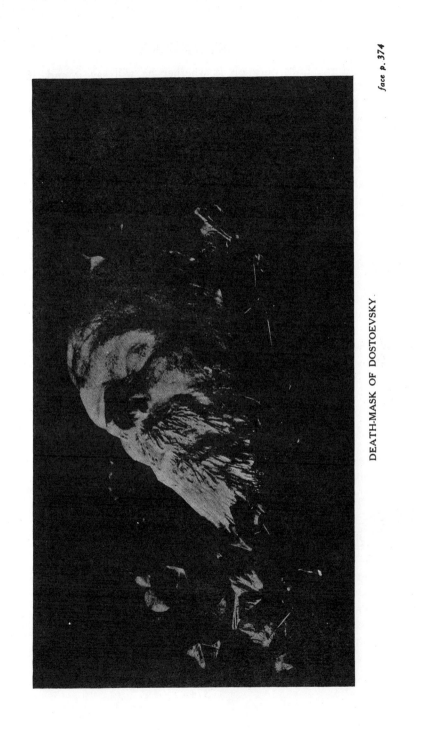

DEATH-MASK OF DOSTOEVSKY.

not the struggle of the two women with their hatred, nor Katya's understanding with Dmitri, but the speech at the burial of little Ilyusha. The schoolboys, led by Alyosha, carry the coffin, and the captain, the wisp of tow, follows busily and stupidly behind. At the grave the boys have to cling to his coat to prevent him from falling in. Smurov, the left-handed boy, also weeps, and even Kolya. Many tears flow on to the snow and on the return home. When Smurov has stopped crying for a moment he quickly flings a stone at a sparrow, and then cries all the more because he has missed the sparrow. Tears, which elsewhere were forgotten, flow profusely over the earth. The boys take the captain home; Kolya bids him pull himself together, for it looks bad to give way to despair. At home things go from bad to worse. The captain catches sight of the orphaned boots of his mordant youngster.

Alyosha makes a speech at the big stone under which Ilyusha is to be buried. If we should become wicked, which, of course, we cannot foresee, let us remember this day. For the rest, why should we become wicked? Ilyusha was good despite everything and life is good despite tears. In spite of everything, long life to life! and Kolya cries, hurrah for Karamazov!

Alyosha's funeral oration is the artlessly improvised sermon of a disciple of Zossima, not lacking in the banalities peculiar to an inexperienced speaker on such occasions. Prosecutor and defending counsel spoke better. But the boys are enthusiastic and none of them thinks of the jokes which were made in the body of the court. The prosecutor and the great Petersburg counsel for the defence weighed their words, for in this case Dmitri was judged by words. But Ilyusha's comrades found it depended only on feeling and redeemed the wickedness of the adults.

This epilogue after the twelfth book is not up to Dostoevsky's usual standard, for the few scenes are chronologically an immediate sequel to the last incidents and must therefore be reckoned part of the novel-drama. Allusion to the future is confined to the hurrahs of Alyosha and the boys. These healthy boyish voices which applaud Ilyusha's devotion to his father are in striking contrast to the words of the madman. Who would not fight for his father? Youth has the last word.

With the burial scene Dostoevsky reverts once again to his past and recapitulates a passage of his youth. The captain is out of *Poor Folk*. In the same way another father followed a coffin whilst the books of his beloved son, with which he had loaded himself, tumbled into the mud. The wisp of tow is an immediate successor to old Pokrovsky. This fact reveals the long path right back to his *début* a generation ago. All paths lead to the realm of the Karamazovs.

.　　.　　.　　.　　.　　.

Dostoevsky is said to have contemplated a continuation of the novel and even, in the course of conversation with his wife and friends, to have sketched his idea in which Alyosha was to have played the principal part. N. Hoffman has dealt with this sketch (62), but it must be taken with a grain of salt. It is quite possible that Dostoevsky mentioned something of the sort; but the question is, when? During his work or afterwards? In any circumstances it need not be taken seriously. We know what to expect of Dostoevsky's first sketches. Everything is changed later on. A continuation of *The Brothers Karamazov* is as little possible as building a second storey on a temple. If Dostoevsky had lived he would have unquestionably have gone on writing. But his whole work is so complete and perfect that to suggest a return of Alyosha, to become in the sequel the standard-bearer of the Karamazovs, is senseless; it would have been almost trespass, for it would have changed the structure of the work and of the whole of Dostoevsky's development. The positions of the characters in the drama are unchangeable, particularly Alyosha's. He is mediator, not hero. If anyone is to be labelled hero, it is not the successor to the Idiot from whom the " positive " hero was to evolve, but Dmitri, the eldest of the Karamazovs, a man in every fibre of his being, in good and in evil, a

CONTINUATION

man in the broadest sense of the word. In the course of our consideration of *The Idiot* we indicated the passage from which this ideal figure might have been developed, subject to certain limitations. Such a development was possible only up to the time of *The Brothers Karamazov*. Undoubtedly this ideal figure was one of Dostoevsky's fairest dreams, and any discussion of doubtful points in this dream inevitably entails discussion of the limitations of Christianity. The flaw which the poet could not avoid—and by that may now be understood, apart from the tragic turn at the end, also to a certain extent conditions which Myshkin's illness veiled—this flaw becomes obvious by its correction in *The Brothers Karamazov* and is one of Dostoevsky's many improvements at his zenith. Any attempt at making the Christ-man hero would be aiming too high. Alyosha, the divine emissary, must remain an emissary, a brilliant but subordinate theme, beside the earthly action from which his hidden wings restrain him; a poem, a marvellous poem. To his limitations belongs his renunciation of the violent reality of the Karamazovs. Frequent reference has been made here to Dostoevsky's discretion. The correction of the Idiot by means of Alyosha is a case in point. It is perfectly certain that had Dostoevsky lived longer he would have made a further attempt at creating a positive hero. However long he had lived nothing would have seemed a greater aim. The novel *Alyosha* would have been a new novel like *The Idiot* which emerged from *Crime and Punishment*. But it is difficult to visualize the repainting of the scenery. It is easier to imagine as a sequel a work on Christ such as, according to a note in his diary, he had in mind.

Nevertheless there is continuation of Alyosha in the spirit of the Idiot, and we possess it. The poet did not need to write it, for it bears the stamp of historical reality. Its name is Dostoevsky.

CHAPTER XV

From Dostoevsky's development is obvious the gradual perfecting of his form. What we are mainly concerned with is the æstheticism of the work freed, as far as possible, from extraneous matter. Already in *Poor Folk* the creative impulse was purely poetical. Those letters are the variations of a lyric poet which encircle the theme in ever-mounting spirals, like mountains surrounding the little church in the valley. The lyric quality is more important than the action. Things are just as they appear through the eyes of these two simple persons in the novel, thus and thus only, and their stolid mentality does not detract from the reality of events.

Dostoevsky adhered to variations. The subject-matter becomes richer and the mentality, the objective which focuses, becomes more and more complicated. The more the variations are differentiated the more the spirals extend, and again and again the *motif* resembles that of the church in the valley. The lyrical note in *Poor Folk* and other later stories would have been incompatible with the tension of the principal works, and had to be modified. The novel-drama developed from the monologues of the under-worldling, his most audacious stroke, and was brought to perfection in his last work.

The history of the form is convincing because it portrays the history of Dostoevsky's thought. The novel-drama was not the invention of an artist seeking to display some new literary method, but of a visionary forced by the momentum of his figures to dramatic expression in order to achieve his variations. In most works until the last the subject-matter overshadowed the form and enforced a continuation. Not till *The Brothers Karamazov* was final balance attained.

The process of construction in each individual work is

378

repeated in a masterly way in his work as a whole. The twofold *début*, *Poor Folk* and *The Double*, constitutes the fundamental theme which is worked out in immense variations and finally appears as the church in the valley. His profusion is overwhelming at first sight. There is breathless succession of events. It would be impossible for us to bring order into this chaos if Dostoevsky had not created it, if there were not the beginning he found, the middle he set, and the end he achieved. But this order resists the surge and thunder of chaos, and yields the creative symbolism which permeates his work. There are fifty characters in each of the principal works. That would make many hundreds if one had to add them up. But fifty characters would amply illustrate his entire works. The same thing is true of his themes. Dostoevsky constantly introduced new people and new themes, but, as in real life, they are mostly the same people and the same themes. Yet at every turn we experience something new. The inventive factor lies, not in the novelty, but in the variety of what is presented.

We have found four or five stages of development which are by no means chronological. His remarkable *début* was scarcely excelled till the underworld den, and in the long interval—particularly before and after the *katorga*—his work fell beneath that level. And if the underworld memoirs, as a novelty, as the bold flight of a man of genius, hold us much more forcibly than the *début*, yet they collapse formally, and at a superficial glance bear out the widely held opinion that they are not literature, but the work of a psychologist of peculiar intuition. Attempts have been made to read into Dostoevsky a new form of artistic expression: the poet-psychologist. Those who hold this view probably think that what is true of any other art is equally true of literature, that a Russian, carried away by psychological intuition, is as justified in sweeping aside the indispensable technique of the novel as a German, inflamed by mediæval mysticism, in violating operatic convention. It cannot be over-emphasized that Dostoevsky has dispelled many inadequate notions without obliterating any art boundaries. His novel-drama remains within the realm of literature—that is the essential difference between his creation and that of Wagner.

Not till *Crime and Punishment*, twenty years after his *début*, is a new level ensured, so far superior to the beginning that we might well believe him already to have reached maturity. *The Idiot* promptly carries the curve far higher and presents a new stage. The form discovered in *Crime and Punishment* is now capable of sustaining vast ramifications of thought. With *The Possessed* there is a sudden, though voluntary, descent, like an airman stalling to put his machine to a test. Just as we think he is going to crash the pilot laughs, climbs again, and vanishes in another direction. The climbs are invariably in different directions. *The Idiot* was not a vertical climb from *Crime and Punishment*, except in the drafts; that would have been impossible to carry out.

We would not like to have missed even the least important of the interludes, for there was always something in them worth while, if only the process of development which reveals Dostoevsky's most phenomenal characteristic: growth of art without conscious effort; growth of idea which leads to consolidation; growth of tendency which emancipates. Were the interludes absent we should still have the whole of Dostoevsky in his last work. In *The Brothers Karamazov* he exhausts himself so completely that everything preceding could be regarded merely as preparatory sketches. When his first work was written he seems already to have been thinking of his last, he who mocked at the conscientious worrying about their collected editions, he the prolific writer and literary hack, who gave what crossed his mind. We know the pen was always only a means to him, and, if anyone called him, he put it aside. He was persecuted by experiences of unique horror.

The poet's procedure can be roughly divided into two categories. Generally his progress is a process of expansion in the same plane rather than of ascent to a higher plane. It is the number of the works which grows, not the poet.

MORAL OF THE DEVELOPMENT

That is what happens with the French novel which is made tolerable by its polish and taste. If consciousness of development preponderates the story suffers, and there is nothing left but stilted phrases—that is the way with the German novel. Dostoevsky was threatened by both these possibilities. The nearest thing to such an intrepid thinker is the German. His *verve* guarded him against falling into either trap. He thought and wrote hurriedly, and dodged from one thing to another. In the realm of painting he could be compared to an artist who toils at the same picture year after year without growing stale. Such paradoxical types exist. The picture has passed through countless stages and the painter has begun it afresh time after time. He aims at keeping the figures static without making them rigid. That is why, as the composition progresses, the painter again and again passes rapidly over the surface with light coats the colour of the air, of the foliage, and of the earth, and in this way breaks up the flesh. In the finished work the surface still retains an appearance of spontaneity. Dostoevsky's episodes served the purpose of light coats of paint. His original thought and structure were clearer, but there was not so much vitality. We were apt to become impatient because the process was overdone. The noisy episodes in particular were disconcerting to our sensitiveness. We have, of course, to see the episodes in proper perspective: noisy streets surrounding the cathedral which towers above them and encompasses us with the restful curves of its high vaults. The streets surge and heave till the very end, in the end more forcibly than ever. Dostoevsky is not more pure and noble in *The Brothers Karamazov* than in earlier works, but attains the peak of creative life. Purity and nobility are inadequate conceptions.

The attempt at analogy in the world of painting is not unfruitful. The fact that he attained the pinnacle of his creation at the end of his life is unique in world-literature, and similar examples are to be found but rarely in the world of painting. Rembrandt, beginning far more modestly, described a similar curve, and the similarity of their courses

once again confirms the mysterious relationship. In the
nineteenth century only the development of Delacroix,
whose *début* reminded us of Dostoevsky's first public appearance, can be considered in any way equivalent. The thriller
element in the Russian is the counterpart to the popular
themes which the painter of Dante's Bark chose in order to
be in touch with the world around him, and the Schilleresque
in him was Raphael. In old age Delacroix's genius became
entirely spiritual. The painter's progress entailed sacrifices
which in French art have to be considered the natural
accompaniments to the development of the artist. Who,
when looking at his later work, thinks of that Dantesque
attitude with which Delacroix embraced both art and people?
What cultured eye would fail to notice his purification?
What cultured eye would not secretly rejoice and forgo
communion with the people for the sake of communion
with the elect who are susceptible to such spiritual beauty?
Would it not accept the exchange as a just and divine
ordinance? Yet this is true only until a Dostoevsky
illustrates that ultimate purification is not incompatible
with communion, and that it is quite possible to begin as
courageously as Delacroix and yet to discover the Dante's
Bark at the end of one's path. In such conservation of
power there is balance transcending artistic canons. With
a final and overwhelming embrace of his people Dostoevsky
perfects his creation.

His creation. By that is not to be understood an idea
or a sum-total of ideas, for the idea of a composition is
only part of the work, and the sum-total of ideas in a series
of works is invariably only part of the entire works. In
every great man, particularly in Dostoevsky, this part has
its interest which must not be undervalued, but it can never
be substituted for the whole work. The detachment of
the idea from a work must always be an extremely delicate
process, never accomplished without effort. But should we
consider only aspects of the idea which seem peculiarly
suited to some demonstration or other, and regard them
fallaciously as typical of Dostoevsky, there may be disaster.

MORAL OF THE DEVELOPMENT

The demonstration succeeds, but the work of art is destroyed, an invariable result of perceiving the thinker in Dostoevsky and overlooking the poet. Disparagement of him is not always evil in origin; it may result from some such need as prompted Arkady, who expected something from the father he had learnt to appreciate; despite, in fact, because of his love, his father refused to enlighten him. One philosopher has said (63) that since Luther no influence has been so widespread as Dostoevsky's, and therefore nothing is more natural than that such a man, a poet who broke away from the pomp of the roof-garden and recognized his calling in active communion with all sinners, insulted and injured, should to-day be regarded as a wise Zossima to whom people go with their troubles and expect an answer. This much is clear: if the wise man were approached in vain, the poet would also be worthless. Otto Kaus has demonstrated convincingly that it is impossible to deduce a theoretical dualism of thinker and poet. " The moment we reject Dostoevsky's *weltanschauung* and deem it false, dated and aimless, we are equally bound to feel his artistic achievements aimless and insincere, otherwise we should be in a quandary from which there is no legitimate escape. If he repel us by his tone of voice or mannerisms, if we discover anything obtuse in him which goes against the grain, and can indicate no point in his previous history which accounts for it, we are bound to feel just as great a bias against Dostoevsky the poet as against Dostoevsky the politician . . . What manifests itself in one place as retrogressive or dead cannot in another place have a quickening effect. What annoys us in one place cannot educate us in another " (64). That is very much to the point, but introducing arguments which are not inherent in the composition is a dangerous procedure. Kaus, for example, has already overshot the mark when he deduces that " if we unmask Dostoevsky's thoughts and thus show them to be false interpretation of historical events, we cannot expect any positive influence in the future." Fortunately he does not unmask Dostoevsky, but in a roundabout way vindicates the poet. To reject

383

The Possessed on the ground of historical inaccuracy would be a lame argument.

We are not in a position to ask of Zossima enlightenment by word of mouth, but are faced with countless printed pages which become unintelligible when judged by our own standards. This difficulty is increased if we are to consider Dostoevsky's journalistic effusions as of equal importance, and to regard the outpourings of the chance moods of the politician, doubtless justifiable at some given moment, as the apodeictic statements of the sage.

A great deal could be said about the politician; what is important has already been mentioned. Significant as was his political activity, considerable as was the part it played in his life, to judge him merely from the political aspect would be worthless. The apparent as well as actual contradictions in his attitude towards East and West, in his pan-Slavism, in his communism and tsarism, are natural actions and reactions, and incidentally frequently indicate only the vast range of understanding in a man of genius. There is never a fundamental contradiction. When he renounces a small truth it is only to expose a greater. If admirers perceive only aberration and irresponsibility in his polarity they are imputing more than his worst enemies. It is rather that the thinker's exaggerated sense of responsibility has at times become a bar to his æsthetic expression.

To illustrate the errors of interpreters one might seek analogy in a metronome which necessarily measures only the time in which events occur, and not the events themselves. A definite space of time is no measure of the importance of the events enacted in it. Interpreters turn minims, crotchets and quavers into breves, and vice versa. They all attempt to write his works while they read them. That is excellent in principle; Dostoevsky would be the first to approve. But there is one vital condition—not necessarily involving intellectual approach. There is no simpler or lighter reading. Any common-sensed person can find his way about; if one thing escapes him there is always something else he can grasp. Far more than intellect a reader needs sense of touch and hearing. But if we do wish to introduce intellectual criticism we must let him present his own case without interference and accept what he offers, otherwise the error of judgment in Dmitri's case will be constantly repeated. There was a temptation to discern in his supposed contradictions, not only fallacies, but even lack of conviction. So ardent an admirer as Nötzel has not quite escaped such an interpretation. It seems to me that the depth of Dostoevsky's problem has been underestimated in such cases, above all his fanatical participation in his problems. Only when one gazes on the world with the simplicity of Tolstoy, who regarded everything as "much simpler" than it was in fact, (65) will Dostoevsky appear arbitrary. Kaus has thrown a ray of light on many apparently confused situations and revealed a view-point of modern criticism by his analysis of a capitalism which Dostoevsky wanted to spare his country (66). Even if imagination plays a part both here and in many of Kaus' inferences, imagination of a man who struggled with might and main against his poet—who does not hate his poet!— yet the example furnishes us with a measure of Dostoevsky's boundless devotion to his task. Not he but the world in which he was set was confused. Dostoevsky's hour did not strike till rationalism held us firmly in its clutches and there were warrants out for the arrest of the meditation of the good old times.

Will the myth of the inconsolable poet last much longer? Will Dostoevsky and Tolstoy, the brightest and most obscure of spirits, always be bracketed together? Foreigners occasionally smile at our monument in Weimar which draws attention to at least representative, even if unequal forces, and testifies to a biographical fact.[1] Only slovenly thinking, otherwise quite foreign to the modern Russian, contrives to couple the two Russians. Even Berdyaev cannot make up his mind to separate the pair

---

[1] The reference is to the Goethe-Schiller statue at Weimar. The two poets worked hand in hand for fifteen years and their intimate association was severed only by Schiller's death.—TR.

who were never together in life. Undoubtedly he makes short work of Tolstoy's religious hot air and establishes that the Christian Dostoevsky was far and away superior, but all the same still assumes that he has to treat them as equals in poetry, probably because their poetic aspect was of less interest to him. The poetic difference seems to us more important on account of its greater range; as the element of religion enters into the works of both, any argument which disposes of an association between the religious feelings of the two apostles must of necessity apply equally to their creative works. The attempt to apply Nietzsche's " Apollo-Dionysos " idea to the case obscures the problematic element in Tolstoy. We are forced to recognize in Dostoevsky the sole unproblematic representative of our age.

.   .   .   .   .   .

On the 8th of November 1880 the poet sent the end of *The Brothers Karamazov* to the *Russian Messenger*. He wrote to Lyubinov, the editor, that he hoped to live another two years and to create something else by that time. His hope was not fulfilled. A few weeks later, on the 28th of January 1881, he was dead. He devoted the last days to the *Journal*. He was worrying whether the censorship would pass his essay on the grey smocks. Only the people in smocks knew the truth, themselves knew best what was good for them and had a right to be trusted. The censorship was favourable.

The last word was with the journalist; that is how it should be with a Dostoevsky. After his unexampled artistic effort he smiled and once again came back to earth. Our outburst of admiration is interrupted. Nothing great in that! he says. Enough then, let us talk of something else. Let us discuss, what do you think?

The Pushkin festival, at which he lived through his day of honour in the service of someone else, occurred during his work on the last part of *The Brothers Karamazov*. Sober witnesses, whom one cannot accuse of romanticism, talk even to-day of this event. Moreover, it was not a

THE PUSHKIN SPEECH

matter of war and peace, but the consecration of a monument, even so to a poet who is a stranger to us and was at that time no longer familiar to many a Russian. That was referred to in the speech. Turgenev was the first of the official speakers. He was still the foremost writer in the public mind. He had spoken with emotion of the importance of the occasion, in a dignified and cultured manner, from a camp in which form and reserve were esteemed. Pushkin's originality was beyond dispute, especially his Russian originality. He belonged to his native land and represented an unassailable height. All that was said with Turgenev's captivating complaisance without attempting to gloss over his Western influences. The speech culminated in the question: did Pushkin belong to Europe? Was this great Russian universal? Turgenev was gentlemanly enough not to make any sacrifice to rhetorical considerations. He put the question at the end whereby it was bound to jeopardize the success of his speech. We are all of his opinion. The question has long been settled.

Then came Dostoevsky. He had scarcely thought of Turgenev's literary standpoint in preparing his speech which he read out from the manuscript. His theme was Pushkin and Russia. The fact that Turgenev had accepted as a foregone conclusion that the poet was national lent weight to Dostoevsky's argument, and Pushkin's national position was thus assured. Up to that time the author of *Eugène Onyegin* had seemed far too Western to ingrained Slavophils, and therefore the most radical of them refrained from attending the festival. Dostoevsky revealed Pushkin's origin. With his shrewd psychology which for once in a way was turned on a well-known figure, already legendary, he showed the development of the Russian element in Pushkin by referring to typical works. The fate of his heroes was acknowledged to be typical of the fate of Russians, and Pushkin himself, with his meteoric appearance and disappearance, seemed to be borne on a similar wave. Dostoevsky only appeared to overrate him, for in reality he loved him. One of the many results of his speech was

corroboration of this simple fact. Love and criticism had
nothing to do with one another. Dostoevsky's love did not
carry the object of his adulation on to the lonely heights of
Parnassus where, crowned with a laurel, it would have been
hidden from mortal gaze, but chose the obvious course and
brought him into human contact. What he stressed in
Pushkin was not literature but the man, the Russian. The
speaker also revealed characteristics in the poet which
might have seemed to indicate a lack of independence.
The influence of Byron and other Western and Oriental
poetry illustrated Pushkin's need and ability to enter into
the spirit of other peoples; another truly Russian trait.

For a professor of literature to talk like that would
have been questionable. In the mouth of Dostoevsky, the
creator, it was thoroughly pertinent and became good tidings.
Poets had better things to do than to erect pedestals in
their own honour, and any criticism directed towards that
end was idle chatter. No one, whatever his vocation, could
do without the rest of humanity, and if in his arrogance he
believed he could dispense with it, he was deceiving himself
more than humanity. A poet who behaved in that way was
acting without rhyme or reason. If he was not one with
the people, what was he? Pushkin was one with the
people. " Bow down, arrogant man, and lower your pride!
Bow down, idle man, and work on your soil! " Thus spoke
Pushkin in *The Gipsies*. These words became winged. A
venerable voice from the past lived in the present and
conjured up the future. The audience heard it. There
were remarkable scenes. People who had been sworn
enemies from time immemorial became reconciled and
vowed they would live as brothers from now on. The
emaciated, frail speaker was in danger of being overwhelmed by the general enthusiasm.

As in Dostoevsky's novels, the effect was the result of
the inexorable reality of his vision. He spoke just as he
wrote, without thinking of speech or writing, inspired by
what he saw. Moreover, it was a solemn occasion, but
words in themselves did not suffice to do justice to the

THE PUSHKIN SPEECH

solemnity. The words out of the poem, which every one had heard often enough, assumed an undreamt-of force, and the whole of Pushkin was revealed in a new and significant light. Doſtoevsky took him down from the bookshelves, reſtored his influence, and set a human being amongſt human beings. People no longer clung to the rhythm of the verse for the pleasure they found in it, no longer abandoned themselves dreamily to audacious fantasies, but accepted out of the diſtance a reality which enhanced their consciousness. There was a vital Pushkin queſtion of the moment and that was why they had assembled. The settlement of this queſtion was not the affair of an academic clique. What they could say about it was only theory and concerned only their limited circle. The sole queſtion was: was the demand contained in Pushkin's words right, and were people disposed to bow down and to work on their soil, not in some special inſtance, not in some special calling or in any abſtraĉt way, but physically and concretely?

That was the solution of the Pushkin queſtion, and the Slavophil poet Aksakov, who was ſtill on the liſt of speakers, declined to speak because he could not usefully add to what had been said. Thus Pushkin became a tendentious poet and, ſtrange to relate, far from reproaching the speaker with exaggeration, every liſtener perceived in this conception only an elevation of Pushkin. When in the next few days there was some isolated objeĉtion, rationalism was defending itself againſt the supposed voice of the people in Pushkin. The long discussion with Gradovsky in the *Journal* turns on the old queſtion of emotion or reason, and Doſtoevsky ſtruggled againſt " Euclidean reasoning," but did not have to defend himself againſt the reproach of being politically partisan. Even his opponent felt there was no personal intereſt here and that a whole world ſtood behind the speaker's passionate words. Doſtoevsky did not contradiĉt the Slavophils, but deprived them of their narrow slogan, ſtressed the importance of native land, not only Russian but native land generally, the right to community and the obligations of community. This revelation of native land was part of his attitude, as was also his plausible reasoning which established the need for community, and his tone which proved amongst man's other rights his right to common dreams. The audience was carried away and a very ordinary function was turned into a solemn ceremony.

This act of piety illumines Dostoevsky's humble humanity. He dealt with Pushkin as the poet and illiterate in *The Brothers Karamazov* dealt with Schiller, let him speak for him. That is how he always set about, went to small folk, looked at them, revealed them and whispered thoughts and feelings to them. Then he would pretend that the vagabonds, drunkards and murderers were expressing only their own thoughts. He did this with such consummate artifice that we regard these people as real and are led to believe that all drunkards and murderers behave in that way. The thoughts were of every hue, could not be divided into ugly and beautiful, for all were appropriate to the people to whom he gave them and were therefore good, and if people were not better as a result, the thoughts were nevertheless nourishment to them, set them free and made them happy. His entire work can be described as an act of piety.

That in itself means a great deal. Dostoevsky is ranked high, not because his work was significant, but because he was so much the consummate poet. As we know, he created other things as well, including his life, and those who were present at the Pushkin speech may have noticed it. There was nothing except the poet in him. The scope of this idea is lost to us. We too have once had such poets, talent apart. Why we no longer have them and cannot even imagine them any more is particularly bound up with the lost piety. Rationalists prefer more tangible reasons and point to his abnormal talent, a tempting excuse in this instance, for seldom has anyone been endowed with greater gifts. Dostoevsky fulfilled all expectations. Delacroix required of the painter to paint a person flinging himself out of the window within the space of time occupied by his fall. In that space of time Dostoevsky would have produced the entire history of a suicide and his family including a hundred variations. He invented facilely and to the point. The episode was at hand on the spot where he needed it. It was only necessary to write it down. Extremely pleasant both for him and for us, but at bottom only one of the minor features of his greatness.

For many of us his work scarcely ranks as poetry to-day. We accept it as once the exile accepted the Book from the good Siberian woman before he was imprisoned. He kept it by him, read and re-read it and made use of it on every special occasion, opened it at hazard, read the words he happened to strike, or had it read to him by others, just like the humorous Stepan Trofimovitch. It was always under his pillow at night, and thus it was at hand on the last day of honour. He made Anna Grigorevna open the book and read the first line of the page she chanced on. " Do not restrain me ! " it ran,[1] the passage in which John and Jesus exchange civilities before John baptizes Him. " Do you hear ? " said Dostoevsky to his wife. His life ebbed away slowly. The whole of Russia followed him to the grave. No Tsar has had such a burial.

He still comforts and teaches us, helps us, laughs with us, a brother, and every youthful heart yearns for him. And strange to say, what occurs to us to-day as most lovable in him is not the significance of his personality which is more closely bound than any with its own time and with ours. We do not think of the hero or of the seer who, at those first tremors in Europe in 1870, foresaw their eventual and inexorable consequences and leapt into the breach with the full violence of his eloquence. We are standing in the dearest cemetery of all and, although we are shaken by the pealing of bells, we do not think of the seer or of the Russian whom we have to thank for the purification and preservation of German cultural values which we let fall into decay. No one amongst us Germans has thought of that yet. We are standing in the dearest cemetery of all. The peal of the bells shakes us. We cannot control ourselves, our tears

---

[1] The English equivalent is " suffer it now ! "—Tr.

flow. Do what we will they flow and flow as if ice **were** melting within us. It is good to let our tears flow. **We** have never felt so comforted. Someone leads us **away.** We trudge along our path next to schoolboys. No **one** knows whither. Only straight ahead! At the great stone there resounds a hurrah!

NOTES

(1) In view of our inability to check the original text it is impossible to appreciate the difficulties which translation presents. In the face of the bowdlerized versions of English and French books in their German translations there is good reason for being sceptical. Serious errors were disclosed in a translation, universally recognized, in the course of a check which Marik Kallin made for me here and there. What is left of Flaubert in the German translation? In any case there is more of Dostoevsky. He gives so much that an occasional slip does not materially affect the general impression. On the other hand even the best translation cannot overcome certain ethnographic peculiarities which make reading difficult for the European. Translators seem to be particularly careless in their handling of his letters, and many a discordant note in the correspondence may perhaps be attributed to that.

(2) His second wife, to whom he dictated all his works from *The Gambler* onwards, says : " sometimes the first three chapters of the novel were printed, the fourth was set up and the fifth in course of post when the sixth had only just been written, and none of the later chapters had even been thought out." (Madame Dostoevsky's *Reminiscences*.) The last words are not correct, at least not to the extent implied. That is proved by the sketches for the main works which date back to a period long anterior to their execution. The works were thought out long before Dostoevsky started to write them.

(3) Compare the well-known letter of Strachov who expressed these objections in the mildest form and immediately added the inferences : " your novels would be more effective if their texture were simpler. *The Gambler*, for example, and *The Cuckold* (*The Eternal Husband*) evoked the clearest impressions, whilst all you have put into *The Idiot* was lost." (!) " This failing is, of course, closely connected with your redeeming features. . . ."

(4) In a letter of Turgenev to Saltikov of the 24th September 1882, that is, after Dostoevsky's death.

(5) *Goethe and Tolstoy*, essay by Thomas Mann (*Deutsche Rundschau* of the 22nd March 1922).

(6) Merejkovsky, *Tolstoy and Dostoevsky*.

(7) Letter of Tolstoy of 1881, quoted in the *Letters*.

(8) The second letter to Strachov is the reply to Strachov's libellous attack on Dostoevsky which will be referred to later.

(9) In the fragments from Dostoevsky's notebooks it is said of Oblomov:

393

DOSTOEVSKY

" an idler and an egoist too. That does not exist amongst Russians. He is only a *Junker* and at that only a Petersburg, not even a Russian *Junker!* " Oblomov also belongs to the " literature of the squirearchy," even if to the best of that class.

(10) On the other hand Kassner exaggerates when he asserts that " what was begun in *The Cloak* attained fruition " in *The Brothers Karamazov*. For in *The Brothers Karamazov* there is surely far too much of which Gogol had never dreamt. Here is the fitting conclusion. " The first complete conquest of the eighteenth century man is the man in *The Cloak*. It is he, and not the romantics, or Edgar Allan Poe, or Balzac's man."

(11) Compare Dostoevsky's long letter to Maikov from Geneva of the 16th August 1867 in which he speaks of his meeting with Goncharov and the quarrel with Turgenev in Baden-Baden. Turgenev told him his novel *Smoke* culminated in the sentence, " if Russia were to vanish to-day off the face of the earth, it would be no loss to humanity, humanity would not even notice it." That was, Turgenev explained to him, " his fundamental view about Russia." His letter continues in that strain.

(12) In the same letter there is convincing proof of it. When Turgenev has finished abusing Russia and declared himself an atheist and the hour of departure has arrived, Dostoevsky " quite accidentally on parting " bursts out about the natives of Baden-Baden. " Do you know what swindlers and rogues they are here ? Really the common people here are far worse and more dishonest than amongst us. That they are also stupider is beyond dispute. They talk all the time of civilization. What has this civilization given to the Germans and in what way are they superior to us ? " Turgenev turns pale and replies : " When you speak like that you insult me personally. You know, of course, that I have settled down here and that I consider myself a German and not a Russian and am proud of it."
About this conversation compare also the *Diary* of Madame Dostoevsky. Turgenev himself referred to his meeting with Dostoevsky in a letter to Polonsky. He alleges that Dostoevsky was loud in abuse of him on account of his novel *Smoke*, that the book was only fit to be publicly burnt. Turgenev adds, " I have not the slightest doubt that Dostoevsky is mad."

(13) Dostoevsky portrayed by his daughter, Aimée Dostoevsky.

(14) The person responsible for the Paris legend is a Russian writer living in Paris at the moment, a contemporary of both Dostoevsky and Turgenev, who seeks to associate Stavrogin's confession with the poet's own transgressions. This passage Dostoevsky struck out of *The Possessed* and it has only recently been published. He alleges that Dostoevsky, as an act of self-debasement, admitted to Turgenev, his arch-enemy, that he himself had committed the crime of which he had made Stavrogin guilty. (André Gide. *Dostoevsky.*) If this fantastic confession was ever made, one might go still further and assume that for the sake of self-debasement Dostoevsky put himself in Stavrogin's place without having perpetrated the crime. Nötzel has shown the improbability of the legend and has rightly condemned the careless methods of such " research." He asserts that he has followed

394

NOTES

up reports of this nature and invariably found them "untenable gossip."

The story that Dostoevsky once assaulted a young girl can be traced back to a letter of Strachov to Leo Tolstoy of 28th November 1883. This appeared in the October 1913 number of the periodical *Ssovremenni Mir*, and Madame Dostoevsky is to be thanked for reprinting it in her *Reminiscences*. Strachov states that he heard the story from Professor Viskovatov who never knew Dostoevsky intimately. This letter, full of calumny and stupidity, is so obviously dictated by the wish to flatter Tolstoy with the crudest arguments at the expense of Dostoevsky that the libel condemns itself. Madame Dostoevsky has spared no pains to show up the inconceivable felony of this friend of his youth, who had every reason to be thankful to Dostoevsky, and to prove the utter improbability of this story.

Moreover Stavrogin's crime is already referred to in *Crime and Punishment*. In the conversation with Raskolnikov's mother Luzhin refers to the rumour that Svidrigailov is suspected of having similarly maltreated a deaf and dumb girl of fourteen or fifteen and had driven her to suicide.

(15) In the volume of essays on Dostoevsky by Bahr, Merejkovsky and Bierbaum.

(16) In his detailed defence, reprinted in the biography of N. Hoffman, Dostoevsky has completely denied criminal guilt, but has forcibly rejected the opportunity offered him of exonerating himself at someone else's expense. As his daughter states in her biography, he is supposed later to have explained that there was actually a plot to overthrow the Tsar and institute a republic of the *intelligentsia* (?).

In his Dostoevsky-biography Nötzel has gone very thoroughly into the whole story. He considers Petrachevsky a person of very limited influence but nevertheless the originator of the Russian revolutionary organization, who would not have shrunk from any kind of terrorism. Nötzel has also not found any reference by Dostoevsky to the extent of his participation but, like the daughter and others, considers it possible that Dostoevsky was assigned a prominent part in the plot. The only authentic evidence is Dostoevsky's statement that in certain circumstances he favoured abolition of serfdom by violence. Nötzel traces Dostoevsky's connexion with the Russian revolution to his acquaintance with Belinsky who was enthusiastic about the poet's first work. Belinsky made Dostoevsky familiar with socialism and tried, unsuccessfully, to convert him to atheism. Dostoevsky soon severed his connexion with Belinsky and later became his bitterest opponent.

Dostoevsky's participation in the Petrachevsky conspiracy is explained by adherents of psycho-analysis as an outcome of his Œdipus-complex. The attempt throws amusing light on methods of psycho-analytical research. In order to construct a pathological contradiction between Dostoevsky's rôle as conspirator and his love for a legitimate constitution, events which took place after one another in the poet's life are put next to one another. That Dostoevsky identified his father with the Tsar whom he wanted to remove is demonstrated by the popular reference to the Tsar as little father and so forth.

(17) Pauline Suslov's reminiscences are shortly to be published by Piper and Co., of Munich.

DOSTOEVSKY

(18) With its attitude common to-day Kurt Kersten's preface to Madame Dostoevsky's *Diary* forestalls the reader's impression and attempts, in a manner familiar to us, to nail down Dostoevsky to certain self-accusatory utterances. Incidental anomalies, contradictions which the authoress herself rectifies are taken as definite lines of argument. Kersten would like to attack the " Dostoevsky-Byzantines." It is a question whether this obscure intention justifies an editor in unfairly disparaging the poet who ought to be, if not respected, at least fairly treated. With his psycho-analytical thesis about Dostoevsky's " flight " Otto Kaus has had a devastating effect. Like other editors of the literary remains Kersten also harps on Dostoevsky's passion for gambling. We shall deal with that later. Occupation with this detail obscures every other issue including the poet's work. I think that still very little trouble has been taken in Germany to get closer to Dostoevsky.

In order to paint the demon as black as possible Anna Grigorevna is exalted to the level of being Dostoevsky's " saviour." This procedure is as little justified as the more customary and equally thoughtless underrating of the brave woman. Anna Grigorevna certainly brought happiness into Dostoevsky's life but did not, as Kersten says, sacrifice herself in the process. It would have been useless. There is more justification for calling Hendrickje Stoffels the saviour of Rembrandt. Dostoevsky's wife ideally fulfilled her duties towards the great man and was therefore an extremely happy woman and greatly to be envied. It is difficult entirely to follow Nötzel in his portrayal of their relationship. He constantly insists that Dostoevsky's first wife was his only love. Even if it is admitted that his release from imprisonment inspired in him a unique passion for Maria Dmitrievna, there is still the question whether the decisive factor was the woman herself or the circumstances in which he came to know her. The motives of the second marriage may have been less significant and purely utilitarian ; but its results eclipse any other poet's marriage of which we have any knowledge. Work was the basis of their companionship. Dostoevsky learnt to value his wife as a shorthand writer ; in this and other capacities she was an ideal companion, a fact which contributed to set the marriage on a solid foundation. But Dostoevsky never at any time regarded her as only an assistant in his work ; in fact that side of her existence was inclined to be assimilated into the background.

Her *Reminiscences* which cover an extensive period and were written at a time when she was a mature though still quite simple woman are an essential auxiliary to the *Diary*. In this also there is no perpetual halo round him. " He was a human being to me as well as a god, he had his faults and his good points like every one else, and he was not always great. He was often, very often just a great child, an invalid, pretentious, self-willed, unable to understand life." She repeatedly emphasizes the joyousness and inoffensiveness of his character and countless minor episodes incidentally confirm her statements. His violent and youthful jealousy of which he never ridded himself, his simplicity which was taken in by every joke, his deep affection for his wife and children, his enjoyment of the slightest fun, these are all indications of his childlike mind which endured till the end of his life. He never ceased to be anxious and irritable but the nature of his moods, which as time went on he learnt to control, testifies that he was not the gloomy person cursory observation makes him out to be. Madame Dostoevsky denounces the stereotyped strain of most posthumous descriptions

NOTES

and attempts to show that these errors are the result of personal misunderstanding. The primary cause is probably the influence of his works. The misanthropists did not know how to read his works even in his lifetime.

(19) Dostoevsky has never made more than cursory use of the *motif*; the description is most complete in *The Idiot* when the prince, immediately on his arrival, describes first to the servant at the general's, then to the ladies the thoughts of a man led to execution. Even here not much space is devoted to description in view of the importance of the episode. Dostoevsky is said rarely to have spoken of the scene, and then without any special emphasis.

(20) Compare the preface to the popular edition of my *Van Gogh* in which a similar comparison is attempted.

(21) That is what he writes to his brother Michael about his analytical portrayal on 1st February 1846.

(22) Letter to his brother Michael of 16th November 1845.

(23) Stephan Zweig. *Drei Meister, Balzac, Dickens, Dostojewski.*

(24) Letter to his brother Michael, undated, 1847.

(25) *Dostojewskis Kindergeschichten.* The episodes are collated from *The Idiot, The Brothers Karamazov, The Insulted and Injured* and *A Raw Youth.* Nötzel has confined himself to episodes which it was possible to remove from the context.

(26) Letter to Maikov from Semipalatinsk of 18th January 1856.

(27) In a letter to his brother Michael of 31st May 1858 he speaks of a novel which is to be written after his return from Siberia. "The fundamental idea is excellent. Moreover there is a new thought in it which I have never come across. Since, however, this character is in all probability very widespread in actual Russian life, particularly at the moment, at least so far as can be judged from the activities and ideas with which every one seems filled, I am convinced that I shall be able to enrich my novel with fresh observations after my return to Russia." This novel to which he repeatedly refers, also again in October 1859 in a letter from Tver, is universally and perhaps justifiably assumed to be *Crime and Punishment,* but can at that time hardly have had the content of the later work, although Dostoevsky, as he says, planned it on a vast scale. Otherwise, in his letter to his brother of 9th May 1859 he would not have spoken in such glowing terms of *The Friend of the Family.*

(28) About the political situation compare Nötzel's detailed exposition in the chapters " The Journal Vremya " and " The period and its events."

(29) *Dostojewski and Nietzsche, Philosophie der Tragödie.*

(30) Serge Persky. *La vie et l'œuvre de Dostoevsky.*

397

DOSTOEVSKY

(31) Dostoevsky does not omit adding that Raskolnikov has frequently perceived such thought-processes in circles of young people.

(32) On the stairway at Marmeladov's after the scene at the drunkard's deathbed Raskolnikov experiences " a unique immeasurable feeling," and he feels " like a man condemned to death who has unexpectedly been informed of his reprieve." The feeling fortifies him and drives him to a solemn proclamation to himself against " the imaginary terrors and phantoms " in ·favour of " the realm of understanding and light " which is now coming. " ' And now we shall see ! we will measure our strength ! ' he adds defiantly, as if addressing some dark power and challenging it to battle."
This proclamation has no bearing on the episode at Marmeladov's. What has happened ? Sonia was brought to her dying father. She appears in her garb of a whore with the red feather in her ridiculously fashionable hat. Marmeladov, as he has told Raskolnikov himself at the beginning of the novel, is responsible for Sonia's misfortune. In order to go on indulging in his drinking he has raised no objection when his wife, Sonia's stepmother, forced the girl on to the streets. He entreats Sonia's forgiveness and dies in her arms. Nothing happens between Raskolnikov and Sonia, there is not the slightest contact, and Raskolnikov's rhetorical allegation that he has just " lived " is all the more awkward because his whole outlay up to this time has been limited to paying for the burial. Probably Dostoevsky himself found his hero's conclusion too " hasty " and wanted to allude to the exaggeration of this episode, and that was his obvious opportunity to introduce the second principal character of the novel who till this time had only been referred to indirectly. Nevertheless, we are still left with the impression that he has dealt with an essential point too cursorily. This is one of those passages which make the reader regret his ignorance of Russian because inexact translation of a few words may be misleading. It is just in *Crime and Punishment* that Dostoevsky frequently proves his ability to express such delicate things.

(33) Moreover, in the third chapter of the sixth part Svidrigailov repeatedly calls Raskolnikov Schiller. This conversation recalls the prince's discussion with the narrator in *The Insulted and Injured*.

(34) Moeller Van Den Bruck, the translator of the Piper edition, considers the title " Crime and Punishment " a stop-gap, and thinks the work does not solve the problem which the title indicates ; this was reserved for a second part which Dostoevsky did not write.

(35) Shestov thinks this question can be used as proof of the identity of Raskolnikov with Ivan Karamazov and that he can thus establish his Nietzsche parallel. " This question," he writes, " makes one's hair stand on end. There are indeed horrors in the world of which we have never dreamt. Ivan's stories of the brutality of the Turks, maltreatment of children, etc., pale before such horrors." Such an interpretation is incomprehensible, unless we are simple enough to assume that Raskolnikov regarded the murder as a kind of minor lapse. Is anything else possible for a man who foresees the effect of his deed on others, particularly on his headstrong sister, than to separate from his people, quite apart from his inability to continue his

NOTES

previous life ? Always the same notion—as if the poet wrote only for the sake of proving ideas which his critics think fit to read into his works. The crudity is in the interpretation.

(36) The unusual terseness of this passage is partly due to the complicated re-writing which was forced on Dostoevsky by the editor of the *Russian Messenger*, for it was foreseen that there would be difficulties with the censor about this Gospel scene. Dostoevsky stresses the trouble he had in re-writing (see his letter to Milyukov, June 1866). Probably the re-writing involved considerable abbreviation.

(37) The importance of these monetary details is striking. Although nothing depends on them and although the visions of this night between two eventful days pile up all kinds of horrors, there is detailed explanation how Svidrigailov distributed his money. Since he is determined to kill himself, there is positively no expiation in this generosity—at that with the money of the wife he had tortured to death.

Raskolnikov's generosity is also frequently illustrated in a manner ill-suiting Dostoevsky's amazing discretion. The details are not insignificant. They can be recognized as reflexes of experiences which were later to be set out in more legitimate form.

(38) Dostoevsky paid the debts of his brother and of the *Epoca* until within a year of his death. Details of this state of affairs are to be found in Hoffman's biography and particularly in his wife's reminiscences. It may be assumed that the greater part of these debts was the direct outcome of Dostoevsky's kindliness and credulity. He gave bills without any evidence of indebtedness, and it often turned out later that these accounts had already been paid by his brother. Thereupon Dostoevsky declares : " that shows what need may drive a man to." He behaved like his Idiot : he satisfied them all, although his friends represented to him that none of these dishonest gentlemen had the slightest claim on him. His only reason for satisfying them was that, as it turned out, some of them would otherwise have suffered a certain amount of loss in other ways. (*The Idiot*, Part II, Chapter I.)

(39) Letter to Milyukov. June 1866.

(40) The book *Dostojewski am Roulette*, edited by René Fülöp-Miller and Friedrich Eckstein, contains the documents for this chapter. It begins with passages out of *The Gambler* which the editors think autobiographical. This procedure is doubtful. Even when, as happens here, certain details do refer to actual experiences, no one has the right, least of all an editor of Dostoevsky, to tear passages out of their context. When these passages are removed from *The Gambler* nothing but tedium is left. *The Gambler* ought to be read in Dostoevsky's form, not in this re-arrangement. The documents consist of Dostoevsky's letters and his wife's diary. The form of publication exaggerates the importance of the documents. Incidental moods are over-emphasized. Moreover, one cannot grasp what the reader gains by this protracted dissertation on the subject of the lost money. It would be difficult to conceive a duller book about the most vivacious person of our times.

In the detailed preface one of the editors treats the gambling mania as one of Dostoevsky's most fundamental features and almost makes out that the poet, till he finally gave it up, spent his time exclusively at the roulette-table and that he did not become a poet till he had ruined himself by gambling. Dostoevsky only gambled abroad, and of the time abroad (the journeys in 1862, 1863, 1865 and the long sojourn from 1867 till 1871) only a fraction was spent in gambling resorts, altogether four months. In 1862 he spent four days in Wiesbaden ; in 1863 some six days in the same place ; in 1865 a few weeks in Baden-Baden. The principal gambling year was 1867, which happened to be the year of his greatest output, a fact which should give furiously to think ! first in Homburg, from the end of April till the end of May, then with his wife in Baden-Baden, from 5th July till 30th August. In the autumn of the same year and in April of the following year he went three or four times from Geneva to Saxon-les-Bains, each time for a few days. In September 1869 he spent one day in Homburg and in April 1871 a few days in Wiesbaden. He lost a thousand to two thousand roubles. Apart from advances from his publisher he borrowed fifty thalers from Turgenev, a similar amount from Baron Vrangel and three ducats from Goncharov. His need was the outcome, not of his gambling losses, but of the above-mentioned situation which was forced on him. Had he not voluntarily shouldered these obligations his need would never have been so serious. Dostoevsky gambled to escape poverty. It is impossible to deduce a diseased and vicious disposition from this simple and widespread frivolity, and the demoniacal nihilism of the underworldling certainly does not lead to Roulettenburg. Compare the gambling chapter in *A Raw Youth* which, for some incomprehensible reason, has been ignored by the editors.

(41) Letter to Sofia Alexandrovna Ivanova-Chymyrova, 1st January 1868.

(42) *Idem.*

(43) Strachov's report about Dostoevsky's communication which portrays the condition preceding an epileptic attack : " for a few seconds you experience ecstasy such as is normally impossible and of which others can have no inkling. You feel complete harmony in yourself and in the world, and this feeling is so sweet and so powerful that for a few seconds of this bliss you would give ten years of your life, indeed your whole life." Quoted by N. Hoffman in her biography. Here there is also a reference to the excellent study of the psychiatrist Tchiz, *Dostoevsky as psychopathologist* (Moscow, 1885), and an interesting extract is translated. With constant reference to the works of Dostoevsky this study shows the stupidity of the dictum about the border-line of genius and insanity and seems written for our days.

(44) Letter to Kovner from Petersburg of 14th February 1877.

(45) For example with Danilevsky, the author of the long article *Europe and Russia* in the periodical *Sarya* who, as Dostoevsky writes to Strachov on 18th March 1869, so accords with his own views and convictions that here and there he is astounded at the identity of their conclusions. " I await," he writes from Florence, " with such excitement the continuation of this article that I run daily to the post office and make systematic

calculations as to the probable date of arrival of the next number of the *Sarya*."

(46) Letter to his niece, 7th May 1870.

(47) According to his letter to Maikov from Dresden of 12th February 1870 he is " now working on a magnificent idea." The editor's surmise that the reference is to *The Possessed* may be accurate, for in his letter to Strachov of 9th October 1870 the date of the beginning of the work is given as the " end of last year." On 8th July 1871 Dostoevsky returned to Petersburg. The novel was not finished by a long way. It was not till the eleventh and twelfth numbers of the *Russian Messenger* in 1872 that the end appeared. Thus Madame Dostoevsky's statement in her reminiscences that Dostoevsky spent three years on the work tallies approximately.

(48) Letter to Strachov, 24th March 1870.

(49) According to Madame Dostoevsky a considerable influence on the substance and tendency of the novel were the conversations with her brother, at the time a student intimately acquainted with revolutionary activities, who visited them in Dresden. For his character of Shatov Dostoevsky drew on the student Ivanov who was murdered by Netchaev in the park of the Academy of Agriculture on 21st November 1869 in similar circumstances. The significance of this incident is confirmed by his letter to Katkov of 8th December 1870. Here doubt is cast on the influence which Madame Dostoevsky attributes to her brother. The letter runs : " the murder of Ivanov by Netchaev, so much discussed in Moscow, belongs to the most prominent events of my story. I will at once assert that my only source of knowledge about Netchaev and Ivanov and all the circumstances of the murder is newspapers. Even had I known them it would never have occurred to me to make a story of them. I take only the complete fact as such. I am thoroughly able to detach myself from this event as it actually occurred, and my Pyotr Verhovensky will not bear the least resemblance to Netchaev. I believe all the same that by dint of imagination I shall create in my mind, which has been affected by this occurrence, a person and a type capable of such a crime. Undoubtedly the portrayal of such a type is not futile ; even so it was not he alone who attracted me. To my mind examples of this deplorable species of humanity are not worthy of literary handling. To my own astonishment this person appeared to me half humorous, which accounts for the fact that, although the incident occurs right in the foreground of the novel, the figure is valid only as accessory in the sphere of activity of another personality ; it is the latter who is to constitute the principal character of the novel. This other character (Nikolay Stavrogin) is likewise a gloomy apparition, an evil-doer. I consider him all the same a tragic figure although many, on reading about him, will exclaim ; ' what does all that signify ? ' So I have set to on the artistic working-out of this person because I have long wanted to portray some character of that sort . . ." [Here Mr Meier-Graefe apologizes for his inability to correct the bad German translation. I do likewise.—Tr.]

Apart from Netchaev four other members of the society were concerned in the murder. The names of these accomplices are known. I have no

DOSTOEVSKY

evidence whether Dostoevsky drew on them as well. Ivanov had opposed the wishes of Netchaev. the founder of the revolutionary society in question. The principal accomplice escaped abroad. All the other eighty-seven members of the society were condemned.

Apart from what he read in the newspapers Dostoevsky may have learnt from his brother-in-law about the acts of incendiarism, too; these will be mentioned later. He had previously passed less unfavourable judgment upon such things. In June 1862 he wrote an article for the *Vremya, Incendiaries and Incendiarism*, in which he contested the view that the outbreak of incendiarism in Petersburg in the spring of that year was the sequel to the appearance of the terrorist pamphlet *Young Russia*, and proved by documentary evidence that such epidemics had occurred in Russia at all times. Previously they had been erroneously attributed to the Poles or the Jews, just as now to the nihilists. The pamphlet was certainly revolutionary, but had in no way inspired the Petersburg conflagrations. With the perspicacity of a criminologist and psychopathologist he attributed them to the imitative instinct and to pathological and criminal tendencies, and recommended the citizens to keep an eye on their houses.

The article was suppressed by the censor. It was found a short while ago by Professor M. Lemke in the Moscow State Archives.

(50) Karl Nötzel. *The Social Movement in Russia.*

(51) Hans Prager. *Die Weltanschauung Dostojewskis.*

(52) In the letter to Strachov of 9th October 1870 is the following: ". . . I am only at the beginning. It is true that many passages in the middle of the novel are already written and isolated passages which I have scratched out I shall still be able to make use of. All the same I am still working on the first chapters. That is a bad omen. . . . At the beginning of the work I considered the novel very artificial and rather looked down on it. But later I became genuinely enthusiastic. Suddenly I fell quite in love with my work and set to strenuously in order to put all I had written into good order. But in the summer there came a change; a new and vital character sprang up in the novel who claimed to be the real hero. The previous hero, a thoroughly interesting figure though not worthy of the name of hero, dropped into the background. The new hero so inspired me that once again I began to re-write the whole thing. And now that I have sent the beginning to the *Russian Messenger* I am suddenly filled with horror: I fear that I am not equal to the theme I have chosen. This fear tortures me horribly, although the introduction of my hero is by no means from the blue . . ."

(53) Letter to Maikov, 2nd March 1871.

(54) *Idem.*

(55) Sketch for *The Possessed.*

(56) Compare the letter to Lyubikov of 10th March 1879 in which he speaks of Ivan's representative rôle.

NOTES

(57) Dostoevsky confirms that in the same letter.

(58) Theophile von Bodisco : *Dostojewski als religiöse Erscheinung.*

(59) As Dostoevsky's daughter relates in her biography, he used at that time to read *The Robbers* aloud to his children.

(60) A. L. Wolynsky. *Das Reich der Karamazoff.*

(61) N. Berdyaev : *Die Weltanschauung Dostojewskis.* Moreover, his opinion that Dostoevsky had lost his youthful faith in Schiller, "the humanitarian idealism," and that Christ and not Schiller had stood the test, is not appropriate. Of course Berdyaev is right when he suggests that we could no longer share Schiller's "idealism in the old sense." But Dostoevsky was able to, as was shown here, and that seems to me one of his claims to fame.

(62) In the quoted work of N. Hoffman is the following : "According to the poet's plan Alyosha was to return to the world in obedience to old Zossima's command and to assume its pain and guilt. He marries Lisa, then abandons her for the sake of the pretty sinner Grushenka and, since he has remained childless, returns, purified, to the monastery after a turbulent period of erring and denying life. There he surrounds himself with a bevy of children whom he loves and teaches and guides until his death." This seems a little doubtful. The relationship to the Idiot certainly does not need to be underlined. It is obvious from the moment of Alyosha's first appearance.

(63) Count Keyserling in the preface to : Nikolaus Berdyaev, *Der Sinn der Geschichte.*

(64) Otto Kaus. *Dostojewski, Zur Kritik der Persönliehkeit.*

(65) As mentioned above. Compare Maxim Gorky : *Reminiscences of Tolstoy.*

(66) Besides the book quoted, also Otto Kaus : *Dostojewski und sein Shicksal.* By the same author : *Flaubert und Dostojewski.* Spengler also has alluded to Kaus' thoughts on Dostoevsky's relationship to capitalism. (*The Decline of the West.*)

BIBLIOGRAPHY

The Novels of Dostoevsky. *The Brothers Karamazov; The Idiot; The Possessed; Crime and Punishment; The House of the Dead; The Insulted and Injured; A Raw Youth; The Eternal Husband and other Stories; The Gambler and other Stories; White Nights and other Stories; An Honest Thief and other Stories; The Friend of the Family and another Story.* Tr. by Constance Garnett. (Heinemann, 1912 to 1920.)

Stavrogin's Confession and The Plan of the Life of a Great Sinner. Tr. by S. S. Koteliansky and Virginia Woolf. (The Hogarth Press, 1922.)

Pages from the Journal of an Author. Tr. by S. S. Koteliansky and J. Middleton Murry. (Maunsel, 1916.)

Letters from the Underworld. Tr. by C. J. Hogarth. (Everyman's Library, 1913.)

Letters of Fyodor Michailovitch Dostoevsky to his Family and Friends. Tr. by Ethel Colburn Mayne. (Chatto & Windus, 1914.)

Dostoevsky : Letters and Reminiscences. Tr. by S. S. Koteliansky and J. Middleton Murry. (Chatto & Windus, 1923.)

Dostoevsky Portrayed by his Wife : the Diary and Reminiscences of Mme Dostoevsky. Tr. from the Russian by S. S. Koteliansky. (Routledge, 1926.)

Fyodor Dostoevsky : a Critical Study. By J. Middleton Murry. (Secker, 1916.)

Dostoevsky and His Creation : a Psycho-critical Study. By Janko Lavrin. (Collins, 1920.)

Tolstoy as Man and Artist ; with an Essay on Dostoievski. Merejkowski. (Constable, 1902.)

Dostoevsky. By André Gide. Tr. from the French. (Dent, 1925.)

Dostoievsky : his Life and Literary Activity. By E. Soloviev. Tr. by C. J. Hogarth. (George Allen & Unwin, 1916.)

DOSTOEVSKY

A Great Russian Realist. By J. A. T. Lloyd. (Stanley Paul, 1912.)

Fyodor Dostoevsky : a Study. By Aimée Dostoevsky. (Heinemann, 1921.)

In Sight of Chaos. By Hermann Hesse. Tr. by Stephen Hudson. (Verlag Seldwyla. Zürich, 1923.)

Dostoievski. From the Russian of Merejkowski. Tr. by G. A. Mounsey. (Moring.)